OXFORD WORLD'S CLASSICS

THE CONDITION OF THE WORKING CLASS IN ENGLAND

FRIEDRICH ENGELS (1820–95) was born into a prosperous business family in Barmen near Dusseldorf. Although apprenticed to his father's business firm, Engels's sympathies moved quickly in the direction of Communism, an orientation which was cemented by the beginning of his lifelong collaboration with Marx in 1844. They jointly published *The Communist Manifesto* on the eve of the 1848 revolutions. In 1850 Engels moved to Manchester where he eventually became a partner in his father's firm, continuing to help Marx who was engaged in writing *Das Kapital*. On retirement in 1870, he settled in London from where his books such as *Anti-Dühring* had an immense influence on the nascent Marxist movement.

DAVID MCLELLAN is Professor of Political Theory at the University of Kent and author of numerous studies of Marx and Marxism. Among his most recent books are *Simone Weil: Utopian Pessimist* and *Unto Caesar: The Political Relevance of Christianity*.

OXFORD WORLD'S CLASSICS

*For over 100 years Oxford World's Classics have brought
readers closer to the world's great literature. Now with over 700
titles—from the 4,000-year-old myths of Mesopotamia to the
twentieth century's greatest novels—the series makes available
lesser-known as well as celebrated writing.*

*The pocket-sized hardbacks of the early years contained
introductions by Virginia Woolf, T. S. Eliot, Graham Greene,
and other literary figures which enriched the experience of reading.
Today the series is recognized for its fine scholarship and
reliability in texts that span world literature, drama and poetry,
religion, philosophy and politics. Each edition includes perceptive
commentary and essential background information to meet the
changing needs of readers.*

OXFORD WORLD'S CLASSICS

FRIEDRICH ENGELS

The Condition of the Working Class in England

Edited with an Introduction and Notes by
DAVID McLELLAN

OXFORD
UNIVERSITY PRESS

OXFORD
UNIVERSITY PRESS

Great Clarendon Street, Oxford OX2 6DP

Oxford University Press is a department of the University of Oxford.
It furthers the University's objective of excellence in research, scholarship,
and education by publishing worldwide in

Oxford New York

Auckland Bangkok Buenos Aires Cape Town Chennai
Dar es Salaam Delhi Hong Kong Istanbul Karachi Kolkata
Kuala Lumpur Madrid Melbourne Mexico City Mumbai Nairobi
São Paulo Shanghai Singapore Taipei Tokyo Toronto

and an associated company in Berlin

Oxford is a registered trade mark of Oxford University Press
in the UK and in certain other countries

Published in the United States
by Oxford University Press Inc., New York

British Library Cataloguing in Publication Data

Data available

Library of Congress Cataloging in Publication Data

Engels, Friedrich, 1820–1895.
[Lage der Arbeitenden Klasse in England. English]
The condition of the working class in England—Friedrich Engels;
edited with an introduction by David McLellan.
p.   cm.—(Oxford world's classics)
Translation of Die Lage der Arbeitenden Klasse in England.
Includes bibliographical references.
1. Working class—England.   2. England—Economic conditions—19th
century.   I. McLellan, David.   II. Title.   III. Series.
HD8389.E515   1993   305.5′62′0942—dc20   92–18294

ISBN 0–19–283688–9

6

Printed in Great Britain by
Clays Ltd, St Ives plc

I wish to record my gratitude to my friend and colleague, Fred Whitemore, for invaluable help with the Introduction.

CONTENTS

INTRODUCTION

ENGELS's study of the condition of the working class is a classic partly because he was in the right place at the right time. From 1842 to 1844 he worked at a branch of his father's cotton mills in Manchester. The textile business was the driving force of the Industrial Revolution and its heart was Manchester. And it was during the 1830s and 1840s that the dramatic social effects of the Frankenstein monster that was early industrial capitalism could be most vividly seen. The fluency of his writing, the personal nature of his observations, his talent for mordant satire combined to make his account of the life of the victims of the early Industrial Revolution into a classic—a historical study to parallel and complement literary classics of the times such as Elizabeth Gaskell's *Mary Barton* (1848) or Charles Dickens's *Hard Times* (1854). What Cobbett had done for agricultural poverty in his *Rural Rides* (1830), Engels did—and more—in his study of the plight of industrial workers in the England of the early 1840s.

Engels was only 24 years old when he wrote *The Condition of the Working Class in England* which accounts for its freshness and its basic optimism, as well as for some of its deficiencies. Engels, the eldest of eight children, was born in 1820 in Barmen in the Wupper Valley near Dusseldorf in the Rhineland. His father was a partner in a prosperous enterprise manufacturing sewing thread, with factories both in Barmen and in Manchester. His mother, a much more sensitive, cultured, and humorous person than her husband, came from a family of Dutch schoolteachers. The area around Barmen was the most industrialized in Germany, indeed Barmen itself was known as 'Little Manchester', and afforded constant evidence of the progress and effects of the Industrial Revolution. It was also a centre of a strict Pietism which flourished in the early nineteenth century as a reaction against the rationalism of the French Revolution. Like the English Puritans, the Pietists held to the literal truth of the Bible, were intolerant of differing views, and frowned on the pursuit of worldly pleasures. The enthusiasm of Engels's

father for business was matched only by his attachment to
the Church, and his son's early life was shaped by a struggle
against both.

The young Engels was eager to devote himself to literature
but his father, contemptuous of bookish pursuits, insisted
that he leave school at the early age of 16 and begin to learn
the rudiments of the family business. The following year
Engels was sent to Bremen to further his business appren-
ticeship working in the office of his father's export agent
there. Engels remained there for two and a half years
and absorbed the cosmopolitan atmosphere of the large
trading port, so different from the narrow horizons of the
Wupper Valley. His business duties were not onerous; he
began to read widely and his own views evolved rapidly.
Under the influence of the radical theologians Strauss and
Schleiermacher he resolved 'only to treat a teaching as divine
if it can defend itself before the bar of reason'. His developing views were expressed in the articles he began to get
published while he was in Bremen. These consisted mainly of
vivid descriptions of that city's social life but included a
series with some biting criticism of social conditions in the
Wupper Valley. Engels declared himself a disciple of the
Young German Movement, a literary group whose members
(the most prominent being the poet Heinrich Heine) were
radical in politics, very liberal in religion, and had a marked
interest in those social questions that were to form the
subject-matter of Engels's great book. His first published
articles, entitled 'Letters from the Wupper Valley', appeared
anonymously in the spring of 1839 in the *Telegraph für
Deutschland*. They anticipate the structure of *The Condition
of the Working Class in England* by concentrating first on
the physical appearance of the Wupper Valley, going on to
discuss the circumstances of the working class, and ending
with a lengthy satirical comment on the middle classes of the
region in which Engels took revenge for the frustrations he
had suffered in his home town.

While still in Bremen, Engels had begun to read Hegel and
was glad, in the spring of 1841, to move to Berlin to do his
year's military service in the Guards Foot Artillery. Hegel
himself had taught in Berlin, Germany's premier university,
from 1818 until his death in 1831 and his influence was

paramount in intellectual circles there. Engels arrived in Berlin just at the time of the brief flowering of the Young Hegelians, as the radically progressive disciples of Hegel were known. The Young Hegelians were a group of young intellectuals who wished to use Hegel's ideas, particularly those of dialectic and negativity, to develop a critique of contemporary religion and politics. Hegel had viewed history as the progress of Spirit in which each historical epoch with its attendant ideas was only a passing stage due to be negated and transcended dialectically by the next stage. The Young Hegelians wished to explore the way in which the religious and political ideas of their own age were destined to give rise to a more satisfactory view of the world. *The Condition of the Working Class in England* is informed by the Young Hegelian enterprise of helping humanity in its appointed task of making rationality unfold itself in history.

On leaving Berlin Engels acquired his definitive political orientation. The Young Hegelians had no coherent attitude to politics, apart from a rather ironic libertarian anarchism. But on the way home from Berlin, Engels stopped in Cologne to meet the editors of the *Rheinische Zeitung*, a radical newspaper founded by Rhenish industrialists to propagate their liberal doctrines, which had opened its columns to the Berlin Young Hegelians. The moving spirit behind the paper—at least in its inception—was Moses Hess, known as 'the Communist Rabbi'. Like Engels, Hess came from a prosperous business family but had educated himself towards Communism. In a series of books written in a meandering style and almost Messianic tone, he had been the first of the Young Hegelians to proclaim a version of Communism. Strongly influenced by French sociology and particularly by the utopian socialism of Saint-Simon, with its positive emphasis on the development of industry, Hess turned Hegel's philosophy towards the future and asserted that Feuerbach's philosophical humanism and the French political notions of class struggle were about to be put into practice through a Communist revolution in the most economically advanced country—England. These ideas had a profound effect on Engels. Hess wrote concerning their meeting: 'We talked of questions of the day. Engels, who was revolutionary to the core when he met me, left as a passionate

Communist.' Someone else Engels met in Cologne that autumn was Karl Marx. Two years old than Engels, Marx had left Berlin after five years of study there. Recent Prussian government clamp-down on the Young Hegelians persuaded Marx to abandon the university career for which he had hoped and he moved back to the more liberal atmosphere of Cologne to become editor of the *Rheinische Zeitung*. With his passionate commitment to Communism, Engels decided to unite his business career and political interest by going to work for a time in his father's factory in Manchester, situated in the industrial heartland of the country of the future.

Arriving at the time of severe economic slump, Engels spent almost two years in Manchester. It was in Manchester, he wrote later, that

it was forcibly brought to my notice that economic factors, hitherto ignored or at least underestimated by historians, play a decisive role in the development of the modern world. I learnt that economic factors were the basic cause of the clash between different classes in society. And I realized that in a highly industrialized country like England the clash of social classes lay at the very root of the rivalry between parties and was of fundamental significance in tracing the course of modern history.[1]

He continued his correspondence for German papers and in particular sent two articles to the *Deutsch–Französische Jahrbücher* which Marx was editing in Paris following the suppression of the *Rheinische Zeitung*. One of these, entitled 'Outlines of a Critique of Political Economy', proclaimed in a stark and simple language the idea of the inevitable impoverishment of the working class and consequent revolution. It was this article which directed Marx's attention to the subject of economics. The other was a long and favourable review of *Past and Present* by Thomas Carlyle whose passionate denunciation of early industrialism left a lasting impression on Engels. When not clerking in the family firm's office, Engels got to know the intricate labyrinths of the working-class areas so vividly described in his book. According to the Address 'To the Working Classes of Great Britain', which prefaces the book:

[1] K. Marx and F. Engels, *Werke* (Berlin, 1957), xxxi. 341.

I wanted more than a mere *abstract* knowledge of my subject, I wanted to see you in your own homes, to observe you in your everyday life, to chat with you on your condition and grievances, to witness your struggles against the social and political power of your oppressors. I have done so: I forsook the company and the dinner parties, the port wine and champagne of the middle classes, and devoted my leisure hours almost exclusively to the intercourse with plain working men.

He thus got to know Manchester 'as intimately as my own native town, more intimately than most of its residents'. He was inducted into many of the secrets of the city by an illiterate Irish servant girl, Mary Burns, with whom he lived on and off until her death some twenty years later. This personal observation was supported by reading masses of parliamentary papers, statistical reports, and pamphlets, as well as the increasing number of books dealing with the social question. He also got to know the Chartists and Owenites and involved himself in local politics.

Thus when Engels returned home to Barmen in September 1844 he brought with him a mass of material which he already planned to turn into a book. On his way he stopped in Paris and met Marx for the second time. 'When I visited Marx in Paris in the summer of 1844', Engels remembered, 'we found ourselves in complete agreement on questions of theory and our collaboration began at that time.' Ironically, Engels composed his anti-bourgeois philippic while living in the family home in Barmen from September 1844 until March 1845.

I am buried up to my ears in English newspapers and books from which I am composing my book on the condition of the English proletarians.... I shall be presenting the English with a fine bill of indictment; I accuse the English bourgeoisie before the entire world of murder, robbery and other crimes on a massive scale, and I am writing an English preface which I shall have printed separately and sent to English party leaders, men of letters, and Members of Parliament. That'll give those fellows something to remember me by. It need hardly be said that my blows ... are meant for ... the German bourgeoisie, to whom I make it plain enough that they are as bad as their English counterparts.[2]

---

[2] Marx and Engels, *Werke*, xxvii. 10.

But the atmosphere was increasingly unconducive to quiet study. He wrote to Marx in March:

I live a dog's life here. All the religious fanaticism of my old man has been aroused by the Communist meetings and by the 'dissolute character' of several of our local Communists with whom I am of course in close contact. And the old man's wrath has been increased by my firm refusal to go into petty trading. Finally my appearance in public as an avowed Communist has aroused in him a truly middle-class fury. Now try to put yourself in my place. Since I want to leave in a fortnight or so, I cannot afford to have a row. So I simply ignore all the criticisms of the family. They are not used to that so they get even angrier . . . you can have no notion of the sheer malice that lies behind this wild Christian hunt after my 'soul'.[3]

Finished in March 1845, the book was published in Leipzig the following June.

Engels's 'fine bill of indictment' begins with a strikingly concise and coherent history of the Industrial Revolution as a process of increasing class polarization between the proletariat and the bourgeoisie involving the building of ever-larger factories and the spread of chaotic urbanization. From this discussion follows what is in many ways the core of the book—the third chapter with its phenomenology of the great towns. Engels starts with London and after discussing Dublin, Glasgow, Edinburgh, and the major towns of Yorkshire, concentrates on the Manchester–Salford conurbation with its half a million people. After describing the geographical situation of the city, he then analyses its social geography, its transport system, and its class apartheid, before penetrating the working-class ghettos and rehearsing the combination of filth, sickness, starvation, and death. His conclusion is that.

the working class of the great cities offers a graduated scale of conditions in life, in the best cases a temporarily endurable existence for hard work and good wages, good and endurable, that is, from the worker's standpoint; in the worst cases, bitter want, reaching even homelessness and death by starvation. The average is much nearer the worst case than the best. (p. 85)

He produces his effects by an attention to detail in a powerful and vivid language which at times rivals that of Dickens and reproduces the passion of Carlyle.

[3] Marx and Engels, *Werke*, xxvii. 26.

In the following chapters Engels analyses the underlying economic mechanism which produces such appalling
phenomena: competition and the pursuit of profit and profit
alone. The economic war of all against all results in all-
pervasive insecurity, atomization, and total demoralization.

Competition is the completest expression of the battle of all against
all which rules in modern civil society. This battle, a battle for life,
for existence, for everything, in case of need a battle of life and
death, is fought not between the different classes of society only, but
also between the individual members of these classes. Each is in the
way of the other, and each seeks to crowd out all who are in his
way, and to put himself in their place. The workers are in constant
competition among themselves. (p. 87)

The necessary preconditions of this competitive universe are
periodic crises; surplus population and a reserve army of
labour are its necessary conditions. After a short chapter on
Irish immigration which serves to highlight the noxious
effects of competition, Engels presents a systematic account
of the effects of capitalist industrialization on the minds and
bodies of the workers. He returns here to the themes of the
third chapter in more detail in order to press home his charge
of social murder against the English bourgeoisie. He details
the diseases, particularly consumption, that produced 'pale,
lank, narrow-chested, hollow-eyed ghosts' (p. 93). (In
Manchester at that time more than half the children of
working-class parents died before the age of 5.) He describes
the illiteracy that has its counterpart in bigotry and fanaticism, and the alcoholism that fosters sexual immorality
and ever-increasing crime. There follows an account of the
factory system with its exploitation of women and children
as cheap labour, and its spate of accidents and spinal injuries. Engels particularly emphasizes the power of the mill-
owners over their operatives in obtaining everything from
sexual favours to rent and the price of food in the factory-
owned shops. He then completes his account by dealing in
the same manner with the mines and the agricultural sector.

As well as this socio-historical account, there is running
through Engels's book (and particularly present towards the
end in chapters on the labour movement and on the bourgeoisie) a description and evaluation of the political struggles
of the working class against the conditions described. Engels
arrived in England at a time when political tension deriving

from working-class unrest was at its height. In 1838 a People's Charter had been drawn up demanding universal suffrage for men, a secret ballot, and annual parliaments with the abolition of a property qualification. In 1842 a petition to Parliament on behalf of the Charter gained 3,500,000 signatures and, in the same year, Chartist agitation resulted in a general strike known as the 'plug riots' since workers pulled the plugs out of boilers to force the shut-down of factories. Engels took recent strikes as evidence that 'the decisive battle between the proletariat and the bourgeoisie is approaching'. He was enthusiastic in his support for Chartism as the political expression of the growing trade union movement which could eventually bring about a socialist revolution after successfully introducing a form of democracy which, unlike the bourgeois form, was social as well as political. The Chartists themselves were divided between those who wished to remain within the boundaries of the law and those who advocated resort to force. This same ambivalence is reflected in Engels: the pacifism that he inherited from Hess leads him in the conclusion to the book to see Communism as a healing doctrine which could transcend class struggle, while at the same time he predicts a war of poor against rich which will be the bloodiest ever waged.

From the date of its publication Engels's book attracted considerable attention in Germany and, to a lesser extent, Russia. There was much praise for its style and its accurate observation but much opposition to its revolutionary conclusions. There is no evidence that it had any effect on the conduct of the German business class who nevertheless, owing to their later economic development and a more cohesive socio-political culture, managed to avoid the excesses so bitterly attacked by Engels. *The Condition of the Working Class in England* was reprinted in 1848 but had to wait until 1887 for a translation to be published in the United States and 1892 for the same translation to appear in Britain. It was only with the spread of socialism that Engels's book became widely read. In recent decades, the controversy that marked its first publication has reappeared: in the introduction to their new translation and critical edition which appeared in 1958, Chaloner and Henderson attacked

Engels for poor methodology, and factual inaccuracy. From the exchanges which followed, Engels emerged rather better than his editors. In 1974 Steven Marcus produced a brilliant study of the book and its author from a literary and psychological perspective which, by placing Engels's book firmly in the context of his own life and times, showed how the problems of urban poverty and the dislocations of industrial society—and the reactions of the young Engels to them—are patterns of question and response which still haunt us. And the last few years have seen several scholarly discussions of Engels's ideas on machinery and poverty. Two of the most striking are Maxine Berg's study of Engels's view of technology as the principle source of unemployment and creator of the reserve army of labour, and Gertrude Himmelfarb's analysis of how the proletarian condition transforms 'poverty' from a passive to a revolutionary concept.

The continuing controversy about *The Condition of the Working Class in England* is the inevitable result of the forthrightness of Engels's views. Critics have rightly pointed to the ludicrously idyllic picture of pre-industrial England at the beginning of the book, a short passage that might have come straight out of the pages of Burke. His attack on the greed and hypocrisy of the middle classes as exemplified in the Poor Law is convincing; but his view of the bourgeoisie as 'a deeply demoralized class, incurably corrupted by selfishness, corroded in their very being' is undoubtedly harsh. Engels perhaps does not give enough space to the profoundly Hegelian irony that the horrors he describes were the result of the actions of those who were, in many respects, virtuous men of sterling character and purpose. As a consequence, he misassesses the nature of the bourgeoisie. He vastly underrates its drive and vitality as a class. He misses the significance of movements such as the Anti-Corn Law League and so fails to see that the bourgeoisie is in the process of remoulding British society economically (and politically) in a way that helps create the basis for the period of stability and progress which followed in the 1850s. Very occasionally, too, Engels garbles his sources, but his account has stood up surprisingly well to subsequent scholarship. He is also too impressed by the 'iron law' of wages and thus self-contradictory on the ability of trade unions to improve wages and working conditions (an issue which is still a matter of contemporary debate), preferring to emphasize their role as schools of working-class organization. In addition he adopts the current English derogatory stereotype of the Irish. Engels's point is, of course, that the lower Irish standard of living enables, through competition, a lowering of workers' wages and working conditions below that which the English would find tolerable. But the modern reader might well find the way Engels presents this—his emphasis on 'Irish filth' etc.—rather shocking. In a similar vein, certain of Engels's remarks on the respective roles of men and women in the workplace show him subject to the prejudices of his age.

More substantially, however, the book contains two main weaknesses. The first is that Engels overestimated the pace and extent to which the diverse sections of the working class were being welded into a single homogeneous block. He talks about the proletariat as though it were a uniform class produced by the introduction of the machine. The spinning-jenny, steam-engine, and power-loom had a powerful effect on the imagination of his contemporaries. The majority of the classical economists had taken the view that machinery, by lowering the cost of production and thus prices, would in the long run increase employment and be to everyone's benefit. Engels, on the contrary, felt that the introduction of machinery caused unemployment and was the root cause of all the social evils that he observed in Manchester. In common with many of his contemporaries, Engels over-emphasized the role of machinery both in creating the factory system and in introducing the employment of women and children. If he had spent more time in London, where manufacture was still dominated by artisans, he would have got a different picture. In fact, the impact of machinery was incremental rather than cataclysmic: factories had existed without machines and the employment of women and children in them had predated the introduction of machinery with results which were, in any case, more complex than Engels portrays them. Underlying his approach is a technological determinism that was to remain with Engels all his life.

The second weakness of *The Condition of the Working*

Class in England lies in its predictions. The Young Hegelians were given to over-optimistic views of what the near future would bring and Engels was no exception. On this, the best comment is that of Marx, writing to his friend some twenty years later:

I have read your book again and I have realized that I am not getting any younger. What power, what incisiveness and what passion drove you to work in those days! That was a time when you were never worried by academic scholarly reservations! Those were the days when you made the reader feel that your theory would become hard fact, if not tomorrow then at any rate on the day after. Yet that very illusion gave the whole work a human warmth and a touch of humour that makes our later writings—where 'black and white' have become 'grey and grey'—seem positively distasteful.[4]

Engels wrote in the immediate aftermath of what was the worst economic slump of the nineteenth century—which was to be followed in the next two decades by the golden age of Victorian capitalism. He expected an imminent revolution—a replay of the French Revolution, but on socialist principles. His Young Hegelian perspective led him to view history as the inevitable unfolding of progressive rationality through social conflict. This radical Hegelianism, together with the truly appalling social misery he witnessed and his over-estimation of the cataclysmic effects of the introduction of machinery, led to the revolutionary and millennial conclusions to his book.

Yet despite these weaknesses—indeed sometimes because of them—Engels's book retains its force as a classic of early social geography and a pioneering study of the effects of early uncontrolled industrialization. However much Engels relied on contemporary scholarly sources (sometimes too much), he was justified in his own claim to have written the first book to have dealt comprehensively with the industrial working class as a whole rather than just with particular groups or industries. Rich and complex, Engels's book combines economics, philosophy, and labour history to provide an empirical basis for several of Marx's later theories. It was the foundation document of what was to

[4] Marx and Engels, *Werke*, xxx. 343.

become the Marxian socialist tradition. Engels lived until 1895 and contributed much to that tradition. But he never surpassed his early achievements: his youthful book remains the classic work on the effects of early industrial capitalism and the struggle against them.

NOTE ON THE TEXT

THE German original was first published in 1845. The text here follows the Moscow edition of the English translation made by Florence Kelley-Wischnewetsky, revised by Engels himself and first published in New York in 1887. It has been checked against the original German for accuracy. The Prefaces by Engels to the separate English edition are included.

SELECT BIBLIOGRAPHY

Commentaries

Maxine Berg, *The Machinery Question and the Making of Political Economy, 1815–1848* (Cambridge University Press: Cambridge, 1980), ch. 14

Asa Briggs, *Victorian Cities* (Odhams: London, 1963), ch. 3

Terrell Carver, *Marx and Engels: The Intellectual Relationship* (Wheatsheaf: Brighton, 1983), ch. 2

—— *Friedrich Engels: His Life and Thought* (Macmillan: London, 1989), ch. 4

Alan Gilbert, *Marx's Politics: Communists and Citizens* (Rutgers University Press: Rutgers, 1981), ch. 3

W. O. Henderson, *The Life of Friedrich Engels* (Frank Cass: London, 1976), vol. i, ch. 2

—— and W. H. Chaloner, 'Introduction' to *The Condition of the Working Class in England* (Macmillan: New York, 1958)

Gertrude Himmelfarb, *The Idea of Poverty: England in the Early Industrial Age* (Faber: London, 1984), ch. 12

Eric Hobsbawm, *Labouring Men* (Weidenfeld & Nicolson: London, 1964), ch. 6

—— 'Introduction' to *The Condition of the Working Class in England* (Granada: St Albans, 1969)

J. D. Hunley, *The Life and Thought of Friedrich Engels: A Reinterpretation* (Yale University Press: New Haven, Conn., 1991)

Richard Hunt, *The Political Ideas of Marx and Engels* (University of Pittsburgh Press: Pittsburgh, 1974–84), vol. 1, ch. 8

Victor Kiernan, 'Introduction' to *The Condition of the Working Class in England* (Penguin: Harmondsworth, 1987)

Steven Marcus, *Engels, Manchester and the Working Class* (Random House: New York, 1974)

S. T. Rigby, *Engels and the Formation of Marxism* (Manchester University Press: Manchester, 1992), ch. 3

John Sherwood, 'Engels, Marx, Malthus, and the Machine', *American Historical Review*, 90 (1985)

Gareth Stedman Jones, 'Engels and the Genesis of Marxism', *New Left Review*, 106 (1977)

Roy Whitfield, *Frederich Engels in Manchester: The Search for a Shadow* (Manchester Free Press: Manchester, 1988)

Karl Williams, *From Pauperism to Poverty* (Routledge & Kegan Paul: London, 1981), ch. 6

A CHRONOLOGY OF
FRIEDRICH ENGELS

The Condition of the
Working Class in England

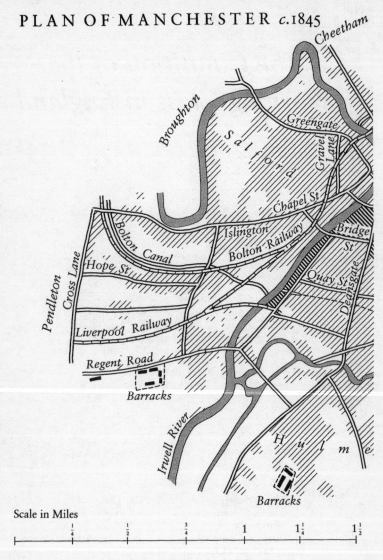

PLAN OF MANCHESTER *c.*1845

Cheetham

Broughton

Salford

Greengate

Gravel Lane

Chapel St

Islington

Bridge St

Bolton Canal

Bolton Railway

Pendleton

Cross Lane

Hope St

Quay St

Deansgate

Liverpool Railway

Regent Road

Barracks

Irwell River

H u l m e

Barracks

Scale in Miles

$\frac{1}{4}$ $\frac{1}{2}$ $\frac{3}{4}$ 1 $1\frac{1}{4}$ $1\frac{1}{2}$

The commercial quarter is distinguished by etching from left to right

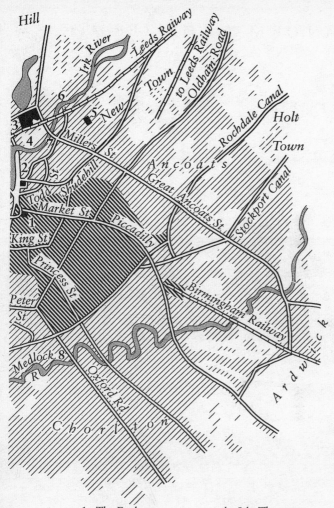

1. The Exchange
2. The Old Church
3. Workhouse
4. Paupers' Cemetery
5. St Michael's Church
6. Scotland Bridge over

the Irk. The street
from 2 to 6 is called
Long Millgate.
7. Ducie Bridge over the
Irk
8. Little Ireland

CONTENTS

over the Bourgeois—The Unfavourable Sides of
the Proletarian Character—Drunkenness—Sexual
Irregularities—Neglect of Family Duties—Contempt
for the Existing Social Order—Crimes—Description
of the Social War

To the Working Classes of Great Britain*

Working Men!

To you I dedicate a work, in which I have tried to lay before my German Countrymen a faithful picture of your condition, of your sufferings and struggles, of your hopes and prospects. I have lived long enough amidst you to know something about your circumstances; I have devoted to their knowledge my most serious attention, I have studied the various official and non-official documents as far as I was able to get hold of them—I have not been satisfied with this, I wanted more than a mere *abstract* knowledge of my subject, I wanted to see you in your own homes, to observe you in your everyday life, to chat with you on your condition and grievances, to witness your struggles against the social and political power of your oppressors. I have done so: I forsook the company and the dinner-parties, the port wine and champagne of the middle classes, and devoted my leisure hours almost exclusively to the intercourse with plain Working Men; I am both glad and proud of having done so. Glad, because thus I was induced to spend many a happy hour in obtaining a knowledge of the realities of life—many an hour, which else would have been wasted in fashionable talk and tiresome etiquette; proud, because thus I got an opportunity of doing justice to an oppressed and calumniated class of men who, with all their faults and under all the disadvantages of their situation, yet command the respect of everyone but an English money-monger; proud, too, because thus I was placed in a position to save the English people from the growing contempt which on the Continent has been the necessary consequence of the brutally selfish policy and general behaviour of your ruling middle class.

Having, at the same time, ample opportunity to watch the middle classes, your opponents, I soon came to the conclusion that you are right, perfectly right in expecting no support whatever from them. Their interest is diametrically opposed to yours, though they always will try to maintain the contrary and to make you believe in their most hearty sympathy with your fates. Their doings give them the lie. I hope to have collected more than sufficient evidence of the fact that—be their words what they please—the middle classes intend in reality nothing else but to enrich themselves by your labour while they can sell its produce, and to abandon you to starvation as soon as they cannot make a profit by this indirect trade in human flesh. What have they done to prove their professed goodwill towards you? Have they ever paid any serious attention to your grievances? Have they done more than paying the expenses of half a dozen commissions of inquiry, whose voluminous reports are damned to everlasting slumber among heaps of waste paper on the shelves of the Home Office? Have they even done as much as to compile from those rotting Blue Books a single readable book from which everybody might easily get some information on the condition of the great majority of 'free-born Britons'? Not they indeed, those are things they do not like to speak of—they have left it to a foreigner to inform the civilized world of the degrading situation you have to live in.

A foreigner to *them*, not to *you*, I hope. Though my English may not be pure, yet, I hope, you will find it *plain* English. No working man in England—nor in France either, by the by—ever treated me as a foreigner. With the greatest pleasure I observed you to be free from that blasting curse, national prejudice and national pride, which after all means nothing but *wholesale selfishness*—I observed you to sympathize with everyone who earnestly applies his powers to human progress—may he be an Englishman or not—to admire everything great and good, whether nursed on your native soil or not—I found you to be more than mere *English*men, members of a single, isolated nation, I found you to be *Men*, members of the great and universal family of Mankind, who know their interests and that of all the human race to be the same. And as such, as members of this Family of 'One and Indivisible' Mankind, as Human Beings in the most emphatic meaning of the word, as such I, and many others on the Continent, hail your progress in every direction and wish you speedy success. Go on then, as you have done hitherto. Much remains to be undergone; be firm, be undaunted—your success is certain, and no step you will have to take in your onward march will be lost to our common cause, the cause of Humanity!

Friedrich Engels

Barmen (Rhenan Prussia)
15 March 1845

Preface to the First German Edition

THE book prefaced by the following pages treats of a subject which I originally intended to deal with in a single chapter of a more comprehensive work on the social history of England. However, the importance of that subject soon made it necessary for me to investigate it separately.

The condition of the working class is the real basis and point of departure of all social movements of the present because it is the highest and most unconcealed pinnacle of the social misery existing in our day. French and German working-class Communism are its direct, Fourierism and English Socialism, as well as the Communism of the German educated bourgeoisie, are its indirect products. A knowledge of proletarian conditions is absolutely necessary to be able to provide solid ground for socialist theories, on the one hand, and for judgements about their right to exist, on the other; and to put an end to all sentimental dreams and fancies pro and con. But proletarian conditions exist in their *classical form*, in their perfection, only in the British Empire, particularly in England proper. Besides, only in England has the necessary material been so completely collected and put on record by official enquiries as is essential for any in the least exhaustive presentation of the subject.

Twenty-one months I had the opportunity to become acquainted with the English proletariat, its strivings, its sorrows, and its joys, to see them from near, from personal observation and personal intercourse, and at the same time to supplement my observations by recourse to the requisite authentic sources. What I have seen, heard, and read has been worked up in the present book. I am prepared to see not only my standpoint attacked in many quarters but also the facts I have cited, particularly when the book gets into the hands of the English. I know equally well that here and there I may be proved wrong in some particular of no importance, something that in view of the comprehensive nature of the subject and its far-reaching assumptions even an Englishman might be unable to avoid; so much the more so since even in England there exists as yet not a single piece of writing which, like mine, takes up *all* the workers. But without a moment's hesitation I challenge the English bourgeoisie to prove that even in a single instance of any consequence for the exposition of my point of view as a whole I have been guilty of any inaccuracy, and to prove it by data as authentic as mine.

A description of the classical form which the conditions of existence of the proletariat have assumed in Britain is very important, particularly for Germany and precisely at the present moment. German Socialism and Communism have proceeded, more than any other, from theoretical premisses; we German theoreticians still knew much too little of the real world to be driven directly by the real relations to reforms of this 'bad reality'. At any rate almost none of the avowed champions of such reforms arrived at Communism otherwise than by way of the Feuerbachean dissolution of Hegelian speculation. The real conditions of life of the proletariat are so little known among us that even the well-meaning 'societies for the uplift of the working classes', in which our bourgeoisie is now mistreating the social question, constantly start out from the most ridiculous and preposterous judgements concerning the condition of the workers. We Germans more than anybody else stand in need of a knowledge of the facts concerning this question. And while the conditions of existence of Germany's proletariat have not assumed the classical form that they have in England, we nevertheless have, at bottom, the same social order, which sooner or later must necessarily reach the same degree of acuteness as it has already attained across the North Sea, unless the intelligence of the nation brings about the adoption of measures that will provide a new basis for the whole social system. The root-causes whose effect in England has been the misery and oppression of the proletariat exist also in Germany and in the long run must engender the same results. In the mean time, however, the established fact of wretched conditions in *England* will impel us to establish also the fact of wretched conditions in *Germany* and will provide us with a yardstick wherewith to measure their extent and the magnitude of the danger—brought to light by the Silesian and Bohemian disturbances*—which directly threatens the tranquillity of Germany from that quarter.

Finally, there are still two remarks I wish to make. First, that I have used the word *Mittelklasse* all along in the sense of the English word *middle class* (or *middle classes*, as is said almost always). Like the French word *bourgeoisie* it means the possessing class, specifically that possessing class which is differentiated from the so-called aristocracy—the class which in France and England is directly and in Germany, figuring as 'public opinion', indirectly in possession of political power. Similarly, I have continually used the expressions working men (*Arbeiter*) and proletarians, working class, propertyless class, and proletariat as equivalents. Secondly, that in the case of most of the quotations I have indicated the party to which the respective authors belong, because in nearly every instance the Liberals try to emphasize the distress in the rural areas and to argue away that which exists in the factory districts, while the Conservatives, conversely, acknowledge the misery in the factory districts but disclaim any knowledge of it in the agricultural areas. For the same reason, whenever I lacked official documents for describing the condition of the industrial workers, I always preferred to present proof from *Liberal* sources in order to defeat the liberal bourgeoisie by casting their own words in their teeth. I cited Tories or Chartists in my support only when I could confirm their correctness from personal observation or was convinced of the truthfulness of the facts quoted because of the personal or literary reputation of the authorities I referred to.

F. Engels

Barmen, 15 March 1845

Introduction

THE history of the proletariat in England begins with the second half of the last century, with the invention of the steam-engine and of machinery for working cotton. These inventions gave rise, as is well known, to an industrial revolution, a revolution which altered the whole civil society; one, the historical importance of which is only now beginning to be recognized. England is the classic soil of this transformation, which was all the mightier, the more silently it proceeded; and England is, therefore, the classic land of its chief product also, the proletariat. Only in England can the proletariat be studied in all its relations and from all sides.

We have not, here and now, to deal with the history of this revolution, nor with its vast importance for the present and the future. Such a delineation must be reserved for a future, more comprehensive work. For the moment, we must limit ourselves to the little that is necessary for understanding the facts that follow, for comprehending the present state of the English proletariat.

Before the introduction of machinery, the spinning and weaving of raw materials was carried on in the working man's home. Wife and daughter spun the yarn that the father wove or that they sold, if he did not work it up himself. These weaver families lived in the country in the neighbourhood of the towns, and could get on fairly well with their wages, because the home market was almost the only one, and the crushing power of competition that came later, with the conquest of foreign markets and the extension of trade, did not yet press upon wages. There was, further, a constant increase in the demand for the home market, keeping pace with the slow increase in population and employing all the workers; and there was also the impossibility of vigorous competition of the workers among themselves, consequent upon the rural dispersion of their homes. So it was that the weaver was usually in a position to lay by something, and rent a little piece of land, that he cultivated in his leisure hours, of which he had as many as he chose to take, since he could weave whenever and as long as he pleased. True, he was a bad farmer and managed his land inefficiently, often obtaining but poor crops; nevertheless, he was no proletarian, he had a stake in the country, he was permanently settled, and stood one step higher in society than the English workman of to-day.

So the workers vegetated throughout a passably comfortable existence, leading a righteous and peaceful life in all piety and probity; and their material position was far better than that of their successors. They did not need to overwork; they did no more than they chose to do, and yet earned what they needed. They had leisure for healthful work in garden or field, work which, in itself, was recreation for them, and they could take part besides in the recreations and games of their neighbours, and all these games—bowling, cricket, football, etc., contributed to their physical health and vigour. They were, for the most part, strong, well-built people, in whose physique little or no difference from that of their peasant neighbours was discoverable. Their children grew up in the fresh country air, and, if they could help their parents at work, it was only occasionally; while of eight or twelve hours work for them there was no question.

What the moral and intellectual character of this class was may be guessed. Shut off from the towns, which they never entered, their yarn and woven stuff being delivered to travelling agents for payment of wages—so shut off that old people who lived quite in the neighbourhood of the town never went thither until they were robbed of their trade by the introduction of machinery and obliged to look about them in the towns for work—the weavers stood upon the moral and intellectual plane of the yeomen with whom they were usually immediately connected through their little holdings. They regarded their squire, the greatest landholder of the region, as their natural superior; they asked advice of him, laid their small disputes before him for settlement, and gave him all honour, as this patriarchal relation involved. They were 'respectable' people, good husbands and fathers, led moral lives because they had no temptation to be immoral, there being no gin palaces or low houses in their vicinity, and because the host, at whose inn they now and then quenched their thirst, was also a respectable man, usually a large tenant farmer who took pride in his good order, good beer, and early hours. They had their children the whole day at home, and brought them up in obedience and the fear of God; the patriarchal relationship remained undisturbed so long as the children were unmarried. The young people grew up in idyllic simplicity and intimacy with their playmates until they married; and even though sexual intercourse before marriage almost unfailingly took place, this happened only when the moral obligation of marriage was recognized on both sides, and a subsequent wedding made everything good. In short, the English industrial workers of those days lived and thought after the fashion still to be found here and there in Germany, in retirement and seclusion, without mental activity and without violent fluctuations in their position in life. They could rarely read and far more rarely write; went regularly to church, never talked politics, never conspired, never thought, delighted in physical exercises, listened with inherited reverence when the Bible was read, and were, in their unquestioning humility, exceedingly well-disposed towards the 'superior' classes. But intellectually, they were dead; lived only for their petty, private interest, for their looms and gardens, and knew nothing of the mighty movement which, beyond their horizon, was sweeping through mankind. They were comfortable in their silent vegetation, and but for the industrial revolution they would never have emerged from this existence, which, cosily romantic as it was, was nevertheless not worthy of human beings. In truth, they were not human beings; they were merely toiling machines in the service of the few aristocrats who had guided history down to that time. The industrial revolution has simply carried this out to its logical end by making the workers machines pure and simple, taking from them the last trace of independent activity, and so forcing them to think and demand a position worthy of men. As in France politics, so in England manufacture, and the movement of civil society in general drew into the whirl of history the last classes which had remained sunk in apathetic indifference to the universal interests of mankind.

The first invention which gave rise to a radical change in the state of the English workers was the jenny, invented in the year 1764 by a weaver, James Hargreaves, of Standhill, near Blackburn, in North Lancashire. This machine was the rough beginning of the later invented mule, and was moved by hand. Instead of one spindle like the ordinary spinning-wheel, it carried sixteen or eighteen manipulated by a single workman. This invention made it possible to deliver more yarn than heretofore. Whereas, though one weaver had employed three spinners, there had never been enough yarn, and the weaver had often been obliged to wait for it, there was now more yarn to be had than could be woven by the available workers. The demand for woven goods, already increasing, rose yet more in consequence of the cheapness of these goods, which cheapness, in turn, was the outcome of the diminished cost of producing the yarn. More weavers were needed, and weavers' wages rose. Now that the weaver could earn more at his loom, he gradually abandoned his farming, and gave his whole time to weaving. At that time a family of four grown persons and two children (who were set to spooling) could earn, with ten hours' daily work, £4 in a week, and often more if trade was good and work pressed. It happened often enough that a single weaver earned £2 a week at his loom. By degrees the class of farming weavers wholly disappeared, and was merged in the newly arising class of weavers who lived wholly upon wages, had no property whatever, not even the pretended property of a holding, and so became working men, proletarians. More-over, the old relation between spinner and weaver was destroyed. Hitherto, so far as this had been possible, yarn had been spun and woven under one roof. Now that the jenny as well as the loom required a strong hand, men began to spin, and whole families lived by spinning, while others laid the antiquated, superseded spinning-wheel aside; and, if they had not means of purchasing a jenny, were forced to live upon the wages of the father alone. Thus began with spinning and weaving that division of labour which has since been so infinitely perfected.

While the industrial proletariat was thus developing with the first still very imperfect machine, the same machine gave rise to the agricultural proletariat. There had, hitherto, been a vast number of small landowners, yeomen, who had vegetated in the same unthinking quiet as their neighbours, the farming weavers. They cultivated their scraps of land

quite after the ancient and inefficient fashion of their ancestors, and opposed every change with the obstinacy
peculiar to such creatures of habit, after remaining stationary
from generation to generation. Among them were many
smallholders also, not tenants in the present sense of the
word, but people who had their land handed down from
their fathers, either by hereditary lease, or by force of ancient
custom, and had hitherto held it as securely as if it had
actually been their own property. When the industrial
workers withdrew from agriculture, a great number of
smallholdings fell idle, and upon these the new class of large
tenants established themselves, tenants-at-will, holding fifty,
one hundred, two hundred or more acres, liable to be turned
out at the end of the year, but able by improved tillage and
larger farming to increase the yield of the land. They could
sell their produce more cheaply than the yeoman, for whom
nothing remained when his farm no longer supported him
but to sell it, procure a jenny or a loom, or take service as an
agricultural labourer in the employ of a large farmer. His
inherited slowness and the inefficient methods of cultivation
bequeathed by his ancestors, and above which he could not
rise, left him no alternative when forced to compete with
men who managed their holdings on sounder principles and
with all the advantages bestowed by farming on a large scale
and the investment of capital for the improvement of the soil.

Meanwhile, the industrial movement did not stop here.
Single capitalists began to set up spinning-jennies in great
buildings and to use water-power for driving them, so
placing themselves in a position to diminish the number
of workers, and sell their yarn more cheaply than single
spinners could do who moved their own machines by hand.
There were constant improvements in the jenny, so that
machines continually became antiquated, and must be
altered or even laid aside; and though the capitalists could
hold out by the application of water-power even with the old
machinery, for the single spinner this was impossible. And
the factory system, the beginning of which was thus made,
received a fresh extension in 1767, through the spinning
throstle invented by Richard Arkwright, a barber, in Preston,
in North Lancashire. After the steam-engine, this is the most
important mechanical invention of the eighteenth century. It

was calculated from the beginning for mechanical motive power, and was based upon wholly new principles. By the combination of the peculiarities of the jenny and throstle, Samuel Crompton, of Firwood, Lancashire, contrived the mule in 1785, and as Arkwright invented the carding engine, and preparatory ('slubbing and roving') frames about the same time, the factory system became the prevailing one for the spinning of cotton. By means of trifling modifications these machines were gradually adapted to the spinning of wool and later (in the first decade of the present century) also of flax, and so to the superseding of hand-work here, too. But even then, the end was not yet. In the closing years of the last century, Dr Cartwright, a country parson, had invented the power-loom, and about 1804 had so far perfected it, that it could successfully compete with the hand-weaver; and all this machinery was made doubly important by James Watt's steam-engine, invented in 1764, and used for supplying motive power for spinning since 1785.

With these inventions, since improved from year to year, the victory of machine-work over hand-work in the chief branches of English industry was won; and the history of the latter from that time forward simply relates how the hand-workers have been driven by machinery from one position after another. The consequences of this were, on the one hand, a rapid fall in price of all manufactured commodities, prosperity of commerce and manufacture, the conquest of nearly all the unprotected foreign markets, the sudden multiplication of capital and national wealth; on the other hand, a still more rapid multiplication of the proletariat, the destruction of all property-holding and of all security of employment for the working class, demoralization, political excitement, and all those facts so highly repugnant to Englishmen in comfortable circumstances, which we shall have to consider in the following pages. Having already seen what a transformation in the social condition of the lower classes a single such clumsy machine as the jenny had wrought, there is no cause for surprise as to that which a complete and interdependent system of finely adjusted machinery has brought about, machinery which receives raw material and turns out woven goods.

Meanwhile, let us trace the development of English

manufacture[1] somewhat more minutely, beginning with the cotton industry. In the years 1771–5, there were annually imported into England rather less than 5,000,000 pounds of raw cotton; in the year 1841 there were imported 528,000,000 pounds, and the import for 1844 will reach at least 600,000,000 pounds. In 1834 England exported 556,000,000 yards of woven cotton goods, 76,500,000 pounds of cotton yarn, and cotton hosiery of the value of £1,200,000. In the same year over 8,000,000 mule spindles were at work, 110,000 power and 250,000 hand-looms, throstle spindles not included, in the service of the cotton industry; and, according to MacCulloch's reckoning, nearly a million and a half human beings were supported by this branch, of whom but 220,000 worked in the mills; the power used in these mills was steam, equivalent to 33,000 horse-power, and water, equivalent to 11,000 horse-power. At present these figures are far from adequate, and it may be safely assumed that, in the year 1845, the power and number of the machines and the number of the workers is greater by one-half than it was in 1834. The chief centre of this industry is Lancashire, where it originated; it has thoroughly revolutionized this county, converting it from an obscure, ill-cultivated swamp into a busy, lively region, multiplying its population tenfold in eighty years, and causing giant cities such as Liverpool and Manchester, containing together 700,000 inhabitants, and their neighbouring towns, Bolton with 60,000, Rochdale with 75,000, Oldham with 50,000, Preston with 60,000, Ashton and Stalybridge with 40,000, and a whole list of other manufacturing towns to spring up as if by a magic touch. The history of South Lancashire contains some of the greatest marvels of modern times, yet no one ever mentions them, and all these miracles are the product of the cotton industry. Glasgow, too, the centre for the cotton district of Scotland, for Lanarkshire and Renfrewshire, has increased in population, from 30,000 to

[1] According to Porter's *Progress of the Nation*, i (London, 1836); ii (1838); iii (1843); (official data), and other sources, chiefly official. [The historical outline of the industrial revolution given above is not exact in certain details; but in 1843–4 no better sources were available. (*Added in the German edition of 1892.*)]

300,000, since the introdution of the industry. The hosiery manufacture of Nottingham and Derby also received one fresh impulse from the lower price of yarn, and a second one from an improvement of the stocking loom, by means of which two stockings could be woven at once. The manufacture of lace, too, became an important branch of industry after the invention of the lace machine in 1777; soon after that date Lindley invented the point-net machine, and in 1809 Heathcoat invented the bobbin-net machine, in consequence of which the production of lace was greatly simplified, and the demand increased proportionately in consequence of the diminished cost, so that now, at least 200,000 persons are supported by this industry. Its chief centres are Nottingham, Leicester, and the West of England, Wiltshire, Devonshire, etc. A corresponding extension has taken place in the branches dependent upon the cotton industry, in dyeing, bleaching, and printing. Bleaching by the application of chlorine in place of the oxygen of the atmosphere; dyeing and printing by the rapid development of chemistry, and printing by a series of most brilliant mechanical inventions, a yet greater advance which, with the extension of these branches caused by the growth of the cotton industry, raised them to a previously unknown degree of prosperity.

The same activity manifested itself in the manufacture of wool. This had hitherto been the leading department of English industry, but the quantities formerly produced are as nothing in comparison with that which is now manufactured. In 1782 the whole wool crop of the preceding three years lay unused for want of workers, and would have continued so to lie if the newly invented machinery had not come to its assistance and spun it. The adaptation of this machinery to the spinning of wool was most successfully accomplished. Then began the same sudden development in the wool districts which we have already seen in the cotton districts. In 1738 there were 75,000 pieces of woollen cloth produced in the West Riding of Yorkshire; in 1817 there were 490,000 pieces, and so rapid was the extension of the industry that in 1834, 450,000 more pieces were produced than in 1825. In 1801, 101,000,000 pounds of wool (7,000,000 pounds of it imported) were worked up; in 1835,

180,000,000 pounds were worked up; of which 42,000,000 pounds were imported. The principal centre of this industry is the West Riding of Yorkshire, where, especially at Bradford, long English wool is converted into worsted yarns, etc.; while in the other cities, Leeds, Halifax, Huddersfield, etc., short wool is converted into hard-spun yarn and cloth. Then come the adjacent part of Lancashire, the region of Rochdale, where in addition to the cotton industry much flannel is produced, and the West of England which supplies the finest cloths. Here also the growth of population is worthy of observation [see Figure], a population which, since 1831, must have increased at least 20 to 25 per cent further. In 1835 the spinning of wool employed in the United Kingdom 1,313 mills, with 71,300 workers, these last being but a small portion of the multitude who are supported directly or indirectly by the manufacture of wool, and excluding nearly all weavers.

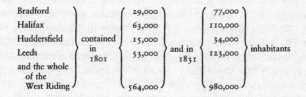

Bradford		29,000		77,000	
Halifax		63,000		110,000	
Huddersfield	contained in 1801	15,000	and in 1831	34,000	inhabitants
Leeds		53,000		123,000	
and the whole of the West Riding		564,000		980,000	

Progress in the linen trade developed later, because the nature of the raw material made the application of spinning machinery very difficult. Attempts had been made in the last years of the last century in Scotland, but the Frenchman, Girard, who introduced flax-spinning in 1810, was the first who succeeded practically, and even Girard's machines first attained on British soil the importance they deserved by means of improvements which they underwent in England, and of their universal application in Leeds, Dundee, and Belfast. From this time the British linen trade rapidly extended. In 1814, 3,000 tons of flax were imported; in 1833, nearly 19,000 tons of flax and 3,400 tons of hemp. The export of Irish linen to Great Britain rose from 32,000,000 yards in 1800 to 53,000,000 in 1825, of which a large part was re-exported. The export of English and Scottish woven linen goods rose from 24,000,000 yards in 1820 to 51,000,000 yards in 1833. The number of flax-spinning establishments in 1835 was 347, employing 33,000 workers, of which one-half were in the South of Scotland, more than 60 in the West Riding of Yorkshire, Leeds, and its environs, 25 in Belfast, Ireland, and the rest in Dorset and Lancashire. Weaving is carried on in the South of Scotland, here and there in England, but principally in Ireland.

With like success did the English turn their attention to the manufacture of silk. Raw material was imported from Southern Europe and Asia ready spun, and the chief labour lay in the twisting of fine threads. Until 1824 the heavy import duty, four shillings per pound on raw material, greatly retarded the development of the English silk industry, while only the markets of England and the Colonies were protected for it. In that year the duty was reduced to one penny, and the number of mills at once largely increased. In a single year the number of throwing spindles rose from 780,000 to 1,180,000; and, although the commercial crisis of 1825 crippled this branch of industry for the moment, yet in 1827 more was produced than ever, the mechanical skill and experience of the English having secured their twisting machinery the supremacy over the awkward devices of their competitors. In 1835 the British Empire possessed 263 twisting mills, employing 30,000 workers, located chiefly in Cheshire, in Macclesfield, Congleton, and the surrounding districts, and in Manchester and Somersetshire. Besides these, there are numerous mills for working up waste, from which a peculiar article known as spun silk is manufactured, with which the English supply even the Paris and Lyons weavers. The weaving of the silk so twisted and spun is carried on in Paisley and elsewhere in Scotland, and in Spitalfields, London, but also in Manchester and elsewhere. Nor is the gigantic advance achieved in English manufacture since 1760 restricted to the production of clothing materials. The impulse, once given, was communicated to all branches of industrial activity, and a multitude of inventions wholly unrelated to those here cited, received double importance from the fact that they were made in the midst of the universal movement. But as soon as the immeasurable

importance of mechanical power was practically demon-
strated, every energy was concentrated in the effort to exploit
this power in all directions, and to exploit it in the interest of
individual inventors and manufacturers; and the demand for
machinery, fuel, and materials called a mass of workers and
a number of trades into redoubled activity. The steam-engine
first gave importance to the broad coalfields of England; the
production of machinery began now for the first time, and
with it arose a new interest in the iron mines which supplied
raw material for it. The increased consumption of wool
stimulated English sheep-breeding, and the growing importation of wool, flax, and silk called forth an extension of
the British ocean carrying trade. Greatest of all was the
growth of production of iron. The rich iron deposits of the
English hills had hitherto been little developed; iron had
always been smelted by means of charcoal, which became
gradually more expensive as agriculture improved and forests
were cut away. The beginning of the use of coke in iron
smelting had been made in the last century, and in 1780
a new method was invented of converting into available
wrought-iron coke-smelted iron, which up to that time had
been convertible into cast iron only. This process, known as
'puddling', consists in withdrawing the carbon which had
mixed with the iron during the process of smelting and
opened a wholly new field for the production of English iron.
Smelting furnaces were built fifty times larger than before,
the process of smelting was simplified by the introduction of
hot blasts, and iron could thus be produced so cheaply that a
multitude of objects which had before been made of stone or
wood were now made of iron.

In 1788 Thomas Paine, the famous democrat, built in
Yorkshire the first iron bridge,* which was followed by a
great number of others, so that now nearly all bridges,
especially for railroad traffic, are built of cast iron, while in
London itself a bridge across the Thames, the Southwark
bridge, has been built of this material. Iron pillars, supports
for machinery, ect., are universally used, and since the
introduction of gas-lighting and railroads, new outlets for
English iron products are opened. Nails and screws gradually
came to be made by machinery. Huntsman, a Sheffielder,
discovered in 1760 a method for casting steel, by which

much labour was saved, and the production of wholly new cheap goods rendered practicable; and through the greater purity of the material placed at its disposal, and the more perfect tools, new machinery, and minute division of labour, the metal trade of England now first attained importance. The population of Birmingham grew from 73,000 in 1801 to 200,000 in 1844; that of Sheffield from 46,000 in 1801 to 110,000 in 1844, and the consumption of coal in the latter city alone reached in 1836, 515,000 tons. In 1805 there were exported 4,300 tons of iron products and 4,600 tons of pig-iron; in 1834, 16,200 tons of iron products and 107,000 tons of pig-iron, while the whole iron product, reaching in 1740 but 17,000 tons, had risen in 1834 to nearly 700,000 tons. The smelting of pig-iron alone consumes yearly more than 3,000,000 tons of coal, and the importance which coal-mining has attained in the course of the last sixty years can scarcely be conceived. All the English and Scottish deposits are now worked, and the mines of Northumberland and Durham alone yield annually more than 5,000,000 tons for shipping, and employ from 40 to 50,000 men. According to the *Durham Chronicle*, there were worked in these two counties: In 1753, 14 mines; in 1800, 40 mines; in 1836, 76 mines; in 1843, 130 mines. Moreover, all mines are now much more energetically worked than formerly. A similarly increased activity was applied to the working of tin, copper, and lead, and alongside of the extension of glass manufacture arose a new branch of industry in the production of pottery, rendered important by the efforts of Josiah Wedgwood, about 1763. This inventor placed the whole manufacture of stoneware on a scientific basis, introduced better taste, and founded the potteries of North Staffordshire, a district of eight English square miles, which, formerly a desert waste, is now sown with works and dwellings, and supports more than 60,000 people.

Into this universal whirl of activity everything was drawn. Agriculture made a corresponding advance. Not only did landed property pass, as we have already seen, into the hands of new owners and cultivators, agriculture was affected in still another way. The great holders applied capital to the improvement of the soil, tore down needless fences, drained, manured, employed better tools, and applied a rotation of crops. The progress of science came to their assistance also; Sir Humphry Davy applied chemistry to agriculture with success, and the development of mechanical science bestowed a multitude of advantages upon the large farmer. Further, in consequence of the increase of population, the demand for agricultural products increased in such measure that from 1760 to 1834, 6,840,540 acres of waste land were reclaimed; and, in spite of this, England was transformed from a grain exporting to a grain importing country.

The same activity was developed in the establishment of communication. From 1818 to 1829, there were built in England and Wales, 1,000 English miles of roadway of the width prescribed by law, 60 feet, and nearly all the old roads were reconstructed on the new system of McAdam. In Scotland, the Department of Public Works built since 1803 nearly 900 miles of roadway and more than 1,000 bridges, by which the population of the Highlands was suddenly placed within reach of civilization. The Highlanders had hitherto been chiefly poachers and smugglers; they now became farmers and hand-workers. And, though Gaelic schools were organized for the purpose of maintaining the Gaelic language, yet Gaelic-Celtic customs and speech are rapidly vanishing before the approach of English civilization. So, too, in Ireland; between the counties of Cork, Limerick, and Kerry lay hitherto a wilderness wholly without passable roads, and serving, by reason of its inaccessibility, as the refuge of all criminals and the chief protection of the Celtic Irish nationality in the South of Ireland. It has now been cut through by public roads, and civilization has thus gained admission even to this savage region. The whole British Empire, and especially England, which, sixty years ago, had as bad roads as Germany or France then had, is now covered by a network of the finest roadways; and these, too, like almost everything else in England, are the work of private enterprise, the State having done very little in this direction.

Before 1755 England possessed almost no canals. In that year a canal was built in Lancashire from Sankey Brook to St Helens; and in 1759 James Brindley built the first important one, the Duke of Bridgewater's canal from Manchester, and the coal-mines of the district to the mouth of the Mersey passing, near Barton, by aqueduct, over the river Irwell. From this achievement dates the canal building of England, to which Brindley first gave importance. Canals were now built, and rivers made navigable in all directions. In England alone, there are 2,200 miles of canals and 1,800 miles of navigable river. In Scotland, the Caledonian Canal was cut directly across the country, and in Ireland several canals were built. These improvements, too, like the railroads and roadways, are nearly all the work of private individuals and companies.

The railroads have been only recently built. The first great one was opened from Liverpool to Manchester in 1830, since which all the great cities have been connected by rail. London with Southampton, Brighton, Dover, Colchester, Exeter, and Birmingham, Birmingham with Gloucester, Liverpool, Lancaster (via Newton and Wigan, and via Manchester and Bolton); also with Leeds (via Manchester and Halifax, and via Leicester, Derby, and Sheffield); Leeds with Hull and Newcastle (via York). There are also many minor lines building or projected, which will soon make it possible to travel from Edinburgh to London in one day.

As it had transformed the means of communication by land, so did the introduction of steam revolutionize travel by sea. The first steamboat was launched in 1807, in the Hudson, in North America; the first in the British Empire, in 1811, on the Clyde. Since then, more than 600 have been built in England; and in 1836 more than 500 were plying to and from British ports.

Such, in brief, is the history of English industrial development in the past sixty years, a history which has no counterpart in the annals of humanity. Sixty, eighty years ago, England was a country like every other, with small towns, few and simple industries, and a thin but *proportionally* large agricultural population. Today it is a country like *no* other, with a capital of two and a half million inhabitants; with vast manufacturing cities; with an industry that supplies the world, and produces almost everything by means of the most complex machinery; with an industrious, intelligent, dense population, of which two-thirds are employed in trade and commerce, and composed of classes wholly different; forming, in fact, with other customs and other needs, a different nation from the England of those days. The industrial revolution is of the same importance for England as the political revolution for France, and the philosophical revolution for Germany; and the difference between England in 1760 and in 1844 is at least as great as that between France, under the *ancien régime* and during the revolution of July. But the mightiest result of this industrial transformation is the English proletariat.

We have already seen how the proletariat was called into existence by the introduction of machinery. The rapid extension of manufacture demanded hands, wages rose, and troops of workmen migrated from the agricultural districts to the towns. Population multiplied enormously, and nearly all the increase took place in the proletariat. Further, Ireland had entered upon an orderly development only since the beginning of the eighteenth century. There, too, the population, more than decimated by English cruelty in earlier disturbances, now rapidly multiplied, especially after the advance in manufacture began to draw masses of Irishmen towards England. Thus arose the great manufacturing and commercial cities of the British Empire, in which at least three-fourths of the population belong to the working class, while the lower middle class consists only of small shopkeepers, and very very few handicraftsmen. For, though the rising manufacture first attained importance by transforming tools into machines, workrooms into factories, and consequently, the toiling lower middle class into the toiling proletariat, and the former large merchants into manufacturers, though the lower middle class was thus early crushed out, and the population reduced to the two opposing elements, workers and capitalists, this happened outside of the domain of manufacture proper, in the province of handicraft and retail trade as well. In the place of the former masters and apprentices, came great capitalists and working men who had no prospect of rising above their class. Handwork was carried on after the fashion of factory work, the division of labour was strictly applied, and small employers who could not compete with great establishments were forced down into the proletariat. At the same time the destruction of the former organization of hand-work, and the disappearance of the lower middle class deprived the working man of all possibility of rising into the middle class himself. Hitherto he had always had the prospect of establishing himself somewhere as master artificer, perhaps employing journeymen and apprentices; but now, when master artificers were crowded out by manufacturers, when large capital had become necessary for carrying on work independently, the working class became, for the first time, an integral, permanent class of the population, whereas it has formerly often been merely a transition leading to the bourgeoisie. Now, he who was born to toil had no other prospect than that of remaining a toiler all his life. Now, for the first time, therefore, the proletariat was in a position to undertake an independent movement.

In this way were brought together those vast masses of working men who now fill the whole British Empire, whose social condition forces itself every day more and more upon the attention of the civilized world. The condition of the working class is the condition of the vast majority of the English people. The question: What is to become of those destitute millions, who consume today what they earned yesterday; who have created the greatness of England by their inventions and their toil; who become with every passing day more conscious of their might, and demand, with daily increasing urgency, their share of the advantages of society?—This, since the Reform Bill,* has become the national question. All parliamentary debates of any importance may be reduced to this; and, though the English middle class will not as yet admit it, though they try to evade this great question, and to represent their own particular interests as the truly national ones, their action is utterly useless. With every session of Parliament the working class gains ground, the interests of the middle class diminish in importance; and, in spite of the fact that the middle class is the chief, in fact, the only power in Parliament, the last session of 1844 was a continuous debate upon subjects affecting the working class, the Poor Relief Bill, the Factory Act, the Masters' and Servants' Act; and Thomas Duncombe, the representative of the working men in the House of Commons, was the great man of the session; while the Liberal middle class with its motion for repealing the Corn Laws, and the Radical middle class with its resolution for refusing the taxes, played pitiable roles. Even the debates about Ireland were at bottom debates about the Irish proletariat, and the means of coming to its assistance. It is high time, too, for the English middle class to make some concessions to the working men who no longer plead but threaten; for in a short time it may be too late.

In spite of all this, the English middle class, especially the manufacturing class, which is enriched directly by means of the poverty of the workers, persists in ignoring this poverty. This class, feeling itself the mighty representative class of the nation, is ashamed to lay the sore spot of England bare before the eyes of the world; will not confess, even to itself, that the workers are in distress, because it, the property-holding, manufacturing class, must bear the moral responsibility for this distress. Hence the scornful smile which intelligent Englishmen (and they, the middle class, alone are known on the Continent) assume when anyone begins to speak of the condition of the working class; hence the utter ignorance on the part of the whole middle class of everything which concerns the workers; hence the ridiculous blunders which men of this class, in and out of Parliament, make when the position of the proletariat comes under discussion; hence the absurd freedom from anxiety, with which the middle class dwells upon a soil that is honeycombed, and may any day collapse, the speedy collapse of which is as certain as a mathematical or mechanical demonstration; hence the miracle that the English have as yet no single book upon the condition of their workers, although they have been examining and mending the old state of things no one knows how many years. Hence also the deep wrath of the whole working class, from Glasgow to London, against the rich, by whom they are systematically plundered and mercilessly left to their fate, a wrath which before too long a time goes by, a time almost within the power of man to predict, must break out into a Revolution in comparison with which the French Revolution, and the year 1794, will prove to have been child's play.

The Industrial Proletariat

THE order of our investigation of the different sections of the proletariat follows naturally from the foregoing history of its rise. The first proletarians were connected with manufacture, were engendered by it, and accordingly, those employed in manufacture, in the working up of raw materials, will first claim our attention. The production of raw materials and of fuel for manufacture attained importance only in consequence of the industrial change, and engendered a new proletariat, the coal and metal miners. Then, in the third place, manufacture influenced agriculture, and in the fourth, the condition of Ireland; and the fractions of the proletariat belonging to each, will find their place accordingly. We shall find, too, that with the possible exception of the Irish, the degree of intelligence of the various workers is in direct proportion to their relation to manufacture; and that the factory-hands are most enlightened as to their own interests, the miners somewhat less so, the agricultural labourers scarcely at all. We shall find the same order again among the industrial workers, and shall see how the factory-hands, eldest children of the industrial revolution, have from the beginning to the present day formed the nucleus of the Labour Movement, and how the others have joined this movement just in proportion as their handicraft has been invaded by the progress of machinery. We shall thus learn from the example which England offers, from the equal pace which the Labour Movement has kept with the movement of industrial development, the historical significance of manufacture.

Since, however, at the present moment, pretty much the whole industrial proletariat is involved in the movement, and the condition of the separate sections has much in common, because they all are industrial, we shall have first to examine the condition of the industrial proletariat as a whole, in order later to notice more particularly each separate division with its own peculiarities.

It has been already suggested that manufacture centralizes property in the hands of the few. It requires large capital with which to erect the colossal establishments that ruin the petty trading bourgeoisie and with which to press into its service the forces of Nature, so driving the hand-labour of the independent workman out of the market. The division of labour, the application of water and especially steam, and the application of machinery, are the three great levers with which manufacture, since the middle of the last century, has been busy putting the world out of joint. Manufacture, on a small scale, created the middle class; on a large scale, it created the working class, and raised the elect of the middle class to the throne, but only to overthrow them the more surely when the time comes. Meanwhile, it is an undenied and easily explained fact that the numerous petty middle class of the 'good old times' has been annihilated by manufacture, and resolved into rich capitalists on the one hand and poor workers on the other.[1]

The centralizing tendency of manufacture does not, however, stop here. Population becomes centralized just as capital does; and, very naturally, since the human being, the worker, is regarded in manufacture simply as a piece of capital for the use of which the manufacturer pays interest under the name of wages. A manufacturing establishment requires many workers employed together in a single building, living near each other and forming a village of themselves in the case of a good-sized factory. They have needs for satisfying which other people are necessary; handicraftsmen, shoemakers, tailors, bakers, carpenters, stonemasons, settle at hand. The inhabitants of the village, especially the younger generation, accustom themselves to factory work, grow skilful in it, and when the first mill can no longer employ them all, wages fall, and the immigration of fresh manufacturers is the consequence. So the village grows into a small town, and the small town into a large

[1] Compare on this point my 'Outlines of a Critique of Political Economy' in the *Deutsch-Französische Jahrbücher*. [In this essay 'free competition' is the starting-point; but industry is only the practice of free competition and the latter is only the principle of industry. (*Added in the German edition.*)]

one. The greater the town, the greater its advantages. It offers roads, railroads, canals; the choice of skilled labour increases constantly, new establishments can be built more cheaply because of the competition among builders and machinists who are at hand, than in remote country districts, whither timber, machinery, builders, and operatives must be brought; it offers a market to which buyers crowd, and direct communication with the markets supplying raw material or demanding finished goods. Hence the marvellously rapid growth of the great manufacturing towns. The country, on the other hand, has the advantage that wages are usually lower than in town, and so town and country are in constant competition; and, if the advantage is on the side of the town today, wages sink so low in the country tomorrow that new investments are most profitably made there. But the centralizing tendency of manufacture continues in full force, and every new factory built in the country bears in it the germ of a manufacturing town. If it were possible for this mad rush of manufacture to go on at this rate for another century, every manufacturing district of England would be one great manufacturing town, and Manchester and Liverpool would meet at Warrington or Newton; for in commerce, too, this centralization of the population works in precisely the same way, and hence it is that one or two great harbours, such as Hull and Liverpool, Bristol and London, monopolize almost the whole maritime commerce of Great Britain.

Since commerce and manufacture attain their most complete development in these great towns, their influence upon the proletariat is also most clearly observable here. Here the centralization of property has reached the highest point; here the morals and customs of the good old times are most completely obliterated; here it has gone so far that the name Merry Old England conveys no meaning, for Old England itself is unknown to memory and to the tales of our grandfathers. Hence, too, there exist here only a rich and a poor class, for the lower middle class vanishes more completely with every passing day. Thus the class formerly most stable has become the most restless one. It consists today of a few remnants of a past time, and a number of people eager to make fortunes, industrial Micawbers* and speculators of whom one may amass a fortune, while ninety-nine become insolvent, and more than half of the ninety-nine live by perpetually repeated failure.

But in these towns the proletarians are the infinite majority, and how they fare, what influence the great town exercises upon them, we have now to investigate.

The Great Towns

A TOWN, such as London, where a man may wander for hours together without reaching the beginning of the end, without meeting the slightest hint which could lead to the inference that there is open country within reach, is a strange thing. This colossal centralization, this heaping together of two and a half millions of human beings at one point, has multiplied the power of this two and a half millions a hundredfold; has raised London to the commercial capital of the world, created the giant docks and assembled the thousand vessels that continually cover the Thames. I know nothing more imposing than the view which the Thames offers during the ascent from the sea to London Bridge. The masses of buildings, the wharves on both sides, especially from Woolwich upwards, the countless ships along both shores, crowding ever closer and closer together, until, at last, only a narrow passage remains in the middle of the river, a passage through which hundreds of steamers shoot by one another; all this is so vast, so impressive, that a man cannot collect himself, but is lost in the marvel of England's greatness before he sets foot upon English soil.[1]

But the sacrifices which all this has cost become apparent later. After roaming the streets of the capital a day or two, making headway with difficulty through the human turmoil and the endless lines of vehicles, after visiting the slums of the metropolis, one realizes for the first time that these Londoners have been forced to sacrifice the best qualities of their human nature, to bring to pass all the marvels of civilization which crowd their city; that a hundred powers which slumbered within them have remained inactive, have been suppressed in order that a few might be developed more fully and multiply through union with those of others. The very turmoil of the streets has something repulsive, some-

---

[1] This applies to the time of sailing vessels. The Thames now is a dreary collection of ugly steamers.

thing against which human nature rebels. The hundreds of thousands of all classes and ranks crowding past each other, are they not all human beings with the same qualities and powers, and with the same interest in being happy? And have they not, in the end, to seek happiness in the same way, by the same means? And still they crowd by one another as though they had nothing in common, nothing to do with one another, and their only agreement is the tacit one, that each keep to his own side of the pavement, so as not to delay the opposing streams of the crowd, while it occurs to no man to honour another with so much as a glance. The brutal indifference, the unfeeling isolation of each in his private interest becomes the more repellent and offensive, the more these individuals are crowded together, within a limited space. And, however much one may be aware that this isolation of the individual, this narrow self-seeking is the fundamental principle of our society everywhere, it is nowhere so shamelessly barefaced, so self-conscious as just here in the crowding of the great city. The dissolution of mankind into monads, of which each one has a separate principle and a separate purpose, the world of atoms, is here carried out to its utmost extreme.

Hence it comes, too, that the social war, the war of each against all, is here openly declared. Just as in Stirner's recent book,* people regard each other only as useful objects; each exploits the other, and the end of it all is, that the stronger treads the weaker under foot, and that the powerful few, the capitalists, seize everything for themselves, while to the weak many, the poor, scarcely a bare existence remains.

What is true of London, is true of Manchester, Birmingham, Leeds, is true of all great towns. Everywhere barbarous indifference, hard egotism on one hand, and nameless misery on the other, everywhere social warfare, every man's house in a state of siege, everywhere reciprocal plundering under the protection of the law, and all so shameless, so openly avowed that one shrinks before the consequences of our social state as they manifest themselves here undisguised, and can only wonder that the whole crazy fabric still hangs together.

Since capital, the direct or indirect control of the means of subsistence and production, is the weapon with which this social warfare is carried on, it is clear that all the disadvantages of such a state must fall upon the poor. For him no man has the slightest concern. Cast into the whirlpool, he must struggle through as well as he can. If he is so happy as to find work, i.e. if the bourgeoisie does him the favour to enrich itself by means of him, wages await him which scarcely suffice to keep body and soul together; if he can get no work he may steal, if he is not afraid of the police, or starve, in which case the police will take care that he does so in a quiet and inoffensive manner. During my residence in England, at least twenty or thirty persons have died of simple starvation under the most revolting circumstances, and a jury has rarely been found possessed of the courage to speak the plain truth in the matter. Let the testimony of the witnesses be never so clear and unequivocal, the bourgeoisie, from which the jury is selected, always finds some back door through which to escape the frightful verdict, death from starvation. The bourgeoisie dare not speak the truth in these cases, for it would speak its own condemnation. But indirectly, far more than directly, many have died of starvation, where long continued want of proper nourishment has called forth fatal illness, when it has produced such debility that causes which might otherwise have remained inoperative brought on severe illness and death. The English working men call this 'social murder', and accuse our whole society of perpetrating this crime perpetually. Are they wrong?

True, it is only individuals who starve, but what security has the working man that it may not be his turn tomorrow? Who assures him employment, who vouches for it that, if for any reason or no reason his lord and master discharges him tomorrow, he can struggle along with those dependent upon him, until he may find someone else 'to give him bread'? Who guarantees that willingness to work shall suffice to obtain work, that uprightness, industry, thrift, and the rest of the virtues recommended by the bourgeoisie, are really his road to happiness? No one. He knows that he has something today, and that it does not depend upon himself whether he shall have something tomorrow. He knows that every breeze that blows, every whim of his employer, every bad turn of trade may hurl him back into the fierce whirlpool from which he has temporarily saved himself, and in which it is hard and often impossible to keep his head above water. He knows that, though he may have the means of living today, it is very uncertain whether he shall tomorrow.

Meanwhile, let us proceed to a more detailed investigation of the position, in which the social war has placed the non-possessing class. Let us see what pay for his work society does give the working man in the form of dwelling, clothing, food, what sort of subsistence it grants those who contribute most to the maintenance of society; and, first, let us consider the dwellings.

Every great city has one or more slums, where the working class is crowded together. True, poverty often dwells in hidden alleys close to the palaces of the rich; but, in general, a separate territory has been assigned to it, where, removed from the sight of the happier classes, it may struggle along as it can. These slums are pretty equally arranged in all the great towns of England, the worst houses in the worst quarters of the towns; usually one- or two-storeyed cottages in long rows, perhaps with cellars used as dwellings, almost always irregularly built. These houses of three or four rooms and a kitchen form, throughout England, some parts of London excepted, the general dwellings of the working class. The streets are generally unpaved, rough, dirty, filled with vegetable and animal refuse, without sewers or gutters, but supplied with foul, stagnant pools instead. Moreover, ventilation is impeded by the bad, confused method of building of the whole quarter, and since many human beings here live crowded into a small space, the atmosphere that prevails in these working-men's quarters may readily be imagined. Further, the streets serve as drying grounds in fine weather; lines are stretched across from house to house, and hung with wet clothing.

Let us investigate some of the slums in their order. London comes first,[1] and in London the famous rookery of St Giles

---

[1] The description given below had already been written when I came across an article in the *Illuminated Magazine* (October 1844) dealing with the working-class districts in London which coincides—in many places almost literally and everywhere in general tenor—with what I had said. The article was entitled 'The Dwellings of the Poor, from the note-book of an M. D.'. (*Note in the German edition.*)

which is now, at last, about to be penetrated by a couple of broad streets. St Giles is in the midst of the most populous part of the town, surrounded by broad, splendid avenues in which the gay world of London idles about, in the immediate neighbourhood of Oxford Street, Regent Street, of Trafalgar Square and the Strand. It is a disorderly collection of tall, three or four-storeyed houses, with narrow, crooked, filthy streets, in which there is quite as much life as in the great thoroughfares of the town, except that, here, people of the working class only are to be seen. A vegetable market is held in the street, baskets with vegetables and fruits, naturally all bad and hardly fit to use, obstruct the sidewalk still further, and from these, as well as from the fish-dealers' stalls, arises a horrible smell. The houses are occupied from cellar to garret, filthy within and without, and their appearance is such that no human being could possibly wish to live in them. But all this is nothing in comparison with the dwellings in the narrow courts and alleys between the streets, entered by covered passages between the houses, in which the filth and tottering ruin surpass all description. Scarcely a whole window-pane can be found, the walls are crumbling, door-posts and window-frames loose and broken, doors of old boards nailed together, or altogether wanting in this thieves' quarter, where no doors are needed, there being nothing to steal. Heaps of garbage and ashes lie in all directions, and the foul liquids emptied before the doors gather in stinking pools. Here live the poorest of the poor, the worst paid workers with thieves and the victims of prostitution indiscriminately huddled together, the majority Irish, or of Irish extraction, and those who have not yet sunk in the whirlpool of moral ruin which surrounds them, sinking daily deeper, losing daily more and more of their power to resist the demoralizing influence of want, filth, and evil surroundings.

Nor is St Giles the only London slum. In the immense tangle of streets, there are hundreds and thousands of alleys and courts lined with houses too bad for anyone to live in, who can still spend anything whatsoever upon a dwelling fit for human beings. Close to the splendid houses of the rich such a lurking-place of the bitterest poverty may often be found. So, a short time ago, on the occasion of a coroner's inquest, a region close to Portman Square, one of the very respectable squares, was characterized as an abode 'of a multitude of Irish demoralized by poverty and filth'. So, too, may be found in streets, such as Long Acre and others, which, though not fashionable, are yet 'respectable', a great number of cellar dwellings out of which puny children and half-starved, ragged women emerge into the light of day. In the immediate neighbourhood of Drury Lane Theatre, the second in London, are some of the worst streets of the whole metropolis, Charles, King, and Park Streets, in which the houses are inhabited from cellar to garret exclusively by poor families. In the parishes of St John and St Margaret there lived in 1840, according to the *Journal of the Statistical Society*, 5,366 working-men's families in 5,294 'dwellings' (if they deserve the name!), men, women, and children thrown together without distinction of age or sex, 26,830 persons all told; and of these families three-fourths possessed but one room. In the aristocratic parish of St George, Hanover Square, there lived, according to the same authority, 1,465 working-men's families, nearly 6,000 persons, under similar conditions, and here, too, more than two-thirds of the whole number crowded together at the rate of one family in one room. And how the poverty of these unfortunates, among whom even thieves find nothing to steal, is exploited by the property-holding class in lawful ways! The abominable dwellings in Drury Lane, just mentioned, bring in the following rents: two cellar dwellings, 3s.; one room, ground-floor, 4s.; second-storey, 4s. 6d.; third-floor, 4s.; garret-room, 3s. weekly, so that the starving occupants of Charles Street alone pay the house-owners a yearly tribute of £2,000, and the 5,366 families above mentioned in Westminster, a yearly rent of £40,000.

The most extensive working-people's district lies east of the Tower in Whitechapel and Bethnal Green, where the greatest masses of London working people live. Let us hear Mr G. Alston, preacher of St Philip's, Bethnal Green, on the condition of his parish. He says:

It contains 1,400 houses, inhabited by 2,795 families, or about 12,000 persons. The space upon which this large population dwells, is less than 400 yards (1,200 feet) square, and in this overcrowding it is nothing unusual to find a man, his wife, four or five children, and, sometimes, both grandparents, all in one single room of ten to twelve square feet, where they eat, sleep, and work. I believe that before the Bishop of London called attention to this most poverty-stricken parish, people at the West End knew as little of it as of the savages of Australia or the South Sea Isles. And if we make ourselves acquainted with these unfortunates, through personal observation, if we watch them at their scanty meal and see them bowed by illness and want of work, we shall find such a mass of helplessness and misery, that a nation like ours must blush that these things can be possible. I was rector near Huddersfield during the three years in which the mills were at their worst, but I have never seen such complete helplessness of the poor as since then in Bethnal Green. Not one father of a family in ten in the whole neighbourhood has other clothing than his working suit, and that is as bad and tattered as possible; many, indeed, have no other covering for the night than these rags, and no bed, save a sack of straw and shavings.

The foregoing description furnishes an idea of the aspect of the interior of the dwellings. But let us follow the English officials, who occasionally stray thither, into one or two of these working men's homes.

On the occasion of an inquest held on 14 November 1843 by Mr Carter, coroner for Surrey, upon the body of Ann Galway, aged 45 years, the newspapers related the following particulars concerning the deceased: She had lived at No. 3 White Lion Court, Bermondsey Street, London, with her husband and a 19-year-old son in a little room, in which neither a bedstead nor any other furniture was to be seen. She lay dead beside her son upon a heap of feathers which were scattered over her almost naked body, there being neither sheet nor coverlet. The feathers stuck so fast over the whole body that the physician could not examine the corpse until it was cleansed, and then found it starved and scarred from the bites of vermin. Part of the floor of the room was torn up, and the hole used by the family as a privy.

On Monday, 15 January 1844 two boys were brought before the police magistrate because, being in a starving condition, they had stolen and immediately devoured a half-cooked calf's foot from a shop. The magistrate felt called upon to investigate the case further, and received the following details from the policeman: The mother of the two boys was the widow of an ex-soldier, afterwards policeman, and had had a very hard time since the death of her husband, to provide for her nine children. She lived at No. 2 Pool's Place, Quaker Court, Spitalfields, in the utmost poverty. When the policeman came to her, he found her with six of her children literally huddled together in a little back room, with no furniture but two old rush-bottomed chairs with the seats gone, a small table with two legs broken, a broken cup, and a small dish. On the hearth was scarcely a spark of fire, and in one corner lay as many old rags as would fill a woman's apron, which served the whole family as a bed. For bed clothing they had only their scanty day clothing. The poor woman told him that she had been forced to sell her bedstead the year before to buy food. Her bedding she had pawned with the victualler for food. In short, everything had gone for food. The magistrate ordered the woman a considerable provision from the poor-box.

In February 1844 Theresa Bishop, a widow 60 years old, was recommended, with her sick daughter, aged 26, to the compassion of the police magistrate in Marlborough Street. She lived at No. 5 Brown Street, Grosvenor Square, in a small back room no larger than a closet, in which there was not one single piece of furniture. In one corner lay some rags upon which both slept; a chest served as table and chair. The mother earned a little by charring. The owner of the house said that they had lived in this way since May 1843, had gradually sold or pawned everything that they had, and had still never paid any rent. The magistrate assigned them £1 from the poor-box.

I am far from asserting that *all* London working people live in such want as the foregoing three families. I know very well that ten are somewhat better off, where one is so totally trodden under foot by society; but I assert that thousands of industrious and worthy people—far worthier and more to be respected than all the rich of London—do find themselves in a condition unworthy of human beings; and that every proletarian, everyone, without exception, is exposed to a similar fate without any fault of his own and in spite of every possible effort.

But in spite of all this, they who have some kind of a shelter are fortunate, fortunate in comparison with the utterly homeless. In London 50,000 human beings get up every morning, not knowing where they are to lay their heads at night. The luckiest of this multitude, those who succeed in keeping a penny or two until evening, enter a lodging-house, such as abound in every great city, where they find a bed. But what a bed! These houses are filled with beds from cellar to garret, four, five, six beds in a room; as many as can be crowded in. Into every bed four, five, or six human beings are piled, as many as can be packed in, sick and well, young and old, drunk and sober, men and women, just as they come, indiscriminately. Then come strife, blows, wounds, or, if these bedfellows agree, so much the worse; thefts are arranged and things done which our language, grown more humane than our deeds, refuses to record. And those who cannot pay for such a refuge? They sleep where they find a place, in passages, arcades, in corners where the police and the owners leave them undisturbed. A few individuals find their way to the refuges which are managed, here and there, by private charity, others sleep on the benches in the parks close under the windows of Queen Victoria. Let us hear the London *Times*:

It appears from the report of the proceedings at Marlborough Street Police Court in our columns of yesterday, that there is an average number of 50 human beings of all ages, who huddle together in the parks every night, having no other shelter than what is supplied by the trees and a few hollows of the embankment. Of these, the majority are young girls who have been seduced from the country by the soldiers and turned loose on the world in all the destitution of friendless penury, and all the recklessness of early vice.

This is truly horrible! Poor there must be everywhere. Indigence will find its way and set up its hideous state in the heart of a great and luxurious city. Amid the thousand narrow lanes and by-streets of a populous metropolis there must always, we fear, be much suffering—much that offends the eye—much that lurks unseen.

But that within the precincts of wealth, gaiety, and fashion, nigh the regal grandeur of St. James, close on the palatial splendour of Bayswater, on the confines of the old and new aristocratic quarters, in a district where the cautious refinement of modern design has refrained from creating one single tenement for poverty; which seems, as it were, dedicated to the exclusive enjoyment of wealth, that *there* want, and famine, and disease, and vice should stalk in all their kindred horrors, consuming body by body, soul by soul!

It is indeed a monstrous state of things! Enjoyment the most absolute, that bodily ease, intellectual excitement, or the more innocent pleasures of sense can supply to man's craving, brought in close contact with the most unmitigated misery! Wealth, from its bright saloons, laughing—an insolently heedless laugh—at the unknown wounds of want! Pleasure, cruelly but unconsciously mocking the pain that moans below! All contrary things mocking one another—all contrary, save the vice which tempts and the vice which is tempted!

But let all men remember this—that within the most courtly precincts of the richest city of God's earth, there may be found, night after night, winter after winter, women—young in years—old in sin and suffering—outcasts from society—ROTTING FROM FAMINE, FILTH, AND DISEASE. Let them remember this, and learn not to theorise but to act. God knows, there is much room for action nowadays.[1]

I have referred to the refuges for the homeless. How greatly overcrowded these are, two examples may show. A newly erected Refuge for the Houseless in Upper Ogle Street, that can shelter 300 persons every night, has received since its opening, 27 January to 17 March 1844, 2,740 persons for one or more nights; and although the season was growing more favourable, the number of applicants in this, as well as in the asylums of Whitecross Street and Wapping, was strongly on the increase, and a crowd of the homeless had to be sent away every night for want of room. In another refuge, the Central Asylum in Playhouse Yard, there were supplied on an average 460 beds nightly, during the first three months of the year 1844, 6,681 persons being sheltered, and 96,141 portions of bread were distributed. Yet the committee of directors declare this institution began to meet the pressure of the needy to a limited extent only when the Eastern Asylum also was opened.

Let us leave London and examine the other great cities of the three kingdoms in their order. Let us take Dublin first, a city the approach to which from the sea is as charming as that of London is imposing. The Bay of Dublin is the most beautiful of the whole British Island Kingdom, and is even compared by the Irish with the Bay of Naples. The city, too, possesses great attractions, and its aristocratic districts are better and more tastefully laid out than those of any other

---

[1] *The Times*, 12 Oct. 1843.

British city. By way of compensation, however, the poorer districts of Dublin are among the most hideous and repulsive to be seen in the world. True, the Irish character, which, under some circumstances, is comfortable only in the dirt, has some share in this; but as we find thousands of Irish in every great city in England and Scotland, and as every poor population must gradually sink into the same uncleanliness, the wretchedness of Dublin is nothing specific, nothing peculiar to Dublin, but something common to all great towns. The poor quarters of Dublin are extremely extensive, and the filth, the uninhabitableness of the houses and the neglect of the streets, surpass all description. Some idea of the manner in which the poor are here crowded together may be formed from the fact that, in 1817, according to the report of the Inspector of Workhouses,[1] 1,318 persons lived in 52 houses with 390 rooms in Barral Street, and 1,997 persons in 71 houses with 393 rooms in and near Church Street; that

In this and the adjoining district there exists a multitude of foul courts and alleys; many cellars receive all their light through the door, while in not a few the inhabitants sleep upon the bare floor, though most of them possess bedsteads at least; Nicholson's Court, for example, contains twenty-eight wretched little rooms with 151 human beings in the greatest want, there being but two bedsteads and two blankets to be found in the whole court.

The poverty is so great in Dublin, that a single benevolent institution, the Mendicity Association, gives relief to 2,500 persons or one per cent of the population daily, receiving and feeding them for the day and dismissing them at night.

Dr Alison describes a similar state of things in Edinburgh, whose superb situation, which has won it the title of the Modern Athens, and whose brilliant aristocratic quarter in the New Town, contrast strongly with the foul wretchedness of the poor in the Old Town. Alison asserts that this extensive quarter is as filthy and horrible as the worst district

[1] Quoted by Dr W. P. Alison, FRSE, Fellow and late President of the Royal College of Physicians, etc., etc., *Observations on the Management of the Poor in Scotland and its Effects on the Health of Great Towns* (Edinburgh, 1840). The author is a religious Tory, brother of the historian, Archibald Alison.

of Dublin, while the Mendicity Association would have as great a proportion of needy persons to assist in Edinburgh as in the Irish capital. He asserts, indeed, that the poor in Scotland, especially in Edinburgh and Glasgow, are worse off than in any other region of the three kingdoms, and that the poorest are not Irish, but Scottish. The preacher of the Old Church of Edinburgh, Dr Lee, testified in 1836, before the Commission of Religious Instruction, that

He had never before seen such misery as in his parish, where the people were without furniture, without everything, two married couples often sharing one room. In a single day he had visited seven houses in which there was not a bed, in some of them not even a heap of straw. Old people of eighty years sleep on the board floor, nearly all slept in their day-clothes. In one cellar room he found two families from a Scotch country district; soon after their removal to the city two of the children had died, and a third was dying at the time of his visit. Each family had a filthy pile of straw lying in a corner; the cellar sheltered besides the two families a donkey, and was, moreover, so dark that it was impossible to distinguish one person from another by day. Dr. Lee declared that it was enough to make a heart of adamant bleed to see such misery in a country like Scotland.

In the Edinburgh *Medical and Surgical Journal*, Dr Hennen reports a similar state of things. From a Parliamentary Report,[1] it is evident that in the dwellings of the poor of Edinburgh a want of cleanliness reigns, such as must be expected under these conditions. On the bed-posts chickens roost at night, dogs and horses share the dwelllings of human beings, and the natural consequence is a shocking stench, with filth and swarms of vermin. The prevailing construction of Edinburgh favours these atrocious conditions as far as possible. The Old Town is built upon both slopes of a hill, along the crest of which runs the High Street. Out of the High Street there open downwards multitudes of narrow, crooked alleys, called wynds from their many turnings, and

[1] 'Report to the Home Secretary from the Poor-Law Commissioners, on an Inquiry into the *Sanitary Condition of the Labouring Classes in Great Britain*, with Appendix.' Presented to both Houses of Parliament in July 1842, 3 vols. Folio. [Assembled and arranged from medical reports by Edwin Chadwick, Secretary of the Poor-Law Commissioners. (*Added in the German edition.*)]

these wynds form the proletarian district of the city. The houses of the Scottish cities, in general, are five- or six-storeyed buildings, like those of Paris, and in contrast with England where, so far as possible, each family has a separate house. The crowding of human beings upon a limited area is thus intensified.

These streets [says an English journal[1] in an article upon the sanitary condition of the working people in cities] are often so narrow that a person can step from the window of one house into that of its opposite neighbour, while the houses are piled so high, storey upon storey, that the light can scarcely penetrate into the court or alley that lies between. In this part of the city there are neither sewers nor other drains, nor even privies belonging to the houses. In consequence, all refuse, garbage, and excrements of at least 50,000 persons are thrown into the gutters every night, so that, in spite of all street sweeping, a mass of dried filth and foul vapours are created, which not only offend the sight and smell, but endanger the health of the inhabitants in the highest degree. Is it to be wondered at, that in such localities all considerations of health, morals, and even the most ordinary decency are utterly neglected? On the contrary, all who are more intimately acquainted with the condition of the inhabitants will testify to the high degree which disease, wretchedness, and demoralisation have here reached. Society in such districts has sunk to a level indescribably low and hopeless. The houses of the poor are generally filthy, and are evidently never cleansed. They consist in most cases of a single room which, while subject to the worst ventilation, is yet usually kept cold by the broken and badly-fitting windows, and is sometimes damp and partly below ground level, always badly furnished and thoroughly uncomfortable, a straw-heap often serving the whole family for a bed, upon which men and women, young and old, sleep in revolting confusion. Water can be had only from the public pumps, and the difficulty of obtaining it naturally fosters all possible filth.

In the other great seaport towns the prospect is no better. Liverpool, with all its commerce, wealth, and grandeur yet treats its workers with the same barbarity. A full fifth of the population, more than 45,000 human beings, live in narrow, dark, damp, badly ventilated cellar dwelllings, of which there are 7,862 in the city. Besides these cellar dwellings there are

[1] The *Artisan*, Oct. 1843. A monthly magazine.

2,270 courts, small spaces built up on all four sides and having but one entrance, a narrow, covered passage-way, the whole ordinarily very dirty and inhabited exclusively by proletarians. Of such courts we shall have more to say when we come to Manchester. In Bristol, on one occasion, 2,800 families were visited, of whom 46 per cent occupied but one room each.

Precisely the same state of things prevails in the factory towns. In Nottingham there are in all 11,000 houses, of which between 7,000 and 8,000 are built back to back with a rear party-wall so that no through ventilation is possible, while a single privy usually serves for several houses. During an investigation made a short time since, many rows of houses were found to have been built over shallow drains covered only by the boards of the ground floor. In Leicester, Derby, and Sheffield, it is no better. Of Birmingham, the article above cited from the *Artisan* states:

In the older quarters of the city there are many bad districts, filthy and neglected, full of stagnant pools and heaps of refuse. Courts are very numerous in Birmingham, reaching two thousand, and containing the greater number of the working-people of the city. These courts are usually narrow, muddy, badly ventilated, ill-drained, and lined with eight to twenty houses, which, by reason of having their rear walls in common, can usually be ventilated from one side only. In the background, within the court, there is usually an ash heap or something of the kind, the filth of which cannot be described. It must, however, be observed that the newer courts are more sensibly built and more decently kept, and that even in the old ones, the cottages are much less crowded than in Manchester and Liverpool, wherefore Birmingham shows even during the reign of an epidemic a far smaller mortality than, for instance, Wolverhampton, Dudley, and Bilston, only a few miles distant. Cellar dwellings are unknown, too, in Birmingham, though a few cellars are misused as work-rooms. The lodging-houses for proletarians are rather numerous (over four hundred), chiefly in courts in the heart of the town. They are nearly all disgustingly filthy and ill-smelling, the refuge of beggars, thieves, tramps, and prostitutes, who eat, drink, smoke, and sleep here without the slightest regard to comfort or decency in an atmosphere endurable to these degraded beings only.

Glasgow is in many respects similar to Edinburgh, possessing the same wynds, the same tall houses. Of this city the *Artisan* observes:

The working-class forms here some 78% of the whole population [about 300,000], and lives in parts of the city which exceed in wretchedness and squalor the lowest nooks of St. Giles and White-chapel, the Liberties of Dublin, the Wynds of Edinburgh. There are numbers of such localities in the heart of the city, south of the Trongate, westward from the Saltmarket, in Calton and off the High Street, endless labyrinths of lanes or wynds into which open at almost every step, courts or blind alleys, formed by ill-ventilated, high-piled, waterless, and dilapidated houses. These are literally swarming with inhabitants. They contain three or four families upon each floor, perhaps twenty persons. In some cases each storey is let out in sleeping places, so that fifteen to twenty persons are packed, one on top of the other, I cannot say accommodated, in a single room. These districts shelter the poorest, most depraved, and worthless members of the community, and may be regarded as the sources of those frightful epidemics which, beginning here, spread desolation over Glasgow.

Let us hear how J. C. Symons, Government Commissioner for the investigation of the condition of the hand-weavers, describes these portions of the city:[1]

I have seen wretchedness in some of its worse phases both here and upon the Continent, but until I visited the wynds of Glasgow I did not believe that so much crime, misery, and disease could exist in any civilised country. In the lower lodging-houses ten, twelve, sometimes twenty persons of both sexes, all ages and various degrees of nakedness, sleep indiscriminately huddled together upon the floor. These dwellings are usually so damp, filthy, and ruinous, that no one could wish to keep his horse in one of them.

And in another place:

The wynds of Glasgow contain a fluctuating population of fifteen to thirty thousand human beings. This quarter consists wholly of narrow alleys and square courts, in the middle of every one of which there lies a dung heap. Revolting as was the outward appearance of these courts, I was yet not prepared for the filth and wretchedness within. In some of the sleeping-places which we visited at night [the Superintendent of Police, Captain Miller, and Symons] we found a complete layer of human beings stretched upon the floor, often

---

[1] J. C. Symons, *Arts and Artisans at Home and Abroad* (Edinburgh, 1889). The author, as it seems, himself a Scots, is a Liberal, and consequently fanatically opposed to every independent movement of working men. The passages here cited are to be found on pp. 116 ff.

fifteen to twenty, some clad, others naked, men and women indiscriminately. Their bed was a litter of mouldy straw, mixed with rags. There was little or no furniture, and the only thing which gave these dens any shimmer of habitableness was a fire upon the hearth. Theft and prostitution form the chief means of subsistence of this population. No one seemed to take the trouble to cleanse this Augean stable, this Pandemonium, this tangle of crime, filth, and pestilence in the centre of the second city of the kingdom. An extended examination of the lowest districts of other cities never revealed anything half so bad, either in intensity of moral and physical infection, or in comparative density of population. In this quarter most of the houses have been declared by the Court of Guild ruinous and unfit for habitation, but precisely these are the most densely populated, because, according to the law, no rent can be demanded for them.

The great manufacturing district in the centre of the British Isles, the thickly peopled stretch of West Yorkshire and South Lancashire, with its numerous factory towns, yields nothing to the other great manufacturing centres. The woollen district of the West Riding of Yorkshire is a charming region, a beautiful green hill country, whose elevations grow more rugged towards the West until they reach their highest point in the bold ridge of Blackstone Edge, the watershed between the Irish Sea and the North Sea. The valleys of the Aire, along which stretches Leeds, and of the Calder, through which the Manchester—Leeds railway runs, are among the most attractive in England, and are strewn in all directions with the factories, villages, and towns. The houses of rough grey stone look so neat and clean in comparison with the blackened brick buildings of Lancashire, that it is a pleasure to look at them. But on coming into the towns themselves, one finds little to rejoice over. Leeds lies as the *Artisan* describes it, and as I found confirmed upon examination,

... on a gentle slope that descends into the valley of the Aire. This stream flows through the city for about a mile-and-a-half and is exposed to violent floods during thaws or heavy rain. The higher western portions of the city are clean, for such a large town. But the low-lying districts along the river and its tributary becks are narrow, dirty, and enough in themselves to shorten the lives of the inhabitants, especially of little children. Added to this, the disgusting state of the working-men's districts about Kirkgate, Marsh Lane,

Cross Street and Richmond Road, which is chiefly attributable to their unpaved, drainless streets, irregular architecture, numerous courts and alleys, and total lack of the most ordinary means of cleanliness, all this taken together is explanation enough of the excessive mortality in these unhappy abodes of filthy misery. In consequence of the overflows of the Aire [which, it must be added, like all other rivers in the service of manufacture, flows into the city at one end clear and transparent, and flows out at the other end thick, black, and foul, smelling of all possible refuse] the houses and cellars are often so full of water that they have to be pumped out. And at such times the water rises, even where there are sewers, out of them into cellars,[1] engenders miasmatic vapours strongly impregnated with sulphuretted hydrogen, and leaves a disgusting residuum highly injurious to health. During the spring-floods of 1839 the action of such a choking of the sewers was so injurious, that, according to the report of the Registrar of Births and Deaths for this part of the town, there were three deaths to two births, whereas in the same three months, in every other part of the town, there were three births to two deaths. Other thickly populated districts are without any sewers whatsoever, or so badly provided as to derive no benefit from them. In some rows of houses the cellars are seldom dry; in certain districts there are several streets, covered with soft mud a foot deep. The inhabitants have made vain attempts from time to time to repair these streets with shovelfuls of cinders, but in spite of all such attempts, dung-heaps, and pools of dirty water emptied from the houses, fill all the holes until wind and sun dry them up.[2] An ordinary cottage in Leeds occupies not more than five yards square of land, and usually consists of a cellar, a living-room, and one sleeping-room. These contracted dwellings, filled day and night with human beings, are another point dangerous alike to the morals and the health of the inhabitants.

And how greatly these cottages are crowded, the Report on the Health of the Working Classes, quoted above, bears testimony 'In Leeds we found brothers and sisters, and lodgers of both sexes, sharing the parents' sleeping-room, whence arise consequences at the contemplation of which human feeling shudders.'

So, too, Bradford, which, but seven miles from Leeds at the junction of several valleys, lies upon the banks of a small,

---

[1] It must be borne in mind that these cellars are not mere storing-rooms for rubbish, but dwellings of human beings.

[2] Compare Report of the Town Council in the *Statistical Journal*, ii. 404.

coal-back foul-smelling stream. On weekdays the town is enveloped in a grey cloud of coal smoke, but on a fine Sunday it offers a superb picture, when viewed from the surrounding heights. Yet within reigns the same filth and discomfort as in Leeds. The older portions of the town are built upon steep hillsides, and are narrow and irregular. In the lanes, alleys, and courts lie filth and debris in heaps; the houses are ruinous, dirty, and miserable, and in the immediate vicinity of the river and the valley bottom I found many a one, whose ground floor, half-buried in the hillside, was totally abandoned. In general, the portions of the valley bottom in which working-men's cottages have crowded between the tall factories are among the worst built and dirtiest districts of the whole town. In the newer portions of this, as of every other factory town, the cottages are more regular, being built in rows, but they share here, too, all the evils incident to the customary method of providing working-men's dwellings, evils of which we shall have occasions to speak more particularly in discussing Manchester. The same is true of the remaining towns of the West Riding, especially of Barnsley, Halifax, and Huddersfield. The last named, the handsomest by far of all the factory towns of Yorkshire and Lancashire, by reason of its charming situation and modern architecture, has yet its bad quarter; for a committee, appointed by a meeting of citizens to survey the town, reported on 5 August 1844:

It is notorious that in Huddersfield whole streets and many lanes and courts are neither paved nor supplied with sewers nor other drains; that in them refuse, *débris*, and filth of every sort lies accumulating, festers and rots, and that, nearly everywhere, stagnant water accumulates in pools, in consequence of which the adjoining dwellings must inevitably be bad and filthy, so that in such places diseases arise and threaten the health of the whole town.

If we cross Blackstone Edge or penetrate it with the railroad, we enter upon that classic soil on which English manufacture has achieved its masterwork and from which all labour movements emanate, namely, South Lancashire with its central city Manchester. Again we have beautiful hill country sloping gently from the watershed westwards towards the Irish Sea, with the charming green valleys of the Ribble, the Irwell, the Mersey, and their tributaries, a country which, a hundred years ago chiefly swamp land, thinly populated, is now sown with towns and villages, and is the most densely populated strip of country in England. In Lancashire, and especially in Manchester, English manufacture finds at once its starting-point and its centre. The Manchester Exchange is the thermometer for all the fluctuations of trade. The modern art of manufacture has reached its perfection in Manchester. In the cotton industry of South Lancashire, the application of the forces of Nature, the superseding of hand-labour by machinery (especially by the power-loom and the self-acting mule), and the division of labour, are seen at the highest point; and, if we recognize in these three elements that which is characteristic of modern manufacture, we must confess that the cotton industry has remained in advance of all other branches of industry from the beginning down to the present day. The effects of modern manufacture upon the working class must necessarily develop here most freely and perfectly, and the manufacturing proletariat present itself in its fullest classic perfection. The degradation to which the application of steam-power, machinery, and the division of labour reduce the working man, and the attempts of the proletariat to rise above this abasement, must likewise be carried to the highest point and with the fullest consciousness. Hence because Manchester is the classic type of a modern manufacturing town, and because I know it as intimately as my own native town, more intimately than most of its residents know it, we shall make a longer stay here.

The towns surrounding Manchester vary little from the central city, so far as the working people's quarters are concerned, except that the working class forms, if possible, a larger proportion of their population. These towns are purely industrial and conduct all their business through Manchester upon which they are in every respect dependent, whence they are inhabited only by working men and petty tradesmen, while Manchester has a very considerable commercial population, especially of commission and 'respectable' retail dealers. Hence Bolton, Preston, Wigan, Bury, Rochdale, Middleton, Heywood, Oldham, Ashton, Stalybridge, Stockport, etc., though nearly all towns of thirty, fifty, seventy to ninety thousand inhabitants, are almost wholly working-people's districts, interspersed only with factories, a few thoroughfares lined with shops, and a few lanes along which the gardens and houses of the manufacturers are scattered like villas. The towns themselves are badly and irregularly built with foul courts, lanes, and back alleys, reeking of coal smoke, and especially dingy from the originally bright red brick, turned black with time, which is here the universal building material. Cellar dwellings are general here; wherever it is in any way possible, these subterranean dens are constructed, and a very considerable portion of the population dwells in them.

Among the worst of these towns after Preston and Oldham is Bolton, eleven miles north-west of Manchester. It has, so far as I have been able to observe in my repeated visits, but one main street, a very dirty one, Deansgate, which serves as a market, and is even in the finest weather a dark, unattractive hole in spite of the fact that, except for the factories, its sides are formed by low one- and two-storeyed houses. Here, as everywhere, the older part of the town is especially ruinous and miserable. A dark-coloured body of water, which leaves the beholder in doubt whether it is a brook or a long string of stagnant puddles, flows through the town and contributes its share to the total pollution of the air, by no means pure without it.

There is Stockport, too, which lies on the Cheshire side of the Mersey, but belongs nevertheless to the manufacturing district of Manchester. It lies in a narrow valley along the Mersey, so that the streets slope down a steep hill on one side and up an equally steep one on the other, while the railway from Manchester to Birmingham passes over a high viaduct above the city and the whole valley. Stockport is renowned throughout the entire district as one of the duskiest, smokiest holes, and looks, indeed, especially when viewed from the viaduct, excessively repellent. But far more repulsive are the cottages and cellar dwellings of the working class, which stretch in long rows through all parts of the town from the valley bottom to the crest of the hill. I do not remember to have seen so many cellars used as dwellings in any other town of this district.

A few miles north-east of Stockport is Ashton-under-Lyne,

one of the newest factory towns of this region. It stands on the slope of a hill at the foot of which are the canal and the river Tame, and is, in general, built on the newer, more regular plan. Five or six parallel streets stretch along the hill intersected at right angles by others leading down into the valley. By this method, the factories would be excluded from the town proper, even if the proximity of the river and the canal-way did not draw them all into the valley where they stand thickly crowded, belching forth black smoke from their chimneys. To this arrangement Ashton owes a much more attractive appearance than that of most factory towns; the streets are broad and cleaner, the cottages look new, bright red, and comfortable. But the modern system of building cottages for working men has its own disadvantages; every street has its concealed back lane to which a narrow paved path leads, and which is all the dirtier. And, although I saw no buildings, except a few on entering, which could have been more than fifty years old, there are even in Ashton streets in which the cottages are getting bad, where the bricks in the house-corners are no longer firm but shift about, in which the walls have cracks and will not hold the chalk whitewash inside; streets, whose dirty, smoke-begrimed aspect is nowise different from that of the other towns of the district, except that in Ashton, this is the exception, not the rule.

A mile eastward lies Stalybridge, also on the Tame. In coming over the hill from Ashton, the traveller has, at the top, both right and left, fine large gardens with superb villa-like houses in their midst, built usually in the Elizabethan style, which is to the Gothic precisely what the Anglican Church is to the Apostolic Roman Catholic. A hundred paces farther and Stalybridge shows itself in the valley, in sharp contrast with the beautiful country seats, in sharp contrast even with the modest cottages of Ashton! Stalybridge lies in a narrow, crooked ravine, much narrower even than the valley at Stockport, and both sides of this ravine are occupied by an irregular group of cottages, houses, and mills. On entering, the very first cottages are narrow, smoke-begrimed, old and ruinous; and as the first houses, so the whole town. A few streets lie in the narrow valley bottom, most of them run criss-cross, pell-mell, up hill and down, and in nearly all the houses, by reason of this sloping situation, the ground floor is half-buried in the earth; and what multitudes of courts, back lanes, and remote nooks arise out of this confused way of building may be seen from the hills, whence one has the town, here and there, in a bird's-eye view almost at one's feet. Add to this the shocking filth, and the repulsive effect of Stalybridge, in spite of its pretty surroundings, may be readily imagined.

But enough of these little towns. Each has its own peculiarities, but in general, the working people live in them just as in Manchester. Hence I have especially sketched only their peculiar construction, and would observe, that all more general observations as to the condition of the labouring population in Manchester are fully applicable to these surrounding towns as well.

Manchester lies at the foot of the southern slope of a range of hills, which stretch hither from Oldham, their last peak, Kersallmoor, being at once the racecourse and the Mons Sacer of Manchester.* Manchester proper lies on the left bank of the Irwell, between that stream and the two smaller ones, the Irk and the Medlock, which here empty into the Irwell. On the right bank of the Irwell, bounded by a sharp curve of the river, lies Salford, and farther westward Pendleton; northward from the Irwell lie Upper and Lower Broughton; northward of the Irk, Cheetham Hill; south of the Medlock lies Hulme; farther east Chorlton on Medlock; still farther, pretty well to the east of Manchester, Ardwick. The whole assemblage of buildings is commonly called Manchester, and contains about 400,000 inhabitants, rather more than less. The town itself is peculiarly built, so that a person may live in it for years, and go in and out daily without coming into contact with a working-people's quarter or even with workers, that is, so long as he confines himself to his business or to pleasure walks. This arises chiefly from the fact, that by unconscious tacit agreement, as well as with outspoken conscious determination, the working-people's quarters are sharply separated from the sections of the city reserved for the middle class; or, if this does not succeed, they are concealed with the cloak of charity. Manchester contains, at its heart, a rather extended commercial district, perhaps half a mile long and about as broad, and consisting almost wholly of offices and warehouses. Nearly the whole district is abandoned by dwellers, and is lonely and deserted at night; only watchmen and policemen traverse its narrow lanes with their dark lanterns. This district is cut through by certain main thoroughfares upon which the vast traffic concentrates, and in which the ground level is lined with brilliant shops. In these streets the upper floors are occupied, here and there, and there is a good deal of life upon them until late at night. With the exception of this commercial district, all Manchester proper, all Salford and Hulme, a great part of Pendleton and Chorlton, two-thirds of Ardwick, and single stretches of Cheetham Hill and Broughton are all unmixed working-people's quarters, stretching like a girdle, averaging a mile and a half in breadth, around the commercial district. Outside, beyond this girdle, lives the upper and middle bourgeoisie, the middle bourgeoisie in regularly laid out streets in the vicinity of the working quarters, especially in Chorlton and the lower lying portions of Cheetham Hill; the upper bourgeoisie in remoter villas with gardens in Chorlton and Ardwick, or on the breezy heights of Cheetham Hill, Broughton, and Pendleton, in free, wholesome country air, in fine, comfortable homes, passed once every half or quarter hour by omnibuses going into the city. And the finest part of the arrangement is this, that the members of this money aristocracy can take the shortest road through the middle of all the labouring districts to their places of business, without ever seeing that they are in the midst of the grimy misery that lurks to the right and the left. For the thoroughfares leading from the Exchange in all directions out of the city are lined, on both sides, with an almost unbroken series of shops, and are so kept in the hands of the middle and lower bourgeoisie, which, out of self-interest, cares for a decent and cleanly external appearance and *can* care for it. True, these shops bear some relation to the districts which lie behind them, and are more elegant in the commercial and residential quarters than when they hide grimy working-men's dwellings; but they suffice to conceal from the eyes of the wealthy men and women of strong stomachs and weak nerves the misery and grime which form the complement of their wealth. So, for instance, Deansgate, which leads from the Old Church directly southward, is lined first with mills and warehouses, then with second-rate shops and alehouses; farther south, when it leaves the commercial district, with less inviting shops, which grow dirtier and more interrupted by beerhouses and gin palaces the farther one goes, until at the southern end the appearance of the shops leaves no doubt that workers and workers only are their customers. So Market Street running south-east from the Exchange; at first brilliant shops of the best sort, with counting-houses or warehouses above; in the continuation, Piccadilly, immense hotels and warehouses; in the farther continuation, London Road, in the neighbourhood of the Medlock, factories, beerhouses, shops for the humbler bourgeoisie and the working population; and from this point onward, large gardens and villas of the wealthier merchants and manufacturers. In this way any one who knows Manchester can infer the adjoining districts, from the appearance of the thoroughfare, but one is seldom in a position to catch from the street a glimpse of the real labouring districts. I know very well that this hypocritical plan is more or less common to all great cities; I know, too, that the retail dealers are forced by the nature of their business to take possession of the great highways; I know that there are more good buildings than bad ones upon such streets everywhere, and that the value of land is greater near them than in remoter districts; but at the same time I have never seen so systematic a shutting out of the working class from the thoroughfares, so tender a concealment of everything which might affront the eye and the nerves of the bourgeoisie, as in Manchester. And yet, in other respects, Manchester is less built according to a plan, after official regulations, is more an outgrowth of accident, than any other city; and when I consider in this connection the eager assurances of the middle class, that the working class is doing famously, I cannot help feeling that the liberal manufacturers, the 'Big Wigs' of Manchester, are not so innocent after all, in the matter of this sensitive method of construction.

I may mention just here that the mills almost all adjoin the rivers or the different canals that ramify throughout the city, before I proceed at once to describe the labouring quarters. First of all, there is the Old Town of Manchester, which lies between the northern boundary of the commercial district and the Irk. Here the streets, even the better ones, are narrow and winding, as Todd Street, Long Millgate, Withy Grove, and Shude Hill, the houses dirty, old, and tumble-down, and the construction of the side streets utterly horrible. Going from the Old Church to Long Millgate, the stroller has at once a row of old-fashioned houses at the right, of which not one has kept its original level; these are remnants of the old pre-manufacturing Manchester, whose former inhabitants have removed with their descendants into better-built districts, and have left the houses, which were not good enough for them, to a working-class population strongly mixed with Irish blood. Here one is in an almost undisguised working-men's quarter, for even the shops and beerhouses hardly take the trouble to exhibit a trifling degree of cleanliness. But all this is nothing in comparison with the courts and lanes which lie behind, to which access can be gained only through covered passages, in which no two human beings can pass at the same time. Of the irregular cramming together of dwellings in ways which defy all rational plan, of the tangle in which they are crowded literally one upon the other, it is impossible to convey an idea. And it is not the buildings surviving from the old times of Manchester which are to blame for this; the confusion has only recently reached its height when every scrap of space left by the old way of building has been filled up and patched over until not a foot of land is left to be further occupied.

To confirm my statement I have drawn a small section of the plan of Manchester—not the worst spot and not one-tenth of the whole Old Town [see Figure].

This drawing will suffice to characterize the irrational manner in which the entire district was built, particularly the part near the Irk.

The south bank of the Irk is here very steep and between 15 and 30, feet high. On this declivitous hillside there are planted three rows of houses, of which the lowest rise directly out of the river, while the front walls of the highest stand on the crest of the hill in Long Millgate. Among them are mills on the river, in short, the method of construction is as crowded and disorderly here as in the lower part of Long Millgate. Right and left a multitude of covered passages lead

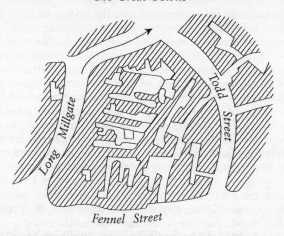

Fennel Street

from the main street into numerous courts, and he who turns in thither gets into a filth and disgusting grime, the equal of which is not to be found—especially in the courts which lead down to the Irk, and which contain unqualifiedly the most horrible dwellings which I have yet beheld. In one of these courts there stands directly at the entrance, at the end of the covered passage, a privy without a door, so dirty that the inhabitants can pass into and out of the court only by passing through foul pools of stagnant urine and excrement. This is the first court on the Irk above Ducie Bridge—in case anyone should care to look into it. Below it on the river there are several tanneries which fill the whole neighbourhood with the stench of animal putrefaction. Below Ducie Bridge the only entrance to most of the houses is by means of narrow, dirty stairs and over heaps of refuse and filth. The first court below Ducie Bridge, known as Allen's Court, was in such a state at the time of the cholera that the sanitary police ordered it evacuated, swept, and disinfected with chloride of lime. Dr Kay gives a terrible description of the state of this court at that time.[1] Since then, it seems to have

---

[1] *The Moral and Physical Condition of the Working-Class Employed in the Cotton Manufacture in Manchester*, James Ph. Kay, MD, (2nd edn., 1832). Dr Kay confuses the working class in general with the factory workers, otherwise an excellent pamphlet.

been partially torn away and rebuilt; at least looking down from Ducie Bridge, the passer-by sees several ruined walls and heaps of debris with some newer houses. The view from this bridge, mercifully concealed from mortals of small stature by a parapet as high as a man, is characteristic for the whole district. At the bottom flows, or rather stagnates, the Irk, a narrow, coal-black, foul-smelling stream, full of debris and refuse, which it deposits on the shallower right bank. In dry weather, a long string of the most disgusting, blackish-green, slime pools are left standing on this bank, from the depths of which bubbles of miasmatic gas constantly arise and give forth a stench unendurable even on the bridge 40 or 50 feet above the surface of the stream. But besides this, the stream itself is checked every few paces by high weirs, behind which slime and refuse accumulate and rot in thick masses. Above the bridge are tanneries, bonemills, and gasworks, from which all drains and refuse find their way into the Irk, which receives further the contents of all the neighbouring sewers and privies. It may be easily imagined, therefore, what sort of residue the stream deposits. Below the bridge you look upon the piles of debris, the refuse, filth, and offal from the courts on the steep left bank; here each house is packed close behind its neighbour and a piece of each is visible, all black, smoky, crumbling, ancient, with broken panes and window-frames. The background is furnished by old barrack-like factory buildings. On the lower right bank stands a long row of houses and mills; the second house being a ruin without a roof, piled with debris; the third stands so low that the lowest floor is uninhabitable, and therefore without windows or doors. Here the background embraces the pauper burial-ground, the station of the Liverpool and Leeds railway, and, in the rear of this, the Workhouse, the 'Poor-Law Bastille' of Manchester, which, like a citadel, looks threateningly down from behind its high walls and parapets on the hilltop, upon the working-people's quarter below.

Above Ducie Bridge, the left bank grows more flat and the right bank steeper, but the condition of the dwellings on both banks grows worse rather than better. He who turns to the left here from the main street, Long Millgate, is lost; he wanders from one court to another, turns countless corners, passes nothing but narrow, filthy nooks and alleys, until after a few minutes he has lost all clue, and knows not whither to turn. Everywhere half or wholly ruined buildings, some of them actually uninhabited, which means a great deal here; rarely a wooden or stone floor to be seen in the houses, almost uniformly broken, ill-fitting windows and doors, and a state of filth! Everywhere heaps of debris, refuse, and offal; standing pools for gutters, and a stench which alone would make it impossible for a human being in any degree civilized to live in such a district. The newly built extension of the Leeds railway, which crosses the Irk here, has swept away some of these courts and lanes, laying others completely open to view. Immediately under the railway bridge there stands a court, the filth and horrors of which surpass all the others by far, just because it was hitherto so shut off, so secluded that the way to it could not be found without a good deal of trouble. I should never have discovered it myself, without the breaks made by the railway, though I thought I knew this whole region thoroughly. Passing along a rough bank, among stakes and washing-lines, one penetrates into this chaos of small one-storeyed, one-roomed huts, in most of which there is no artificial floor; kitchen, living- and sleeping-room all in one. In such a hole, scarcely 5 feet long by 6 broad, I found two beds—and such bedsteads and beds!—which, with a staircase and chimney-place, exactly filled the room. In several others I found absolutely nothing, while the door stood open, and the inhabitants leaned against it. Everywhere before the doors refuse and offal; that any sort of pavement lay underneath could not be seen but only felt, here and there, with the feet. This whole collection of cattle-sheds for human beings was surrounded on two sides by houses and a factory, and on the third by the river, and besides the narrow stair up the bank, a narrow doorway alone led out into another almost equally ill-built, ill-kept labyrinth of dwellings.

Enough! The whole side of the Irk is built in this way, a planless, knotted chaos of houses, more or less on the verge of uninhabitableness, whose unclean interiors fully correspond with their filthy external surroundings. And how could the people be clean with no proper opportunity for satisfying the most natural and ordinary wants? Privies are so rare here that they are either filled up every day, or are too remote for most of the inhabitants to use. How can people wash when they have only the dirty Irk water at hand, while pumps and water-pipes can be found in decent parts of the city alone? In truth, it cannot be charged to the account of these helots of modern society if their dwellings are not more clean than the pigsties which are here and there to be seen among them. The landlords are not ashamed to let dwellings like the six or seven cellars on the quay directly below Scotland Bridge, the floors of which stand at least 2 feet below the low-water level of the Irk that flows not 6 feet away from them; or like the upper floor of the corner-house on the opposite shore directly above the bridge, where the ground floor, utterly uninhabitable, stands deprived of all fittings for doors and windows, a case by no means rare in this region, when this open ground floor is used as a privy by the whole neighbourhood for want of other facilities!

If we leave the Irk and penetrate once more on the opposite side from Long Millgate into the midst of the working-men's dwellings, we shall come into a somewhat newer quarter, which stretches from St Michael's Church to Withy Grove and Shude Hill. Here there is somewhat better order. In place of the chaos of buildings, we find at least long straight lanes and alleys or courts, built according to a plan and usually square. But if, in the former case, every house was built according to caprice, here each lane and court is so built, without reference to the situation of the adjoining ones. The lanes run now in this direction, now in that, while every two minutes the wanderer gets into a blind alley, or, on turning a corner, finds himself back where he started from; certainly no one who has not lived a considerable time in this labyrinth can find his way through it.

If I may use the word at all in speaking of this district, the ventilation of these streets and courts is, in consequence of this confusion, quite as imperfect as in the Irk region; and if this quarter may, nevertheless, be said to have some advantage over that of the Irk, the houses being newer and the streets occasionally having gutters, nearly every house has, on the other hand, a cellar dwelling, which is rarely found in the Irk district, by reason of the greater age and more careless construction of the houses. As for the rest, the filth, debris, and offal heaps, and the pools in the streets are common to both quarters, and in the district now under discussion, another feature most injurious to the cleanliness of the inhabitants is the multitude of pigs walking about in all the alleys, rooting into the offal heaps, or kept imprisoned in small pens. Here, as in most of the working-men's quarters of Manchester, the pork-raisers rent the courts and build pigpens in them. In almost every court one or even several such pens may be found, into which the inhabitants of the court throw all refuse and offal, whence the swine grow fat; and the atmosphere, confined on all four sides, is utterly corrupted by putrefying animal and vegetable substances. Through this quarter, a broad and measurably decent street has been cut, Millers Street, and the background has been pretty successfully concealed. But if anyone should be led by curiosity to pass through one of the numerous passages which lead into the courts, he will find this piggery repeated at every twenty paces.

Such is the Old Town of Manchester, and on rereading my description, I am forced to admit that instead of being exaggerated, it is far from black enough to convey a true impression of the filth, ruin, and uninhabitableness, the defiance of all considerations of cleanliness, ventilation, and health which characterize the construction of this single district, containing at least twenty to thirty thousand inhabitants. And such a district exists in the heart of the second city of England, the first manufacturing city of the world. If anyone wishes to see in how little space a human being can move, how little air—and *such* air!—he can breathe, how little of civilization he may share and yet live, it is only necessary to travel hither. True, this is the *Old* Town, and the people of Manchester emphasize the fact whenever anyone mentions to them the frightful condition of this Hell upon Earth; but what does that prove? Everything which here arouses horror and indignation is of recent origin, belongs to the *industrial epoch*. The couple of hundred houses, which belong to old Manchester, have been long since abandoned by their original inhabitants; the industrial epoch alone has crammed into them the swarms of workers whom they now shelter; the industrial epoch alone has built up every spot between these old houses to win a covering for the masses whom it has conjured hither from the agricultural districts and from Ireland; the industrial epoch alone enables the owners of these cattlesheds to rent them for high prices to human beings, to plunder the poverty of the workers, to undermine the health of thousands, in order that they *alone*, the owners, may grow rich. In the industrial epoch alone has it become possible that the worker scarcely freed from feudal servitude could be used as mere material, a mere chattel; that he must let himself be crowded into a dwelling too bad for every other, which he for his hard-earned wages buys the right to let go utterly to ruin. This manufacture has achieved, which, without these workers, this poverty, this slavery could not have lived. True, the original construction of this quarter was bad, little good could have been made out of it; but, have the landowners, has the municipality done anything to improve it when rebuilding? On the contrary, wherever a nook or corner was free, a house has been run up; where a superfluous passage remained, it has been built up; the value of land rose with the blossoming out of manufacture, and the more it rose, the more madly was the work of building up carried on, without reference to the health or comfort of the inhabitants, with sole reference to the highest possible profit on the principle that *no hole is so bad but that some poor creature must take it who can pay for nothing better*. However, it is the Old Town, and with this reflection the bourgeoisie is comforted. Let us see, therefore, how much better it is in the New Town.

The New Town, known also as Irish Town, stretches up a hill of clay, beyond the Old Town, between the Irk and St George's Road. Here all the features of a city are lost. Single rows of houses or groups of streets stand, here and there, like little villages on the naked, not even grass-grown clay soil; the houses, or rather cottages, are in bad order, never repaired, filthy, with damp, unclean, cellar dwellings; the lanes are neither paved nor supplied with sewers, but harbour numerous colonies of swine penned in small sties or yards, or wandering unrestrained through the neighbourhood. The mud in the streets is so deep that there is never a chance, except in the driest weather, of walking without sinking into it ankle deep at every step. In the vicinity of St

George's Road, the separate groups of buildings approach each other more closely, ending in a continuation of lanes, blind alleys, back lanes, and courts, which grow more and more crowded and irregular the nearer they approach the heart of the town. True, they are here oftener paved or supplied with paved sidewalks and gutters; but the filth, the bad order of the houses, and especially of the cellars remain the same.

It may not be out of place to make some general observations just here as to the customary construction of working-men's quarters in Manchester. We have seen how in the Old Town pure accident determined the grouping of the houses in general. Every house is built without reference to any other, and the scraps of space between them are called courts for want of another name. In the somewhat newer portions of the same quarter, and in other working-men's quarters, dating from the early days of industrial activity, a somewhat more orderly arrangement may be found. The space between two streets is divided into more regular, usually square courts [see Figure].

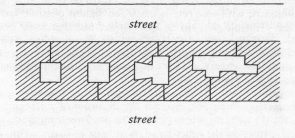

These courts were built in this way from the beginning, and communicate with the streets by means of covered passages. If the totally planless construction is injurious to the health of the workers by preventing ventilation, this method of shutting them up in courts surrounded on all sides by buildings is far more so. The air simply cannot escape; the chimneys of the houses are the sole drains for the imprisoned atmosphere of the courts, and they serve the purpose only so

long as fire is kept burning.[1] Moreover, the houses surrounding such courts are usually built back to back, having
the rear wall in common; and this alone suffices to prevent
any sufficient through ventilation. And, as the police charged
with care of the streets does not trouble itself about the
condition of these courts, as everything quietly lies where it is
thrown, there is no cause for wonder at the filth and heaps of
ashes and offal to be found here. I have been in courts, in
Millers Street, at least half a foot below the level of the
thoroughfare, and without the slightest drainage for the
water that accumulates in them in rainy weather! More
recently another different method of building was adopted,
and has now become general. Working-men's cottages are
almost never built singly, but always by the dozen or score; a
single contractor building up one or two streets at a time.
These are then arranged as follows: One front is formed of
cottages of the best class, so fortunate as to possess a back
door and small court, and these command the highest rent.
In the rear of these cottages runs a narrow alley, the back
street, built up at both ends, into which either a narrow
roadway or a covered passage leads from one side. The
cottages which face this back street command least rent, and
are most neglected. These have their rear walls in common
with the third row of cottages which face a second street,
and command less rent than the first row and more than the
second. The streets are laid out somewhat in the following
manner [see Figure].

By this method of construction, comparatively good
ventilation can be obtained for the first row of cottages, and
the third row is no worse off than in the former method. The
middle row, on the other hand, is at least as badly ventilated
as the houses in the courts, and the back street is always in
the same filthy, disgusting condition as they. The contractors
prefer this method because it saves them space, and furnishes

---

[1] And yet an English Liberal wiseacre asserts, in the Report of the
Children's Employment Commission, that these courts are the master-
piece of municipal architecture, because, like a multitude of little parks,
they improve ventilation, the circulation of air! Certainly, if each court
had two or four broad open entrances facing each other, through which
the air could pour; but they never have two, rarely one, and usually only
a narrow covered passage.

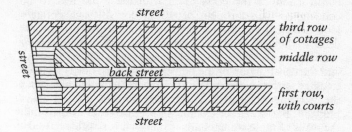

the means of fleecing better paid workers through the higher
rents of the cottages in the first and third rows. These three
different forms of cottage building are found all over
Manchester and throughout Lancashire and Yorkshire, often
mixed up together, but usually separate enough to indicate
the relative age of parts of towns. The third system, that of
the back alleys, prevails largely in the great working-men's
district east of St George's Road and Ancoats Street, and
is the one most often found in the other working-men's
quarters of Manchester and its suburbs.

In the last-mentioned broad district included under the
name Ancoats, stand the largest mills of Manchester lining
the canals, colossal six- and seven-storeyed buildings tower-
ing with their slender chimneys far above the low cottages
of the workers. The population of the district consists,
therefore, chiefly of mill-hands, and in the worst streets, of
hand-weavers. The streets nearest the heart of the town are
the oldest, and consequently the worst; they are, however,
paved, and supplied with drains. Among them I include
those nearest to and parallel with Oldham Road and Great
Ancoats Street. Farther to the north-east lie many newly
built-up streets; here the cottages look neat and cleanly,
doors and windows are new and freshly painted, the rooms
within newly whitewashed; the streets themselves are better
aired, the vacant building lots between them larger and more
numerous. But this can be said of a minority of the houses
only, while cellar dwellings are to be found under almost
every cottage; many streets are unpaved and without sewers;
and, worse than all, this neat appearance is all pretence, a
pretence which vanishes within the first ten years. For the

construction of the cottages individually is no less to be condemned than the plan of the streets. All such cottages look neat and substantial at first; their massive brick walls deceive the eye, and, on passing through a *newly built* working-men's street, without remembering the back alleys and the construction of the houses themselves, one is inclined to agree with the assertion of the Liberal manufacturers that the working population is nowhere so well housed as in England. But on closer examination, it becomes evident that the walls of these cottages are as thin as it is possible to make them. The outer walls, those of the cellar, which bear the weight of the ground floor and roof, are one whole brick thick at most, the bricks lying with their long sides touching ([▯▯▯▯▯]); but I have seen many a cottage of the same height, some in process of building, whose outer walls were but one-half brick thick, the bricks lying not sidewise but lengthwise, their narrow ends touching ([▭▭▭▭▭]). The object of this is to spare material, but there is also another reason for it; namely, the fact that the contractors never own the land but lease it, according to the English custom for twenty, thirty, forty, fifty, or ninety-nine years, at the expiration of which time it falls, with everything upon it, back into the possession of the original holder, who pays nothing in return for improvements upon it. The improvements are therefore so calculated by the lessee as to be worth as little as possible at the expiration of the stipulated term. And as such cottages are often built but twenty or thirty years before the expiration of the term, it may easily be imagined that the contractors make no unnecessary expenditures upon them. Moreover, these contractors, usually carpenters and builders, or manufacturers, spend little or nothing in repairs, partly to avoid diminishing their rent receipts, and partly in view of the approaching surrender of the improvement to the landowner; while in consequence of commercial crises and the loss of work that follows them, whole streets often stand empty, the cottages falling rapidly into ruin and uninhabitableness. It is calculated in general that working-men's cottages last only forty years on the average. This sounds strangely enough when one sees the beautiful, massive walls of newly built ones, which seem to give promise of lasting a couple of centuries; but the fact remains that the niggardliness of the original expenditure, the neglect of all repairs, the frequent periods of emptiness, the constant change of inhabitants, and the destruction carried on by the dwellers during the final ten years, usually Irish families, who do not hesitate to use the wooden portions for firewood—all this, taken together, accomplishes the complete ruin of the cottages by the end of forty years. Hence it comes that Ancoats, built chiefly since the sudden growth of manufacture, chiefly indeed within the present century, contains a vast number of ruinous houses, most of them being, in fact, in the last stages of inhabitableness. I will not dwell upon the amount of capital thus wasted, the small additional expenditure upon the original improvement and upon repairs which would suffice to keep this whole district clean, decent, and inhabitable for years together. I have to deal here with the state of the houses and their inhabitants, and it must be admitted that no more injurious and de-moralizing method of housing the workers has yet been discovered than precisely this. The working man is con-strained to occupy such ruinous dwellings because he cannot pay for others, and because there are no others in the vicinity of his mill; perhaps, too, because they belong to the em-ployer, who engages him only on condition of his taking such a cottage. The calculation with reference to the forty years' duration of the cottage is, of course, not always perfectly strict; for, if the dwellings are in a thickly built-up portion of the town, and there is a good prospect of finding steady occupants for them, while the ground rent is high, the contractors do a little something to keep the cottages inhabitable after the expiration of the forty years. They never do anything more, however, than is absolutely unavoidable, and the dwellings so repaired are the worst of all. Occa-sionally when an epidemic threatens, the otherwise sleepy conscience of the sanitary police is a little stirred, raids are made into the working-men's districts, whole rows of cellars and cottages are closed, as happened in the case of several lanes near Oldham Road; but this does not last long: the condemned cottages soon find occupants again, the owners are much better off by letting them, and the sanitary police won't come again so soon. These east and north-east sides of Manchester are the only ones on which the bourgeoisie has not built, because ten or eleven months of the year the west and south-west wind drives the smoke of all the factories hither, and that the working-people alone may breathe.

Southward from Great Ancoats Street lies a great, straggling, working-men's quarter, a hilly, barren stretch of land, occupied by detached, irregularly built rows of houses or squares, between these, empty building lots, uneven, clayey, without grass and scarcely passable in wet weather. The cottages are all filthy and old, and recall the New Town to mind. The stretch cut through by the Birmingham railway is the most thickly built-up and the worst. Here flows the Medlock with countless windings through a valley, which is, in places, on a level with the valley of the Irk. Along both sides of the stream, which is coal-black, stagnant, and foul, stretches a broad belt of factories and working-men's dwellings, the latter all in the worst condition. The bank is chiefly declivitous and is built over to the water's edge, just as we saw along the Irk; while the houses are equally bad, whether built on the Manchester side or in Ardwick, Chorlton, or Hulme. But the most horrible spot (if I should describe all the separate spots in detail I should never come to the end) lies on the Manchester side, immediately south-west of Oxford Road, and is known as Little Ireland. In a rather deep hole, in a curve of the Medlock and surrounded on all four sides by tall factories and high embankments, covered with buildings, stand two groups of about 200 cottages, built chiefly back to back, in which live about 4,000 human beings, most of them Irish. The cottages are old, dirty, and of the smallest sort, the streets uneven, fallen into ruts and in part without drains or pavement; masses of refuse, offal, and sickening filth lie among standing pools in all directions; the atmosphere is poisoned by the effluvia from these, and laden and darkened by the smoke of a dozen tall factory chimneys. A horde of ragged women and children swarm about here, as filthy as the swine that thrive upon the garbage heaps and in the puddles. In short, the whole rookery furnishes such a hateful and repulsive spectacle as can hardly be equalled in the worst court on the Irk. The race that lives in these ruinous cottages, behind broken windows, mended with oilskin, sprung doors, and rotten door-posts, or in dark, wet cellars, in measureless filth and stench, in this atmosphere penned in as if with a purpose, this race must really have reached the lowest stage of humanity. This is the impression and the line of thought which the exterior of this district forces upon the beholder. But what must one think when he hears that in each of these pens, containing at most two rooms, a garret and perhaps a cellar, on the average twenty human beings live; that in the whole region, for each 120 persons, one usually inaccessible privy is provided; and that in spite of all the preachings of the physicians, in spite of the excitement into which the cholera epidemic plunged the sanitary police by reason of the condition of Little Ireland, in spite of everything, in this year of grace 1844, it is in almost the same state as in 1831! Dr Kay asserts[1] that not only the cellars but the first floors of all the houses in this district are damp; that a number of cellars once filled up with earth have now been emptied and are occupied once more by Irish people; that in one cellar the water constantly wells up through a hole stopped with clay, the cellar lying below the river level, so that its occupant, a hand-loom weaver, had to bale out the water from his dwelling every morning and pour it into the street!

Farther down, on the left side of the Medlock, lies Hulme, which, properly speaking, is one great working-people's district, the condition of which coincides almost exactly with that of Ancoats; the more thickly built-up regions chiefly bad and approaching ruin, the less populous of more modern structure, but generally sunk in filth. On the other side of the Medlock, in Manchester proper, lies a second great working-men's district which stretches on both sides of Deansgate as far as the business quarter, and in certain parts rivals the Old Town. Especially in the immediate vicinity of the business quarter, between Bridge and Quay Streets, Princess and Peter Streets, the crowded construction exceeds in places the narrowest courts of the Old Town. Here are long, narrow lanes between which run contracted, crooked courts and passages, the entrances to which are so irregular that the explorer is caught in a blind alley at every few steps, or comes out where he least expects to, unless he knows every court and every alley exactly and separately. According to Dr

---

[1] Kay, *The Moral and Physical Condition of the Working-Class.*

Kay, the most demoralized class of all Manchester lived in these ruinous and filthy districts, people whose occupations are thieving and prostitution; and, to all appearance, his assertion is still true at the present moment. When the sanitary police made its expedition hither in 1831, it found the uncleanness as great as in Little Ireland or along the Irk (that it is not much better today, I can testify); and among other items, they found in Parliament Street for 380 persons, and in Parliament Passage for thirty thickly populated houses, but a single privy.

If we cross the Irwell to Salford, we find on a peninsula formed by the river, a town of 80,000 inhabitants, which, properly speaking, is one large working-men's quarter, penetrated by a single wide avenue. Salford, once more important than Manchester, was then the leading town of the surrounding district to which it still gives its name, Salford Hundred. Hence it is that an old and therefore very unwholesome, dirty, and ruinous locality is to be found here, lying opposite the Old Church of Manchester, and in as bad a condition as the Old Town on the other side of the Irwell. Farther away from the river lies the newer portion, which is, however, already beyond the limit of its forty years of cottage life, and therefore ruinous enough. All Salford is built in courts or narrow lanes, so narrow, that they remind me of the narrowest I have ever seen, the little lanes of Genoa. The average construction of Salford is in this respect much worse than that of Manchester, and so, too, in respect to cleanliness. If, in Manchester, the police, from time to time, every six or ten years, makes a raid upon the working-people's districts, closes the worst dwellings, and causes the filthiest spots in these Augean stables to be cleansed, in Salford it seems to have done absolutely nothing. The narrow side lanes and courts of Chapel Street, Greengate, and Gravel Lane have certainly never been cleansed since they were built. Of late, the Liverpool railway has been carried through the middle of them, over a high viaduct, and has abolished many of the filthiest nooks; but what does that avail? Whoever passes over this viaduct and looks down, sees filth and wretchedness enough; and, if anyone takes the trouble to pass through these lanes, and glance through the open doors and windows into the houses and cellars, he can convince himself afresh with every step that the workers of Salford live in dwellings in which cleanliness and comfort are impossible. Exactly the same state of affairs is found in the more distant regions of Salford, in Islington, along Regent Road, and back of the Bolton railway. The working-men's dwellings between Oldfield Road and Gross Lane, where a mass of courts and alleys are to be found in the worst possible state, vie with the dwellings of the Old Town in filth and overcrowding. In this district I found a man, apparently about 60 years old, living in a cow-stable. He had constructed a sort of chimney for his square pen, which had neither windows, floor, nor ceiling, had obtained a bedstead and lived there, though the rain dripped through his rotten roof. This man was too old and weak for regular work, and supported himself by removing manure with a hand-cart; the dung-heaps lay next door to his palace!

Such are the various working-people's quarters of Manchester as I had occasion to observe them personally during twenty months. If we briefly formulate the result of our wanderings, we must admit that 350,000 working people of Manchester and its environs live, almost all of them, in wretched, damp, filthy cottages, that the streets which surround them are usually in the most miserable and filthy condition, laid out without the slightest reference to ventilation, with reference solely to the profit secured by the contractor. In a word, we must confess that in the working-men's dwellings of Manchester, no cleanliness, no convenience, and consequently no comfortable family life is possible; that in such dwellings only a physically degenerate race, robbed of all humanity, degraded, reduced morally and physically to bestiality, could feel comfortable and at home. And I am not alone in making this assertion. We have seen that Dr Kay gives precisely the same description; and, though it is superfluous, I quote further the words of a Liberal, recognized and highly valued as an authority by the manufacturers, and a fanatical opponent of all independent movements of the workers:[1]

---

[1] Nassau W. Senior, *Letters on the Factory Act to the Rt. Hon., the President of the Board of Trade* (Chas. Poulett Thomson, Esq.) (London, 1837), 24.

As I passed through the dwellings of the mill-hands in Irish Town, Ancoats, and Little Ireland, I was only amazed that it is possible to maintain a reasonable state of health in such homes. These towns, for in extent and number of inhabitants they are towns, have been erected with the utmost disregard of everything except the immediate advantage of the speculating builder. A carpenter and builder unite to buy a series of building sites (i.e. they lease them for a number of years), and cover them with so-called houses. In one place we found a whole street following the course of a ditch, because in this way deeper cellars could be secured without the cost of digging, cellars not for storing wares or rubbish, but for dwellings for human beings. *Not one house of this street escaped the cholera.* In general, the streets of these suburbs are unpaved, with a dung-heap or ditch in the middle; the houses are built back to back, without ventilation or drainage, and whole families are limited to a corner of a cellar or a garret.

I have already referred to the unusual activity which the sanitary police manifested during the cholera visitation. When the epidemic was approaching, a universal terror seized the bourgeoisie of the city. People remembered the unwholesome dwellings of the poor, and trembled before the certainty that each of these slums would become a centre for the plague, whence it would spread desolation in all directions through the houses of the propertied class. A Health Commission was appointed at once to investigate these districts, and report upon their condition to the Town Council. Dr Kay, himself a member of this Commission, who visited in person every separate police district except one, the eleventh, quotes extracts from their reports: There were inspected, in all, 6,951 houses—naturally in Manchester proper alone, Salford and the other suburbs being excluded. Of these, 6,565 urgently needed whitewashing within; 960 were out of repair; 939 had insufficient drains; 1,435 were damp; 452 were badly ventilated; 2,221 were without privies. Of the 687 streets inspected, 248 were unpaved, 53 but partially paved, 112 ill-ventilated, 352 containing standing pools, heaps of debris, refuse, etc. To cleanse such an Augean stable before the arrival of the cholera was, of course, out of the question. A few of the worst nooks were therefore cleansed, and everything else left as before. In the cleansed spots, as Little Ireland proves, the old filthy condition was naturally restored in a couple of months. As to the internal condition of these houses, the same Commission reports a state of things similar to that which we have already met with in London, Edinburgh, and other cities.[1]

It often happens that a whole Irish family is crowded into one bed; often a heap of filthy straw or quilts of old sacking cover all in an indiscriminate heap, where all alike are degraded by want, stolidity, and wretchedness. Often the inspectors found, in a single house, two families in two rooms. All slept in one, and used the other as a kitchen and dining-room in common. Often more than one family lived in a single damp cellar, in whose pestilent atmosphere twelve to sixteen persons were crowded together. To these and other sources of disease must be added that pigs were kept, and other disgusting things of the most revolting kind were found.

We must add that many families, who had but one room for themselves, receive boarders and lodgers in it, that such lodgers of both sexes by no means rarely sleep in the same bed with the married couple; and that the single case of a man and his wife and his adult sister-in-law sleeping in one bed was found, according to the 'Report concerning the sanitary condition of the working-class', six times repeated in Manchester. Common lodging-houses, too, are very numerous; Dr Kay gives their number in 1831 as 267 in Manchester proper, and they must have increased greatly since then. Each of these receives from twenty to thirty guests, so that they shelter all told, nightly, from five to seven thousand human beings. The character of the houses and their guests is the same as in other cities. Five to seven beds in each room lie on the floor—without bedsteads, and on these sleep, mixed indiscriminately, as many persons as apply. What physical and moral atmosphere reigns in these holes I need not state. Each of these houses is a focus of crime, the scene of deeds against which human nature revolts, which would perhaps never have been executed but for this forced centralization of vice.[2] Gaskell gives the

---

[1] Kay, *The Moral and Physical Condition of the Working-Class*, 32.

[2] P. Gaskell, *The Manufacturing Population of England: Its Moral, Social and Physical Condition, and the Changes which have arisen from the Use of Steam Machinery; with an Examination of Infant Labour,*

number of persons living in cellars in Manchester proper as 20,000. The *Weekly Dispatch* gives the number, 'according to official reports', as 12 per cent of the working-class, which agrees with Gaskell's number; the workers being estimated at 175,000, 21,000 would form 12 per cent of it. The cellar dwellings in the suburbs are at least as numerous, so that the number of persons living in cellars in Manchester—using its name in the broader sense—is not less than forty to fifty thousand. So much for the dwellings of the workers in the largest cities and towns. The manner in which the need of a shelter is satisfied furnishes a standard for the manner in which all other necessities are supplied. That in these filthy holes a ragged, ill-fed population alone can dwell is a safe conclusion, and such is the fact. The clothing of the working people, in the majority of cases, is in a very bad condition. The material used for it is not of the best adapted. Wool and linen have almost vanished from the wardrobe of both sexes, and cotton has taken their place. Shirts are made of bleached or coloured cotton goods; the dresses of the women are chiefly of cotton print goods, and woollen petticoats are rarely to be seen on the washline. The men wear chiefly trousers of fustian or other heavy cotton goods, and jackets or coats of the same. Fustian has become the proverbial costume of the working men, who are called 'fustian jackets', and call themselves so in contrast to the gentlemen who wear broadcloth, which latter words are used as characteristic for the middle class. When Feargus O'Connor, the Chartist leader, came to Manchester during the insurrection of 1842,

---

'Fiat Justitia' (1833), depicting chiefly the state of the working class in Lancashire. The author is a Liberal, but wrote at a time when it was not a feature of Liberalism to chant the happiness of the workers. He is therefore unprejudiced, and can afford to have eyes for the evils of the present state of things, and especially for the factory system. On the other hand, he wrote before the Factories Enquiry Commission, and adopts from untrustworthy sources many assertions afterwards refuted by the Report of the Commission. This work, although on the whole a valuable one, can therefore only be used with discretion, especially as the author, like Kay, confuses the whole working class with the mill-hands. The history of the development of the proletariat, contained in the introduction to the present work, is chiefly taken from this work of Gaskell's.

he appeared, amidst the deafening applause of the working men, in a fustian suit of clothing. Hats are the universal head-covering in England, even for working men, hats of the most diverse forms, round, high, broad-brimmed, narrow-brimmed, or without brims—only the younger men in factory towns wearing caps. Anyone who does not own a hat folds himself a low, square paper cap.

The whole clothing of the working class, even assuming it to be in good condition, is little adapted to the climate. The damp air of England with its sudden changes of temperature, more calculated than any other to give rise to colds, obliges almost the whole middle class to wear flannel next the skin, about the body, and flannel scarves and shirts are in almost universal use. Not only is the working class deprived of this precaution, it is scarcely ever in a position to use a thread of woollen clothing; and the heavy cotton goods, though thicker, stiffer, and heavier than woollen clothes, afford much less protection against cold and wet, remain damp much longer because of their thickness and the nature of the stuff, and have nothing of the compact density of fulled woollen cloths. And, if a working man once buys himself a woollen coat for Sunday, he must get it from one of the cheap shops where he finds bad, so-called 'Devil's-dust' cloth, manufactured for sale and not for use, and liable to tear or grow threadbare in a fortnight, or he must buy of an old-clothes-dealer a half-worn coat which has seen its best days, and lasts but a few weeks. Moreover, the working-man's clothing is, in most cases, in bad condition, and there is the oft-recurring necessity for placing the best pieces in the pawnbroker's shop. But among very large numbers, especially among the Irish, the prevailing clothing consists of perfect rags often beyond all mending, or so patched that the original colour can no longer be detected. Yet the English and Anglo-Irish go on patching, and have carried this art to a remarkable pitch, putting wool or bagging on fustian, or the reverse—it's all the same to them. But the true, transplanted Irish hardly ever patch except in the extremest necessity, when the garment would otherwise fall apart. Ordinarily the rags of the shirt protrude through the rents in the coat or trousers. They wear, as Thomas Carlyle says, 'A suit of tatters, the getting on or off which is said to be a difficult operation, transacted only in festivals and the high tides of the calendar'.[1] The Irish have introduced, too, the custom previously unknown in England, of going barefoot. In every manufacturing town there is now to be seen a multitude of people, especially women and children, going about barefoot, and their example is gradually being adopted by the poorer English.

As with clothing, so with food. The workers get what is too bad for the property-holding class. In the great towns of England everything may be had of the best, but it costs money; and the workman, who must keep house on a couple of pence, cannot afford much expense. Moreover, he usually receives his wages on Saturday evening, for, although a beginning has been made in the payment of wages on Friday, this excellent arrangement is by no means universal; and so he comes to market at five or even seven o'clock, while the buyers of the middle class have had the first choice during the morning, when the market teems with the best of everything. But when the workers reach it, the best has vanished, and, if it was still there, they would probably not be able to buy it. The potatoes which the workers buy are usually poor, the vegetables wilted, the cheese old and of poor quality, the bacon rancid, the meat lean, tough, taken from old, often diseased, cattle, or such as have died a natural death, and not fresh even then, often half decayed. The sellers are usually small hucksters who buy up inferior goods, and can sell them cheaply by reason of their badness. The poorest workers are forced to use still another device to get together the things they need with their few pence. As nothing can be sold on Sunday, and all shops must be closed at twelve o'clock on Saturday night, such things as would not keep until Monday are sold at any price between ten o'clock and midnight. But nine-tenths of what is sold at ten o'clock is past using by Sunday morning, yet these are precisely the provisions which make up the Sunday dinner of the poorest class. The meat which the workers buy is very often past using; but having bought it, they must eat it. On 6 January 1844 (if I am not greatly mistaken), a court leet was held in Manchester, when eleven meat-sellers were fined for having sold tainted meat.

[1] Thomas Carlyle, *Chartism* (London, 1840), 28.

Each of them had a whole ox or pig, or several sheep, or from 50 to 60 pounds of meat, which were all confiscated in a tainted condition. In one case, sixty-four stuffed Christmas geese were seized which had proved unsaleable in Liverpool, and had been forwarded to Manchester, where they were brought to market foul and rotten. All the particulars, with names and fines, were published at the time in the *Manchester Guardian*. In the six weeks, from 1 July to 14 August, the same sheet reported three similar cases. According to the *Guardian* for 3 August, a pig, weighing 200 pounds, which had been found dead and decayed, was cut up and exposed for sale by a butcher at Heywood, and was then seized. According to the number for 31 July, two butchers at Wigan, of whom one had previously been convicted of the same offence, were fined £2 and £4 respectively, for exposing tainted meat for sale; and, according to the number for 10 August, twenty-six tainted hams seized at a dealer's in Bolton, were publicly burnt, and the dealer fined 20s. But these are by no means all the cases; they do not even form a fair average for a period of six weeks, according to which to form an average for the year. There are often seasons in which every number of the semi-weekly *Guardian* mentions a similar case found in Manchester or its vicinity. And when one reflects upon the many cases which must escape detection in the extensive markets that stretch along the front of every main street, under the slender supervision of the market inspectors—and how else can one explain the boldness with which whole animals are exposed for sale?—when one considers how great the temptation must be, in view of the incomprehensibly small fines mentioned in the foregoing cases; when one reflects what condition a piece of meat must have reached to be seized by the inspectors, it is impossible to believe that the workers obtain good and nourishing meat as a usual thing. But they are victimized in yet another way by the money-greed of the middle class. Dealers and manufacturers adulterate all kinds of provisions in an atrocious manner, and without the slighest regard to the health of the consumers. We have heard the *Manchester Guardian* upon this subject, let us hear another organ of the middle class—I delight in the testimony of my opponents—let us hear the *Liverpool Mercury*:

Salted butter is sold for fresh, the lumps being covered with a coating of fresh butter, or a pound of fresh being laid on top to taste, while the salted article is sold after this test, or the whole mass is washed and then sold as fresh. With sugar, pounded rice and other cheap adulterating materials are mixed, and the whole sold at full price. The refuse of soap-boiling establishments also is mixed with other things and sold as sugar. Chicory and other cheap stuff is mixed with ground coffee, and artificial coffee beans with the unground article. Cocoa is often adulterated with fine brown earth, treated with fat to render it more easily mistakable for real cocoa. Tea is mixed with the leaves of the sloe and with other refuse, or dry tea-leaves are roasted on hot copper plates, so returning to the proper colour and being sold as fresh. Pepper is mixed with pounded nut-shells; port-wine is manufactured outright (out of alcohol, dye-stuffs, etc.), while it is notorious that more of it is consumed in England alone than is grown in Portugal; and tobacco is mixed with disgusting substances of all sorts and in all possible forms in which the article is produced.

I can add that several of the most respected tobacco dealers in Manchester announced publicly last summer, that, by reason of the universal adulteration of tobacco, no firm could carry on business without adulteration, and that no cigar costing less than 3*d.* is made wholly from tobacco. These frauds are naturally not restricted to articles of food, though I could mention a dozen more, the villainy of mixing gypsum or chalk with flour among them. Fraud is practised in the sale of articles of every sort: flannel, stockings, etc. are stretched, and shrink after the first washing; narrow cloth is sold as being from one and a half to three inches broader than it actually is; stoneware is so thinly glazed that the glazing is good for nothing, and cracks at once, and a hundred other rascalities, *tout comme chez nous.** But the lion's share of the evil results of these frauds falls to the workers. The rich are less deceived, because they can pay the high prices of the large shops which have a reputation to lose, and would injure themselves more than their customers if they kept poor or adulterated wares; the rich are spoiled, too, by habitual good eating, and detect adulteration more easily with their sensitive palates. But the poor, the working people, to whom a couple of farthings are important, who must buy many things with little money, who cannot afford to enquire too closely into the quality of their purchases, and cannot do so in any case because they have had no opportunity of cultivating their taste—to their share fall all the adulterated, poisoned provisions. They must deal with the small retailers, must buy perhaps on credit, and these small retail dealers who cannot sell even the same quality of goods so cheaply as the largest retailers because of their small capital and the large proportional expenses of their business, must knowingly or unknowingly buy adulterated goods in order to sell at the lower prices required, and to meet the competition of the others. Further, a large retail dealer who has extensive capital invested in his business is ruined with his ruined credit if detected in a fraudulent practice; but what harm does it do a small grocer, who has customers in a single street only, if frauds are proved against him? If no one trusts him in Ancoats, he moves to Chorlton or Hulme, where no one knows him, and where he continues to defraud as before; while legal penalties attach to very few adulterations unless they involve revenue frauds. Not in the quality alone, but in the quantity of his goods as well, is the English working man defrauded. The small dealers usually have false weights and measures, and an incredible number of convictions for such offences may be read in the police reports. How universal this form of fraud is in the manufacturing districts, a couple of extracts from the *Manchester Guardian* may serve to show. They cover only a short period, and, even here, I have not all the numbers at hand:

16 June 1844, Rochdale Sessions—Four dealers fined 5s. to 10s. for using light weights. Stockport Sessions—Two dealers fined 1s., one of them having seven light weights and a false scale, and both having been warned.

19 June, Rochdale Sessions—One dealer fined 5s., and two farmers 10s.

22 June, Manchester Justices of the Peace—Nineteen dealers fined 2s. 6d. to £2.

26 June, Ashton Sessions—Fourteen dealers and farmers fined 2s. 6d. to £1. Hyde Petty Sessions—Nine farmers and dealers condemned to pay costs and 5s. fines.

9 July, Manchester—Sixteen dealers condemned to pay costs and fines not exceeding 10s.

13 July, Manchester—Nine dealers fined from 2s. 6d. to 20s.

24 July, Rochdale—Four dealers fined 10s. to 20s.

27 July, Bolton—Twelve dealers and innkeepers condemned to pay costs.

3 August, Bolton—Three dealers fined 2s. 6d., and 5s.

10 August, Bolton—One dealer fined 5s.

And the same causes which make the working class the chief sufferers from frauds in the quality of goods make them the usual victims of frauds in the question of quantity too.

The habitual food of the individual working man naturally varies according to his wages. The better paid workers, especially those in whose families every member is able to earn something, have good food as long as this state of things lasts; meat daily and bacon and cheese for supper. Where wages are less, meat is used only two or three times a week, and the proportion of bread and potatoes increases. Descending gradually, we find the animal food reduced to a small piece of bacon cut up with the potatoes; lower still, even this disappears, and there remain only bread, cheese, porridge, and potatoes, until on the lowest round of the ladder, among the Irish, potatoes form the sole food. As an accompaniment, weak tea, with perhaps a little sugar, milk, or spirits, is universally drunk. Tea is regarded in England, and even in Ireland, as quite as indispensable as coffee in Germany, and where no tea is used, the bitterest poverty reigns. But all this presupposes that the workman has work. When he has none, he is wholly at the mercy of accident, and eats what is given him, what he can beg or steal. And, if he gets nothing, he simply starves, as we have seen. The quantity of food varies, of course, like its quality, according to the rate of wages, so that among ill-paid workers, even if they have no large families, hunger prevails in spite of full and regular work; and the number of the ill-paid is very large. Especially in London, where the competition of the workers rises with the increase of population, this class is very numerous, but it is to be found in other towns as well. In these cases all sorts of devices are used; potato parings, vegetable refuse, and rotten vegetables[1] are eaten for want of

---

[1] *Weekly Dispatch*, April or May 1844, according to a report by Dr Southwood Smith on the condition of the poor in London. (*Note in the German edition.*)

other food, and everything greedily gathered up which may possibly contain an atom of nourishment. And, if the week's wages are used up before the end of the week, it often enough happens that in the closing days the family gets only as much food, if any, as is barely sufficient to keep off starvation. Of course such a way of living unavoidably engenders a multitude of diseases, and when these appear, when the father from whose work the family is chiefly supported, whose physical exertion most demands nourishment, and who therefore first succumbs—when the father is utterly disabled, then misery reaches its height, and then the brutality with which society abandons its members, just when their need is greatest, comes out fully into the light of day.

To sum up briefly the facts thus far cited. The great towns are chiefly inhabited by working people, since in the best case there is one bourgeois for two workers, often for three, here and there for four; these workers have no property whatsoever of their own, and live wholly upon wages, which usually go from hand to mouth. Society, composed wholly of atoms, does not trouble itself about them; leaves them to care for themselves and their families, yet supplies them no means of doing this in an efficient and permanent manner. Every working man, even the best, is therefore constantly exposed to loss of work and food, that is to death by starvation, and many perish in this way. The dwellings of the workers are everywhere badly planned, badly built, and kept in the worst condition, badly ventilated, damp, and unwholesome. The inhabitants are confined to the smallest possible space, and at least one family usually sleeps in each room. The interior arrangement of the dwellings is poverty-stricken in various degrees, down to the utter absence of even the most necessary furniture. The clothing of the workers, too, is generally scanty, and that of great multitudes is in rags. The food is, in general, bad; often almost unfit for use, and in many cases, at least at times, insufficient in quantity, so that, in extreme cases, death by starvation results. Thus the working class of the great cities offers a graduated scale of conditions in life, in the best cases a temporarily endurable existence for hard work and good wages, good and endurable, that is, from the worker's standpoint; in the worst cases, bitter want, reaching even homelessness and death by starvation. The average is much nearer the worst case than the best. And this series does not fall into fixed classes, so that one can say, this fraction of the working class is well off, has always been so, and remains so. If that is the case here and there, if single branches of work have in general an advantage over others, yet the condition of the workers in each branch is subject to such great fluctuations that a single working man may be so placed as to pass through the whole range from comparative comfort to the extremest need, even to death by starvation, while almost every English working man can tell a tale of marked changes of fortune. Let us examine the causes of this somewhat more closely.

Competition

WE have seen in the introduction how competition created the proletariat at the very beginning of the industrial movement, by increasing the wages of weavers in consequence of the increased demand for woven goods, so inducing the weaving peasants to abandon their farms and earn more money by devoting themselves to their looms. We have seen how it crowded out the small farmers by means of the large farm system, reduced them to the rank of proletarians, and attracted them in part into the towns; how it further ruined the small bourgeoisie in great measure and reduced its members also to the ranks of the proletariat; how it centralized capital in the hands of the few, and population in the great towns. Such are the various ways and means by which competition, as it reached its full manifestation and free development in modern industry, created and extended the proletariat. We shall now have to observe its influence on the working class already created. And here we must begin by tracing the results of competition of single workers with one another.

Competition is the completest expression of the battle of all against all which rules in modern civil society. This battle, a battle for life, for existence, for everything, in case of need a battle of life and death, is fought not between the different classes of society only, but also between the individual members of these classes. Each is in the way of the other, and each seeks to crowd out all who are in his way, and to put himself in their place. The workers are in constant competition among themselves as the members of the bourgeoisie among themselves. The power-loom weaver is in competition with the hand-loom weaver, the unemployed or ill-paid hand-loom weaver with him who has work or is better paid, each trying to supplant the other. But this competition of the workers among themselves is the worst side of the present state of things in its effect upon the worker, the sharpest weapon against the proletariat in the hands of the bourgeoisie. Hence the effort of the workers to nullify this competition by associations, hence the hatred of the bourgeoisie towards these associations, and its triumph in every defeat which befalls them.

The proletarian is helpless; left to himself, he cannot live a single day. The bourgeoisie has gained a monopoly of all means of existence in the broadest sense of the word. What the proletarian needs, he can obtain only from this bourgeoisie, which is protected in its monopoly by the power of the State. The proletarian is, therefore, in law and in fact, the slave of the bourgeoisie, which can decree his life or death. It offers him the means of living, but only for an 'equivalent' for his work. It even lets him have the appearance of acting from a free choice, of making a contract with free, unconstrained consent, as a responsible agent who has attained his majority.

Fine freedom, where the proletarian has no other choice than that of either accepting the conditions which the bourgeoisie offers him, or of starving, of freezing to death, of sleeping naked among the beasts of the forests! A fine 'equivalent' valued at pleasure by the bourgeoisie! And if one proletarian is such a fool as to starve rather than agree to the equitable propositions of the bourgeoisie, his 'natural superiors',[1] another is easily found in his place; there are proletarians enough in the world, and not all so insane as to prefer dying to living.

Here we have the competition of the workers among themselves. If *all* the proletarians announced their determination to starve rather than work for the bourgeoisie, the latter would have to surrender its monopoly. But this is not the case—is, indeed, a rather impossible case—so that the bourgeoisie still thrives. To this competition of the worker there is but one limit; no worker will work for less than he needs to subsist. If he must starve, he will prefer to starve in idleness rather than in toil. True, this limit is relative; one needs more than another, one is accustomed to more comfort than another; the Englishman who is still somewhat civilized, needs more than the Irishman who goes in rags,

---

[1] A favourite expression of the English manufacturers. (*Note in the German edition.*)

eats potatoes, and sleeps in a pigsty. But that does not hinder the Irishman's competing with the Englishman, and gradually forcing the rate of wages, and with it the Englishman's level of civilization, down to the Irishman's level. Certain kinds of work require a certain grade of civilization, and to these belong almost all forms of industrial occupation; hence the interest of the bourgeoisie requires in this case that wages should be high enough to enable the workman to keep himself upon the required plane.

The newly immigrated Irishman, encamped in the first stable that offers, or turned out in the street after a week because he spends everything upon drink and cannot pay rent, would be a poor mill-hand. The mill-hand must, therefore, have wages enough to enable him to bring up his children to regular work; but no more, lest he should be able to get on without the wages of his children, and so make something else of them than mere working men. Here, too, the limit, the minimum wage, is relative. When every member of the family works, the individual worker can get on with proportionately less, and the bourgeoisie has made the most of the opportunity of employing and making profitable the labour of women and children afforded by machine-work. Of course it is not in every family that every member can be set to work, and those in which the case is otherwise would be in a bad way if obliged to exist upon the minimum wage possible to a wholly employed family. Hence the usual wages form an average according to which a fully employed family gets on pretty well, and one which embraces few members able to work, pretty badly. But in the worst case, every working man prefers surrendering the trifling luxury to which he was accustomed to not living at all; prefers a pigpen to no roof, wears rags in preference to going naked, confines himself to a potato diet in preference to starvation. He contents himself with half-pay and the hope of better times rather than be driven into the street to perish before the eyes of the world, as so many have done who had no work whatever. This trifle, therefore, this something more than nothing, is the minimum of wages. And if there are more workers at hand than the bourgeoisie thinks well to employ—if at the end of the battle of competition there yet remain workers who find nothing to do, they must simply starve; for the bourgeois will hardly give them work if he cannot sell the produce of their labour at a profit.

From this it is evident what the minimum of wages is. The maximum is determined by the competition of the bourgeoisie among themselves; for we have seen how they, too, must compete with each other. The bourgeois can increase his capital only in commerce and manufacture, and in both cases he needs workers. Even if he invests his capital at interest, he needs them indirectly; for without commerce and manufacture, no one would pay him interest upon his capital, no one could use it. So the bourgeois certainly needs workers, not indeed for his immediate living, for at need he could consume his capital, but as we need an article of trade or a beast of burden—as a means of profit. The proletarian produces the goods which the bourgeois sells with advantage. When, therefore, the demand for these goods increases so that all the competing working men are employed, and a few more might perhaps be useful, the competition among the workers falls away, and the bourgeoisie begin to compete among themselves. The capitalist in search of workmen knows very well that his profits increase as prices rise in consequence of the increased demand for his goods, and pays a trifle higher wages rather than let the whole profit escape him. He sends the butter to fetch the cheese, and getting the latter, leaves the butter ungrudgingly to the workers. So one capitalist after another goes in chase of workers, and wages rise; but only as high as the increasing demand permits. If the capitalist, who willingly sacrificed a part of his extraordinary profit, runs into danger of sacrificing any part of his ordinary average profit, he takes very good care not to pay more than average wages.

From this we can determine the average rate of wages. Under average circumstances, when neither workers nor capitalists have reason to compete, especially among themselves, when there are just as many workers at hand as can be employed in producing precisely the goods that are demanded, wages stand a little above the minimum. How far they rise above the minimum will depend upon the average needs and the grade of civilization of the workers. If the workers are accustomed to eat meat several times in the week, the capitalists must reconcile themselves to paying wages enough to make this food attainable, not less, because the workers are not competing among themselves and have no occasion to content themselves with less; not more, because the capitalists, in the absence of competition among themselves, have no occasion to attract working men by extraordinary favours.

This standard of the average needs and the average civilization of the workers has become very complicated by reason of the complications of English industry, and is different for different sorts of workers, as has been pointed out. Most industrial occupations demand a certain skill and regularity, and for these qualities which involve a certain grade of civilization, the rate of wages must be such as to induce the worker to acquire such skill and subject himself to such regularity. Hence it is that the average wages of industrial workers are higher than those of mere porters, day-labourers, etc., higher especially than those of agricultural labourers, a fact to which the additional cost of the necessities of life in cities contributes somewhat. In other words, the worker is, in law and in fact, the slave of the property-holding class, so effectually a slave that he is sold like a piece of goods, rises and falls in value like a commodity. If the demand for workers increases, the price of workers rises; if it falls, their price falls. If it falls so greatly that a number of them become unsaleable, if they are left in stock, they are simply left idle; and as they cannot live upon that, they die of starvation. For, to speak in the words of the economists, the expense incurred in maintaining them would not 'be reproduced', would be money thrown away, and to this end no man advances capital; and, so far, Malthus was perfectly right in his theory of population. The only difference as compared with the old, outspoken slavery is this, that the worker of today seems to be free because he is not sold once for all, but piecemeal by the day, the week, the year, and because no one owner sells him to another, but he is forced to sell himself in this way instead, being the slave of no particular person, but of the whole property-holding class. For him the matter is unchanged at bottom, and if this semblance of liberty necessarily gives him some real freedom on the one hand, it entails on the other the disadvantage that no one guarantees him a subsistence, he is in danger of being repudiated at any moment by his master, the bourgeoisie, and left to die of starvation, if the bourgeoisie ceases to have an interest in his employment, his existence. The bourgeoisie, on the other hand, is far better off under the present arrangement than under the old slave system; it can dismiss its employees at discretion without sacrificing invested capital, and gets its work done much more cheaply than is possible with slave labour, as Adam Smith comfortingly pointed out.[1]

Hence it follows, too, that Adam Smith was perfectly right in making the assertion 'That the demand for men, like that for any other commodity, necessarily regulates the production of men, quickens it when it goes on too slowly, and stops it when it advances too fast'.

Just as in the case of any other commodity! If there are too few labourers at hand, prices, i.e. wages, rise, the workers are more prosperous, marriages multiply, more children are born and more live to grow up, until a sufficient number of labourers has been secured. If there are too many on hand, prices fall, want of work, poverty, and starvation, and consequent diseases arise, and the 'surplus population' is put out of the way. And Malthus, who carried the foregoing proposition of Smith further, was also right, in his way, in asserting that there is always a surplus population; that there are always too many people in the world; he is wrong only when he asserts that there are more people on hand than can be maintained from the available means of subsistence. Surplus population is engendered rather by the competition of the workers among themselves, which forces each separate worker to labour as much each day as his strength can

---

[1] Adam Smith, *Wealth of Nations*, ed. I., MacCulloch, 1-vol. edn. (London, 1841), sect. 8, p. 36: 'The wear and tear of a slave, it has been said, is at the expense of his master, but that of a free servant is at his own expense. The wear and tear of the latter, however, is, in reality, as much at the expense of his master as that of the former. The wages paid to journeymen and servants of every kind, must by such as may enable them, one with another, to continue the race of journeymen and servants, according as the increasing, diminishing, or stationary demand of the society may happen to require. But though the wear and tear of a free servant be equally at the expense of his master, it generally costs him much less than that of a slave. The fund for replacing or repairing, if I may say so, the wear and tear of the slave, is commonly managed by a negligent master or careless overseer.'

possibly admit. If a manufacturer can employ ten hands nine hours daily, he can employ nine if each works ten hours, and the tenth goes hungry. And if a manufacturer can force the nine hands to work an extra hour daily for the same wages by threatening to discharge them at a time when the demand for hands is not very great, he discharges the tenth and saves so much wages. This is the process on a small scale, which goes on in a nation on a large one. The productiveness of each hand raised to the highest pitch by the competition of the workers among themselves, the division of labour, the introduction of machinery, the subjugation of the forces of Nature, deprive a multitude of workers of bread. These starving workers are then removed from the market, they can buy nothing, and the quantity of articles of consumption previously required by them is no longer in demand, need no longer be produced; the workers previously employed in producing them are therefore driven out of work, and are also removed from the market, and so it goes on, always the same old round, or rather, so it would go if other circumstances did not intervene. The introduction of the industrial forces already referred to for increasing production leads, in the course of time, to a reduction of prices of the articles produced and to consequent increased consumption, so that a large part of the displaced workers finally, after long suffering, find work again. If, in addition to this, the conquest of foreign markets constantly and rapidly increases the demand for manufactured goods, as has been the case in England during the past sixty years, the demand for hands increases, and, in proportion to it, the population. Thus, instead of diminishing, the population of the British Empire has increased with extraordinary rapidity, and is still increasing. Yet, in spite of the extension of industry, in spite of the demand for working men which, in general, has increased, there is, according to the confession of all the official political parties (Tory, Whig, and Radical), permanent surplus, superfluous population; the competition among the workers is constantly greater than the competition to secure workers.

Whence comes this incongruity? It lies in the nature of industrial competition and the commercial crises which arise from it. In the present unregulated production and distribution of the means of subsistence, which is carried on not directly for the sake of supplying needs, but for profit, in the system under which every one works for himself to enrich himself, disturbances inevitably arise at every moment. For example, England supplies a number of countries with most diverse goods. Now, although the manufacturer may know how much of each article is consumed in each country annually, he cannot know how much is on hand at every given moment, much less can he know how much his competitors export thither. He can only draw most uncertain inferences from the perpetual fluctuations in prices, as to the quantities on hand and the needs of the moment. He must trust to luck in exporting his goods. Everything is done blindly, as guess-work, more or less at the mercy of accident. Upon the slightest favourable report, each one exports what he can, and before long such a market is glutted, sales stop, capital remains inactive, prices fall, and English manufacture has no further employment for its hands. In the beginning of the development of manufacture, these checks were limited to single branches and single markets; but the centralizing tendency of competition which drives the hands thrown out of one branch into such other branches as are most easily accessible, and transfers the goods which cannot be disposed of in one market to other markets, has gradually brought the single minor crises nearer together and united them into one periodically recurring crisis. Such a crisis usually recurs once in five years after a brief period of activity and general prosperity; the home market, like all foreign ones, is glutted with English goods, which it can only slowly absorb, the industrial movement comes to a standstill in almost every branch, the small manufacturers and merchants who cannot survive a prolonged inactivity of their invested capital fail, the larger ones suspend business during the worst season, close their mills or work short time, perhaps half the day; wages fall by reason of the competition of the unemployed, the diminution of working-time, and the lack of profitable sales; want becomes universal among the workers, the small savings, which individuals may have made, are rapidly consumed, the philanthropic institutions are overburdened, the poor-rates are doubled, trebled, and still insufficient, the number of the starving increases, and the whole multitude of 'surplus' population presses in terrific numbers into the foreground. This continues for a time; the 'surplus' exist as best they may, or perish; philanthropy and the Poor Law help many of them to a painful prolongation of their existence. Others find scant means of subsistence here and there in such kinds of work as have been least open to competition, are most remote from manufacture. And with how little can a human being keep body and soul together for a time! Gradually the state of things improves; the accumulations of goods are consumed, the general depression among the men of commerce and manufacture prevents a too hasty replenishing of the markets, and at last rising prices and favourable reports from all directions restore activity. Most of the markets are distant ones; demand increases and prices rise constantly while the first exports are arriving; people struggle for the first goods, the first sales enliven trade still more, the prospective ones promise still higher prices; expecting a further rise, merchants begin to buy upon speculation, and so to withdraw from consumption the articles intended for it, just when they are most needed. Speculation forces prices still higher, by inspiring others to purchase, and appropriating new importations at once. All this is reported to England, manufacturers begin to produce with a will, new mills are built, every means is employed to make the most of the favourable moment. Speculation arises here, too, exerting the same influence as upon foreign markets, raising prices, withdrawing goods from consumption, spurring manufacture in both ways to the highest pitch of effort. Then come the daring speculators working with fictitious capital, living upon credit, ruined if they cannot speedily sell; they hurl themselves into this universal, disorderly race for profits, multiply the disorder and haste by their unbridled passion, which drives prices and production to madness. It is a frantic struggle, which carries away even the most experienced and phlegmatic; goods are spun, woven, hammered, as if all mankind were to be newly equipped, as though two thousand million new consumers had been discovered in the moon. All at once the shaky speculators abroad, who must have money, begin to sell, below market price, of course, for their need is urgent; one sale is followed by others, prices fluctuate, speculators throw their goods upon the market in terror, the market is disordered, credit shaken, one house after another stops payments, bankruptcy follows bankruptcy, and the discovery is made that three times more goods are on hand or under way than can be consumed. The news reaches England, where production has been going on at full speed meanwhile, panic seizes all hands, failures abroad cause others in England, the panic crushes a number of firms, all reserves are thrown upon the market here, too, in the moment of anxiety, and the alarm is still further exaggerated. This is the beginning of the crisis, which then takes precisely the same course as its predecessor, and gives place in turn to a season of prosperity. So it goes on perpetually—prosperity, crisis, prosperity, crisis, and this perennial round in which English industry moves is, as has been before observed, usually completed once in five or six years.

From this it is clear that English manufacture must have, at all times save the brief periods of highest prosperity, an unemployed reserve army of workers, in order to be able to produce the masses of goods required by the market in the liveliest months. This reserve army is larger or smaller, according as the state of the market occasions the employment of a larger or smaller proportion of its members. And if at the moment of highest activity of the market the agricultural districts, Ireland, and the branches least affected by the general prosperity temporarily supply to manufacture a number of workers, these are a mere minority, and these too belong to the reserve army, with the single difference that the prosperity of the moment was required to reveal their connection with it. When they enter upon the more active branches of work, their former employers draw in somewhat, in order to feel the loss less, work longer hours, employ women and younger workers, and when the wanderers discharged at the beginning of the crisis return, they find their places filled and themselves superfluous—at least in the majority of cases. This reserve army, which embraces an immense multitude during the crisis and a large number during the period which may be regarded as the average between the highest prosperity and the crisis, is the 'surplus population' of England, which keeps body and soul together by begging, stealing, street-sweeping, collecting manure, pushing hand-carts, driving donkeys, peddling, or performing occasional small jobs. In every great town a multitude of such people may be found. It is astonishing in what devices this 'surplus population' takes refuge. The London crossing-sweepers are known all over the world; but hitherto the principal streets in all the great cities, as well as the crossings, have been swept by people out of other work, and employed by the Poor Law guardians or the municipal authorities for the purpose. Now, however, a machine has been invented which rattles through the streets daily, and has spoiled this source of income for the unemployed. Along the great highways leading into the cities, on which there is a great deal of waggon traffic, a large number of people may be seen with small carts, gathering fresh horse-dung at the risk of their lives among the passing coaches and omnibuses, often paying a couple of shillings a week to the authorities for the privilege. But this occupation is forbidden in many places, because the ordinary street-sweepings thus impoverished cannot be sold as manure. Happy are such of the 'surplus' as can obtain a push-cart and go about with it. Happier still those to whom it is vouchsafed to possess an ass in addition to the cart. The ass must get his own food or is given a little gathered refuse, and can yet bring in a trifle of money. Most of the 'surplus' betake themselves to huckstering. On Saturday afternoons, especially, when the whole working population is on the streets, the crowd who live from huckstering and peddling may be seen. Shoe and corset laces, braces, twine, cakes, oranges, every kind of small articles are offered by men, women, and children; and at other times also, such peddlers are always to be seen standing at the street corners or going about with cakes and ginger-beer or nettle-beer.[1] Matches and such things, sealing-wax, and patent mixtures for lighting fires are further resources of such vendors. Others, so-called jobbers, go about the streets seeking small jobs. Many of these succeed in getting a day's work, many are not so fortunate.

[1] Two cooling effervescent drinks, the former made of water, sugar, and some ginger, the latter of water, sugar, and nettles. They are much liked by the workers, especially the teetotallers. (*Note in the German edition.*)

At the gates of all the London docks, [says the Rev. W. Champneys, preacher of the East End] hundreds of the poor appear every morning in winter before daybreak, in the hope of getting a day's work. They await the opening of the gates; and, when the youngest and strongest and best known have been engaged, hundreds cast down by disappointed hope, go back to their wretched homes.

When these people find no work and will not rebel against society, what remains for them but to beg? And surely no one can wonder at the great army of beggars, most of them able-bodied men, with whom the police carries on perpetual war. But the beggary of these men has a peculiar character. Such a man usually goes about with his family singing a pleading song in the streets or appealing, in a speech, to the benevolence of the passers-by. And it is a striking fact that these beggars are seen almost exclusively in the working-people's districts, that it is almost exclusively the gifts of the poor from which they live. Or the family takes up its position in a busy street, and without uttering a word, lets the mere sight of its helplessness plead for it. In this case, too, they reckon upon the sympathy of the workers alone, who know from experience how it feels to be hungry, and are liable to find themselves in the same situation at any moment; for this dumb, yet most moving appeal, is met with almost solely in such streets as are frequented by working men, and at such hours as working men pass by; but especially on Saturday evenings, when the 'secrets' of the working-people's quarters are generally revealed, and the middle class withdraws as far as possible from the district thus polluted. And he among the 'surplus' who has courage and passion enough openly to resist society, to reply with declared war upon the bourgeoisie to the disguised war which the bourgeoisie wages upon him, goes forth to rob, plunder, murder, and burn!

Of this surplus population there are, according to the reports of the Poor Law commissioners, on an average, a million and a half in England and Wales; in Scotland the number cannot be ascertained for want of Poor Law regulations, and with Ireland we shall deal separately. Moreover, this million and a half includes only those who actually apply to the parish for relief; the great multitude who struggle on without recourse to this most hated expedient, it does not embrace. On the other hand, a good part of the number belongs to the agricultural districts, and does not enter into the present discussion. During a crisis this number naturally increases markedly, and want reaches its highest pitch. Take, for instance, the crisis of 1842, which, being the latest, was the most violent; for the intensity of the crisis increases with each repetition, and the next, which may be expected not later than 1847,[1] will probably be still more violent and lasting. During this crisis the poor-rates rose in every town to a hitherto unknown height. In Stockport, among other towns, for every pound paid in house-rent, 8s. of poor-rate had to be paid, so that the rate alone formed 40 per cent of the house-rent. Moreover, whole streets stood vacant, so that there were at least 20,000 fewer inhabitants than usual, and on the doors of the empty houses might be read: 'Stockport to let'. In Bolton, where, in ordinary years, the rents from which rates are paid average £86,000, they sank to £36,000. The number of the poor to be supported rose, on the other hand, to 14,000, or more than 20 per cent of the whole number of inhabitants. In Leeds, the Poor Law guardians had a reserve fund of £10,000. This, with a contribution of £7,000, was wholly exhausted before the crisis reached its height. So it was everywhere. A report drawn up in January 1843, by a committee of the Anti-Corn Law League, on the condition of the industrial districts in 1842, which was based upon detailed statements of the manufacturers, asserts that the poor-rate was, taking the average, twice as high as in 1839, and that the number of persons requiring relief has trebled, even quintupled, since that time; that a multitude of applicants belong to a class which had never before solicited relief; that the working class commands more than two-thirds less of the means of subsistence than from 1834 to 1836; that the consumption of meat had been decidedly less, in some places 20 per cent, in others reaching 60 per cent less; that even handicraftsmen, smiths, bricklayers, and others, who usually have full employment in the most depressed periods, now suffered greatly from want of work and reduction of wages; and that, even now, in January 1843, wages are still steadily falling. And these are the

---

[1] And it came in 1847.

reports of manufacturers! The starving workmen, whose mills were idle, whose employers could give them no work, stood in the streets in all directions, begged singly or in crowds, besieged the sidewalks in armies, and appealed to the passers-by for help; they begged, not cringing like ordinary beggars, but threatening by their numbers, their gestures, and their words. Such was the state of things in all the industrial districts, from Leicester to Leeds, and from Manchester to Birmingham. Here and there disturbances arose, as in the Staffordshire potteries, in July. The most frightful excitement prevailed among the workers until the general insurrection broke out throughout the manufacturing districts in August. When I came to Manchester in November 1842, there were crowds of unemployed working men at every street corner, and many mills were still standing idle. In the following months these unwilling corner loafers gradually vanished, and the factories came into activity once more.

To what extent want and suffering prevail among these unemployed during such a crisis, I need not describe. The poor-rates are insufficient, vastly insufficient; the philanthropy of the rich is a rain-drop in the ocean, lost in the moment of falling; beggary can support but few among the crowds. If the small dealers did not sell to the working people on credit at such times as long as possible—paying themselves liberally afterwards, it must be confessed—and if the working people did not help each other, every crisis would remove a multitude of the surplus through death by starvation. Since, however, the most depressed period is brief, lasting, at worst, but one, two, or two and a half years, most of them emerge from it with their lives after dire privations. But indirectly by disease, etc., every crisis finds a multitude of victims, as we shall see. First, however, let us turn to another cause of abasement to which the English worker is exposed, a cause permanently active in forcing the whole class downwards.

4

Irish Immigration

WE have already referred several times in passing to the Irish who have immigrated into England; and we shall now have to investigate more closely the causes and results of this immigration.

The rapid extension of English industry could not have taken place if England had not possessed in the numerous and impoverished population of Ireland a reserve at command. The Irish had nothing to lose at home, and much to gain in England; and from the time when it became known in Ireland that the east side of St George's Channel offered steady work and good pay for strong arms, every year has brought armies of the Irish hither. It has been calculated that more than a million have already immigrated, and not far from 50,000 still come every year, nearly all of whom enter the industrial districts, especially the great cities, and there form the lowest class of the population. Thus there are in London, 120,000; in Manchester, 40,000; in Liverpool, 34,000; Bristol, 24,000; Glasgow, 40,000; Edinburgh, 29,000, poor Irish people.[1] These people having grown up almost without civilization, accustomed from youth to every sort of privation, rough, intemperate, and improvident, bring all their brutal habits with them among a class of the English population which has, in truth, little inducement to cultivate education and morality. Let us hear Thomas Carlyle upon this subject.[2]

The wild Milesian* features, looking false ingenuity, restlessness, unreason, misery, and mockery, salute you on all highways and byways. The English coachman, as he whirls past, lashes the Milesian with his whip, curses him with his tongue; the Milesian is

[1] Archibald Alison, *Principles of Population and Their Connection with Human Happiness*, 2 vols. (1840). This Alison is the historian of the French Revolution, and, like his brother, Dr W. P. Alison, a religious Tory.

[2] *Chartism*, 28, 31 etc.

holding out his hat to beg. He is the sorest evil this country has to strive with. In his rags and laughing savagery, he is there to undertake all work that can be done by mere strength of hand and back—for wages that will purchase him potatoes. He needs only salt for condiment, he lodges to his mind in any pig-hutch or dog-hutch, roosts in outhouses, and wears a suit of tatters, the getting on and off of which is said to be a difficult operation, transacted only in festivals and the high tides of the calendar. The Saxon-man, if he cannot work on these terms, finds no work. The uncivilised Irishman, not by his strength, but by the opposite of strength, drives the Saxon native out, takes possession in his room. There abides he, in his squalor and unreason, in his falsity and drunken violence, as the ready-made nucleus of degradation and disorder. Whoever struggles, swimming with difficulty, may now find an example how the human being can exist not swimming, but sunk. That the condition of the lower multitude of English labourers approximates more and more to that of the Irish, competing with them in all the markets: that whatsoever labour, to which mere strength with little skill will suffice, is to be done, will be done not at the English price, but at an approximation to the Irish price; at a price superior as yet to the Irish, that is, superior to scarcity of potatoes for thirty weeks yearly; superior, yet hourly, with the arrival of every new steamboat, sinking nearer to an equality with that.

If we except his exaggerated and one-sided condemnation of the Irish national character, Carlyle is perfectly right. These Irishmen who migrate for 4*d.* to England, on the deck of a steamship on which they are often packed like cattle, insinuate themselves everywhere. The worst dwellings are good enough for them; their clothing causes them little trouble, so long as it holds together by a single thread; shoes they know not; their food consists of potatoes and potatoes only; whatever they earn beyond these needs they spend upon drink. What does such a race want with high wages? The worst quarters of all the large towns are inhabited by Irishmen. Whenever a district is distinguished for especial filth and especial ruinousness, the explorer may safely count upon meeting chiefly those Celtic faces which one recognizes at the first glance as different from the Saxon physiognomy of the native, and the singing, aspirate brogue which the true Irishman never loses. I have occasionally heard the Irish-Celtic language spoken in the most thickly populated parts of Manchester. The majority of the families who live in cellars are almost everywhere of Irish origin. In short, the Irish have, as Dr Kay says, discovered the minimum of the necessities of life, and are now making the English workers acquainted with it. Filth and drunkenness, too, they have brought with them. The lack of cleanliness, which is not so injurious in the country, where population is scattered, and which is the Irishman's second nature, becomes terrifying and gravely dangerous through its concentration here in the great cities. The Milesian deposits all garbage and filth before his house door here, as he was accustomed to do at home, and so accumulates the pools and dirt-heaps which disfigure the working-people's quarters and poison the air. He builds a pigsty against the house wall as he did at home, and if he is prevented from doing this, he lets the pig sleep in the room with himself. This new and unnatural method of cattle-raising in cities is wholly of Irish origin. The Irishman loves his pig as the Arab his horse, with the difference that he sells it when it is fat enough to kill. Otherwise, he eats and sleeps with it, his children play with it, ride upon it, roll in the dirt with it, as anyone may see a thousand times repeated in all the great towns of England. The filth and comfortlessness that prevail in the houses themselves it is impossible to describe. The Irishman is unaccustomed to the presence of furniture; a heap of straw, a few rags, utterly beyond use as clothing, suffice for his nightly couch. A piece of wood, a broken chair, an old chest for a table, more he needs not; a tea-kettle, a few pots and dishes, equip his kitchen, which is also his sleeping and living room. When he is in want of fuel, everything combustible within his reach, chairs, doorposts, mouldings, flooring, finds its way up the chimney. Moreover, why should he need much room? At home in his mud-cabin there was only one room for all domestic purposes; more than one room his family does not need in England. So the custom of crowding many persons into a single room, now so universal, has been chiefly implanted by the Irish immigration. And since the poor devil must have one en- joyment, and society has shut him out of all others, he betakes himself to the drinking of spirits. Drink is the only thing which makes the Irishman's life worth having, drink and his cheery care-free temperament; so he revels in drink to the point of the most bestial drunkenness. The southern facile character of the Irishman, his crudity, which places him but little above the savage, his contempt for all humane enjoyments, in which his very crudeness makes him incapable of sharing, his filth and poverty, all favour drunkenness. The temptation is great, he cannot resist it, and so when he has money he gets rid of it down his throat. What else should he do? How can society blame him when it places him in a position in which he almost of necessity becomes a drunkard; when it leaves him to himself, to his savagery?

With such a competitor the English working man has to struggle, with a competitor upon the lowest plane possible in a civilized country, who for this very reason requires less wages than any other. Nothing else is therefore possible than that, as Carlyle says, the wages of the English working man should be forced down further and further in every branch in which the Irish compete with him. And these branches are many. All such as demand little or no skill are open to the Irish. For work which requires long training or regular, pertinacious application, the dissolute, unsteady, drunken Irishman is on too low a plane. To become a mechanic, a mill-hand, he would have to adopt the English civilization, the English customs, become, in the main, an Englishman. But for all simple, less exact work, wherever it is a question more of strength than skill, the Irishman is as good as the Englishman. Such occupations are therefore especially overcrowded with Irishmen: hand-weavers, bricklayers, porters, jobbers, and such workers, count hordes of Irishmen among their number, and the pressure of this race has done much to depress wages and lower the working class. And even if the Irish, who have forced their way into other occupations, should become more civilized, enough of the old habits would cling to them to have a strong degrading influence upon their English companions in toil, especially in view of the general effect of being surrounded by the Irish. For when, in almost every great city, a fifth or a quarter of the workers are Irish, or children of Irish parents, who have grown up among Irish filth, no one can wonder if the life, habits, intelligence, moral status—in short, the whole character of the working class assimilates a great part of the Irish characteristics. On the contrary, it is easy to understand how the degrading position of the English workers, engendered by our modern history, and its immediate consequences, has been still more degraded by the presence of Irish competition.

5

Results

HAVING now investigated, somewhat in detail, the conditions under which the English working class lives, it is time to draw some further inferences from the facts presented, and then to compare our inferences with the actual state of things. Let us see what the workers themselves have become under the given circumstances, what sort of people they are, what their physical, mental, and moral status.

When one individual inflicts bodily injury upon another, such injury that death results, we call the deed manslaughter; when the assailant knew in advance that the injury would be fatal, we call his deed murder. But when society[1] places hundreds of proletarians in such a position that they inevitably meet a too early and an unnatural death, one which is quite as much a death by violence as that by the sword or bullet; when it deprives thousands of the necessaries of life, places them under conditions in which they *cannot* live—forces them, through the strong arm of the law, to remain in such conditions until that death ensues which is the inevitable consequence—knows that these thousands of victims must perish, and yet permits these conditions to remain, its deed is murder just as surely as the deed of the single individual; disguised, malicious murder, murder against which none can defend himself, which does not seem what it

[1] When as here and elsewhere I speak of society as a responsible whole, having rights and duties, I mean, of course, the ruling power of society, the class which at present holds social and political control, and bears, therefore, the responsibility for the condition of those to whom it grants no share in such control. This ruling class in England, as in all other civilized countries, is the bourgeoisie. But that this society, and especially the bourgeoisie, is charged with the duty of protecting every member of society, at least, in his life, to see to it, for example, that no one starves, I need not now prove to my *German* readers. If I were writing for the English bourgeoisie, the case would be different. (And so it is now in Germany. Our German capitalists are fully up to the English level, in this respect at least, in the year of grace, 1886.)

is, because no man sees the murderer, because the death of the victim seems a natural one, since the offence is more one of omission than of commission. But murder it remains. I have now to prove that society in England daily and hourly commits what the working-men's organs, with perfect correctness, characterize as social murder, that it has placed the workers under conditions in which they can neither retain health nor live long; that it undermines the vital force of these workers gradually, little by little, and so hurries them to the grave before their time. I have further to prove that society knows how injurious such conditions are to the health and the life of the workers, and yet does nothing to improve these conditions. That it *knows* the consequences of its deeds; that its act is, therefore, not mere manslaughter, but murder, I shall have proved, when I cite official documents, reports of Parliament and of the Government, in substantiation of my charge.

That a class which lives under the conditions already sketched and is so ill-provided with the most necessary means of subsistence, cannot be healthy and can reach no advanced age, is self-evident. Let us review the circumstances once more with especial reference to the health of the workers. The centralization of population in great cities exercises of itself an unfavourable influence; the atmosphere of London can never be so pure, so rich in oxygen, as the air of the country; two and a half million pairs of lungs, two hundred and fifty thousand fires, crowded upon an area three to four miles square, consume an enormous amount of oxygen, which is replaced with difficulty, because the method of building cities in itself impedes ventilation. The carbonic acid gas, engendered by respiration and fire, remains in the streets by reason of its specific gravity, and the chief air current passes over the roofs of the city. The lungs of the inhabitants fail to receive the due supply of oxygen, and the consequence is mental and physical lassitude and low vitality. For this reason, the dwellers in cities are far less exposed to acute, and especially to inflammatory, affections than rural populations, who live in a free, normal atmosphere; but they suffer the more from chronic affections. And if life in large cities is, in itself, injurious to health, how great must be the harmful influence of an abnormal atmosphere in the working-people's quarters, where, as we have seen, everything combines to poison the air. In the country, it may, perhaps, be comparatively innoxious to keep a dung-heap adjoining one's dwelling, because the air has free ingress from all sides; but in the midst of a large town, among closely built lanes and courts that shut out all movement of the atmosphere, the case is different. All putrefying vegetable and animal substances give off gases decidedly injurious to health, and if these gases have no free way of escape, they inevitably poison the atmosphere. The filth and stagnant pools of the working-people's quarters in the great cities have, therefore, the worst effect upon the public health, because they produce precisely those gases which engender disease; so, too, the exhalations from contaminated streams. But this is by no means all. The manner in which the great multitude of the poor is treated by society today is revolting. They are drawn into the large cities where they breathe a poorer atmosphere than in the country; they are relegated to districts which, by reason of the method of construction, are worse ventilated than any others; they are deprived of all means of cleanliness, of water itself, since pipes are laid only when paid for, and the rivers so polluted that they are useless for such purposes; they are obliged to throw all offal and garbage, all dirty water, often all disgusting drainage and excrement into the streets, being without other means of disposing of them; they are thus compelled to infect the region of their own dwellings. Nor is this enough. All conceivable evils are heaped upon the heads of the poor. If the population of great cities is too dense in general, it is they in particular who are packed into the least space. As though the vitiated atmosphere of the streets were not enough, they are penned in dozens into single rooms, so that the air which they breathe at night is enough in itself to stifle them. They are given damp dwellings, cellar dens that are not waterproof from below, or garrets that leak from above. Their houses are so built that the clammy air cannot escape. They are supplied bad, tattered, or rotten clothing, adulterated and indigestible food. They are exposed to the most exciting changes of mental condition, the most violent vibrations between hope and fear; they are hunted like game, and not permitted to attain peace of mind and quiet enjoyment of life. They are deprived of all enjoyments except that of sexual indulgence and drunkenness, are worked every day to the point of complete exhaustion of their mental and physical energies, and are thus constantly spurred on to the maddest excess in the only two enjoyments at their command. And if they surmount all this, they fall victims to want of work in a crisis when all the little is taken from them that had hitherto been vouchsafed them.

How is it possible, under such conditions, for the lower class to be healthy and long lived? What else can be expected than an excessive mortality, an unbroken series of epidemics, a progressive deterioration in the physique of the working population? Let us see how the facts stand.

That the dwellings of the workers in the worst portions of the cities, together with the other conditions of life of this class, engender numerous diseases, is attested on all sides. The article already quoted from the *Artisan* asserts with perfect truth, that lung diseases must be the inevitable consequence of such conditions, and that, indeed, cases of this kind are disproportionately frequent in this class. That the bad air of London, and especially of the working-people's districts, is in the highest degree favourable to the development of consumption, the hectic appearance of great numbers of persons sufficiently indicates. If one roams the streets a little in the early morning, when the multitudes are on their way to their work, one is amazed at the number of persons who look wholly or half-consumptive. Even in Manchester the people have not the same appearance; these pale, lank, narrow-chested, hollow-eyed ghosts, whom one passes at every step, these languid, flabby faces, incapable of the slightest energetic expression, I have seen in such startling numbers only in London, though consumption carries off a horde of victims annually in the factory towns of the North. In competition with consumption stands typhus, to say nothing of scarlet fever, a disease which brings most frightful devastation into the ranks of the working class. Typhus, that universally diffused affliction, is attributed by the official report on the sanitary condition of the working class directly to the bad state of the dwellings in the matters of ventilation, drainage, and cleanliness. This report, compiled, it must not be forgotten, by the leading physicians of

England from the testimony of other physicians, asserts that a single ill-ventilated court, a single blind alley without drainage, is enough to engender fever, and usually does engender it, especially if the inhabitants are greatly crowded. This fever has the same character almost everywhere, and develops in nearly every case into specific typhus. It is to be found in the working-people's quarters of all great towns and cities, and in single ill-built, ill-kept streets of smaller places, though it naturally seeks out single victims in better districts also. In London it has now prevailed for a considerable time; its extraordinary violence in the year 1837 gave rise to the report already referred to. According to the annual report of Dr Southwood Smith on the London Fever Hospital, the number of patients in 1843 was 1,462, or 418 more than in any previous year. In the damp, dirty regions of the north, south, and east districts of London, this disease raged with extraordinary violence. Many of the patients were working people from the country, who had endured severest privation while migrating, and, after their arrival, had slept hungry and half-naked in the streets, and so fallen victims to the fever. These people were brought into the hospital in such a state of weakness, that unusual quantities of wine, cognac, and preparations of ammonia and other stimulants were required for their treatment; 16.5 per cent of all patients died. This malignant fever is to be found in Manchester; in the worst quarters of the Old Town, Ancoats, Little Ireland, etc., it is rarely extinct; though here, as in the *English* towns generally, it prevails to a less extent than might be expected. In Scotland and Ireland, on the other hand, it rages with a violence that surpasses all conception. In Edinburgh and Glasgow it broke out in 1817, after the famine, and in 1826 and 1837 with especial violence, after the commercial crisis, subsiding somewhat each time after having raged about three years. In Edinburgh about 6,000 persons were attacked by the fever during the epidemic of 1817, and about 10,000 in that of 1837, and not only the number of persons attacked but the violence of the disease increased with each repetition.[1]

But the fury of the epidemic in all former periods seems to

---

[1] W. P. Alison, *Management of the Poor in Scotland.*

have been child's play in comparison with its ravages after the crisis of 1842. One-sixth of the whole indigent population of Scotland was seized by the fever, and the infection was carried by wandering beggars with fearful rapidity from one locality to another. It did not reach the middle and upper classes of the population, yet in two months there were more fever cases than in twelve years before. In Glasgow, 12 per cent of the population were seized in the year 1843; 32,000 persons, of whom 32 per cent perished, while this mortality in Manchester and Liverpool does not ordinarily exceed 8 per cent. The illness reached a crisis on the seventh and fifteenth days; on the latter, the patient usually became yellow, which our authority[1] regards as an indication that the cause of the malady was to be sought in mental excitement and anxiety. In Ireland, too, these fever epidemics have become domesticated. During twenty-one months of the years 1817−18, 39,000 fever patients passed through the Dublin hospital; and in a more recent year, according to Sheriff Alison,[2] 60,000. In Cork the fever hospital received one-seventh of the population in 1817−18, in Limerick in the same time one-fourth, and in the bad quarter of Waterford, nineteen-twentieths of the whole population were ill of the fever at one time.[3]

When one remembers under what conditions the working people live, when one thinks how crowded their dwellings are, how every nook and corner swarms with human beings, how sick and well sleep in the same room, in the same bed, the only wonder is that a contagious disease like this fever does not spread yet further. And when one reflects how little medical assistance the sick have at command, how many are without any medical advice whatsoever, and ignorant of the most ordinary precautionary measures, the mortality seems actually small. Dr Alison, who has made a careful study of this disease, attributes it directly to the want and the wretched condition of the poor, as in the report already

[1] A. Alison, *Principles of Population*, vol. ii.

[2] A. Alison in an article read before the British Association for the Advancement of Science, Oct. 1844, in York.

[3] W. P. Alison, *Management of the Poor in Scotland*. (*Note in the German edition.*)

quoted. He asserts that privations and the insufficient satisfaction of vital needs are what prepare the frame for contagion and make the epidemic wide-spread and terrible. He proves that a period of privation, a commercial crisis or a bad harvest, has each time produced the typhus epidemic in Ireland as in Scotland, and that the fury of the plague has fallen almost exclusively on the working class. It is a note-worthy fact, that according to his testimony, the majority of persons who perish by typhus are fathers of families, precisely the persons who can least be spared by those dependent upon them; and several Irish physicians whom he quotes bear the same testimony.

Another category of diseases arises directly from the food rather than the dwellings of the workers. The food of the labourer, indigestible enough in itself, is utterly unfit for young children, and he has neither means nor time to get his children more suitable food. Moreover, the custom of giving children spirits, and even opium, is very general; and these two influences, with the rest of the conditions of life pre-judicial to bodily development, give rise to the most diverse affections of the digestive organs, leaving life-long traces behind them. Nearly all workers have stomachs more or less weak, and are yet forced to adhere to the diet which is the root of the evil. How should they know what is to blame for it? And if they knew, how could they obtain a more suitable regimen so long as they cannot adopt a different way of living and are not better educated? But new disease arises during childhood from impaired digestion. Scrofula is almost universal among the working class, and scrofulous parents have scrofulous children, especially when the original in-fluences continue in full force to operate upon the inherited tendency of the children. A second consequence of this insufficient bodily nourishment, during the years of growth and development, is rachitis, which is extremely common among the children of the working class. The hardening of the bones is delayed, the development of the skeleton in general is restricted, and deformities of the legs and spinal column are frequent, in addition to the usual rachitic affec-tions. How greatly all these evils are increased by the changes to which the workers are subject in consequence of fluctu-ations in trade, want of work, and the scanty wages in time of crisis, it is not necessary to dwell upon. Temporary want of sufficient food, to which almost every working man is exposed at least once in the course of his life, only contributes to intensify the effect of his usually sufficient but bad diet. Children who are half-starved, just when they most need ample and nutritious food—and how many such there are during every crisis and even when trade is at its best—must inevitably become weak, scrofulous, and rachitic in a high degree. And that they do become so, their appearance amply shows. The neglect to which the great mass of working-men's children are condemned leaves ineradicable traces and brings the enfeeblement of the whole race of workers with it. Add to this the unsuitable clothing of this class, the impossibility of precautions against colds, the necessity of toiling so long as health permits, want made more dire when sickness appears, and the only too common lack of all medical assistance; and we have a rough idea of the sanitary condition of the English working class. The injurious effects peculiar to single employments as now conducted, I shall not deal with here.

Besides these, there are other influences which enfeeble the health of a great number of workers, intemperance most of all. All possible temptations, all allurements combine to bring the workers to drunkenness. Liquor is almost their only source of pleasure, and all things conspire to make it accessible to them. The working man comes from his work tired, exhausted, finds his home comfortless, damp, dirty, repulsive; he has urgent need of recreation, he *must* have something to make work worth his trouble, to make the prospect of the next day endurable. His unnerved, uncomfortable, hypochondriac state of mind and body arising from his unhealthy condition, and especially from indigestion, is aggravated beyond endurance by the general conditions of his life, the uncertainty of his existence, his dependence upon all possible accidents and chances, and his inability to do anything towards gaining an assured position. His enfeebled frame, weakened by bad air and bad food, violently demands some external stimulus; his social need can be gratified only in the public house, he has absolutely no other place where he can meet his friends. How can he be expected to resist the temptation? It is morally and physically inevitable that, under such circumstances, a very large number of working men should fall into intemperance. And apart from the chiefly physical influences which drive the working man into drunkenness, there is the example of the great mass, the neglected education, the impossibility of protecting the young from temptation, in many cases the direct influence of intemperate parents, who give their own children liquor, the certainty of forgetting for an hour or two the wretchedness and burden of life, and a hundred other circumstances so mighty that the workers can, in truth, hardly be blamed for yielding to such overwhelming pressure. Drunkenness has here ceased to be a vice, for which the vicious can be held responsible; it becomes a phenomenon, the necessary, inevitable effect of certain conditions upon an object possessed of no volition in relation to those conditions. They who have degraded the working man to a mere object have the responsibility to bear. But as inevitably as a great number of working men fall a prey to drink, just so inevitably does it manifest its ruinous influence upon the body and mind of its victims. All the tendencies to disease arising from the conditions of life of the workers are promoted by it, it stimulates in the highest degree the development of lung and digestive troubles, the rise and spread of typhus epidemics.

Another source of physical mischief to the working class lies in the impossibility of employing skilled physicians in cases of illness. It is true that a number of charitable institutions strive to supply this want, that the infirmary in Manchester, for instance, receives or gives advice and medicine to 22,000 patients annually. But what is that in a city in which, according to Gaskell's calculation,[1] three-fourths of the population need medical aid every year? English doctors charge high fees, and working men are not in a position to pay them. They can therefore do nothing, or are compelled to call in cheap charlatans, and use quack remedies, which do more harm than good. An immense number of such quacks thrive in every English town, securing their clientele among the poor by means of advertisements, posters, and other such devices. Besides these, vast quantities of patent medicines are sold, for all conceivable ailments:

[1] *Manufacturing Population*, ch. 8.

Morrison's Pills, Parr's Life Pills, Dr Mainwaring's Pills, and a thousand other pills, essences, and balsams, all of which have the property of curing all the ills that flesh is heir to. These medicines rarely contain actually injurious substances, but, when taken freely and often, they affect the system prejudicially; and as the unwary purchasers are always recommended to take as much as possible, it is not to be wondered at that they swallow them wholesale whether wanted or not.

It is by no means unusual for the manufacture of Parr's Life Pills to sell twenty to twenty-five thousand boxes of these salutary pills in a week, and they are taken for constipation by this one, for diarrhoea by that one, for fever, weakness, and all possible ailments. As our German peasants are cupped or bled at certain seasons, so do the English working people now consume patent medicines to their own injury and the great profit of the manufacturer. One of the most injurious of these patent medicines is a drink prepared with opiates, chiefly laudanum, under the name Godfrey's Cordial. Women who work at home, and have their own and other people's children to take care of, give them this drink to keep them quiet, and, as many believe, to strengthen them. They often begin to give this medicine to newly-born children, and continue, without knowing the effects of this 'heart's-ease', until the children die. The less susceptible the child's system to the action of the opium, the greater the quantities administered. When the cordial ceases to act, laudanum alone is given, often to the extent of fifteen to twenty drops at a dose. The Coroner of Nottingham testified before a Parliamentary Commission[1] that one apothecary had, according to his own statement, used thirteen hundredweight of laudanum in one year in the preparation of

[1] Report of Commission of Inquiry into the Employment of Children and Young Persons in Mines and Collieries and in the Trades and Manufactures in which numbers of them work together, not being included under the terms of the Factories' Regulation Act. First and Second Reports, Grainger's Report. Second Report usually cited as 'Children's Employment Commission's Report'. [This is one of the best official reports, containing, as it does, a mass of the most valuable but also most frightful facts. (*Added in the German edition.*)] First Report, 1841; Second Report, 1843.

Godfrey's Cordial. The effects upon the children so treated may be readily imagined. They are pale, feeble, wilted, and usually die before completing the second year. The use of this cordial is very extensive in all great towns and industrial districts in the kingdom.

The result of all these influences is a general enfeeblement of the frame in the working class. There are few vigorous, well-built, healthy persons among the workers, i.e. among the factory operatives, who are employed in confined rooms, and we are here discussing these only. They are almost all weakly, of angular but not powerful build, lean, pale, and of relaxed fibre, with the exception of the muscles especially exercised in their work. Nearly all suffer from indigestion, and consequently from a more or less hypochondriac, melancholy, irritable, nervous condition. Their enfeebled constitutions are unable to resist disease, and are therefore seized by it on every occasion. Hence they age prematurely, and die early. On this point the mortality statistics supply unquestionable testimony.

According to the Report of Registrar-General Graham, the annual death-rate of all England and Wales is something less than 2.25 per cent. That is to say, out of 45 persons, one dies every year.[1] This was the average for the year 1839–40. In 1840–1 the mortality diminished somewhat, and the death-rate was but one in 46. But in the great cities the proportion is wholly different. I have before me official tables of mortality (*Manchester Guardian*, 31 July 1844), according to which the death-rate of several large towns is as follows: In Manchester, including Chorlton and Salford, one in 32.72; and excluding Chorlton and Salford, one in 30.75. In Liverpool, including West Derby (suburb), 31.90, and excluding West Derby, 29.90; while the average of all the districts of Cheshire, Lancashire, and Yorkshire cited, including a number of wholly or partially rural districts and many small towns, with a total population of 2,172,506 for the whole, is one death in 39.80 persons. How unfavourably the workers are placed in the great cities, the mortality for

[1] Fifth Annual Report of the Registrar-General of Births, Deaths, and Marriages.

Prescott in Lancashire shows; a district inhabited by miners, and showing a lower sanitary condition than that of the agricultural districts, mining being by no means a healthful occupation. But these miners live in the country, and the death-rate among them is but one in 47.54, or nearly 2.5 per cent better than that for all England. All these statements are based upon the mortality tables for 1843. Still higher is the death-rate in the Scottish cities; in Edinburgh, in 1838–9, one in 29; in 1831, in the Old Town alone, one in 22. In Glasgow, according to Dr Cowen,[1] the average has been, since 1830, one in 30; and in single years, one in 22 to 24. That this enormous shortening of life falls chiefly upon the working class, that the general average is improved by the smaller mortality of the upper and middle classes, is attested upon all sides. One of the most recent depositions is that of a physician, Dr P. N. Holland, in Manchester, who investigated Chorlton-on-Medlock, a suburb of Manchester, under official commission. He divided the houses and streets into three classes each, and ascertained the following variations in the death-rate [see Figure]. It is clear from other tables given by Holland that the mortality in the *streets* of the second class is 18 per cent greater, and in the streets of the third class 68 per cent greater than in those of the first class; that the mortality in the *houses* of the second class is 31 per cent greater, and in the third class 78 per cent greater than in those of the first class; that the mortality in those bad

First class of streets: houses, class	I	Mortality 1 in	51
	II		45
	III		36
Second class of streets: houses, class	I		55
	II		38
	III		35
Third class of streets: houses, class	I		—
	II		35
	III		25

[1] Dr Cowen, 'Vital Statistics of Glasgow', *Journal of the Statistical Society of London.* (Oct. 1840).

streets which were improved, decreased 25 per cent. He closes with the remark, very frank for an English bourgeois:[1]

When we find the rate of mortality four times as high in some streets as in others, and twice as high in whole classes of streets as in other classes, and further find that it is all but invariably high in those streets which are in bad condition, and almost invariably low in those whose condition is good, we cannot resist the conclusion that multitudes of our fellow-creatures, *hundreds of our immediate neighbours*, are annually destroyed for want of the most evident precautions.

The Report on the Sanitary Condition of the Working Class contains information which attests the same fact. In Liverpool, in 1840, the average longevity of the upper classes, gentry, professional men, etc., was 35 years; that of the business men and better-placed handicraftsmen, 22 years; and that of the operatives, day-labourers, and serviceable class in general, but 15 years. The Parliamentary reports contain a mass of similar facts.

The death-rate is kept so high chiefly by the heavy mortality among young children in the working class. The tender frame of a child is least able to withstand the unfavourable influences of an inferior lot in life; the neglect to which they are often subjected, when both parents work or one is dead, avenges itself promptly, and no one need wonder that in Manchester, according to the report last quoted, more than 57 per cent of the children of the working class perish before the fifth year, while but 20 per cent of the children of the higher classes, and not quite 32 per cent of the children of all classes in the country die under five years of age.[2] The article of the *Artisan*, already several times referred to, furnishes exacter information on this point, by comparing the city death-rate in single diseases of children with the country death-rate, thus demonstrating that, in general, epidemics in Manchester and Liverpool are three times more fatal than in country districts; that affections of the nervous system are

[1] Report of Commission of Inquiry into the State of Large Towns and Populous Districts. First Report, 1844. Appendix.
[2] Factories' Inquiry Commission's Reports, 3rd vol. Report of Dr Hawkins on Lancashire, in which Dr Roberton is cited—the 'Chief Authority for Statistics in Manchester'.

quintupled, and stomach troubles trebled, while deaths from affections of the lungs in cities are to those in the country as 2.5 to 1. Fatal cases of smallpox, measles, scarlet fever, and whooping cough, among small children, are four times more frequent; those of water on the brain are trebled, and convulsions ten times more frequent. To quote another acknowledged authority, I append the following table. Out of 10,000 persons, there die—[1] [see Table]. Apart from the diverse diseases which are the necessary consequence of the present neglect and oppression of the poorer classes, there are other influences which contribute to increase the mortality among small children. In many families the wife, like the husband, has to work away from home, and the consequence is the total neglect of the children, who are

	Under 5 years	5–19	20–39	40–59	60–69	70–79	80–89	90–99	100+
In Ruthlandshire, a healthy agricultural district	2,865	891	1,275	1,299	1,189	1,428	938	112	3
Essex, marshy agricultural district	3,159	1,110	1,526	1,413	963	1,019	630	177	3
Town of Carlisle, 1779–87, before introduction of mills	4,408	911	1,006	1,201	940	826	533	153	22
Town of Carlisle, after the introduction of mills	4,738	930	1,261	1,134	677	727	452	80	1
Preston, factory town	4,947	1,136	1,379	1,114	553	532	298	38	3
Leeds, factory town	5,286	927	1,228	1,198	593	512	225	29	2

[1] Quoted by Dr Wade from the Report of the Parliamentary Factories' Commission of 1832, in his *History of the Middle and Working-Classes*, 3rd edn., London, 1835.

either locked up or given out to be taken care of. It is, therefore, not to be wondered at if hundreds of them perish through all manner of accidents. Nowhere are so many children run over, nowhere are so many killed by falling, drowning, or burning, as in the great cities and towns of England. Deaths from burns and scalds are especially frequent, such a case occurring nearly every week during the winter months in Manchester, and very frequently in London, though little mention is made of them in the papers. I have at hand a copy of the *Weekly Dispatch* of 15 December 1844, according to which, in the week from 1 December to 7 December inclusive, *six* such cases occurred. These unhappy children, perishing in this terrible way, are victims of our social disorder, and of the property-holding classes interested in maintaining and prolonging this disorder. Yet one is left in doubt whether even this terribly torturing death is not a blessing for the children in rescuing them from a long life of toil and wretchedness, rich in suffering and poor in enjoyment. So far has it gone in England; and the bourgeoisie reads these things every day in the newspapers and takes no further trouble in the matter. But it cannot complain if after the official and non-official testimony here cited which must be known to it, I broadly accuse it of social murder. Let the ruling class see to it that these frightful conditions are ameliorated, or let it surrender the administration of the common interests to the labouring class. To the latter course it is by no means inclined; for the former task, so long as it remains the bourgeoisie crippled by bourgeois prejudice, it has not the needed power. For if, at last, after hundreds of thousands of victims have perished, it manifests some little anxiety for the future, passing a 'Metropolitan Buildings Act',* under which the most unscrupulous overcrowding of dwellings is to be, at least in some slight degree, restricted; if it points with pride to measures which, far from attacking the root of the evil, do not by any means meet the demands of the commonest sanitary police, it cannot thus vindicate itself from the accusation. The English bourgeoisie has but one choice, either to continue its rule under the unanswerable charge of murder and in spite of this charge, or to abdicate in favour of the labouring class. Hitherto it has chosen the former course.

Let us turn from the physical to the mental state of the workers. Since the bourgeoisie vouchsafes them only so much of life as is absolutely necessary, we need not wonder that it bestows upon them only so much education as lies in the interest of the bourgeoisie; and that, in truth, is not much. The means of education in England are restricted out of all proportion to the population. The few day schools at the command of the working class are available only for the smallest minority, and are bad besides. The teachers, worn-out workers, and other unsuitable persons who only turn to teaching in order to live, are usually without the indispensable elementary knowledge, without the moral discipline so needful for the teacher, and relieved of all public supervision. Here, too, free competition rules, and, as usual, the rich profit by it, and the poor, for whom competition is *not* free, who have not the knowledge needed to enable them to form a correct judgement, have the evil consequences to bear. Compulsory school attendance does not exist. In the mills it is, as we shall see, purely nominal; and when in the session of 1843 the Ministry was disposed to make this nominal compulsion effective, the manufacturing bourgeoisie opposed the measure with all its might, though the working class was outspokenly in favour of compulsory school attendance. Moreover, a mass of children work the whole week through in the mills or at home, and therefore cannot attend school. The evening schools, supposed to be attended by children who are employed during the day, are almost abandoned or attended without benefit. It is asking too much, that young workers who have been using themselves up twelve hours in the day should go to school from eight to ten at night. And those who try it usually fall asleep, as is testified by hundreds of witnesses in the Children's Employment Commission's Report. Sunday schools have been founded, it is true, but they, too, are most scantily supplied with teachers, and can be of use to those only who have already learnt something in the day schools. The interval from one Sunday to the next is too long for an ignorant child to remember in the second sitting what it learned in the first, a week before. The Children's Employment Commission's Report furnishes a hundred proofs, and the Commission itself most emphatically expresses the opinion, that neither the weekday nor the Sunday schools, in the least degree, meet the needs of the nation. This report gives evidence of ignorance in the working class of England, such as could hardly be expected in Spain or Italy. It cannot be otherwise; the bourgeoisie has little to hope, and much to fear, from the education of the working class. The Ministry, in its whole enormous budget of £55,000,000, has only the single trifling item of £40,000 for public education, and, but for the fanaticism of the religious sects which does at least as much harm as good, the means of education would be yet more scanty. As it is, the State Church manages its national schools and the various sects their sectarian schools for the sole purpose of keeping the children of the brethren of the faith within the congregation, and of winning away a poor childish soul here and there from some other sect. The consequence is that religion, and precisely the most unprofitable side of religion, polemical discussion, is made the principal subject of instruction, and the memory of the children overburdened with incomprehensible dogmas and theological distinctions; that sectarian hatred and bigotry are awakened as early as possible, and all rational mental and moral training shamefully neglected. The working class has repeatedly demanded of Parliament a system of strictly secular public education, leaving religion to the ministers of the sects; but, thus far, no Ministry has been induced to grant it. The Minister is the obedient servant of the bourgeoisie, and the bourgeoisie is divided into countless sects; but each would gladly grant the workers the otherwise dangerous education on the sole condition of their accepting, as an antidote, the dogmas peculiar to the especial sect in question. And as these sects are still quarrelling among themselves for supremacy, the workers remain for the present without education. It is true that the manufacturers boast of having enabled the majority to read, but the quality of the reading is appropriate to the source of the instruction, as the Children's Employment Commission proves. According to this report, he who knows his letters can read enough to satisfy the conscience of the manufacturers. And when one reflects upon the confused orthography of the English language which makes reading one of the arts, learned only under long instruction, this ignorance is readily understood. Very few working people write readily; and writing orthographically is beyond the powers even of many 'educated' persons. The Sunday schools of the State Church, of the Quakers, and, I think, of several other sects, do not teach writing, 'because it is too worldly an employment for Sunday'. The quality of the instruction offered the workers in other directions may be judged from a specimen or two, taken from the Children's Employment Commission's Report, which unfortunately does not embrace mill-work proper:

'In Birmingham,' says Commissioner Grainger, 'the children examined by me are, as a whole, utterly wanting in all that could be in the remotest degree called a useful education. Although in almost all the schools religious instruction alone is furnished, the profoundest ignorance even upon that subject prevailed.'—'In Wolverhampton,' says Commissioner Horne, 'I found, among others, the following example: A girl of eleven years had attended both day and Sunday school, "had never heard of another world, of Heaven, or another life." A boy, seventeen years old, did not know that twice two are four, nor how many farthings in two pence even when the money was placed in his hand. Several boys had never heard of London nor of Willenhall, though the latter was but an hour's walk from their homes, and in the closest relations with Wolverhampton. Several had never heard the name of the Queen nor other names, such as Nelson, Wellington, Bonaparte; but it was noteworthy that those who had never heard even of St. Paul, Moses, or Solomon, were very well instructed as to the life, deeds, and character of Dick Turpin, the streetrobber, and especially of Jack Sheppard, the thief and gaol-breaker. A youth of sixteen did not know how many twice two are, nor how much four farthings make. A youth of seventeen asserted that four farthings are four half pence; a third, seventeen years old, answered several very simple questions with the brief statement, that he "was ne jedge o'nothin".'[1] These children who are crammed with religious doctrines four or five years at a stretch, know as little at the end as at the beginning. One child 'went to Sunday school regularly for five years; does not know who Jesus Christ is, but had heard the name; had never heard of the twelve Apostles, Samson, Moses, Aaron, etc.'[2] Another 'attended Sunday school regularly six years; knows who Jesus Christ

[1] Children's Employment Commission's Report. App. Part II. Q. 18, No. 216, 217, 226, 233, etc. Horne.

[2] Ibid., evidence, pp. 9, 39; 133.

was; he died on the cross to save our Saviour; had never heard of St. Peter or St. Paul'.[1] A third, 'attended different Sunday schools seven years; can read only the thin, easy books with simple words of one syllable; has heard of the Apostles, but does not know whether St. Peter was one or St. John; the latter must have been St. John Wesley'.[2] To the question who Christ was, Horne received the following answers among others: 'He was Adam', 'He was an Apostle', 'He was the Saviour's Lord's Son', and from a youth of sixteen: 'He was a king of London long ago'. In Sheffield, Commissioner Symons let the children from the Sunday school read aloud; they could not tell what they had read, or what sort of people the Apostles were, of whom they had just been reading. After he had asked them all one after the other about the Apostles without securing a single correct answer, one sly-looking little fellow, with great glee, called out: 'I know, mister; they were the lepers!'[3] From the pottery districts and from Lancashire the reports are similar.

This is what the bourgeoisie and the State are doing for the education and improvement of the working class. Fortunately the conditions under which this class lives are such as give it a sort of practical training, which not only replaces school cramming, but renders harmless the confused religious notions connected with it, and even places the workers in the vanguard of the national movement of England. Necessity is the mother of invention, and what is still more important, of thought and action. The English working man, who can scarcely read and still less write, nevertheless knows very well where his own interest and that of the nation lies. He knows, too, what the especial interest of the bourgeoisie is, and what he has to expect of that bourgeoisie. If he cannot write he can speak, and speak in public; if he has no arithmetic, he can, nevertheless, reckon with the Political Economists enough to see through a Corn-Law-repealing bourgeois, and to get the better of him in argument; if celestial matters remain very mixed for him in spite of all the effort of the preachers, he sees all the more clearly into

[1] Children's Employment Commission's Report, pp. 9, 36; 146.
[2] Ibid., pp. 34, 158.
[3] Symons' Rep. App. Part. 1., pp. E., 22 ff.

terrestrial, political, and social questions. We shall have occasion to refer again to this point; and pass now to the moral characteristics of our workers.

It is sufficiently clear that the instruction in morals can have no better effect than the religious teaching, with which in all English schools it is mixed up. The simple principles which, for plain human beings, regulate the relations of man to man, brought into the direst confusion by our social state, our war of each against all, necessarily remain confused and foreign to the working man when mixed with incomprehensible dogmas, and preached in the religious form of an arbitrary and dogmatic commandment. The schools contribute, according to the confession of all authorities, and especially of the Children's Employment Commission, almost nothing to the morality of the working class. So short-sighted, so stupidly narrow-minded is the English bourgeoisie in its egotism, that it does not even take the trouble to impress upon the workers the morality of the day, which the bourgeoisie has patched together in its own interest for its own protection! Even this precautionary measure is too great an effort for the enfeebled and sluggish bourgeoisie. A time must come when it will repent its neglect, too late. But it has no right to complain that the workers know nothing of its system of morals, and do not act in accordance with it.

Thus are the workers cast out and ignored by the class in power, morally as well as physically and mentally. The only provision made for them is the law, which fastens upon them when they become obnoxious to the bourgeoisie. Like the dullest of the brutes, they are treated to but one form of education, the whip, in the shape of force, not convincing but intimidating. There is, therefore, no cause for surprise if the workers, treated as brutes, actually become such; or if they can maintain their consciousness of manhood only by cherishing the most glowing hatred, the most unbroken inward rebellion against the bourgeoisie in power. They are men so long only as they burn with wrath against the reigning class. They become brutes the moment they bend in patience under the yoke, and merely strive to make life endurable while abandoning the effort to break the yoke.

This, then, is all that the bourgeoisie has done for the education of the proletariat—and when we take into consideration all the circumstances in which this class lives, we shall not think the worse of it for the resentment which it cherishes against the ruling class. The moral training which is not given to the worker in school is not supplied by the other conditions of his life; that moral training, at least, which alone has worth in the eyes of the bourgeoisie; his whole position and environment involves the strongest temptation to immorality. He is poor, life offers him no charm, almost every enjoyment is denied him, the penalties of the law have no further terrors for him; why should he restrain his desires, why leave to the rich the enjoyment of his birthright, why not seize a part of it for himself? What inducement has the proletarian not to steal? It is all very pretty and very agreeable to the ear of the bourgeois to hear the 'sacredness of property' asserted; but for him who has none, the sacredness of property dies out of itself. Money is the god of this world; the bourgeois takes the proletarian's money from him and so makes a practical atheist of him. No wonder, then, if the proletarian retains his atheism and no longer respects the sacredness and power of the earthly God. And when the poverty of the proletarian is intensified to the point of actual lack of the barest necessaries of life, to want and hunger, the temptation to disregard all social order does but gain power. This the bourgeoisie for the most part recognizes. Symons[1] observes that poverty exercises the same ruinous influence upon the mind which drunkenness exercises upon the body; and Dr Alison explains to property-holding readers, with the greatest exactness, what the consequences of social oppression must be for the working class.[2] Want leaves the working man the choice between starving slowly, killing himself speedily, or taking what he needs where he finds it—in plain English, stealing. And there is no cause for surprise that most of them prefer stealing to starvation and suicide.

True, there are, within the working class, numbers too moral to steal even when reduced to the utmost extremity,

[1] *Arts and Artisans.*

[2] *Principles of Population*, ii. 196, 197.

and these starve or commit suicide. For suicide, formerly the enviable privilege of the upper classes, has become fashionable among the English workers, and numbers of the poor kill themselves to avoid the misery from which they see no other means of escape.

But far more demoralizing than his poverty in its influence upon the English working man is the insecurity of his position, the necessity of living upon wages from hand to mouth, that in short which makes a proletarian of him. The smaller peasants in Germany are usually poor, and often suffer want, but they are less at the mercy of accident, they have at least something secure. The proletarian, who has nothing but his two hands, who consumes today what he earned yesterday, who is subject to every possible chance, and has not the slightest guarantee for being able to earn the barest necessities of life, whom every crisis, every whim of his employer may deprive of bread, this proletarian is placed in the most revolting, inhuman position conceivable for a human being. The slave is assured of a bare livelihood by the self-interest of his master, the serf has at least a scrap of land on which to live; each has at worst a guarantee for life itself. But the proletarian must depend upon himself alone, and is yet prevented from so applying his abilities as to be able to rely upon them. Everything that the proletarian can do to improve his position is but a drop in the ocean compared with the floods of varying chances to which he is exposed, over which he has not the slightest control. He is the passive subject of all possible combinations of circumstances, and must count himself fortunate when he has saved his life even for a short time; and his character and way of living are naturally shaped by these conditions. Either he seeks to keep his head above water in this whirlpool, to rescue his manhood, and this he can do solely in rebellion[1] against the class which plunders him so mercilessly and then abandons him to his fate, which strives to hold him in this position so demoralizing to a human being; or he gives up the struggle against his fate as hopeless, and strives to profit, so far as he can, by the most favourable moment. To save is unavailing,

[1] We shall see later how the rebellion of the working class against the bourgeoisie in England is legalized by the right of coalition.

for at the utmost he cannot save more than suffices to sustain life for a short time, while if he falls out of work, it is for no brief period. To accumulate lasting property for himself is impossible; and if it were not, he would only cease to be a working man and another would take his place. What better thing can he do, then, when he gets high wages, than live well upon them? The English bourgeoisie is violently scandalized at the extravagant living of the workers when wages are high; yet it is not only very natural but very sensible of them to enjoy life when they can, instead of laying up treasures which are of no lasting use to them, and which in the end moth and rust (i.e. the bourgeoisie) get possession of. Yet such a life is demoralizing beyond all others. What Carlyle says of the cotton spinners is true of all English industrial workers:[1]

Their trade, now in plethoric prosperity, anon extenuated into inanition and 'short time', is of the nature of gambling; they live by it like gamblers, now in luxurious superfluity, now in starvation. Black, mutinous discontent devours them; simply the miserablest feeling that can inhabit the heart of man. English commerce, with its world-wide, convulsive fluctuations, with its immeasurable Proteus Steam demon, makes all paths uncertain for them, all life a bewilderment; society, steadfastness, peaceable continuance, the first blessings of man are not theirs.—This world is for them no home, but a dingy prison-house, of reckless unthrift, rebellion, rancour, indignation against themselves and against all men. Is it a green, flowery world, with azure everlasting sky stretched over it, the work and government of a god; or a murky, simmering Tophet, of copperas fumes, cotton fuzz, gin riot, wrath and toil, created by a Demon, governed by a Demon?

And elsewhere:[2]

Injustice, infidelity to truth and fact and Nature's order, being properly the one evil under the sun, and the feeling of injustice the one intolerable pain under the sun, our grand question as to the condition of these working-men would be: Is it just? And, first of all, what belief have they themselves formed about the justice of it? The words they promulgate are notable by way of answer; their

---

[1] *Chartism*, 34 f.

[2] Ibid. 40.

actions are still more notable. Revolt, sullen revengeful humour of revolt against the upper classes, decreasing respect for what their temporal superiors command, decreasing faith for what their spiritual superiors teach, is more and more the universal spirit of the lower classes. Such spirit may be blamed, may be vindicated, but all men must recognise it as extant there, all may know that it is mournful, that unless altered it will be fatal.

Carlyle is perfectly right as to the facts and wrong only in censuring the wild rage of the workers against the higher classes. This rage, this passion, is rather the proof that the workers feel the inhumanity of their position, that they refuse to be degraded to the level of brutes, and that they will one day free themselves from servitude to the bourgeoisie. This may be seen in the case of those who do not share this wrath; they either bow humbly before the fate that overtakes them, live a respectful private life as well as they can, do not concern themselves as to the course of public affairs, help the bourgeoisie to forge the chains of the workers yet more securely, and stand upon the plane of intellectual nullity that prevailed before the industrial period began; or they are tossed about by fate, lose their moral hold upon themselves as they have already lost their economic hold, live along from day to day, drink and fall into licentiousness; and in both cases they are brutes. The last-named class contributes chiefly to the 'rapid increase of vice', at which the bourgeoisie is so horrified after itself setting in motion the causes which give rise to it.

Another source of demoralization among the workers is their being condemned to work. As voluntary, productive activity is the highest enjoyment known to us, so is compulsory toil the most cruel, degrading punishment. Nothing is more terrible than being constrained to do some one thing every day from morning until night against one's will. And the more a man the worker feels himself, the more hateful must his work be to him, because he feels the constraint, the aimlessness of it for himself. Why does he work? For love of work? From a natural impulse? Not at all! He works for money, for a thing which has nothing whatsoever to do with the work itself; and he works so long, moreover, and in such unbroken monotony, that this alone must make his work a torture in the first weeks if he has the least human feeling left. The division of labour has multiplied the brutalizing influences of forced work. In most branches the worker's activity is reduced to some paltry, purely mechanical manipulation, repeated minute after minute, unchanged year after year.[1] How much human feeling, what abilities can a man retain in his thirtieth year, who has made needle points or filed toothed wheels twelve hours every day from his early childhood, living all the time under the conditions forced upon the English proletarian? It is still the same thing since the introduction of steam. The worker's activity is made easy, muscular effort is saved, but the work itself becomes unmeaning and monotonous to the last degree. It offers no field for mental activity, and claims just enough of his attention to keep him from thinking of anything else. And a sentence to such work, to work which takes his whole time for itself, leaving him scarcely time to eat and sleep, none for physical exercise in the open air, or the enjoyment of Nature, much less for mental activity, how can such a sentence help degrading a human being to the level of a brute? Once more the worker must choose, must either surrender himself to his fate, become a 'good' workman, heed 'faithfully' the interest of the bourgeoisie, in which case he most certainly becomes a brute, or else he must rebel, fight for his manhood to the last, and this he can only do in the fight against the bourgeoisie.

And when all these conditions have engendered vast demoralization among the workers, a new influence is added to the old, to spread this degradation more widely and carry it to the extremest point. This influence is the centralization of the population. The writers of the English bourgeoisie are crying murder at the demoralizing tendency of the great cities; like perverted Jeremiahs, they sing dirges, not over the destruction, but the growth of the cities. Sheriff Alison attributes almost everything, and Dr Vaughan, author of *The Age of Great Cities*, still more to this influence. And this is

---

[1] Shall I call bourgeois witnesses to bear testimony for me here, too? I select one only, whom everyone may read, namely, Adam Smith, *Wealth of Nations*, ed. J. R. McCulloch, 4 vol. (London, 1828), vol. iii, book 5, ch. 1, p. 297.

natural, for the propertied class has too direct an interest in the other conditions which tend to destroy the worker body and soul. If they should admit that 'poverty, insecurity, overwork, forced work, are the chief ruinous influences', they would have to draw the conclusion, 'then let us give the poor property, guarantee their subsistence, make laws against overwork', and this the bourgeoisie dare not formulate. But the great cities have grown up so spontaneously, the population has moved into them so wholly of its own motion, and the inference that manufacture and the middle class which profits from it alone have created the cities is so remote, that it is extremely convenient for the ruling class to ascribe all the evil to this apparently unavoidable source; whereas the great cities really only secure a more rapid and certain development for evils already existing in the germ. Alison is humane enough to admit this; he is no thoroughbred Liberal manufacturer, but only a half developed Tory bourgeois, and he has, therefore, an open eye, now and then, where the full-fledged bourgeois is still stone blind. Let us hear him:[1]

It is in the great cities that vice has spread her temptations, and pleasure her seductions, and folly her allurements; that guilt is encouraged by the hope of impunity, and idleness fostered by the frequency of example. It is to these great marts of human corruption that the base and the profligate resort from the simplicity of country life; it is here that they find victims whereon to practise their iniquity, and gains to reward the dangers that attend them. Virtue is here depressed from the obscurity in which it is involved. Guilt is matured from the difficulty of its detection; licentiousness is rewarded by the immediate enjoyment which it promises. If any person will walk through St. Giles's, the crowded alleys of Dublin, or the poorer quarters of Glasgow by night, he will meet with ample proof of these observations; he will no longer wonder at the disorderly habits and profligate enjoyments of the lower orders; his astonishment will be, not that there is so much, but that there is so little crime in the world. The great cause of human corruption in these crowded situations is the contagious nature of bad example and the extreme difficulty of avoiding the seductions of vice when they are brought into close and daily proximity with the younger part of the people. Whatever we may think of the strength of virtue, experience proves that the higher orders are indebted for their

[1] *Principles of Population*, ii. 76 ff., 82, 135.

exemption from atrocious crime or disorderly habits chiefly to their fortunate removal from the scene of temptation; and that where they are exposed to the seductions which assail their inferiors, they are noways behind them in yielding to their influence. It is the peculiar misfortune of the poor in great cities that they cannot fly from these irresistible temptations, but that, turn where they will, they are met by the alluring forms of vice, or the seductions of guilty enjoyment. It is the experienced impossibility of concealing the attractions of vice from the younger part of the poor in great cities which exposes them to so many causes of demoralisation. All this proceeds not from any unwonted or extraordinary depravity in the character of these victims of licentiousness, but from the almost irresistible nature of the temptations to which the poor are exposed. The rich, who censure their conduct, would in all probability yield as rapidly as they have done to the influence of similar causes. There is a certain degree of misery, a certain proximity to sin, which virtue is rarely able to withstand, and which the young, in particular, are generally unable to resist. The progress of vice in such circumstances is almost as certain and often nearly as rapid as that of physical contagion.

And elsewhere:

When the higher orders for their own profit have drawn the labouring-classes in great numbers into a small space, the contagion of guilt becomes rapid and unavoidable. The lower orders, situated as they are in so far as regards moral or religious instruction, are frequently hardly more to be blamed for yielding to the temptations which surround them than for falling victims to the typhus fever.

Enough! The half-bourgeois Alison betrays to us, however narrow his manner of expressing himself, the evil effect of the great cities upon the moral development of the workers. Another, a bourgeois *pur sang*,* a man after the heart of the Anti-Corn Law League, Dr Andrew Ure,[1] betrays the other side. He tells us that life in great cities facilitates cabals among the workers and confers power on the Plebs. If here the workers are not educated (i.e. to obedience to the bourgeoisie), they may view matters one-sidedly, from the standpoint of a sinister selfishness, and may readily permit themselves to be hoodwinked by sly demagogues; nay, they might even be capable of viewing their greatest benefactors,

[1] *Philosophy of Manufactures* (London, 1835), 406 ff. We shall have occasion to refer further to this reputable work.

the frugal and enterprising capitalists, with a jealous and hostile eye. Here proper training alone can avail, or national bankruptcy and other horrors must follow, since a revolution of the workers could hardly fail to occur. And our bourgeois is perfectly justified in his fears. If the centralization of population stimulates and develops the property-holding class, it forces the development of the workers yet more rapidly. The workers begin to feel as a class, as a whole; they begin to perceive that, though feeble as individuals, they form a power united; their separation from the bourgeoisie, the development of views peculiar to the workers and corresponding to their position in life, is fostered, the consciousness of oppression awakens, and the workers attain social and political importance. The great cities are the birthplaces of labour movements; in them the workers first began to reflect upon their own condition, and to struggle against it; in them the opposition between proletariat and bourgeoisie first made itself manifest; from them proceeded the Trade Unions, Chartism, and Socialism. The great cities have transformed the disease of the social body, which appears in chronic form in the country, into an acute one, and so made manifest its real nature and the means of curing it. Without the great cities and their forcing influence upon the popular intelligence, the working class would be far less advanced than it is. Moreover, they have destroyed the last remnants of the patriarchal relation between working men and employers, a result to which manufacture on a large scale has contributed by multiplying the employees dependent upon a single employer. The bourgeoisie deplores all this, it is true, and has good reason to do so; for, under the old conditions, the bourgeois was comparatively secure against a revolt on the part of his hands. He could tyrannize over them and plunder them to his heart's content, and yet receive obedience, gratitude, and assent from these stupid people by bestowing a trifle of patronizing friendliness which cost him nothing, and perhaps some paltry present, all apparently out of pure, self-sacrificing, uncalled-for goodness of heart, but really not one-tenth part of his duty. As an individual bourgeois, placed under conditions which he had not himself created, he might do his duty at least in part; but, as a member of the ruling class, which, by the mere fact of its ruling, is responsible for the condition of the whole nation, he did nothing of what his position involved. On the contrary, he plundered the whole nation for his own individual advantage. In the patriarchal relation that hypocritically concealed the slavery of the worker, the latter must have remained an intellectual zero, totally ignorant of his own interest, a mere private individual. Only when estranged from his employer, when convinced that the sole bond between employer and employee is the bond of pecuniary profit, when the sentimental bond between them, which stood not the slightest test, had wholly fallen away, then only did the worker begin to recognize his own interests and develop independently; then only did he cease to be the slave of the bourgeoisie in his thoughts, feelings, and the expression of his will. And to this end manufacture on a grand scale and in great cities has most largely contributed.

Another influence of great moment in forming the character of the English workers is the Irish immigration already referred to. On the one hand it has, as we have seen, degraded the English workers, removed them from civilization, and aggravated the hardship of their lot; but, on the other hand, it has thereby deepened the chasm between workers and bourgeoisie, and hastened the approaching crisis. For the course of the social disease from which England is suffering is the same as the course of a physical disease; it develops, according to certain laws, has its own crises, the last and most violent of which determines the fate of the patient. And as the English nation cannot succumb under the final crisis, but must go forth from it, born again, rejuvenated, we can but rejoice over everything which accelerates the course of the disease. And to this the Irish immigration further contributes by reason of the passionate, mercurial Irish temperament, which it imports into England and into the English working class. The Irish and English are to each other much as the French and the Germans; and the mixing of the more facile, excitable, fiery Irish temperament with the stable, reasoning, persevering English must, in the long run, be productive only of good for both. The rough egotism of the English bourgeoisie would have kept its hold upon the working class much more firmly if the Irish nature, generous to a fault, and ruled primarily by sentiment, had not intervened, and softened the cold, rational English character in part by a mixture of the races, and in part by the ordinary contact of life.

In view of all this, it is not surprising that the working class has gradually become a race wholly apart from the English bourgeoisie. The bourgeoisie has more in common with every other nation of the earth than with the workers in whose midst it lives. The workers speak other dialects, have other thoughts and ideals, other customs and moral principles, a different religion and other politics than those of the bourgeoisie. Thus they are two radically dissimilar nations, as unlike as difference of race could make them, of whom we on the Continent have known but one, the bourgeoisie. Yet it is precisely the other, the people, the proletariat, which is by far the more important for the future of England.[1]

Of the public character of the English working man, as it finds expression in associations and political principles, we shall have occasion to speak later; let us here consider the results of the influences cited above, as they affect the private character of the worker. The workman is far more humane in ordinary life than the bourgeois. I have already mentioned the fact that the beggars are accustomed to turn almost exclusively to the workers, and that, in general, more is done by the workers than by the bourgeoisie for the maintenance of the poor. This fact, which any one may prove for himself any day, is confirmed, among others, by Dr Parkinson, Canon of Manchester, who says:[2]

The poor give one another more than the rich give the poor. I can confirm my statement by the testimony of one of our eldest, most skilful, most observant, and humane physicians, Dr. Bardsley, who has often declared that the total sum which the poor yearly bestow upon one another, surpasses that which the rich contribute in the same time.

[1] The idea that large-scale industry has split the English into two different nations has, as is well known, been carried out about the same time also by Disraeli in his novel, *Sybil, or the Two Nations*. (*Note in the German edition of 1892*.)

[2] *On the Present Condition of the Labouring Poor in Manchester,* ... By the Revd. Rd. Parkinson, Canon of Manchester (3rd edn., London and Manchester, 1841), Pamphlet.

In other ways, too, the humanity of the workers is constantly manifesting itself pleasantly. They have experienced hard times themselves, and can therefore feel for those in trouble; to them every person is a human being, while the worker is less than a human being to the bourgeois; whence they are more approachable, friendlier, and less greedy for money, though they need it far more than the property-holding class. For them money is worth only what it will buy, whereas for the bourgeois it has an especial inherent value, the value of a god, and makes the bourgeois the mean, low money-grubber that he is. The working man who knows nothing of this feeling of reverence for money is therefore less grasping than the bourgeois, whose whole activity is for the purpose of gain, who sees in the accumulations of his money-bags the end and aim of life. Hence the workman is much less prejudiced, has a clearer eye for facts as they are than the bourgeois, and does not look at everything through the spectacles of personal selfishness. His faulty education saves him from religious prepossessions, he does not understand religious questions, does not trouble himself about them, knows nothing of the fanaticism that holds the bourgeoisie bound; and if he chances to have any religion, he has it only in name, not even in theory. Practically he lives for this world, and strives to make himself at home in it. All the writers of the bourgeoisie are unanimous on this point, that the workers are not religious, and do not attend church. From the general statement are to be excepted the Irish, a few elderly people, and the half-bourgeois, the overlookers, foremen, and the like. But among the masses there prevails almost universally a total indifference to religion, or at the utmost, some trace of Deism too undeveloped to amount to more than mere words, or a vague dread of the words infidel, atheist, etc. The clergy of all sects is in very bad odour with the working men, though the loss of its influence is recent. At present, however, the mere cry 'He's a parson!' is often enough to drive one of the clergy from the platform of a public meeting. And like the rest of the conditions under which he lives, his want of religious and other culture contributes to keep the working man more unconstrained, freer from inherited stable tenets and cut-and-dried opinions, than the bourgeois who is saturated with the class prejudices poured into him from his earliest youth. There is nothing to be done with the bourgeois; he is essentially conservative in however liberal a guise, his interest is bound up with that of the property-holding class, he is dead to all active movement; he is losing his position in the forefront of England's historical development. The workers are taking his place, in rightful claim first, then in fact.

All this, together with the correspondent public action of the workers, with which we shall deal later, forms the favourable side of the character of this class; the unfavourable one may be quite as briefly summed up, and follows quite as naturally out of the given causes. Drunkenness, sexual irregularities, brutality, and disregard for the rights of property are the chief points with which the bourgeois charges them. That they drink heavily is to be expected. Sheriff Alison asserts that in Glasgow some 30,000 working men get drunk every Saturday night, and the estimate is certainly not exaggerated; and that in that city in 1830, one house in twelve, and in 1840, one house in ten, was a public house; that in Scotland, in 1823, excise was paid upon 2,300,000 gallons; in 1837, upon 6,620,000 gallons; in England, in 1823, upon 1,976,000 gallons, and in 1837, upon 7,875,000 gallons of spirits.[1] The Beer Act of 1830, which facilitated the opening of beerhouses (jerry shops), whose keepers are licensed to sell beer to be drunk on the premises, facilitated the spread of intemperance by bringing a beerhouse, so to say, to everybody's door. In nearly every street there are several such beerhouses, and among two or three neighbouring houses in the country one is sure to be a jerry shop. Besides these, there are hush-shops in multitudes, i.e. secret drinking-places which are not licensed, and quite as many secret distilleries which produce great quantities of spirits in retired spots, rarely visited by the police, in the great cities. Gaskell estimates these secret distilleries in Manchester alone at more than a hundred, and their product at 156,000 gallons at the least. In Manchester there are, besides, more than a thousand public houses selling all sorts of alcoholic drinks, or quite as many in proportion to the number of inhabitants as in Glasgow. In all other great

[1] *Principles of Population, passim.* (*Note in the German edition.*)

towns, the state of things is the same. And when one considers, apart from the usual consequences of intemperance, that men and women, even children, often mothers with babies in their arms, come into contact in these places with the most degraded victims of the bourgeois regime, with thieves, swindlers, and prostitutes; when one reflects that many a mother gives the baby on her arm gin to drink, the demoralizing effects of frequenting such places cannot be denied.

On Saturday evenings, especially when wages are paid and work stops somewhat earlier than usual, when the whole working class pours from its own poor quarters into the main thoroughfares, intemperance may be seen in all its brutality. I have rarely come out of Manchester on such an evening without meeting numbers of people staggering and seeing others lying in the gutter. On Sunday evening the same scene is usually repeated, only less noisily. And when their money is spent, the drunkards go to the nearest pawnshop, of which there are plenty in every city—over sixty in Manchester, and ten or twelve in a single street of Salford, Chapel Street—and pawn whatever they possess. Furniture, Sunday clothes where such exist, kitchen utensils in masses are fetched from the pawnbrokers on Saturday night only to wander back, almost without fail, before the next Wednesday, until at last some accident makes the final redemption impossible, and one article after another falls into the clutches of the usurer, or until he refuses to give a single farthing more upon the battered, used-up pledge. When one has seen the extent of intemperance among the workers in England, one readily believes Lord Ashley's statement[1] that this class annually expends something like £25,000,000 upon intoxicating liquor; and the deterioration in external conditions, the frightful shattering of mental and physical health, the ruin of all domestic relations which follow may readily be imagined. True, the temperance societies have done much, but what are a few thousand teetotallers among the millions of workers? When Father Mathew, the Irish apostle of temperance, passes through the English cities,

[1] Sitting of the Lower House on 28 Feb. 1843. (*Note in the German edition.*)

from thirty to sixty thousand workers take the pledge; but most of them break it again within a month. If one counts up the immense numbers who have taken the pledge in the last three or four years in Manchester, the total is greater than the whole population of the town—and still it is by no means evident that intemperance is diminishing.

Next to intemperance in the enjoyment of intoxicating liquors, one of the principal faults of English working men is sexual licence. But this, too, follows with relentless logic, with inevitable necessity out of the position of a class left to itself, with no means of making fitting use of its freedom. The bourgeoisie has left the working class only these two pleasures, while imposing upon it a multitude of labours and hardships, and the consequence is that the working men, in order to get something from life, concentrate their whole energy upon these two enjoyments, carry them to excess, surrender to them in the most unbridled manner. When people are placed under conditions which appeal to the brute only, what remains to them but to rebel or to succumb to utter brutality? And when, moreover, the bourgeoisie does its full share in maintaining prostitution—and how many of the 40,000 prostitutes who fill the streets of London[1] every evening live upon the virtuous bourgeoisie! How many of them owe it to the seduction of a bourgeois, that they must offer their bodies to the passers-by in order to live?—surely it has least of all a right to reproach the workers with their sexual brutality.

The failings of the workers in general may be traced to an unbridled thirst for pleasure, to want of providence, and of flexibility in fitting into the social order, to the general inability to sacrifice the pleasure of the moment to a remoter advantage. But is that to be wondered at? When a class can purchase few and only the most sensual pleasures by its wearying toil, must it not give itself over blindly and madly to those pleasures? A class about whose education no one troubles himself, which is a play-ball to a thousand chances, knows no security in life—what incentives has such a class to providence, to 'respectability', to sacrifice the pleasure of the

[1] Sheriff Alison, *Principles of Population*, vol. ii. (*Note in the German edition.*)

moment for a remoter enjoyment, most uncertain precisely by reason of the perpetually varying, shifting conditions under which the proletariat lives? A class which bears all the disadvantages of the social order without enjoying its advantages, one to which the social system appears in purely hostile aspects—who can demand that such a class respect this social order? Verily that is asking much! But the working man cannot escape the present arrangement of society so long as it exists, and when the individual worker resists it, the greatest injury falls upon himself.

Thus the social order makes family life almost impossible for the worker. In a comfortless, filthy house, hardly good enough for mere nightly shelter, ill-furnished, often neither rain-tight nor warm, a foul atmosphere filling rooms over-crowded with human beings, no domestic comfort is possible. The husband works the whole day through, perhaps the wife also and the elder children, all in different places; they meet night and morning only, all under perpetual temptation to drink; what family life is possible under such conditions? Yet the working man cannot escape from the family, must live in the family, and the consequence is a perpetual succession of family troubles, domestic quarrels, most demoralizing for parents and children alike. Neglect of all domestic duties, neglect of the children, especially, is only too common among the English working people, and only too vigorously fostered by the existing institutions of society. And children growing up in this savage way, amidst these demoralizing influences, are expected to turn out goody-goody and moral in the end! Verily the requirements are naïve, which the self-satisfied bourgeois makes upon the working man!

The contempt for the existing social order is most conspicuous in its extreme form—that of offences against the law. If the influences demoralizing to the working man act more powerfully, more concentratedly than usual, he becomes an offender as certainly as water abandons the fluid for the vaporous state at 80 degrees, Réaumur. Under the brutal and brutalizing treatment of the bourgeoisie, the working man becomes precisely as much a thing without volition as water, and is subject to the laws of Nature with precisely the same necessity; at a certain point all freedom ceases. Hence with the extension of the proletariat, crime has increased in England, and the British nation has become the most criminal in the world. From the annual criminal tables of the Home Secretary, it is evident that the increase of crime in England has proceeded with incomprehensible rapidity. The numbers of arrests for *criminal* offences reached in the years: 1805, 4,605; 1810, 5,146; 1815, 7,898; 1820, 13,710; 1825, 14,437; 1830, 18,107; 1835, 20,731; 1840, 27,187; 1841, 27,760; 1842, 31,309 in England and Wales alone. That is to say, they increased sevenfold in thirty-seven years. Of these arrests, in 1842, 4,497 were made in Lancashire alone, or more than 14 per cent of the whole; and 4,094 in Middlesex, including London, or more than 13 per cent. So that two districts which include great cities with large proletarian populations, produced one-fourth of the total amount of crime, though their population is far from forming one-fourth of the whole. Moreover, the criminal tables prove directly that nearly all crime arises within the proletariat; for, in 1842, taking the average, out of 100 criminals, 32.35 could neither read nor write; 58.32 read and wrote imperfectly; 6.77 could read and write well; 0.22 had enjoyed a higher education, while the degree of education of 2.34 could not be ascertained. In Scotland, crime has increased yet more rapidly. There were but 89 arrests of criminal offences in 1819, and as early as 1837 the number had risen to 3,176, and in 1842 to 4,189. In Lanarkshire, where Sheriff Alison himself made out the official report, population has doubled once in thirty years, and crime once in five and a half, or six times more rapidly than the population. The offences, as in all civilized countries, are, in the great majority of cases, against property, and have, therefore, arisen from want in some form; for what a man has, he does not steal. The proportion of offences against property to the population, which in the Netherlands is as 1:7,140, and in France, as 1:804, was in England, when Gaskell wrote, as 1:799. The proportion of offences against persons to the population is, in the Netherlands, 1:28,904; in France, 1:17,573; in England, 1:23,395; that of crimes in general to the population in the agricultural districts, as 1:1,043; in the manufacturing districts as 1:840.[1]

[1] *Manufacturing Population of England*, ch. 10.

In the whole of England today the proportion is 1:660;[1] though it is scarcely ten years since Gaskell's book appeared!

These facts are certainly more than sufficient to bring any one, even a bourgeois, to pause and reflect upon the consequences of such a state of things. If demoralization and crime multiply twenty years longer in this proportion (and if English manufacture in these twenty years should be less prosperous than heretofore, the progressive multiplication of crime can only continue the more rapidly), what will the result be? Society is already in a state of visible dissolution; it is impossible to pick up a newspaper without seeing the most striking evidence of the giving way of all social ties. I look at random into a heap of English journals lying before me; there is the *Manchester Guardian* for 30 October 1844, which reports for three days. It no longer takes the trouble to give exact details as to Manchester, and merely relates the most interesting cases: that the workers in a mill have struck for higher wages without giving notice, and been condemned by a Justice of the Peace to resume work; that in Salford a couple of boys had been caught stealing, and a bankrupt tradesman tried to cheat his creditors. From the neighbouring towns the reports are more detailed: in Ashton, two thefts, one burglary, one suicide; in Bury, one theft; in Bolton, two thefts, one revenue fraud; in Leigh, one theft; in Oldham, one strike for wages, one theft, one fight between Irish women, one non-Union hatter assaulted by Union men, one mother beaten by her son, one attack upon the police, one robbery of a church; in Stockport, discontent of working men with wages, one theft, one fraud, one fight, one wife beaten by her husband; in Warrington, one theft, one fight; in Wigan, one theft, and one robbery of a church. The reports of the London papers are much worse; frauds, thefts, assaults, family quarrels crowd one another. A *Times* of 12 September 1844, falls into my hand, which gives a report of a single day, including a theft, an attack upon the police, a sentence upon a father requiring him to support his illegitimate son, the abandonment of a child by its parents, and the poisoning of a man by his wife. Similar reports are to be

---

[1] The total of population, about 15 millions, divided by the number of convicted criminals (22,733).

found in all the English papers. In this country, social war is under full headway, every one stands for himself, and fights for himself against all comers, and whether or not he shall injure all the others who are his declared foes, depends upon a cynical calculation as to what is most advantageous for himself. It no longer occurs to any one to come to a peaceful understanding with his fellow-man; all differences are settled by threats, violence, or in a law-court. In short, every one sees in his neighbour an enemy to be got out of the way, or, at best, a tool to be used for his own advantage. And this war grows from year to year, as the criminal tables show, more violent, passionate, irreconcilable. The enemies are dividing gradually into two great camps—the bourgeoisie on the one hand, the workers on the other. This war of each against all, of the bourgeoisie against the proletariat, need cause us no surprise, for it is only the logical sequel of the principle involved in free competition. But it may very well surprise us that the bourgeoisie remains so quiet and composed in the face of the rapidly gathering storm-clouds, that it can read all these things daily in the papers without, we will not say indignation at such a social condition, but fear of its consequences, of a universal outburst of that which manifests itself symptomatically from day to day in the form of crime. But then it is the bourgeoisie, and from its standpoint it cannot even see the facts, much less perceive their consequences. One thing only is astounding, that class prejudice and preconceived opinions can hold a whole class of human beings in such perfect, I might almost say, such mad blindness. Meanwhile, the development of the nation goes its way whether the bourgeoisie has eyes for it or not, and will surprise the property-holding class one day with things not dreamed of in its philosophy.

6

Single Branches of Industry:
Factory-Hands

IN dealing now with the more important branches of the English manufacturing proletariat, we shall begin, according to the principle already laid down, with the factory-workers, i.e. those who are comprised under the Factory Act. This law regulates the length of the working day in mills in which wool, silk, cotton, and flax are spun or woven by means of water or steam-power, and embraces, therefore, the more important branches of English manufacture. The class employed by them is the most intelligent and energetic of all the English workers, and, therefore, the most restless and most hated by the bourgeoisie. It stands as a whole, and the cotton-workers pre-eminently stand, at the head of the labour movement, as their masters the manufacturers, especially those of Lancashire, take the lead of the bourgeois agitation.

We have already seen in the introduction how the population employed in working up the textile materials were first torn from their former way of life. It is, therefore, not surprising that the progress of mechanical invention in later years also affected precisely these workers most deeply and permanently. The history of cotton manufacture as related by Ure,[1] Baines,[2] and others is the story of improvements in every direction, most of which have become domesticated in the other branches of industry as well. Hand-work is superseded by machine-work almost universally, nearly all manipulations are conducted by the aid of steam or water, and every year is bringing further improvements.

In a well-ordered state of society, such improvements could only be a source of rejoicing; in a war of all against all,

[1] Dr A. Ure, *The Cotton Manufacture of Great Britain* (1836).

[2] E. Baines, *History of the Cotton Manufacture of Great Britain* (1835).

individuals seize the benefit for themselves, and so deprive the majority of the means of subsistence. Every improvement in machinery throws workers out of employment, and the greater the advance, the more numerous the unemployed; each great improvement produces, therefore, upon a number of workers the effect of a commercial crisis, creates want, wretchedness, and crime. Take a few examples. The very first invention, the jenny, worked by one man, produced at least sixfold what the spinning-wheel had yielded in the same time; thus every new jenny threw five spinners out of employment. The throstle, which, in turn, produced much more than the jenny, and like it, was worked by one man, threw still more people out of employment. The mule, which required yet fewer hands in proportion to the product, had the same effect, and every improvement in the mule, every multiplication of its spindles, diminished still further the number of workers employed. But this increase of the number of spindles in the mule is so great that whole armies of workers have been thrown out of employment by it. For, whereas one spinner, with a couple of children for piecers, formerly set 600 spindles in motion, he could now manage 1,400 to 2,000 spindles upon two mules, so that two adult spinners and a part of the piecers whom they employed were thrown out. And since self-acting mules have been introduced into a very large number of spinning-mills, the spinners' work is wholly performed by the machine. There lies before me a book from the pen of James Leach,[1] one of the recognized leaders of the Chartists in Manchester. The author has worked for years in various branches of industry, in mills and coal-mines, and is known to me personally as an honest, trustworthy, and capable man. In consequence of his political position, he had at command extensive detailed information as to the different factories, collected by the workers themselves, and he publishes tables from which it is clear that in 1841, in 35 factories, 1,060 fewer mule spinners were employed than in 1829, though the number of spindles in these 35 factories had increased by 99,239. He cites

---

[1] W. Rashleigh, MP, *Stubborn Facts from the Factories by a Manchester Operative*. Published and dedicated to the working classes. (London, 1844), 28 ff.

five factories in which no spinners whatever are employed, self-actors only being used. While the number of spindles increased by 10 per cent, the number of spinners diminished more than 60 per cent. And Leach adds that since 1841, so many improvements have been introduced by double-decking and other means, that in some of the factories named, half the operatives have been discharged. In one factory alone, where eighty spinners were employed a short time ago, there are now but twenty left; the others having been discharged or set at children's work for children's wages. Of Stockport Leach tells a similar story, that in 1835, 800 spinners were employed, and in 1843 but 140, though the manufacture of Stockport has greatly increased during the last eight or nine years. Similar improvements have now been made in carding-frames, by which one-half the operatives have been thrown out of employment. In one factory improved frames have been set up, which have thrown four hands out of eight out of work, besides which the employer reduced the wages of the four retained from 8s. to 7s. The same process has gone on in the weaving industry; the power-loom has taken possession of one branch of hand-weaving after another, and since it produces much more than the hand-loom, while one weaver can work two looms, it has superseded a multitude of working-people. And in all sorts of manufacture, in flax- and wool-spinning, in silk-twisting, the case is the same. The power-loom, too, is beginning to appropriate one branch after another of wool- and linen-weaving; in Rochdale alone, there are more power- than hand-looms in flannel and other wool-weaving branches. The bourgeoisie usually replies to this, that improvements in machinery, by decreasing the cost of production, supply finished goods at lower prices, and that these reduced prices cause such an increase in con-sumption that the unemployed operatives soon find full employment in newly founded factories.[1] The bourgeoisie is so far correct that under certain conditions favourable for the general development of manufacture, every reduction in price of goods *in which the raw material is cheap*, greatly increases consumption, and gives rise to the building of new factories; but every further word of the assertion is a lie. The

[1] Compare Factories' Inquiry Commission's Report.

bourgeoisie ignores the fact that it takes years for these results of the decrease in price to follow and for new factories to be built; it is silent upon the point that every improvement in machinery throws the real work, the expenditure of force, more and more upon the machine, and so transforms the work of full-grown men into mere supervision, which a feeble woman or even a child can do quite as well, and does for half or even one-third the wages; that, therefore, grown men are constantly more and more supplanted and *not re-employed* by the increase in manufacture; it conceals the fact that whole branches of industry fall away, or are so changed that they must be learned afresh; and it takes good care not to confess what it usually harps upon, whenever the question of forbidding the work of children is broached, that factory-work must be learned in earliest youth in order to be learned properly. It does not mention the fact that the process of improvement goes steadily on, and that as soon as the operative has succeeded in making himself at home in a new branch, if he actually does succeed in so doing, this, too, is taken from him, and with it the last remnant of security which remained to him for winning his bread. But the bourgeoisie gets the benefit of the improvements in machinery; it has a capital opportunity for piling up money during the first years while many old machines are still in use, and the improvement not yet universally introduced; and it would be too much to ask that it should have an open eye for the disadvantages inseparable from these improvements.

The fact that improved machinery reduces wages has also been as violently disputed by the bourgeoisie, as it is constantly reiterated by the working men. The bourgeoisie insists that although the price of piece-work has been reduced, yet the total of wages for the week's work has rather risen than fallen, and the condition of the operatives rather improved than deteriorated. It is hard to get to the bottom of the matter, for the operatives usually dwell upon the price of piece-work. But it is certain that the weekly wage, also, has, in many branches of work, been reduced by the improvement of machinery. The so-called fine spinners (who spin fine mule yarn), for instance, do receive high wages, 30–40s. a week, because they have a powerful association for keeping wages up, and their craft requires long training; but the coarse spinners who have to compete against self-actors (which are not as yet adapted for fine spinning), and whose association was broken down by the introduction of these machines, receive very low wages. A mule spinner told me that he does not earn more than 14s. a week, and his statement agrees with that of Leach, that in various factories the coarse spinners earn less than 16s. 6d. a week, and that a spinner, who three years ago earned 30s., can now hardly scrape up 12s. 6d., and had not earned more on an average in the past year. The wages of women and children may perhaps have fallen less, but only because they were not high from the beginning. I know several women, widows with children, who have trouble enough to earn 8–9s. a week; and that they and their families cannot live decently upon that sum, everyone must admit who knows the price of the barest necessaries of life in England. That wages in general have been reduced by the improvement of machinery is the unanimous testimony of the operatives. The bourgeois assertion that the condition of the working class has been improved by machinery is most vigorously proclaimed a falsehood in every meeting of working men in the factory districts. And even if it were true that the relative wage, the price of piece-work only, has fallen, while the absolute wage, the sum to be earned in the week, remained unchanged, what would follow? That the operatives have had quietly to look on while the manufacturers filled their purses from every improvement without giving the hands the smallest share in the gain. The bourgeois forgets, in fighting the working man, the most ordinary principles of his own Political Economy. He who at other times swears by Malthus, cries out in his anxiety before the workers: 'Where could the millions by which the population of England has increased find work, without the improvements in machinery?'[1] As though the bourgeois did not know well enough that without machinery and the expansion of industry which it produced, these 'millions' would never have been brought into the world and grown up! The service which machinery has rendered the workers is simply this: that it has

[1] J. Symons, in *Arts and Artisans*.

brought home to their minds the necessity of a social reform by means of which machinery shall no longer work against but for them. Let the wise bourgeois ask the people who sweep the streets in Manchester and elsewhere (though even this is past now, since machines for the purpose have been invented and introduced), or sell salt, matches, oranges, and shoe-strings on the streets, or even beg, what they were formerly, and he will see how many will answer: 'Mill-hands thrown out of work by machinery.' The consequences of improvement in machinery under our present social conditions are, for the working man, solely injurious, and often in the highest degree oppressive. Every new advance brings with it loss of employment, want, and suffering, and in a country like England where, without that, there is usually a 'surplus population' to be discharged from work is the worst that can befall the operative. And what a dispiriting, unnerving influence this uncertainty of his position in life, consequent upon the unceasing progress of machinery, must exercise upon the worker, whose lot is precarious enough without it! To escape despair, there are but two ways open to him; either inward and outward revolt against the bourgeoisie or drunkenness and general demoralization. And the English operatives are accustomed to take refuge in both. The history of the English proletariat relates hundreds of uprisings against machinery and the bourgeoisie; we have already spoken of the moral dissolution which, in itself, is only another form of despair.

The worst situation is that of those workers who have to compete against a machine that is making its way. The price of the goods which they produce adapts itself to the price of the kindred product of the machine, and as the latter works more cheaply, its human competitor has but the lowest wages. The same thing happens to every operative employed upon an old machine in competition with later improvements. And who else is there to bear the hardship? The manufacturer will not throw out his old apparatus, nor will he sustain the loss upon it; out of the dead mechanism he can make nothing, so he fastens upon the living worker, the universal scapegoat of society. Of all the workers in competition with machinery, the most ill-used are the hand-loom cotton weavers. They receive the most trifling wages, and, with full work, are not in a position to earn more than 10s. a week. One class of woven goods after another is annexed by the power-loom, and hand-weaving is the last refuge of workers thrown out of employment in other branches, so that the trade is always overcrowded. Hence it comes that, in average seasons, the hand-weaver counts himself fortunate if he can earn 6s. or 7s. a week, while to reach this sum he must sit at his loom fourteen to eighteen hours a day. Most woven goods require moreover a damp weaving-room, to keep the weft from snapping, and in part, for this reason, in part because of their poverty, which prevents them from paying for better dwellings, the work-rooms of these weavers are usually without wooden or paved floors. I have been in many dwellings of such weavers, in remote, vile courts and alleys, usually in cellars. Often half a dozen of these handloom weavers, several of them married, live together in a cottage with one or two workrooms, and one large sleeping-room. Their food consists almost exclusively of potatoes, with perhaps oatmeal porridge, rarely milk, and scarcely ever meat. Great numbers of them are Irish or of Irish descent. And these poor hand-loom weavers, first to suffer from every crisis, and last to be relieved from it, must serve the bourgeoisie as a handle in meeting attacks upon the factory system. 'See,' cries the bourgeois, triumphantly, 'see how these poor creatures must famish, while the mill operatives are thriving, and *then* judge the factory[1] system!' As though it were not precisely the factory system and the machinery belonging to it which had so shamefully crushed the hand-loom weavers, and as though the bourgeoisie did not know this quite as well as ourselves! But the bourgeoisie has interests at stake, and so a falsehood or two and a bit of hypocrisy won't matter much.

Let us examine somewhat more closely the fact that machinery more and more supersedes the work of men. The human labour, involved in both spinning and weaving, consists chiefly in piecing broken threads, as the machine does all the rest. This work requires no muscular strength, but only flexibility of finger. Men are, therefore, not only not needed for it, but actually, by reason of the greater muscular

[1] See Dr Ure in the *Philosophy of Manufactures*.

development of the hand, less fit for it than women and
children, and are, therefore, naturally almost superseded by
them. Hence, the more the use of the arms, the expenditure
of strength, can be transferred to steam or water-power, the
fewer men need be employed; and as women and children
work more cheaply, and in these branches better than men,
they take their places. In the spinning-mills women and
girls are to be found in almost exclusive possession of the
throstles; among the mules one man, an adult spinner (with
self-actors, he, too, becomes superfluous), and several piecers
for tying the threads, usually children or women, sometimes young men of from 18 to 20 years, here and there
an old spinner[1] thrown out of other employment. At the
power-looms women, from 15 to 20 years, are chiefly
employed, and a few men; these, however, rarely remain
at this trade after their twenty-first year. Among the preparatory machinery, too, women alone are to be found, with here
and there a man to clean and sharpen the carding-frames.
Besides all these, the factories employ numbers of children—
doffers—for mounting and taking down bobbins, and a few
men as overlookers, a mechanic and an engineer for the
steam-engines, carpenters, porters, etc.; but the actual work
of the mills is done by women and children. This the manufacturers deny.

They published last year elaborate tables to prove that
machinery does not supersede adult male operatives. According to these tables, rather more than half of all the factory-
workers employed, viz. 52 per cent, were females and 48 per
cent males, and of these operatives more than half were over
18 years old. So far, so good. But the manufacturers are very
careful not to tell us, how many of the adults were men
and how many women. And this is just the point. Besides
this, they have evidently counted the mechanics, engineers,
carpenters, all the men employed in any way in the factories,

---

[1] Report of Factory Inspector, L. Horner, October 1844: 'The state of
things in the matter of wages is greatly perverted in certain branches of
cotton manufacture in Lancashire; there are hundreds of young men,
between twenty and thirty, employed as piecers and otherwise, who do
not get more than 8 or 9 shillings a week, while children under thirteen
years, working under the same roof, earn 5 shillings and young girls,
from sixteen to twenty years, 10—12 shillings per week.'

perhaps even the clerks, and still they have not the courage to tell the whole truth. These publications teem generally with falsehoods, perversions, crooked statements, with calculations of averages, that prove a great deal for the uninitiated reader and nothing for the initiated, and with suppressions of facts bearing on the most important points; and they prove only the selfish blindness and want of uprightness of the manufacturers concerned. Let us take some of the statements of a speech with which Lord Ashley introduced the Ten Hours Bill,* on 15 March 1844, into the House of Commons. Here he gives some data as to the relations of sex and age of the operatives, not yet refuted by the manufacturers, whose statements, as quoted above, cover moreover only a part of the manufacturing industry of England. Of 419,560 factory operatives of the British Empire in 1839, 192,887, or nearly half, were under 18 years of age, and 242,296 of the female sex, of whom 112,192 were less than 18 years old. There remain, therefore, 80,695 male operatives under 18 years, and 96,569 adult male operatives, *or not one full quarter* of the whole number. In the cotton factories, 56.5 per cent; in the woollen mills, 69.5 per cent; in the silk mills, 70.5 per cent; in the flax-spinning mills, 70.5 per cent of all operatives are of the female sex. These numbers suffice to prove the crowding out of adult males. But you have only to go into the nearest mill to see the fact confirmed. Hence follows of necessity that inversion of the existing social order which, being forced upon them, has the most ruinous consequences for the workers. The employment of women at once breaks up the family; for when the wife spends twelve or thirteen hours every day in the mill, and the husband works the same length of time there or elsewhere, what becomes of the children? They grow up like wild weeds; they are put out to nurse for a shilling or eighteenpence a week, and how they are treated may be imagined. Hence the accidents to which little children fall victims multiply in the factory districts to a terrible extent. The lists of the Coroner of Manchester[1] showed for nine months: 69 deaths from burning, 56 from drowning, 23 from falling, 77 from other

[1] Report of Factories' Inquiry Commission. Testimony of Dr Hawkins, p. 3.

causes, or a total of 225[1] deaths from accidents, while in non-manufacturing Liverpool during twelve months there were but 146 fatal accidents. The mining accidents are excluded in both cases; and since the Coroner of Manchester has no authority in Salford, the population of both places mentioned in the comparison is about the same. The *Manchester Guardian* reports one or more deaths by burning in almost every number. That the general mortality among young children must be increased by the employment of the mothers is self-evident, and is placed beyond all doubt by notorious facts. Women often return to the mill three or four days after confinement, leaving the baby, of course; in the dinner-hour they must hurry home to feed the child and eat something, and what sort of suckling that can be is also evident. Lord Ashley repeats the testimony of several workwomen:

'M. H., twenty years old, has two children, the youngest a baby, that is tended by the other, a little older. The mother goes to the mill shortly after five o'clock in the morning, and comes home at eight at night; all day the milk pours from her breasts, so that her clothing drips with it.' 'H. W. has three children, goes away Monday morning at five o'clock, and comes back Saturday evening; has so much to do for the children then that she cannot get to bed before three o'clock in the morning; often wet through to the skin, and obliged to work in that state.' She said: 'My breasts have given me the most frightful pain, and I have been dripping wet with milk.'

The use of narcotics to keep the children still is fostered by this infamous system, and has reached a great extent in the factory districts. Dr Johns, Registrar-in-Chief for Manchester, is of opinion that this custom is the chief source of the many deaths from convulsions. The employment of the wife dissolves the family utterly and of necessity, and this dissolution, in our present society, which is based upon the family, brings the most demoralizing consequences for parents as well as children. A mother who has no time to trouble herself about her child, to perform the most ordinary loving services for it during its first year, who scarcely indeed sees it, can be no real mother to the child, must inevitably grow indifferent

---

[1] In 1842, among the accidents brought to the Infirmary in Manchester, 189 were from burning.

to it, treat it unlovingly like a stranger. The children who grow up under such conditions are utterly ruined for later family life, can never feel at home in the family which they themselves found, because they have always been accustomed to isolation, and they contribute therefore to the already general undermining of the family in the working class. A similar dissolution of the family is brought about by the employment of the children. When they get on far enough to earn more than they cost their parents from week to week, they begin to pay the parents a fixed sum for board and lodging, and keep the rest for themselves. This often happens from the fourteenth or fifteenth year.[1] In a word, the children emancipate themselves, and regard the paternal dwelling as a lodging-house, which they often exchange for another, as suits them.

In many cases the family is not wholly dissolved by the employment of the wife, but turned upside down. The wife supports the family, the husband sits at home, tends the children, sweeps the room and cooks. This case happens very frequently; in Manchester alone, many hundred such men could be cited, condemned to domestic occupations. It is easy to imagine the wrath aroused among the working men by this reversal of all relations within the family, while the other social conditions remain unchanged. There lies before me a letter from an English working man, Robert Pounder, Baron's Buildings, Woodhouse, Moorside, in Leeds (the bourgeoisie may hunt him up there; I give the exact address for the purpose), written by him to Oastler.[2]

He relates how another working man, being on tramp, came to St Helens, in Lancashire, and there looked up an old friend.

He found him in a miserable, damp cellar, scarcely furnished; and when my poor friend went in, there sat poor Jack near the fire, and what did he, think you? why he sat and mended his wife's stockings with the bodkin; and as soon as he saw his old friend at the doorpost, he tried to hide them. But Joe, that is my friend's name,

---

[1] Factories' Inquiry Commission's Report, Power's Report on Leeds, *passim*; Tufnell Report on Manchester, p. 17, etc.

[2] This letter is re-translated from the German, no attempt being made to reproduce either the spelling or the original Yorkshire dialect.

had seen it, and said: 'Jack, what the devil art thou doing? Where is the missus? Why, is that thy work?' and poor Jack was ashamed, and said: 'No, I know this is not my work, but my poor missus is i' th' factory; she has to leave at half-past five and works till eight at night, and then she is so knocked up that she cannot do aught when she gets home, so I have to do everything for her what I can, for I have no work, nor had any for more nor three years, and I shall never have any more work while I live'; and then he wept a big tear. Jack again said: 'There is work enough for women folks and childer hereabouts, but none for men; thou mayest sooner find a hundred pound on the road than work for men—but I should never have believed that either thou or any one else would have seen me mending my wife's stockings, for it is bad work. But she can hardly stand on her feet; I am afraid she will be laid up, and then I don't know what is to become of us, for it's a good bit that she has been the man in the house and I the woman; it is bad work, Joe;' and he cried bitterly, and said, 'It has not been always so.' 'No,' said Joe; 'but when thou hadn't no work, how hast thou not shifted?' 'I'll tell thee, Joe, as well as I can, but it was bad enough; thou knowest when I got married I had work plenty, and thou knows I was not lazy.' 'No, that thou wert not.' 'And we had a good furnished house, and Mary need not go to work. I could work for the two of us; but now the world is upside down. Mary has to work and I have to stop at home, mind the childer, sweep and wash, bake and mend; and, when the poor woman comes home at night, she is knocked up. Thou knows, Joe, it's hard for one that was used different.' 'Yes, boy, it is hard.' And then Jack began to cry again, and he wished he had never married, and that he had never been born; but he had never thought, when he wed Mary, that it would come to this. 'I have often cried over it', said Jack. Now when Joe heard this, he told me that he had cursed and damned the factories, and the masters, and the Government, with all the curses that he had learned while he was in the factory from a child.

Can any one imagine a more insane state of things than that described in this letter? And yet this condition, which unsexes the man and takes from the woman all womanliness without being able to bestow upon the man true womanliness, or the woman true manliness—this condition which degrades, in the most shameful way, both sexes, and, through them, Humanity, is the last result of our much-praised civilization, the final achievement of all the efforts and struggles of hundreds of generations to improve their own situation and that of their posterity. We must either despair of mankind, and its aims and efforts, when we see all our labour and toil result in such a mockery, or we must admit that human society has hitherto sought salvation in a false direction; we must admit that so total a reversal of the position of the sexes can have come to pass only because the sexes have been placed in a false position from the beginning. If the reign of the wife over the husband, as inevitably brought about by the factory system, is inhuman, the pristine rule of the husband over the wife must have been inhuman too. If the wife can now base her supremacy upon the fact that she supplies the greater part, nay, the whole of the common possession, the necessary inference is that this community of possession is no true and rational one, since one member of the family boasts offensively of contributing the greater share. If the family of our present society is being thus dissolved, this dissolution merely shows that, at bottom, the binding tie of this family was not family affection, but private interest lurking under the cloak of a pretended community of possessions. The same relation exists on the part of those children who support unemployed parents[1] when they do not directly pay board as already referred to. Dr Hawkins testified in the Factories' Inquiry Commission's Report that this relation is common enough, and in Manchester it is notorious. In this case the children are the masters in the house, as the wife was in the former case, and Lord Ashley gives an example of this in his speech:[2] A man berated his two daughters for going to the public house, and they answered that they were tired of being ordered about, saying, 'Damn you, we have to keep you!' Determined to keep the proceeds of their work for themselves, they left the family dwelling, and abandoned their parents to their fate.

The unmarried women, who have grown up in mills, are no better off than the married ones. It is self-evident that a

[1] How numerous married women are in the factories is seen from information furnished by a manufacturer: In 412 factories in Lancashire, 10,721 of them were employed; of the husbands of these women, but 5,314 were also employed in the factories, 3,927 were otherwise employed, 821 were unemployed, and information was wanting as to 659; or two, if not three men for each factory, are supported by the work of their wives.

[2] House of Commons, 15th Mar. 1844.

girl who has worked in a mill from her ninth year is in no position to understand domestic work, whence it follows that female operatives prove wholly inexperienced and unfit as housekeepers. They cannot knit or sew, cook or wash, are unacquainted with the most ordinary duties of a house-keeper, and when they have young children to take care of, have not the vaguest idea how to set about it. The Factories' Inquiry Commission's Report gives dozens of examples of this, and Dr Hawkins, Commissioner for Lancashire, expresses his opinion as follows:[1]

The girls marry early and recklessly; they have neither means, time, nor opportunity to learn the ordinary duties of household life; but if they had them all, they would find no time in married life for the performance of these duties. The mother is more than twelve hours away from her child daily; the baby is cared for by a young girl or an old woman, to whom it is given to nurse. Besides this, the dwelling of the mill-hands is too often no home but a cellar, which contains no cooking or washing utensils, no sewing or mending materials, nothing which makes life agreeable and civilised, or the domestic hearth attractive. For these and other reasons, and especially for the sake of the better chances of life for the little children, I can but wish and hope that a time may come in which married women will be shut out of the factories.[2]

But that is the least of the evil. The moral consequences of the employment of women in factories are even worse. The collecting of persons of both sexes and all ages in a single workroom, the inevitable contact, the crowding into a small space of people, to whom neither mental nor moral educa-tion has been given, is not calculated for the favourable development of the female character. The manufacturer, if he pays any attention to the matter, can interfere only when something scandalous actually happens; the permanent, less conspicuous influence of persons of dissolute character, upon the more moral, and especially upon the younger ones, he cannot ascertain, and consequently cannot prevent. But precisely this influence is the most injurious. The language

[1] Factories' Inquiry Commission's Report, p. 4.

[2] For further examples and information compare Factories' Inquiry Commission's Report, Cowell Evidence, pp. 37, 38, 39, 72, 77, 82; Tufnell Evidence, pp. 9, 15, 45, 54, etc.

used in the mills is characterized by many witnesses in the report of 1833, as 'indecent', 'bad', 'filthy', etc.[1] It is the same process upon a small scale which we have already witnessed upon a large one in the great cities. The centralization of population has the same influence upon the same persons, whether it affects them in a great city or a small factory. The smaller the mill the closer the packing, and the more unavoidable the contact; and the consequences are not wanting. A witness in Leicester said that he would rather let his daughter beg than go into a factory; that they are perfect gates of hell; that most of the prostitutes of the town had their employment in the mills to thank for their present situation.[2] Another, in Manchester, 'did not hesitate to assert that three-fourths of the young factory employees, from fourteen to twenty years of age, were unchaste.'[3] Commissioner Cowell expresses it as his opinion, that the morality of the factory operatives is somewhat below the average of that of the working class in general.[4] And Dr Hawkins says:[5]

An estimate of sexual morality cannot readily be reduced to figures; but if I may trust my own observations and the general opinion of those with whom I have spoken, as well as the whole tenor of the testimony furnished me, the aspect of the influence of factory life upon the morality of the youthful female population is most depressing.

It is, besides, a matter of course that factory servitude, like any other, and to an even higher degree, confers the *jus primae noctis* upon the master. In this respect also the employer is sovereign over the persons and charms of his employees. The threat of discharge suffices to overcome all resistance in nine cases out of ten, if not in ninety-nine out of a hundred, in girls who, in any case, have no strong inducements to chastity. If the master is mean enough, and the official report mentions several such cases, his mill is also his harem; and the fact that not all manufacturers use their power, does not in the least change the position of the girls.

[1] Cowell Evidence, pp. 35, 37, and elsewhere.
[2] Power Evidence, p. 8.　　　[3] Cowell Evidence, p. 57.
[4] Ibid. 82.
[5] Factories' Inquiry Commission's Report, p. 4, Hawkins.

In the beginning of manufacturing industry, when most of the employers were upstarts without education or consideration for the hypocrisy of society, they let nothing interfere with the exercise of their vested rights.

To form a correct judgement of the influence of factory-work upon the health of the female sex, it is necessary first to consider the work of children, and then the nature of the work itself. From the beginning of manufacturing industry, children have been employed in mills, at first almost exclusively by reason of the smallness of the machines, which were later enlarged. Even children from the workhouses were employed in multitudes, being rented out for a number of years to the manufacturers as apprentices. They were lodged, fed, and clothed in common, and were, of course, completely the slaves of their masters, by whom they were treated with the utmost recklessness and barbarity. As early as 1796, the public objection to this revolting system found such vigorous expression through Dr Percival and Sir Robert Peel (father of the Cabinet Minister, and himself a cotton manufacturer), that in 1802 Parliament passed an Apprentices' Bill, by which the most crying evils were removed.* Gradually the increasing competition of free workpeople crowded out the whole apprentice system; factories were built in cities, machinery was constructed on a larger scale, and workrooms were made more airy and wholesome; gradually, too, more work was found for adults and young persons. The number of children in the mills diminished somewhat, and the age at which they began to work rose a little; few children under 8 or 9 years were now employed. Later, as we shall see, the power of the State intervened several times to protect them from the money-greed of the bourgeoisie.

The great mortality among children of the working class, and especially among those of the factory operatives, is proof enough of the unwholesome conditions under which they pass their first years. These influences are at work, of course, among the children who survive, but not quite so powerfully as upon those who succumb. The result in the most favourable case is a tendency to disease, or some check in development, and consequent less than normal vigour of the constitution. A 9-year-old child of a factory operative that has grown up in want, privation, and changing conditions, in cold and damp, with insufficient clothing and unwholesome dwellings, is far from having the working force of a child brought up under healthier conditions. At 9 years of age it is sent into the mill to work 6½ hours (formerly 8, earlier still, 12 to 14, even 16 hours) daily, until the thirteenth year; then twelve hours until the eighteenth year. The old enfeebling influences continue, while the work is added to them. It is not to be denied that a child of 9 years, even an operative's child, can hold out through 6½ hours' daily work, without anyone being able to trace visible bad results in its development directly to this cause; but in no case can its presence in the damp, heavy air of the factory, often at once warm and wet, contribute to good health; and, in any case, it is unpardonable to sacrifice to the greed of an unfeeling bourgeoisie the time of children which should be devoted solely to their physical and mental development, withdraw them from school and the fresh air, in order to wear them out for the benefit of the manufacturers. The bourgeoisie says: 'If we do not employ the children in the mills, they only remain under conditions unfavourable to their development'; and this is true on the whole. But what does this mean if it is not a confession that the bourgeoisie first places the children of the working class under unfavourable conditions, and then exploits these bad conditions for its own benefit, appeals to that which is as much its own fault as the factory system, excuses the sin of today with the sin of yesterday? And if the Factory Act did not in some measure fetter their hands, how this 'humane', this 'benevolent' bourgeoisie, which has built its factories solely for the good of the working class, would take care of the interests of these workers! Let us hear how they acted before the factory inspector was at their heels. Their own admitted testimony shall convict them in the report of the Factories' Inquiry Commission of 1833.

The report of the Central Commission relates that the manufacturers began to employ children rarely of 5 years, often of 6, very often of 7, usually of 8 to 9 years; that the working day often lasted fourteen to sixteen hours, exclusive of meals and intervals; that the manufacturers permitted overlookers to flog and maltreat children, and often took an active part in so doing themselves. One case is related of a

Scots manufacturer, who rode after a 16-year-old runaway, forced him to return, running after the employer as fast as the master's horse trotted, and beat him the whole way with a long whip.[1] In the large towns where the operatives resisted more vigorously, such things naturally happened less often. But even this long working day failed to satisfy the greed of the capitalists. Their aim was to make the capital invested in the building and machinery produce the highest return, by every available means, to make it work as actively as possible. Hence the manufacturers introduced the shameful system of night-work. Some of them employed two sets of operatives, each numerous enough to fill the whole mill, and let one set work the twelve hours of the day, and the other the twelve hours of the night. It is needless to picture the effect upon the frames of young children, and even upon the health of young persons and adults, produced by permanent loss of sleep at night, which cannot be made good by any amount of sleep during the day. Irritation of the whole nervous system, with general lassitude and enfeeblement of the entire frame, were the inevitable results, with the fostering of temptation to drunkenness and unbridled sexual indulgence. One manufacturer testifies[2] that during the two years in which night-work was carried on in his factory, the number of illegitimate children born was doubled, and such general demoralization prevailed that he was obliged to give up night-work. Other manufacturers were yet more barbarous, requiring many hands to work thirty to forty hours at a stretch, several times a week, letting them get a couple of hours sleep only, because the night-shift was not complete, but calculated to replace a part of the operatives only.

The reports of the Commission touching this barbarism surpass everything that is known to me in this line. Such infamies, as are here related, are nowhere else to be found— yet we shall see that the bourgeoisie constantly appeals to the testimony of the Commission as being in its own favour. The consequences of these cruelties became evident quickly enough. The Commissioners mention a crowd of cripples

---

[1] Stuart Evidence, p. 35.

[2] Tufnell Evidence, p. 91.

who appeared before them, who clearly owed their distortion to the long working hours. This distortion usually consists of a curving of the spinal column and legs, and is described as follows by Francis Sharps, MRCS, of Leeds:[1]

I never saw the peculiar bending of the lower ends of the thigh bones before I came to Leeds. At first I thought it was rachitis, but I was soon led to change my opinion in consequence of the mass of patients who presented themselves at the hospital, and the appearances of the disease at an age (from eight to fourteen) in which children are usually not subject to rachitis, as well as by the circumstance that the malady had first appeated after children began to work in the mills. Thus far I have seen about a hundred such cases, and can, most decidedly, express the opinion that they are the consequences of overwork. So far as I know they were all mill children, and themselves attributed the evil to this cause. The number of cases of curvature of the spine which have fallen under my observation, and which were evidently consequent upon too protracted standing, was not less than three hundred.

Precisely similar is the testimony of Dr Hey, for eighteen years physician in the hospital in Leeds:[2]

Malformations of the spine are very frequent among mill-hands; some of them consequent upon mere overwork, others the effect of long work upon constitutions originally feeble, or weakened by bad food. Deformities seem even more frequent than these diseases; the knees were bent inward, the ligaments very often relaxed and enfeebled, and the long bones of the legs bent. The thick ends of these long bones were especially apt to be bent and disproportionately developed, and these patients came from the factories in which long work-hours were of frequent occurrence.

Surgeons Beaumont and Sharp, of Bradford, bear the same testimony. The reports of Drinkwater, Power, and Dr Loudon contain a multitude of examples of such distortions, and those of Tufnell and Sir David Barry, which are less directed to this point, give single examples.[3]

[1] Dr Loudon Evidence, pp. 12, 13.

[2] Dr Loudon Evidence, p. 16.

[3] Drinkwater Evidence, pp. 72, 80, 146, 148, 150 (two brothers); 69 (two brothers); 155, and many others.
Power Evidence, pp. 63, 66, 67 (two cases); 68 (three cases); 69 (two cases); in Leeds, pp. 29, 31, 40, 43, 53 ff.

The Commissioners for Lancashire, Cowell, Tufnell, and Hawkins, have almost wholly neglected this aspect of the physiological results of the factory system, though this district rivals Yorkshire in the number of cripples. I have seldom traversed Manchester without meeting three or four of them, suffering from precisely the same distortions of the spinal columns and legs as that described, and I have often been able to observe them closely. I know one personally who corresponds exactly with the foregoing description of Dr Hey, and who got into this condition in Mr Douglas's factory in Pendleton, an establishment which enjoys an unenviable notoriety among the operatives by reason of the former long working periods continued night after night. It is evident, at a glance, whence the distortions of these cripples come, they all look exactly alike. The knees are bent inward and backwards, the ankles deformed and thick, and the spinal column often bent forwards or to one side. But the crown belongs to the philanthropic manufacturers of the Macclesfield silk district. They employed the youngest children of all, even from 5 to 6 years of age. In the supplementary testimony of Commissioner Tufnell, I find the statement of a certain factory manager Wright, both of whose sisters were most shamefully crippled, and who had once counted the cripples in several streets, some of them the cleanest and neatest streets of Macclesfield. He found in Townley Street ten, George Street five, Charlotte Street four, Watercots fifteen, Bank Top three, Lord Street seven, Mill Lane twelve, Great George Street two, in the workhouse two, Park Green one, Peckford Street two, whose families all unanimously declared that the cripples had become such in consequence of overwork in the silk-twisting mills. One boy is mentioned so crippled as not to be able to go upstairs, and girls deformed in back and hips.

Other deformities also have proceeded from this overwork, especially flattening of the foot, which Sir D. Barry[1]

Loudon Evidence, pp. 4, 7 (four cases); 8 (several cases). etc.

Sir D. Barry Evidence, pp. 6, 8, 13, 21, 22, 44, 55 (three cases), etc. Tufnell Evidence, pp. 5, 6, 16, etc.

[1] Factories' Inquiry Commission's Report, 1833, Sir D. Barry Evidence, p. 21 (two cases).

frequently observed, as did the physicians and surgeons in Leeds.[1] In cases, in which a stronger constitution, better food, and other more favourable circumstances enabled the young operative to resist this effect of a barbarous exploitation, we find, at least, pain in the back, hips, and legs, swollen joints, varicose veins, and large, persistent ulcers in the thighs and calves. These affections are almost universal among the operatives. The reports of Stuart, Mackintosh, and Sir D. Barry contain hundreds of examples; indeed, they know almost no operative who did not suffer from some of these affections; and in the remaining reports, the occurrence of the same phenomena is attested by many physicians. The reports covering Scotland place it beyond all doubt, that a working day of thirteen hours, even for men and women from 18 to 22 years of age, produces at least these consequences, both in the flax-spinning mills of Dundee and Dunfermline, and in the cotton mills of Glasgow and Lanark.

All these affections are easily explained by the nature of factory-work, which is, as the manufacturers say, very 'light', and precisely by reason of its lightness, more enervating than any other. The operatives have little to do, but must stand the whole time. Any one who sits down, say upon a window-ledge or a basket, is fined, and this perpetual upright position, this constant mechanical pressure of the upper portions of the body upon spinal column, hips, and legs, inevitably produces the results mentioned. This standing is not required by the work itself, and at Nottingham chairs have been introduced, with the result that these affections disappeared, and the operatives ceased to object to the length of the working day. But in a factory where the operative works solely for the bourgeois, and has small interest in doing his work well, he would probably use the seats more than would be agreeable and profitable to the manufacturer; and in order that somewhat less raw material may be spoiled for the bourgeois, the operative must sacrifice health and strength.[2] This long protracted upright position, with the

[1] Factories' Inquiry Commission's Report, 1833, Loudon Evidence, pp. 13, 16, etc.

[2] In the spinning-room of a mill at Leeds, too, chairs had been introduced. Drinkwater Evidence, p. 85.

bad atmosphere prevalent in the mills, entails, besides the deformities mentioned, a marked relaxation of all vital energies, and, in consequence, all sorts of other affections general rather than local. The atmosphere of the factories is, as a rule, at once damp and warm, unusually warmer than is necessary, and, when the ventilation is not *very* good, impure, heavy, deficient in oxygen, filled with dust and the smell of the machine oil, which almost everywhere smears the floor, sinks into it, and becomes rancid. The operatives are lightly clad by reason of the warmth, and would readily take cold in case of irregularity of the temperature; a draught is distasteful to them, the general enervation which gradually takes possession of all the physical functions diminishes the animal warmth: this must be replaced from without, and nothing is therefore more agreeable to the operative than to have all the doors and windows closed, and to stay in his warm factory-air. Then comes the sudden change of temperature on going out into the cold and wet or frosty atmosphere, without the means of protection from the rain, or of changing wet clothing for dry, a circumstance which perpetually produces colds. And when one reflects that, with all this, not one single muscle of the body is really exercised, really called into activity, except perhaps those of the legs; that nothing whatsoever counteracts the enervating, relaxing tendency of all these conditions; that every influence is wanting which might give the muscles strength, the fibres elasticity and consistency; that from youth up, the operative is deprived of all fresh air recreation, it is impossible to wonder at the almost unanimous testimony of the physicians in the Factories' Report, that they find a great lack of ability to resist disease, a general depression in vital activity, a constant relaxation of the mental and physical powers. Let us hear Sir D. Barry first:[1]

The unfavourable influences of mill-work upon the hands are the following: (1) The inevitable necessity of forcing their mental and bodily effort to keep pace with a machine moved by a uniform and unceasing motive power. (2) Continuance in an upright position during unnaturally long and quickly recurring periods. (3) Loss of sleep in consequence of too long working-hours, pain in the legs,

[1] General report by Sir D. Barry.

and general physical derangement. To these are often added low, crowded, dusty, or damp work-rooms, impure air, a high temperature, and constant perspiration. Hence the boys especially very soon and with but few exceptions, lose the rosy freshness of childhood, and become paler and thinner than other boys. Even the hand-weaver's bound boy, who sits before his loom with his bare feet resting upon the clay-floor, retains a fresher appearance, because he occasionally goes into the fresh air for a time. But the mill child has not a moment free except for meals, and never goes into the fresh air except on its way to them. All adult male spinners are pale and thin, suffer from capricious appetite and indigestion; and as they are all trained in the mills from their youth up, and there are very few tall, athletic men among them, the conclusion is justified that their occupation is very unfavourable for the development of the male constitution; females bear this work far better. [Very naturally. But we shall see that they have their own diseases.]

So, too, Power:[1]

I can bear witness that the factory system in Bradford has engendered a multitude of cripples, and that the effect of long continued labour upon the physique is apparent not alone in actual deformity, but also, and much more generally, in stunted growth, relaxation of the muscles, and delicacy of whole frame.

So, too, F. Sharp, in Leeds, the surgeon[2] already quoted:

When I moved from Scarborough to Leeds, I was at once struck by the fact that the general appearance of the children was much paler, and their fibre less vigorous here than in Scarborough and its environs. I saw, too, that many children were exceptionally small for their age. I have met with numberless cases of scrofula, lung trouble, mesenteric affections, and indigestion, concerning which I, as a medical man, have no doubt that they arose from mill-work. I believe that the nervous energy of the body is weakened by the long hours, and the foundation of many diseases laid. If people from the country were not constantly coming in, the race of mill-hands would soon be wholly degenerate.

So, too, Beaumont, surgeon in Bradford:

[1] Power Report, p. 74.

[2] The surgeons in England are scientifically educated as well as the physicians, and have, in general, medical as well as surgical practice. They are, in general, for various reasons, preferred to the physicians.

To my thinking, the system, according to which work is done in the mills here, produces a peculiar relaxation of the whole organism, and thereby makes children in the highest degree susceptible to epidemic, as well as to incidental illness. I regard the absence of all appropriate regulations for ventilation and cleanliness in the mills very decidedly as the chief cause of that peculiar tendency or susceptibility to morbid affections which I have so frequently met in my practice.

Similar testimony is borne by Dr Kay:

(1) I have had opportunity of observing the effects of the factory system upon the health of children under the most favourable circumstances [in Wood's mill, in Bradford, the best arranged of the district, in which he was factory surgeon]. (2) These effects are decidedly, and to a very great extent, injurious, even under these most favourable circumstances. (3) In the year 1842, three-fifths of all the children employed in Woods' mill were treated by me. (4) The worst effect is not the predominance of deformities, but of enfeebled and morbid constitutions. (5) All this is greatly improved since the working-hours of children have been reduced at Wood's to ten.

The Commissioner, Dr Loudon himself, who cites these witnesses, says:

In conclusion, I think it has been clearly proved that children have been worked a most unreasonable and cruel length of time daily, and that even adults have been expected to do a certain quantity of labour which scarcely any human being is able to endure. The consequence is that many have died prematurely, and others are afflicted for life with defective constitutions, and the fear of a posterity enfeebled by the shattered constitution of the survivors is but too well founded, from a physiological point of view.

And, finally, Dr Hawkins, in speaking of Manchester:

I believe that most travellers are struck by the lowness of stature, the leanness and the paleness which present themselves so commonly to the eye at Manchester, and above all, among the factory classes. I have never been in any town in Great Britain, nor in Europe, in which degeneracy of form and colour from the national standard has been so obvious. Among the married women all the characteristic peculiarities of the English wife are conspicuously wanting. I must confess that all the boys and girls brought before me from the Manchester mills had a depressed appearance, and were very pale.

In the expression of their faces lay nothing of the usual mobility, liveliness, and cheeriness of youth. Many of them told me that they felt not the slightest inclination to play out of doors on Saturday and Sunday, but preferred to be quiet at home.

I add, at once, another passage of Hawkins's report, which only half belongs here, but may be quoted here as well as anywhere else:

Intemperance, excess, and want of providence are the chief faults of the factory population, and these evils may be readily traced to the habits which are formed under the present system, and almost inevitably arise from it. It is universally admitted that indigestion, hypochondria, and general debility affect this class to a very great extent. After twelve hours of monotonous toil, it is but natural to look about for a stimulant of one sort or another; but when the above-mentioned diseased conditions are added to the customary weariness, people will quickly and repeatedly take refuge in spirituous liquors.

For all this testimony of the physicians and commissioners, the report itself offers hundreds of cases of proof. That the growth of young operatives is stunted, by their work, hundreds of statements testify; among others, Cowell gives the weight of 46 youths of 17 years of age, from one Sunday school, of whom 26 employed in mills, averaged 104.5 pounds, and 20 not employed in mills, 117.7 pounds. One of the largest manufacturers of Manchester, leader of the opposition against the working men, I think Robert Hyde Greg himself, said, on one occasion, that if things went on as at present, the operatives of Lancashire would soon be a race of pigmies.[1] A recruiting officer[2] testified that operatives are little adapted for military service, looked thin and nervous, and were frequently rejected by the surgeons as unfit. In Manchester he could hardly get men of 5 feet 8 inches; they were usually only 5 feet 6 to 7, whereas in the agricultural districts, most of the recruits were 5 feet 8.

The men wear out very early in consequence of the conditions under which they live and work. Most of them are unfit for work at 40 years, a few hold out to 45, almost none to 50 years of age. This is caused not only by the general

---

[1] This statement is not taken from the report.

[2] Tufnell, p. 59.

enfeeblement of the frame, but also very often by a failure of the sight, which is a result of mule-spinning, in which the operative is obliged to fix his gaze upon a long row of fine, parallel threads, and so greatly to strain the sight.

Of 1,600 operatives employed in several factories in Harpur and Lanark, but ten were over 45 years of age; of 22,094 operatives in diverse factories in Stockport and Manchester, but 143 were over 45 years old. Of these 143, sixteen were retained as a special favour, and one was doing the work of a child. A list of 131 spinners contained but seven over 45 years, and yet the whole 131 were rejected by the manufacturers, to whom they applied for work, as 'too old'. Of fifty worked-out spinners in Bolton only two were over 50 and the rest did not yet average 40 and all were without means of support by reason of old age! Mr Ashworth, a large manufacturer, admits in a letter to Lord Ashley, that, towards the fortieth year, the spinners can no longer prepare the required quantity of yarn, and are therefore 'sometimes' discharged; he calls operatives 40 years of age 'old people'![1] Commissioner Mackintosh expresses himself in the same way in the report of 1833: 'Although I was prepared for it from the way the children are employed, I still found it difficult to believe the statements of the older hands as to their ages; they age so very early.'

Surgeon Smellie of Glasgow, who treated operatives chiefly, says that 40 years is old age for them.[2] And similar evidence may be found elsewhere.[3] In Manchester, this premature old age among the operatives is so universal that almost every man of 40 would be taken for ten to fifteen years older, while the prosperous classes, men as well as women, preserve their appearance exceedingly well if they do not drink too heavily.

The influence of factory-work upon the female physique also is marked and peculiar. The deformities entailed by long hours of work are much more serious among women.

[1] All taken from Lord Ashley's speech (sitting of Lower House, 15 Mar. 1844). (*Note in the German edition.*)

[2] Stuart Evidence, p. 101.

[3] Tufnell Evidence, pp. 3, 9, 15; Hawkins Report, p. 4; Evidence, p. 11 etc., etc.

Protracted work frequently causes deformities of the pelvis, partly in the shape of abnormal position and development of the hip bones, partly of malformation of the lower portion of the spinal column. 'Although', says Dr Loudon, in his report, 'no example of malformation of the pelvis and of some other affections came under my notice, these things are nevertheless so common, that every physician must regard them as probable consequences of such working-hours, and as vouched for besides by men of the highest medical credibility.'

That factory operatives undergo more difficult confinement than other women is testified to by several midwives and accoucheurs, and also that they are more liable to miscarriage.[1] Moreover, they suffer from the general enfeeblement common to all operatives, and, when pregnant, continue to work in the factory up to the hour of delivery, because otherwise they lose their wages and are made to fear that they may be replaced if they stop away too soon. It frequently happens that women are at work one evening and delivered the next morning, and the case is none too rare of their being delivered in the factory among the machinery. And if the gentlemen of the bourgeoisie find nothing particularly shocking in this, their wives will perhaps admit that it is a piece of cruelty, an infamous act of barbarism, indirectly to force a pregnant woman to work twelve or thirteen hours daily (formerly still longer), up to the day of her delivery, in a standing position, with frequent stoopings. But this is not all. If these women are not obliged to resume work within two weeks, they are thankful, and count themselves fortunate. Many come back to the factory after eight, and even after three to four days, to resume full work. I once heard a manufacturer ask an overlooker: 'Is so and so not back yet?' 'No.' 'How long since she was confined?' 'A week.' 'She might surely have been back long ago. That one over there only stays three days.' Naturally, fear of being discharged, dread of starvation drives her to the factory in spite of her weakness, in defiance of her pain. The interest of the manufacturer will not brook that his employees stay at home by reason of illness; they must not be ill, they must not venture to lie still through a long confinement, or he

---

[1] Hawkins Evidence, pp. 11, 13.

must stop his machinery or trouble his supreme head with a temporary change of arrangements; and rather than do this, he discharges his people when they begin to be ill. Listen:[1] 'A girl feels very ill, can scarcely do her work. Why does she not ask permission to go home? Ah! the master is very particular, and if we are away a quarter of a day, we risk being sent away altogether.' Or Sir D. Barry:[2] 'Thomas McDurt, workman, has slight fever. Cannot stay at home longer four days, because he would fear of losing his place.'

And so it goes on in almost all the factories. The employment of young girls produces all sorts of irregularities during the period of development. In some, especially those who are better fed, the heat of the factories hastens this process, so that in single cases, girls of 13 and 14 are wholly mature. Roberton, whom I have already cited (mentioned in the Factories' Inquiry Commission's Report as the 'eminent' gynaeocologist of Manchester), relates in the North of England *Medical and Surgical Journal*, that he had seen a girl of 11 years who was not only a wholly developed woman, but pregnant, and that it was by no means rare in Manchester for women to be confined at 15 years of age. In such cases, the influence of the warmth of the factories is the same as that of a tropical climate, and, as in such climates, the abnormally early development revenges itself by correspondingly premature age and debility. On the other hand, retarded development of the female constitution occurs, the breasts mature late or not at all.[3] Menstruation first appears in the seventeenth or eighteenth, sometimes in the twentieth year, and is often wholly wanting.[4] Irregular menstruation, coupled with great pain and numerous affections, especially with anaemia, is very frequent, as the medical reports unanimously state.

Children of such mothers, particularly of those who are obliged to work during pregnancy, cannot be vigorous. They are, on the contrary, described in the report, especially in

[1] Cowell Evidence, p. 77.

[2] Sir D. Barry Evidence, p. 44.

[3] Cowell, p. 35.

[4] Dr Hawkins Evidence, p. 11; Dr Loudon, p. 14, etc.; Sir D. Barry, p. 5, etc.

Manchester, as very feeble; and Barry alone asserts that they are healthy, but says further, that in Scotland, where his inspection lay, almost no married women worked in factories. Moreover, most of the factories there are in the country (with the exception of Glasgow), a circumstance which contributes greatly to the invigoration of the children. The operatives' children in the neighbourhood of Manchester are nearly all thriving and rosy, while those within the city look pale and scrofulous; but with the ninth year the colour vanishes suddenly, because all are then sent into the factories, when it soon becomes impossible to distinguish the country from the city children.

But besides all this, there are some branches of factory-work which have an especially injurious effect. In many rooms of the cotton- and flax-spinning mills, the air is filled with fibrous dust, which produces chest affections, especially among workers in the carding- and combing-rooms. Some constitutions can bear it, some cannot; but the operative has no choice. He must take the room in which he finds work, whether his chest is sound or not. The most common effects of this breathing of dust are bloodspitting, hard, noisy breathing, pains in the chest, coughs, sleeplessness—in short, all the symptoms of asthma ending in the worst cases in consumption.[1] Especially unwholesome is the wet spinning of linen-yarn which is carried on by young girls and boys. The water spirts over them from the spindle so that the front of their clothing is constantly wet through to the skin; and there is always water standing on the floor. This is the case to a less degree in the doubling-rooms of the cotton mills, and the result is a constant succession of colds and affections of the chest. A hoarse, rough voice is common to all operatives, but especially to wet spinners and doublers. Stuart, Mackintosh, and Sir D. Barry express themselves in the most vigorous terms as to the unwholesomeness of this work, and the small consideration shown by most of the manufacturers for the health of the girls who do it. Another effect of flax-spinning is a peculiar deformity of the shoulder, especially a

[1] Compare Stuart, pp. 13, 70, 101; Mackintosh, p. 24, etc.; Power Report on Nottingham, on Leeds; Cowell, p. 33, etc.; Barry, p. 12 (five cases in one factory), pp. 17, 44, 52, 60, etc.; Loudon, p. 13.

projection of the right shoulder-blade, consequent upon the nature of the work. This sort of spinning and the throstle-spinning of cotton frequently produce diseases of the knee-pan, which is used to check the spindle during the joining of broken threads. The frequent stooping and the bending to the low machines common to both these branches of work have, in general, a stunting effect upon the growth of the operative. In the throstle-room of the cotton mill at Manchester, in which I was employed, I do not remember to have seen one single tall, well-built girl; they were all short, dumpy, and badly formed, decidedly ugly in the whole development of the figure. But apart from all these diseases and malformations, the limbs of the operatives suffer in still another way. The work between the machinery gives rise to multitudes of accidents of more or less serious nature, which have for the operative the secondary effect of unfitting him for his work more or less completely. The most common accident is the squeezing off of a single joint of a finger, somewhat less common the loss of the whole finger, half or a whole hand, an arm, etc., in the machinery. Lockjaw very often follows, even upon the lesser among these injuries, and brings death with it. Besides the deformed persons, a great number of maimed ones may be seen going about in Manchester; this one has lost an arm or a part of one, that one a foot, the third half a leg; it is like living in the midst of an army just returned from a campaign. But the most dangerous portion of the machinery is the strapping which conveys motive power from the shaft to the separate machines, especially if it contains buckles which, however, are rarely used now. Whoever is seized by the strap is carried up with lightning speed, thrown against the ceiling above and floor below with such force that there is rarely a whole bone left in the body, and death follows instantly. Between 12 June and 3 August 1843, the *Manchester Guardian* reported the following serious accidents (the trifling ones it does not notice): 12 June, a boy died in Manchester of lockjaw, caused by his hand being crushed between wheels. 16 June, a youth in Saddleworth seized by a wheel and carried away with it; died, utterly mangled. 29 June, a young man at Green Acres Moor, near Manchester, at work in a machine shop, fell under the grindstone, which broke two of his ribs and lacerated him terribly. 24 July, a girl in Oldham died, carried around fifty times by a strap; no bone unbroken. 27 July, a girl in Manchester seized by the blower (the first machine that receives the raw cotton), and died of injuries received. 3 August, a bobbins turner died in Dukenfield, caught in a strap, every rib broken. In the year 1843, the Manchester Infirmary treated 962 cases of wounds and mutilations caused by machinery, while the number of all other accidents within the district of the hospital was 2,426, so that for five accidents from all other causes, two were caused by machinery. The accidents which happened in Salford are not included here, nor those treated by surgeons in private practice. In such cases, whether or not the accident unfits the victim for further work, the employer, at best, pays the doctor, or, in very exceptional cases, he may pay wages during treatment; what becomes of the operative afterwards, in case he cannot work, is no concern of the employer.

The Factory Report says on his subject, that employers must be made responsible for all cases, since children cannot take care, and adults will take care in their own interest. But the gentlemen who write the report are bourgeois, and so they must contradict themselves and bring up later all sorts of bosh on the subject of the culpable temerity of the operatives.

The state of the case is this : If children cannot take care, the employment of children must be forbidden. If adults are reckless, they must be mere overgrown children on a plane of intelligence which does not enable them to appreciate the danger in its full scope and who is to blame for this but the bourgeoisie which keeps them in a condition in which their intelligence cannot develop? Or the machinery is ill-arranged, and must be surrounded with fencing, to supply which falls to the share of the bourgeoisie. Or the operative is under inducements which outweigh the threatened danger; he must work rapidly to earn his wage, has no time to take care, and for this, too, the bourgeoisie is to blame. Many accidents happen, for instance, while the operatives are cleaning machinery in motion. Why? Because the bourgeois would otherwise oblige the worker to clean the machinery during the free hours while it is not going, and the worker naturally is not disposed to sacrifice any part of his free time. Every free hour is so precious to the worker that he often risks his life twice a week rather than sacrifice one of them to the bourgeois. Let the employer take from working hours the time required for cleaning the machinery, and it will never again occur to an operative to clean machinery in motion. In short, from whatever point of view, the blame falls ultimately on the manufacturer, and of him should be required at the very least, lifelong support of the incapacitated operative, and support of the victim's family in case death follows the accident. In the earliest period of manufacture, the accidents were much more numerous in proportion than now, for the machinery was inferior, smaller, more crowded, and almost never fenced. But the number is still large enough, as the foregoing cases prove, to arouse the grave question as to a state of things which permits so many deformities and mutilations for the benefit of a single class, and plunges so many industrious working people into want and starvation by reason of injuries undergone in the service and through the fault of the bourgeoisie.

A pretty list of diseases engendered purely by the hateful money-greed of the manufacturers! Women made unfit for childbearing, children deformed, men enfeebled, limbs crushed, whole generations wrecked, afflicted with disease and infirmity, purely to fill the purses of the bourgeoisie. And when one reads of the barbarism of single cases, how children are seized naked in bed by the overlookers, and driven with blows and kicks to the factory, their clothing over their arms,[1] how their sleepiness is driven off with blows, how they fall asleep over their work nevertheless, how one poor child sprang up, still asleep, at the call of the overlooker, and mechanically went through the operations of its work after its machine was stopped; when one reads how children, too tired to go home, hide away in the wool in the drying-room to sleep there, and could only be driven out of the factory with straps; how many hundreds came home so tired every night, that they could eat no supper for sleepiness and want of appetite, that their parents found them kneeling by the bedside, where they had fallen asleep during their prayers; when one reads all this and a hundred other villainies

[1] Stuart, p. 39.

and infamies in this one report, all testified to on oath, confirmed by several witnesses, deposed by men whom the commissioners themselves declare trustworthy; when one reflects that this is a Liberal report, a bourgeois report, made for the purpose of reversing the previous Tory report, and rehabilitating the pureness of heart of the manufacturers, that the commissioners themselves are on the side of the bourgeoisie, and report all these things against their own will, how can one be otherwise than filled with wrath and resentment against a class which boasts of philanthropy and self-sacrifice, while its one object is to fill its purse *à tout prix*?* Meanwhile, let us listen to the bourgeoisie speaking through the mouth of its chosen apostle, Dr Ure, who relates in his *Philosophy of Manufactures*[1] that the workers have been told that their wages bore no proportion to their sacrifices, the good understanding between masters and men being thus disturbed. Instead of this, the working men should have striven to recommend themselves by attention and industry, and should have rejoiced in the prosperity of their masters. They would then become overseers, superintendents, and finally partners, and would thus—(Oh! Wisdom, thou speakest as the dove!)—'have increased at the same time the demand for their companions' labour in the market!' 'Had it not been for the violent collisions and interruptions resulting from erroneous views among the operatives, the factory system would have been developed still more repidly and beneficially.'[2] Hereupon follows a long Jeremiad upon the spirit of resistance of the operatives, and on the occasion of a strike of the best paid workers, the fine spinners, the following naïve observation:[3] 'In fact, it was their high wages which enabled them to maintain a stipendiary committee in affluence, and to pamper themselves into nervous ailments, by a diet too rich and exciting for their indoor employments.'

Let us hear how the bourgeois describes the work of children:[4]

I have visited many factories, both in Manchester and in the surrounding districts, during a period of several months, entering

---

[1] Dr Andrew Ure, *Philosophy of Manufactures*, 277 ff.

[2] Ibid. 277.   [3] Ibid. 298.   [4] Ibid. 301.

the spinning-rooms unexpectedly, and often alone, at different times of the day, and I never saw a single instance of corporal chastisement inflicted on a child; nor, indeed, did I ever see children in ill-humour. They seemed to be always cheerful and alert; taking pleasure in the light play of their muscles, enjoying the mobility natural to their age. The scene of industry, so far from exciting sad emotions, in my mind, was always exhilarating. It was delightful to observe the nimbleness with which they pieced broken ends, as the mule carriage began to recede from the fixed roller beam, and to see them at leisure, after a few seconds' exercise of their tiny fingers, to amuse themselves in any attitude they chose, till the stretch and winding on were once more completed. The work of these lively elves seemed to resemble a sport, in which habit gave them a pleasing dexterity. Conscious of their skill, they were delighted to show it off to any stranger. As to exhaustion by the day's work, they evinced no trace of it on emerging from the mill in the evening; for they immediately began to skip about any neighbouring playground, and to commence their little games with the same alacrity as boys issuing from a school.

Naturally! As though the immediate movement of every muscle were not an urgent necessity for frames grown at once stiff and relaxed! But Ure should have waited to see whether this momentary excitement had not subsided after a couple of minutes. And besides, Ure could see this whole performance only in the afternoon after five or six hours' work, but not in the evening! As to the health of the operatives, the bourgeois has the boundless impudence to cite the report of 1833 just quoted in a thousand places, as testimony for the excellent health of these people; to try to prove by detached and garbled quotations that no trace of scrofula can be found among them, and what is quite true, that the factory system frees them from all acute diseases (that they have every variety of chronic affection instead he naturally conceals). To explain the impudence with which our friend Ure palms off the grossest falsehoods upon the English public, it must be known that the report consists of three large folio volumes, which it never occurs to a well-fed English bourgeois to study through. Let us hear further how he expresses himself as to the Factory Act of 1834, passed by the Liberal bourgeoisie, and imposing only the most meagre limitations upon the manufacturers, as we shall see. This law, especially its compulsory education clause, he calls an

absurd and despotic measure directed against the manufacturers, through which all children under 12 years of
age have been thrown out of employment; and with what
results? The children thus discharged from their light and
useful occupation receive no education whatsoever; cast out
from the warm spinning-room into a cold world, they subsist
only by begging and stealing, a life in sad contrast with their
steadily improving condition in the factory and in Sunday
school. Under the mask of philanthropy, this law intensifies
the sufferings of the poor, and will greatly restrict the
conscientious manufacturer in his useful work, if, indeed, it
does not wholly stop him:[1]

The ruinous influence of the factory system began at an
early day to attract general attention. We have already
alluded to the Apprentices' Act of 1802. Later, towards
1817, Robert Owen, then a manufacturer in New Lanark, in
Scotland, afterwards founder of English Socialism, began to
call the attention of the Government, by memorials and
petitions, to the necessity of legislative guarantees for the
health of the operatives, and especially of children. The late
Sir Robert Peel and other philanthropists united with him,
and gradually secured the Factory Acts of 1819, 1825, and
1831, of which the first two were never enforced,* and the
last only here and there. This law of 1831, based upon the
motion of Sir J. C. Hobhouse, provided that in cotton mills
no one under 21 should be employed between half-past seven
at night and half-past five in the morning; and that in all
factories young persons under 18 should work no longer
than twelve hours daily, and nine hours on Saturday. But
since operatives could not testify against their masters without being discharged, this law helped matters very little. In
the great cities, where the operatives were more restive, the
larger manufacturers came to an agreement among themselves to obey the law; but even there, there were many who,
like the employers in the country, did not trouble themselves
about it. Meanwhile, the demand for a ten hours' law had
become lively among the operatives; that is, for a law which
should forbid all operatives under 18 years of age to work
longer than ten hours daily; the Trade Unions, by their

[1] Ure, *Philosophy of Manufactures*, 405, 406 ff.

agitation, made this demand general throughout manufacturing population; the philanthropic section of the Tory
party, then led by Michael Sadler, seized upon the plan,
and brought it before Parliament. Sadler obtained a parliamentary committee for the investigation of the factory
system, and this committee reported in 1832. Its report was
emphatically partisan, composed by strong enemies of the
factory system, for party ends. Sadler permitted himself to be
betrayed by his noble enthusiasm into the most distorted and
erroneous statements, drew from his witnesses by the very
form of his questions, answers which contained the truth,
but truth in a perverted form. The manufacturers themselves,
incensed at a report which represented them as monsters,
now demanded an official investigation; they knew that an
exact report must, in this case, be advantageous to them;
they knew that Whigs, genuine bourgeois, were at the helm,
with whom they were upon good terms, whose principles
were opposed to any restriction upon manufacture. They
obtained a commission, in due order, composed of Liberal
bourgeois, whose report I have so often cited. This comes
somewhat nearer the truth than Sadler's, but its deviations
therefrom are in the opposite direction. On every page it
betrays sympathy with the manufacturers, distrust of the
Sadler report, repugnance to the working men agitating
independently and the supporters of the Ten Hours Bill.
It nowhere recognizes the right of the working man to a
life worthy of a human being, to independent activity, and
opinions of his own. It reproaches the operatives that in
sustaining the Ten Hours Bill they thought, not of the children only, but of themselves as well; it calls the working
men engaged in the agitation demagogues, ill-intentioned,
malicious, etc., is written, in short, on the side of the
bourgeoisie; and still it cannot whitewash the manufacturers,
and still it leaves such a mass of infamies upon the shoulders
of the employers, that even after this report, the agitation for
the Ten Hours Bill, the hatred against the manufacturers,
and the committee's severest epithets applied to them are
all fully justified. But there was the one difference, that
whereas the Sadler report accuses the manufacturers of
open, undisguised brutality, it now became evident that this
brutality was chiefly carried on under the mask of civilization

and humanity. Yet Dr Hawkins, the medical commissioner for Lancashire, expresses himself decidedly in favour of the Ten Hours Bill in the opening lines of his report, and Commissioner Mackintosh explains that his own report does not contain the whole truth, because it is very difficult to induce the operatives to testify against their employers, and because the manufacturers, besides being forced into greater concessions towards their operatives by the excitement among the latter, are often prepared for the inspection of the factories, have them swept, the speed of the machinery reduced, etc. In Lancashire especially they resorted to the device of bringing the overlookers of workrooms before the commissioners, and letting them testify as working men to the humanity of the employers, the wholesome effects of the work, and the indifference, if not the hostility of the operatives, towards the Ten Hours Bill. But these are not genuine working men; they are deserters from their class, who have entered the service of the bourgeoisie for better pay, and fight in the interests of the capitalists against the workers. Their interest is that of the capitalists, and they are, therefore, almost more hated by the workers than the manufacturers themselves.

And yet this report suffices wholly to exhibit the most shameful recklessness of the manufacturing bourgeoisie towards its employees, the whole infamy of the industrial exploiting system in its full inhumanity. Nothing is more revolting than to compare the long register of diseases and deformities engendered by overwork, in this report, with the cold, calculating political economy of the manufacturers, by which they try to prove that they, and with them all England, must go to ruin, if they should be forbidden to cripple so and so many children every year. The language of Dr Ure alone, which I have quoted, would be yet more revolting if it were not so preposterous.

The result of this report was the Factory Act of 1834, which forbade the employment of children under 9 years of age (except in silk mills), limited the working hours of children between 9 and 13 years to forty-eight per week, or nine hours in any one day at the utmost; that of young persons from 14 to 18 years of age to sixty-nine per week, or twelve on any one day as the maximum, provided for an hour and a half as the minimum interval for meals, and repeated the total prohibition of night-work for persons under 18 years of age. Compulsory school attendance two hours daily was prescribed for all children under 14 years, and the manufacturer declared punishable in case of employing children without a certificate of age from the factory surgeon, and a certificate of school attendance from the teacher. As recompense, the employer was permitted to withdraw one penny from the child's weekly earnings to pay the teacher. Further, surgeons and inspectors were appointed to visit the factories at all times, take testimony of operatives on oath, and enforce the law by prosecution before a Justice of the Peace. This is the law against which Dr Ure inveighs in such unmeasured terms!

The consequence of this law, and especially of the appointment of inspectors, was the reduction of working hours to an average of twelve to thirteen, and the superseding of children as far as possible. Hereupon some of the most crying evils disappeared almost wholly. Deformities arose now only in cases of weak constitution, and the effects of over-work became much less conspicuous. Nevertheless, enough testimony remains to be found in the Factory Report, that the lesser evils, swelling of the ankles, weakness and pain in the legs, hips, and back, varicose veins, ulcers on the lower extremities, general weakness, especially of the pelvic region, nausea, want of appetite alternating with unnatural hunger, indigestion, hypochondria, affections of the chest in consequence of the dust and foul atmosphere of the factories, etc., etc., all occur among employees subject to the provisions of Sir J. C. Hobhouse's Law (of 1831), which prescribes twelve to thirteen hours as the maximum. The reports from Glasgow and Manchester are especially worthy of attention in this respect. These evils remained too, after the law of 1834, and continue to undermine the health of the working class to this day. Care has been taken to give the brutal profit-greed of the bourgeoisie a hypocritical, civilized form, to restrain the manufacturers through the arm of the law from too conspicuous villainies, and thus to give them a pretext for self-complacently parading their sham philanthropy. That is all. If a new commission were appointed today, it would find things pretty much as before.

As to the extemporized compulsory attendance at school, it remained wholly a dead letter, since the Government failed to provide good schools. The manufacturers employed as teachers worn-out operatives, to whom they sent the children two hours daily, thus complying with the letter of the law; but the children learned nothing. And even the reports of the factory inspectors, which are limited to the scope of the inspector's duties, i.e. the enforcement of the Factory Act, give data enough to justify the conclusion that the old evils inevitably remain. Inspectors Horner and Saunders, in their reports for October and December 1843, state that, in a number of branches in which the employment of children can be dispensed with or superseded by that of adults, the working day is still fourteen to sixteen hours, or even longer. Among the operatives in these branches they found numbers of young people who had just outgrown the provisions of the law. Many employers disregard the law, shorten the meal times, work children longer than is permitted, and risk prosecution, knowing that the possible fines are trifling in comparison with the certain profits derivable from the offence. Just at present especially, while business is exceptionally brisk, they are under great temptation in this respect.

Meanwhile the agitation for the Ten Hours Bill by no means died out among the operatives; in 1839 it was under full headway once more, and Sadler's place, he having died, was filled in the House of Commons by Lord Ashley[1] and Richard Oastler, both Tories. Oastler especially, who carried on a constant agitation in the factory districts, and had been active in the same way during Sadler's life, was the particular favourite of the working men. They called him their 'good old king', 'the king of the factory children', and there is not a child in the factory districts that does not know and revere him, that does not join the procession which moves to welcome him when he enters a town. Oastler vigorously opposed the New Poor Law also, and was therefore imprisoned for debt by a Mr Thornhill, on whose estate he was employed as agent, and to whom he owed money. The Whigs offered repeatedly to pay his debt and confer other

---

[1] Afterwards Earl of Shaftesbury, died 1885.

favours upon him if he would only give up his agitation against the Poor Law. But in vain; he remained in prison, whence he published his Fleet Papers* against the factory system and the Poor Law.

The Tory Goverment of 1841 turned its attention once more to the Factory Acts. The Home Secretary, Sir James Graham, proposed, in 1843, a bill restricting the working hours of children to six and one-half, and making the enactments for compulsory school attendance more effective, the principal point in this connection being a provision for better schools. This bill was, however, wrecked by the jealousy of the dissenters;* for, although compulsory religious instruction was not extended to the children of dissenters, the schools provided for were to be placed under the general supervision of the Established Church, and the Bible made the general reading-book, religion being thus made the foundation of all instruction, whence the dissenters felt themselves threatened. The manufacturers and the Liberals generally united with them; the working men were divided by the Church question, and therefore inactive. The opponents of the bill, though outweighed in the great manufacturing towns, such as Salford and Stockport, and able in others, such as Manchester, to attack certain of its points only, for fear of the working men, collected nevertheless nearly two million signatures for a petition against it, and Graham allowed himself to be so far intimidated as to withdraw the whole bill. The next year he omitted the school clauses, and proposed that, instead of the previous provisions, children between 8 and 13 years should be restricted to six and one-half hours, and so employed as to have either the whole morning or the whole afternoon free; that young people between 13 and 18 years, and all females, should be limited to twelve hours; and that the hitherto frequent evasions of the law should be prevented. Hardly had he proposed this bill, when the ten hours' agitation was begun again more vigorously than ever. Oastler had just then regained his liberty; a number of his friends and a collection among the workers had paid his debt, and he threw himself into the movement with all his might. The defenders of the Ten Hours Bill in the House of Commons had increased in numbers, the masses of petitions supporting it which poured in from all sides brought them allies, and on 19 March 1844 Lord Ashley carried, with a majority of 179 to 170, a resolution that the word 'Night' in the Factory Act should express the time from six at night to six in the morning, whereby the prohibition of night-work came to mean the limitation of working hours to twelve, including free hours, or ten hours of actual work a day. But the ministry did not agree to this. Sir James Graham began to threaten resignation from the Cabinet, and at the next vote on the bill the House rejected by a small majority both ten and twelve hours! Graham and Peel now announced that they should introduce a new bill, and that if this failed to pass they should resign. The new bill was exactly the old Twelve Hours Bill with some changes of form, and the same House of Commons which had rejected the principal points of this bill in March, now swallowed it whole. The reason of this was that most of the supporters of the Ten Hours Bill were Tories who let fall the bill rather than the ministry; but be the motives what they may, the House of Commons by its votes upon this subject, each vote reversing the last, has brought itself into the greatest contempt among all the workers, and proved most brilliantly the Chartists' assertion of the necessity of its reform. Three members, who had formerly voted against the ministry, afterwards voted for it and rescued it. In all the divisions, the bulk of the opposition voted *for* and the bulk of its own party *against* the ministry.[1] The foregoing propositions of Graham touching the employment of children six and one-half and of all other operatives twelve hours are now legislative provisions, and by them and by the limitation of overwork for making up time lost through breakdown of machinery or insufficient water-power by reason of frost or drought, a working day of more than twelve hours has been made well-nigh impossible. There remains, however, no doubt that, in a very short time, the Ten Hours Bill will really be adopted.* The manufacturers are naturally all against it; there are perhaps not ten who are for it; they have

[1] It is notorious that the House of Commons made itself ridiculous a second time in the same session in the same way on the Sugar Question,* when it first voted against the ministry and then for it, after an application of the ministerial whip.

used every honourable and dishonourable means against this dreaded measure, but with no other result than that of drawing down upon them the ever-deepening hatred of the working men. The bill will pass. What the working men will do they can do, and that they will have this bill they proved last spring. The economic arguments of the manufacturers that a Ten Hours Bill would increase the cost of production and incapacitate the English producers for competition in foreign markets, and that wages must fall, are all *half* true; but they prove nothing except this, that the industrial greatness of England can be maintained only through the barbarous treatment of the operatives, the destruction of their health, the social, physical, and mental decay of whole generations. Naturally, if the Ten Hours Bill were a final measure, it must ruin England; but since it must inevitably bring with it other measures which must draw England into a path wholly different from that hitherto followed, it can only prove an advance.

Let us turn to another side of the factory system which cannot be remedied by legislative provisions so easily as the diseases now engendered by it. We have already alluded in a general way to the nature of the employment, and enough in detail to be able to draw certain inferences from the facts given. The supervision of machinery, the joining of broken threads, is no activity which claims the operative's thinking powers, yet it is of a sort which prevents him from occupying his mind with other things. We have seen, too, that this work affords the muscles no opportunity for physical activity. Thus it is, properly speaking, not work, but tedium, the most deadening, wearing process conceivable. The operative is condemned to let his physical and mental powers decay in this utter monotony, it is his mission to be bored every day and all day long from his eighth year. Moreover, he must not take a moment's rest; the engine moves unceasingly; the wheels, the straps, the spindles hum and rattle in his ears without a pause, and if he tries to snatch one instant, there is the overlooker at his back with the book of fines. This condemnation to be buried alive in the mill, to give constant attention to the tireless machine is felt as the keenest torture by the operatives, and its action upon mind and body is in the long run stunting in the highest degree. There is no better means of inducing stupefaction than a period of factory-work, and if the operatives have, nevertheless, not only rescued their intelligence, but cultivated and sharpened it more than other working men, they have found this possible only in rebellion against their fate and against the bourgeoisie, the sole subject on which under all circumstances they can think and feel while at work. Or, if this indignation against the bourgeoisie does not become the supreme passion of the working man, the inevitable consequence is drunkenness and all that is generally called demoralization. The physical enervation and the sickness, universal in consequence of the factory system, were enough to induce Commissioner Hawkins to attribute this demoralization thereto as inevitable; how much more when mental lassitude is added to them, and when the influences already mentioned which tempt every working man to demoralization, make themselves felt here too! There is no cause for surprise, therefore, that in the manufacturing towns especially, drunkenness and sexual excesses have reached the pitch which I have already described.[1]

Further, the slavery in which the bourgeoisie holds the proletariat chained, is nowhere more conspicuous than in the factory system. Here ends all freedom in law and in fact. The operative must be in the mill at half-past five in the morning; if he comes a couple of minutes too late, he is fined; if he comes ten minutes too late, he is not let in until breakfast is

---

[1] Let us hear another competent judge: 'If we consider the example of the Irish in connection with the ceaseless toil of the cotton operative class, we shall wonder less at their terrible demoralization. Continuous exhausting toil, day after day, year after year, is not calculated to develop the intellectual and moral capabilities of the human being. The wearisome routine of endless drudgery, in which the same mechanical process is ever repeated, is like the torture of Sisyphus; the burden of toil, like the rock, is ever falling back upon the worn-out drudge. The mind attains neither knowledge nor the power of thought from the eternal employment of the same muscles. The intellect dozes off in dull indolence, but the coarser part of our nature reaches a luxuriant development. To condemn a human being to such work is to cultivate the animal quality in him. He grows indifferent, he scorns the impulses and customs which distinguish his kind. He neglects the conveniences and finer pleasures of life, lives in filthy poverty with scanty nourishment, and squanders the rest of his earnings in debauchery.'—Dr J. Kay.

over, and a quarter of the day's wages is withheld, though he loses only two and one-half hours' work out of twelve. He must eat, drink, and sleep at command. For satisfying the most imperative needs, he is vouchsafed the least possible time absolutely required by them. Whether his dwelling is a half-hour or a whole one removed from the factory does not concern his employer. The despotic bell calls him from his bed, his breakfast, his dinner.

What a time he has of it, too, inside the factory! Here the employer is absolute law-giver; he makes regulations at will, changes and adds to his codex at pleasure, and even, if he inserts the craziest stuff, the courts say to the working man: 'You were your own master, no one forced you to agree to such a contract if you did not wish to; but now, when you have freely entered into it, you must be bound by it.' And so the working man only gets into the bargain the mockery of the Justice of the Peace who is a bourgeois himself, and of the law which is made by the bourgeoisie. Such decisions have been given often enough. In October 1844 the operatives of Kennedy's mill, in Manchester, struck. Kennedy prosecuted them on the strength of a regulation placarded in the mill, that at no time more than two operatives in one room may quit work at once. And the court decided in his favour, giving the working men the explanation cited above.[1] And such rules as these usually are! For instance: (1) The doors are closed ten minutes after work begins, and thereafter no one is admitted until the breakfast hour; whoever is absent during this time forfeits 3*d.* per loom. (2) Every power-loom weaver detected absenting himself at another time, while the machinery is in motion, forfeits for each hour and each loom, 3*d.* Every person who leaves the room during working hours, without obtaining permission from the overlooker, forfeits 3*d.* (3) Weavers who fail to supply themselves with scissors forfeit, per day, 1*d.* (4) All broken shuttles, brushes, oil-cans, wheels, window-panes, etc., must be paid for by the weaver. (5) No weaver to stop work without giving a week's notice. The manufacturer may dismiss any employee without notice for bad work or improper behaviour. (6) Every operative detected speaking to

---

[1] *Manchester Guardian*, 30 Oct.

another, singing or whistling, will be fined 6*d.*; for leaving his place during working hours, 6*d.*[1] Another copy of factory regulations lies before me, according to which every operative who comes three minutes too late forfeits the wages for a quarter of an hour, and every one who comes twenty minutes too late, for a quarter of a day. Every one who remains absent until breakfast forfeits 1*s.* on Monday, and 6*d.* every other day of the week, etc., etc. This last is the regulation of the Phoenix Works in Jersey Street, Manchester. It may be said that such rules are necessary in a great, complicated factory, in order to insure the harmonious working of the different parts; it may be asserted that such a severe discipline is as necessary here as in an army. This may be so, but what sort of a social order is it which cannot be maintained without such shameful tyranny? Either the end sanctifies the means, or the inference of the badness of the end from the badness of the means is justified. Everyone who has served as a soldier knows what it is to be subjected even for a short time to military discipline. But these operatives are condemned from their ninth year to their death to live under the sword, physically and mentally. They are worse slaves than the Negroes in America, for they are more sharply watched, and yet it is demanded of them that they shall live like human beings, shall think and feel like men! Verily, this they can do only under glowing hatred towards their oppressors, and towards that order of things which places them in such a position, which degrades them to machines. But it is far more shameful yet, that according to the universal testimony of the operatives, numbers of manufacturers collect the fines imposed upon the operatives with the most heartless severity, and for the purpose of piling up extra profits out of the farthings thus extorted from the impoverished proletarians. Leach asserts, too, that the operatives often find the factory clock moved forward a quarter of an hour and the doors shut, while the clerk moves about with the fines-book inside, noting the many names of the absentees. Leach claims to have counted ninety-five operatives thus shut out, standing before a factory, whose clock was a quarter of an hour slower than the town clocks

[1] *Stubborn Facts*, 9 ff.

at night, and a quarter of an hour faster in the morning. The Factory Report relates similar facts. In one factory the clock was set back during working hours, so that the operatives worked overtime without extra pay; in another, a whole quarter of an hour overtime was worked; in a third, there were two clocks, an ordinary one and a machine clock, which registered the revolutions of the main shaft; if the machinery went slowly, working hours were measured by the machine clock until the number of revolutions due in twelve hours was reached; if work went well, so that the number was reached before the usual working hours were ended, the operatives were forced to toil on to the end of the twelfth hour. The witness adds that he had known girls who had good work, and who had worked overtime, who, nevertheless, betook themselves to a life of prostitution rather than submit to this tyranny.[1] To return to the fines, Leach relates having repeatedly seen women in the last period of pregnancy fined 6*d.* for the offence of sitting down a moment to rest. Fines for bad work are wholly arbitrary; the goods are examined in the wareroom, and the supervisor charges the fines upon a list without even summoning the operative, who only learns that he has been fined when the overlooker pays his wages, and the goods have perhaps been sold, or certainly been placed beyond his reach. Leach has in his possession such a fines list, ten feet long, and amounting to £35 17*s.* 10*d.* He relates that in the factory where this list was made, a new supervisor was dismissed for fining too little, and so bringing in £5 too little weekly.[2] And I repeat that I know Leach to be a thoroughly trustworthy man incapable of a falsehood.

But the operative is his employer's slave in still other respects. If his wife or daughter finds favour in the eyes of the master, a command, a hint suffices, and she must place herself at his disposal. When the employer wishes to supply with signatures a petition in favour of bourgeois interests, he need only send it to his mill. If he wishes to decide a parliamentary election, he sends his enfranchised operatives in rank and file to the polls, and they vote for the bourgeois

[1] Drinkwater Evidence, p. 80.

[2] *Stubborn Facts*, 13–17.

candidate whether they will or no. If he desires a majority in a public meeting, he dismisses them half an hour earlier than usual, and secures them places close to the platform, where he can watch them to his satisfaction.

Two further arrangements contribute especially to force the operative under the dominion of the manufacturer; the Truck system and the Cottage system. The truck system, the payment of the operatives in goods, was formerly universal in England. The manufacturer opens a shop, 'for the convenience of the operatives, and to protect them from the high prices of the petty dealers'. Here goods of all sorts are sold to them on credit; and to keep the operatives from going to the shops where they could get their goods more cheaply—the 'Tommy shops' usually charging 25 to 30 per cent more than others—wages are paid in requisitions on the shop instead of money. The general indignation against this infamous system led to the passage of the Truck Act in 1831, by which, for most employees, payment in truck orders was declared void and illegal, and was made punishable by fine; but, like most other English laws, this has been enforced only here and there. In the towns it is carried out comparatively efficiently; but in the country, the truck system, disguised or undisguised, flourishes. In the town of Leicester, too, it is very common. There lie before me nearly a dozen convictions for this offence, dating from the period between November 1843, and June 1844, and reported, in part, in the *Manchester Guardian* and, in part, in the *Northern Star*. The system is, of course, less openly carried on at present; wages are usually paid in cash, but the employer still has means enough at command to force him to purchase his wares in the truck shop and nowhere else. Hence it is difficult to combat the truck system, because it can now be carried on under cover of the law, provided only that the operative receives his wages in money. The *Northern Star* of 27 April 1844 publishes a letter from an operative of Holmfirth, near Huddersfield, in Yorkshire, which refers to a manufacturer of the name of Bowers, as follows (retranslated from the German):

It is very strange to think that the accursed truck system should exist to such an extent as it does in Holmfirth, and nobody be found who has the pluck to make the manufacturer stop it. There are here a great many honest hand-weavers suffering through this damned system; here is one sample from a good many out of the noble-hearted Free Trade Clique. There is a manufacturer who has upon himself the curses of the whole district on account of his infamous conduct towards his poor weavers; if they have got a piece ready which comes to 34 or 36 shillings, he gives them 20s. in money and the rest in cloth or goods, and 40 to 50 per cent dearer than at the other shops, and often enough the goods are rotten into the bargain. But, what says the Free Trade *Mercury*, the *Leeds Mercury*?[1] They are not bound to take them; they can please themselves. Oh, yes, but they must take them or else starve. If they ask for another 20s. in money, they must wait eight or fourteen days for a warp; but if they take the 20s. and the goods, then there is always a warp ready for them. And that is Free Trade. Lord Brougham said we ought to put by something in our young days, so that we need not go to the parish when we are old. Well, are we to put by the rotten goods? If this did not come from a lord, one would say his brains were as rotten as the goods that our work is paid in. When the unstamped papers came out 'illegally', there was a lot of them to report it to the police in Holmfirth, the Blythes, the Edwards, etc.; but where are they now? But this is different. Our truck manufacturer belongs to the pious Free Trade lot; he goes to church twice every Sunday, and repeats devotedly after the parson: 'We have left undone the things we ought to have done, and we have done the things we ought not to have done, and there is no good in us; but, good Lord, deliver us.' Yes, deliver us till tomorrow, and we will pay our weavers again in rotten goods.

The cottage system looks much more innocent and arose in a much more harmless way, though it has the same enslaving influence upon the employee. In the neighbourhood of the mills in the country, there is often a lack of dwelling accommodation for the operatives. The manufacturer is frequently obliged to build such dwellings and does so gladly, as they yield great advantages, besides the interest upon the capital invested. If any owner of working-men's dwellings averages about 6 per cent on his invested capital, it is safe to calculate that the manufacturer's cottages yield twice this rate; for so long as his factory does not stand perfectly idle he is sure of occupants, and of occupants who pay punctually. He is therefore spared the two chief

[1] *Leeds Mercury*: a radical bourgeois newspaper. (*Note in the German edition.*)

disadvantages under which other house-owners labour; his cottages never stand empty, and he runs no risk. But the rent of the cottages is as high as though these disadvantages were in full force, and by obtaining the same rent as the ordinary house-owner, the manufacturer, at cost of the operatives, makes a brilliant investment at 12 to 14 per cent. For it is clearly unjust that he should make twice as much profit as other competing house-owners, who at the same time are excluded from competing with him. But it implies a double wrong, when he draws his fixed profit from the pockets of the non-possessing class, which must consider the expenditure of every penny. He is used to that, however, he whose whole wealth is gained at the cost of his employees. But this injustice becomes an infamy when the manufacturer, as often happens, forces his operatives, who must occupy his houses on pain of dismissal, to pay a higher rent than the ordinary one, or even to pay rent for houses in which they do not live! The *Halifax Guardian*, quoted by the Liberal *Sun*,[1] asserts that hundreds of operatives in Ashton-under-Lyne, Oldham, and Rochdale, etc., are forced by their employers to pay house-rent whether they occupy the house or not. The cottage system is universal in the country districts; it has created whole villages, and the manufacturer usually has little or no competition against his houses, so that he can fix his price regardless of any market rate, indeed at his pleasure. And what power does the cottage system give the employer over his operatives in disagreements between master and men? If the latter strike, he need only give them notice to quit his premises, and the notice need only be a week; after that time the operative is not only without bread but without a shelter, a vagabond at the mercy of the law which sends him, without fail, to the treadmill.

Such is the factory system sketched as fully as my space permits, and with as little partisan spirit as the heroic deeds of the bourgeoisie against the defenceless workers permit—deeds towards which it is impossible to remain indifferent, towards which indifference were a crime. Let us compare the condition of the free Englishman of 1845 with the Saxon serf under the lash of the Norman barons of 1145. The serf was

---

[1] *Sun*, a London daily; end of Nov. 1844.

glebae adscriptus, bound to the soil, so is the free working man through the cottage system. The serf owed his master the *jus primae noctis*, the right of the first night—the free working man must, on demand, surrender to his master not only that, but the right of every night. The serf could acquire no property; everything that he gained, his master could take from him; the free working man has no property, can gain none by reason of the pressure of competition, and what even the Norman baron did not do, the modern manufacturer does. Through the truck system, he assumes every day the administration in detail of the things which the worker requires for his immediate necessities. The relation of the lord of the soil to the serf was regulated by the prevailing customs and by-laws which were obeyed, because they corresponded to them. The free working-man's relation to his master is regulated by laws which are *not* obeyed, because they correspond neither with the interests of the employer nor with the prevailing customs. The lord of the soil could not separate the serf from the land, nor sell him apart from it, and since almost all the land was fief and there was no capital, practically could not sell him at all. The modern bourgeois forces the working man to sell himself. The serf was the slave of the piece of land on which he was born, the working man is the slave of his own necessaries of life and of the money with which he has to buy them—both are *slaves of a thing*. The serf had a guarantee for the means of subsistence in the feudal order of society in which every member had his own place. The free working man has no guarantee whatsoever, because he has a place in society only when the bourgeoisie can make use of him; in all other cases he is ignored, treated as non-existent. The serf sacrificed himself for his master in war, the factory operative in peace. The lord of the serf was a barbarian who regarded his villein as a head of cattle; the employer of operatives is civilized and regards his 'hand' as a machine. In short, the position of the two is not far from equal, and if either is at a disadvantage, it is the free working man. Slaves they both are, with the single difference that the slavery of the one is undissembled, open, honest; that of the other cunning, sly, disguised, deceitfully concealed from himself and everyone else, a hypocritical servitude worse than the old. The philanthropic Tories were right when they gave the operatives the name white slaves. But the hypocritical disguised slavery recognizes the right to freedom, at least in outward form; bows before a freedom-loving public opinion, and herein lies the historic progress as compared with the old servitude, that the *principle* of freedom is affirmed, and the oppressed will one day see to it that this principle is carried out.

At the close a few stanzas of a poem which voices the sentiments of the workers themselves about the factory system. Written by Edward P. Mead of Birmingham, it is a correct expression of the views prevailing among them.

THE STEAM KING*

There is a King, and a ruthless King,
Not a King of the poet's dream;
But a tyrant fell, white slaves know well,
And that ruthless King is Steam.
 He hath an arm, an iron arm,
 And tho' he hath but one,
 In that mighty arm there is a charm,
 That millions hath undone.
Like the ancient Moloch grim, his sire
In Himmon's vale that stood,
His bowels are of living fire,
And children are his food.
 His priesthood are a hungry band,
 Blood-thirsty, proud, and bold;
 'Tis they direct his giant hand,
 In turning blood to gold.
For filthy gain in their servile chain
All nature's rights they bind;
They mock at lovely woman's pain,
And to manly tears are blind.
 The sighs and groans of Labour's sons
 Are music in their ear,
 And the skeleton shades of lads and maids,
 In the Steam King's Hells appear.
Those hells upon earth, since the Steam King's birth,
Have scatter'd around despair;
For the human mind for Heav'n design'd,
With the body, is murdered there.
 Then down with the King, the Moloch King,
 Ye working millions all;

O chain his hand, or our native land
Is destin'd by him to fall.
And his Satraps abhor'd, each proud Mill Lord,
Now gorg'd with gold and blood,
Must be put down by the nation's frown,
As well as their monster God.[1]

---

[1] I have neither time nor space to deal in detail with the replies of the manufacturers to the charges made against them for twelve years past. These men will not learn because their supposed interest blinds them. As, moreover, many of their objections have been met in the foregoing, the following is all that it is necessary for me to add:

You come to Manchester, you wish to make yourself acquainted with the state of affairs in England. You naturally have good introductions to respectable people. You drop a remark or two as to the condition of the workers. You are made acquainted with a couple of the first Liberal manufacturers, Robert Hyde Greg, perhaps, Edmund Ashworth, Thomas Ashton, or others. They are told of your wishes. The manufacturer understands you, knows what he has to do. He accompanies you to his factory in the country; Mr Greg to Quarrybank in Cheshire, Mr Ashworth to Turton near Bolton, Mr Ashton to Hyde. He leads you through a superb, admirably arranged building, perhaps supplied with ventilators, he calls your attention to the lofty, airy rooms, the fine machinery, here and there a healthy looking operative. He gives you an excellent lunch, and proposes to you to visit the operatives' homes; he conducts you to the cottages, which look new, clean, and neat, and goes with you into this one and that one, naturally only to overlookers, mechanics, etc., so that you may see 'families who live wholly from the factory'. Among other families you might find that only wife and children work, and the husband darns stockings. The presence of the employer keeps you from asking indiscreet questions; you find every one well paid, comfortable, comparatively healthy by reason of the country air; you begin to be converted from your exaggerated ideas of misery and starvation. But, that the cottage system makes slaves of the operatives, that there may be a truck shop in the neighbourhood, that the people hate the manufacturer, this they do not point out to you, because he is present. He has built a school, church, reading-room, etc. That he uses the school to train children to subordination, that he tolerates in the reading-room such prints only as represent the interests of the bourgeoisie, that he dismisses his employees if they read Chartist or Socialist papers or books, this is all concealed from you. You see an easy, patriarchal relation, you see the life of the overlookers, you see what the bourgeoisie *promises* the workers if they become its slaves, mentally and morally. This 'country manufacture' has always been what the employers like to show, because in it the disadvantages of the factory system, especially from the point of view of health, are, in part, done away with by the free air and surroundings, and because the patriarchal servitude of the workers can here be longest maintained. Dr Ure sings a dithyramb upon the theme. But woe to the operatives to whom it occurs to think for themselves and become Chartists! For them the paternal affection of the manufacturer comes to a sudden end. Further, if you should wish to be accompanied through the working-people's quarters of Manchester, if you should desire to see the development of the factory system in a factory town, you may wait long before these rich bourgeoisie will help you! These gentlemen do not know in what condition their employees are nor what they want, and they dare not know things which would make them uneasy or even oblige them to act in opposition to their own interests. But, fortunately, that is of no consequence: what the working men have to carry out, they carry out for themselves.

7

The Remaining Branches of Industry

WE were compelled to deal with the factory system somewhat at length, as it is an entirely novel creation of the
industrial period; we shall be able to treat the other workers
the more briefly, because what has been said either of the
industrial proletariat in general, or of the factory system in
particular, will wholly, or in part, apply to them. We shall,
therefore, merely have to record how far the factory system
has succeeded in forcing its way into each branch of industry, and what other peculiarities these may reveal.

The four branches comprised under the Factory Act are
engaged in the production of clothing stuffs. We shall do
best if we deal next with those workers who receive their
materials from these factories; and, first of all, with the
stocking weavers of Nottingham, Derby, and Leicester.
Touching these workers, the Children's Employment Commission reports that the long working hours, imposed by low
wages, with a sedentary life and the strain upon the eyes
involved in the nature of the employment, usually enfeeble
the whole frame, and especially the eyes. Work at night
is impossible without a very powerful light produced by
concentrating the rays of the lamp, making them pass
through glass globes, which is most injurious to the sight. At
40 years of age, nearly all wear spectacles. The children
employed at spooling and hemming usually suffer grave
injuries to the health and constitution. They work from the
sixth, seventh, or eighth year ten to twelve hours daily in
small, close rooms. It is not uncommon for them to faint at
their work, to become too feeble for the most ordinary
household occupation, and so near-sighted as to be obliged
to wear glasses during childhood. Many were found by the
commissioners to exhibit all the symptoms of a scrofulous
constitution, and the manufacturers usually refuse to employ
girls who have worked in this way as being too weak. The
condition of these children is characterized as 'a disgrace to a
Christian country', and the wish expressed for legislative

interference. The Factory Report[1] adds that the stocking weavers are the worst paid workers in Leicester, earning 6s., or with great effort, 7s. a week, for sixteen to eighteen hours' daily work. Formerly they earned 20s. to 21s., but the introduction of enlarged frames has ruined their business; the great majority still work with old, small, single frames, and compete with difficulty with the progress of machinery. Here, too, every progress is a disadvantage for the workers. Nevertheless, Commissioner Power speaks of the pride of the stocking weavers that they are free, and have no factory bell to measure out the time for their eating, sleeping, and working. Their position today is no better than in 1833, when the Factory Commission made the foregoing statements; the competition of the Saxon stocking weavers, who have scarcely anything to eat, takes care of that. This competition is too strong for the English in nearly all foreign markets, and for the lower qualities of goods even in the English market. It must be a source of rejoicing for the patriotic German stocking weaver that his starvation wages force his English brother to starve too! And, verily, will he not starve on, proud and happy, for the greater glory of German industry, since the honour of the Fatherland demands that his table should be bare, his dish half-empty? Ah! it is a noble thing this competition, this 'race of the nations'. In the *Morning Chronicle*, another Liberal sheet, the organ of the bourgeoisie *par excellence*, there were published some letters from a stocking weaver in Hinckley, describing the condition of his fellow-workers. Among other things, he reports 50 families, 321 persons, who were supported by 109 frames; each frame yielded on an average 5s.; each family earned an average of 11s. 4d. weekly. Out of this there was required for house-rent, frame rent, fuel, light, soap, and needles, together 5s. 10d., so that there remained for food, per head daily, 1½d., and for clothing nothing. 'No eye', says the stocking weaver, 'has seen, no ear heard, and no heart felt the half of the sufferings that these poor people endure.' Beds were wanting either wholly or in part, the children ran about ragged and barefoot; the men said, with tears in their eyes: 'It's a long time since we had any meat;

---

[1] Grainger Report. Appendix, Part I, p. F 15. §§ 132–42.

we have almost forgotten how it tastes'; and, finally, some of them worked on Sunday, though public opinion pardons anything else more readily than this, and the rattling noise of the frame is audible throughout the neighbourhood. 'But', said one of them, 'look at my children and ask no questions. My poverty forces me to it; I can't and won't hear my children forever crying for bread, without trying the last means of winning it honestly. Last Monday I got up at two in the morning and worked to near midnight; the other days from six in the morning to between eleven and twelve at night. I have had enough of it; I shan't kill myself; so now I go to bed at ten o'clock, and make up the lost time on Sundays.' Neither in Leicester, Nottingham, nor Derby have wages risen since 1833; and the worst of it is that in Leicester the truck system prevails to a great extent, as I have mentioned. It is, therefore, not to be wondered at that the weavers of this region take a very active part in all working-men's movements, the more active and effective because the frames are worked chiefly by men.

In this stocking weavers' district the lace industry also has its headquarters. In the three counties mentioned there are in all 2,760 lace frames in use, while in all the rest of England there are but 786. The manufacture of lace is greatly complicated by a rigid division of labour, and embraces a multitude of branches. The yarn is first spooled by girls 14 years of age and upwards, winders; then the spools are set up on the frames by boys, 8 years old and upwards, threaders, who pass the thread through fine openings, of which each machine has an average of 1,800, and bring it towards its destination; then the weaver weaves the lace which comes out of the machine like a broad piece of cloth and is taken apart by very little children who draw out the connecting threads. This is called running or drawing lace, and the children themselves lace-runners. The lace is then made ready for sale. The winders, like the threaders, have no specified working-time, being called upon whenever the spools on a frame are empty, and are liable, since the weavers work at night, to be required at any time in the factory or workroom. This irregularity, the frequent night-work, the disorderly way of living consequent upon it, engender a multitude of physical and moral ills, especially early and unbridled sexual licence, upon which point all witnesses are unanimous. The work is very bad for the eyes, and although a permanent injury in the case of the threaders is not universally observable, inflammations of the eye, pain, tears, and momentary uncertainty of vision during the act of threading are engendered. For the winders, however, it is certain that their work seriously affects the eye, and produces, besides the frequent inflammations of the cornea, many cases of amaurosis and cataract. The work of the weavers themselves is very difficult, as the frames have constantly been made wider, until those now in use are almost all worked by three men in turn, each working eight hours, and the frame being kept in use the whole twenty-four. Hence it is that the winders and threaders are so often called upon during the night, and must work to prevent the frame from standing idle. The filling in of 1,800 openings with thread occupies three children at least two hours. Many frames are moved by steam-power, and the work of men thus superseded; and, as the Children's Employment Commission's Report mentions only lace factories to which the children are summoned, it seems to follow either that the work of the weavers has been removed to great factory rooms of late, or that steam-weaving has become pretty general; a forward movement of the factory system in either case. Most unwholesome of all is the work of the runners, who are usually children of 7, and even of 5 and 4, years old. Commissioner Grainger actually found one child of 2 years old employed at this work. Following a thread which is to be withdrawn by a needle from an intricate texture, is very bad for the eyes, especially when, as is usually the case, the work is continued fourteen to sixteen hours. In the least unfavourable case, aggravated near-sightedness follows; in the worst case, which is frequent enough, incurable blindness from amaurosis. But, apart from that, the children, in consequence of sitting perpetually bent up, become feeble, narrow-chested, and scrofulous from bad digestion. Disordered functions of the uterus are almost universal among the girls, and curvature of the spine also, so that 'all the runners may be recognized from their gait'. The same consequences for the eyes and the whole constitution are produced by the embroidery of lace. Medical witnesses are unanimously of the opinion that the health of all children employed in the production of lace suffers seriously, that they are pale, weak, delicate, undersized, and much less able than other children to resist disease. The affections from which they usually suffer are general debility, frequent fainting, pains in the head, sides, back, and hips, palpitation of the heart, nausea, vomiting and want of appetite, curvature of the spine, scrofula, and consumption. The health of the female lacemakers especially, is constantly and deeply undermined; complaints are universal of anaemia, difficult child-birth, and miscarriage.[1] The same subordinate official of the Children's Employment Commission reports further that the children are very often ill-clothed and ragged, and receive insufficient food, usually only bread and tea, often no meat for months together. As to their moral condition, he reports:[2]

All the inhabitants of Nottingham, the police, the clergy, the manufacturers, the working-people, and the parents of the children are all unanimously of opinion that the present system of labour is a most fruitful source of immorality. The threaders, chiefly boys, and the winders, usually girls, are called for in the factory at the same time; and as their parents cannot know how long they are wanted there, they have the finest opportunity to form improper connections and remain together after the close of the work. This has contributed, in no small degree, to the immorality which, according to general opinion, exists to a terrible extent in Nottingham. Apart from this, the quiet of home life, and the comfort of the family to which these children and young people belong, is wholly sacrificed to this most unnatural state of things.

Another branch of lace-making, bobbin-lacework, is carried on in the agricultural shires of Northampton, Oxford, and Bedford, chiefly by children and young persons, who complain universally of bad food, and rarely taste meat. The employment itself is most unwholesome. The children work in small, ill-ventilated, damp rooms, sitting always bent over the lace cushion. To support the body in this wearying position, the girls wear stays with a wooden busk, which, at the tender age of most of them, when the bones are still very soft, wholly displace the ribs, and make narrow chests

[1] Grainger's whole Report.
[2] Grainger Children's Employment Commission's Report.

universal. They usually die of consumption after suffering the severest forms of digestive disorders, brought on by sedentary work in a bad atmosphere. They are almost wholly without education, least of all do they receive moral training. They love finery, and in consequence of these two influences their moral condition is most deplorable, and prostitution almost epidemic among them.[1]

This is the price at which society purchases for the fine ladies of the bourgeoisie the pleasure of wearing lace; a reasonable price truly! Only a few thousand blind working men, some consumptive labourers' daughters, a sickly generation of the vile multitude bequeathing its debility to its equally 'vile' children and children's children. But what does that come to? Nothing, nothing whatsoever! Our English bourgeoisie will lay the report of the Government Commission aside indifferently, and wives and daughters will deck themselves with lace as before. It is a beautiful thing, the composure of an English bourgeois.

A great number of operatives are employed in the cotton-printing establishments of Lancashire, Derbyshire, and the West of Scotland. In no branch of English industry has mechanical ingenuity produced such brilliant results as here, but in no other has it so crushed the workers. The application of engraved cylinders driven by steam-power, and the discovery of a method of printing four to six colours at once with such cylinders, has as completely superseded hand-work as did the application of machinery to the spinning and weaving of cotton, and these new arrangements in the printing-works have superseded the hand-workers much more than was the case in the production of the fabrics. One man, with the assistance of one child, now does with a machine the work done formerly by 200 block printers; a single machine yields 28 yards of printed cloth per minute. The calico printers are in a very bad way in consequence; the shires of Lancaster, Derby, and Chester produced (according to a petition of the printers to the House of Commons), in the year 1842, 11,000,000 pieces of printed cotton goods: of these, 100,000 were printed by hand exclusively, 900,000 in part with machinery and in part

[1] Burns, Children's Employment Commission's Report.

by hand, and 10,000,000 by machinery alone, with four to six colours. As the machinery is chiefly new and undergoes constant improvement, the number of hand-printers is far too great for the available quantity of work, and many of them are therefore starving; the petition puts the number at one-quarter of the whole, while the rest are employed but one or two, in the best case three days in the week, and are ill-paid. Leach[1] asserts of one print-works (Deeply Dale, near Bury, in Lancashire), that the hand-printers did not earn on an average more than 5s., though he knows that the machine-printers were pretty well paid. The print-works are thus wholly affiliated with the factory system, but without being subject to the legislative restrictions placed upon it. They produce an article subject to fashion, and have therefore no regular work. If they have small orders, they work half-time; if they make a hit with a pattern, and business is brisk, they work till ten or twelve o'clock, perhaps even all night. In the neighbourhood of my home, near Manchester, there was a print-works that was often lighted when I returned late at night; and I have heard that the children were obliged at times to work so long there, that they would try to catch a moment's rest and sleep on the stone steps and in the corners of the lobby. I have no legal proof of the truth of the statement, or I should name the firm. The Report of the Children's Employment Commission is very cursory upon this subject, stating merely that in England, at least, the children are mostly pretty well clothed and fed (relatively, according to the wages of the parents), that they receive no education whatsoever, and are morally on a low plane. It is only necessary to remember that these children are subject to the factory system, and then, referring the reader to what has already been said of that, we can pass on.

Of the remaining workers employed in the manufacture of clothing stuffs little remains to be said; the bleachers' work is very unwholesome, obliging them to breathe chlorine, a gas injurious to the lungs. The work of the dyers is in many cases very healthful, since it requires the exertion of the whole body; how these workers are paid is little known, and this is

[1] Leach, *Stubborn Facts from the Factories*, 47.

ground enough for the inference that they do not receive less than the average wages, otherwise they would make complaint. The fustian cutters, who, in consequence of the large consumption of cotton velvet, are comparatively numerous, being estimated at from 3,000 to 4,000, have suffered very severely, indirectly, from the influence of the factory system. The goods formerly woven with hand-looms, were not perfectly uniform, and required a practised hand in cutting the single rows of threads. Since power-looms have been used, the rows run regularly; each thread of the weft is exactly parallel with the preceding one, and cutting is no longer an art. The workers thrown out of employment by the introduction of machinery turn to fustian cutting, and force down wages by their competition; the manufacturers discovered that they could employ women and children, and the wages sank to the rate paid them, while hundreds of men were thrown out of employment. The manufacturers found that they could get the work done in the factory itself more cheaply than in the cutters' workroom, for which they indirectly paid the rent. Since this discovery, the low upper-storey cutters' rooms stand empty in many a cottage, or are let for dwellings, while the cutter has lost his freedom of choice of his working hours, and is brought under the dominion of the factory bell. A cutter of perhaps 45 years of age told me that he could remember a time when he had received 8*d.* a yard for work, for which he now received 1*d.*; true, he can cut the more regular texture more quickly than the old, but he can by no means do twice as much in an hour as formerly, so that his wages have sunk to less than a quarter of what they were. Leach[1] gives a list of wages paid in 1827 and in 1843 for various goods, from which it appears that articles paid in 1827 at the rates of 4*d.*, 2¼*d.*, 2¾*d.*, and 1*d.* per yard, were paid in 1843 at the rate of 1½*d.*, 1*d.*, ¾*d.*, and ⅜*d.* per yard, cutters' wages. The average weekly wage, according to Leach, was as follows: 1827, £1 6*s.* 6*d.*; £1 2*s.* 6*d.*; £1; £1 6*s.* 6*d.*; and for the same goods in 1843, 10*s.* 6*d.*; 7*s.* 6*d.*; 6*s.* 8*d.*; 10*s.*; while there are hundreds of workers who cannot find employment even at these last named rates. Of the handweavers of the cotton

---

[1] Leach, *Stubborn Facts from the Factories*, 35.

industry we have already spoken; the other woven fabrics are almost exclusively produced on hand-looms. Here most of the workers have suffered as the fustian cutters have done from the crowding in of competitors displaced by machinery, and are, moreover, subject like the factory operatives to a severe fine system for bad work. Take, for instance, the silk weavers. Mr Brocklehurst, one of the largest silk manufacturers in all England, laid before a committee of Members of Parliament lists taken from his books, from which it appears that for goods for which he paid wages in 1821 at the rate of 30s., 14s., 3s. 6d., 9d., 1s. 6d., 10s., he paid in 1831 but 9s., 7s. 3d., 2s. 3d., 4d., 6d., 6s. 3d., while in this case no improvement in the machinery has taken place. But what Mr Brocklehurst does may very well be taken as a standard for all. From the same lists it appears that the average weekly wage of his weavers, after all deductions, was, in 1821, 16s. 6d., and, in 1831, but 6s. Since that time wages have fallen still further. Goods which brought in 4d. weavers' wages in 1831, bring in but 2½d. in 1843 (single sarsenets), and a great number of weavers in the country can get work only when they undertake these goods at 1½d.–2d. Moreover, they are subject to arbitrary deductions from their wages. Every weaver who receives materials is given a card, on which is usually to be read that the work is to be returned at a specified hour of the day; that a weaver who cannot work by reason of illness must make the fact known at the office within three days, or sickness will not be regarded as an excuse; that it will not be regarded as a sufficient excuse if the weaver claims to have been obliged to wait for yarn; that for certain faults in the work (if, for example, more weft-threads are found within a given space than are prescribed), not less than half the wages will be deducted; and that if the goods should not be ready at the time specified, one penny will be deducted for every yard returned. The deductions in accordance with these cards are so considerable that, for instance, a man who comes twice a week to Leigh, in Lancashire, to gather up woven goods, brings his employer at least £15 fines every time. He asserts this himself, and he is regarded as one of the most lenient. Such things were formerly settled by arbitration; but as the workers were usually dismissed if they insisted upon that, the custom has been almost wholly abandoned, and the manufacturer acts arbitrarily as prosecutor, witness, judge, lawgiver, and executive in one person. And if the workman goes to a Justice of the Peace, the answer is: 'When you accepted your card you entered upon a contract, and you must abide by it.' The case is the same as that of the factory operatives. Besides, the employer obliges the workman to sign a document in which he declares that he agrees to the deductions made. And if a workman rebels, all the manufacturers in the town know at once that he is a man who, as Leach says,[1] 'resists the lawful order as established by weavers' cards, and, moreover, has the impudence to doubt the wisdom of those who are, as he ought to know, his superiors in society'. Naturally, the workers are perfectly free; the manufacturer does not force them to take his materials and his cards, but he says to them what Leach translates into plain English with the words: 'If you don't like to be frizzled in my frying-pan, you can take a walk into the fire.'

The silk weavers of London, and especially of Spitalfields, have lived in periodic distress for a long time, and that they still have no cause to be satisfied with their lot is proved by their taking a most active part in English labour movements in general, and in London ones in particular. The distress prevailing among them gave rise to the fever which broke out in East London, and called forth the Commission for Investigating the Sanitary Condition of the Labouring Class. But the last report of the London Fever Hospital shows that this disease is still raging.

After the textile fabrics, by far the most important products of English industry are the metal-wares. This trade has its headquarters at Birmingham, where the finer metal goods of all sorts are produced, at Sheffield for cutlery, and in Staffordshire, especially at Wolverhampton, where the coarser articles, locks, nails, etc., are manufactured. In describing the position of the workers employed in these trades, let us begin with Birmingham. The disposition of the work has retained in Birmingham, as in most places where metals are wrought, something of the old handicraft character; the small employers are still to be found, who work with their apprentices in the shop at home, or when

[1] *Stubborn Facts*, 37–40.

they need steam-power, in great factory buildings which are divided into little shops, each rented to a small employer, and supplied with a shaft moved by the engine, and furnishing motive power for the machinery. Léon Faucher, author of a series of articles in the *Revue des deux Mondes*, which at least betray study, and are better than what has hitherto been written upon the subject by Englishmen or Germans, characterizes this relation in contrast with the manufacture of Lancashire and Yorkshire as 'Démocratie industrielle', and observes that it produces no very favourable results for master or men. This observation is perfectly correct, for the many small employers cannot well subsist on the profit divided amongst them, determined by competition, a profit under other circumstances absorbed by a single manufacturer. The centralizing tendency of capital holds them down. For one who grows rich ten are ruined, and a hundred placed at a greater disadvantage than ever, by the pressure of the one upstart who can afford to sell more cheaply than they. And in the cases where they have to compete from the beginning against great capitalists, it is self-evident that they can only toil along with the greatest difficulty. The apprentices are, as we shall see, quite as badly off under the small employers as under the manufacturers, with the single difference that they, in turn, may become small employers, and so attain a certain independence—that is to say, they are at best less directly exploited by the bourgeoisie than under the factory system. Thus these small employers are neither genuine proletarians, since they live in part upon the work of their apprentices, nor genuine bourgeois, since their principal means of support is their own work. This peculiar midway position of the Birmingham iron-workers is to blame for their having so rarely joined wholly and unreservedly in the English labour movements. Birmingham is a politically radical, but not a Chartist, town. There are, however, numerous larger factories belonging to capitalists; and in these the factory system reigns supreme. The division of labour, which is here carried out to the last detail (in the needle industry, for example), and the use of steam-power, admit of the employment of a great multitude of women and children, and we find here[1] precisely the same features

---

[1] Children's Employment Commission's Report.

reappearing which the Factories' Report presented—the work of women up to the hour of confinement, incapacity as housekeepers, neglect of home and children, indifference, actual dislike to family life, and demoralization; further, the crowding out of men from employment, the constant improvement of machinery, early emancipation of children, husbands supported by their wives and children, etc., etc. The children are described as half-starved and ragged, the half of them are said not to know what it is to have enough to eat, many of them get nothing to eat before the midday meal, or even live the whole day upon a penny-worth of bread for a noonday meal—there were actually cases in which children received no food from eight in the morning until seven at night. Their clothing is very often scarcely sufficient to cover their nakedness, many are barefoot even in winter. Hence they are all small and weak for their age, and rarely develop with any degree of vigour. And when we reflect that with these insufficient means of reproducing the physical forces, hard and protracted work in close rooms is required of them, we cannot wonder that there are few adults in Birmingham fit for military service. 'The workingmen', says a recruiting surgeon, 'are small, delicate, and of very slight physical power; many of them deformed, too, in the chest or spinal column.' According to the assertion of a recruiting sergeant, the people of Birmingham are smaller than those anywhere else, being usually 5 feet 4 to 5 inches tall; out of 613 recruits, but 238 were found fit for service. As to education, a series of depositions and specimens taken from the metal districts have already been given,[1] to which the reader is referred. It appears further, from the Children's Employment Commission's Report, that in Birmingham more than half the children between 5 and 15 years attend no school whatsoever, that those who do are constantly changing, so that it is impossible to give them any training of an enduring kind, and that they are all withdrawn from school very early and set to work. The report makes it clear what sort of teachers are employed. One teacher, in answer to the question whether she gave moral instruction, said, No, for threepence a week school fees that was too much to

<hr />

[1] See pp. 123–4 above.

require; several others did not even understand this question and still others did not consider this part of their duty. One of the teachers said that she gave no moral instruction but that she took a great deal of trouble to instil good principles into the children. (And she made a decided slip in her English in saying it.) In the schools the commissioner found constant noise and disorder. The moral state of the children is in the highest degree deplorable. Half of all the criminals are children under 15, and in a single year ninety 10-year-old offenders, among them forty-four serious criminal cases, were sentenced. Unbridled sexual intercourse seems, according to the opinion of the commissioner, almost universal, and that at a very early age.[1]

In the iron district of Staffordshire the state of things is still worse. For the coarse wares made here neither much division of labour (with certain exceptions) nor steampower or machinery can be applied. In Wolverhampton, Willenhall, Bilston, Sedgeley, Wednesfield, Darlaston, Dudley, Walsall, Wednesbury, etc., there are, therefore, fewer factories, but chiefly single forges, where the small masters work alone, or with one or more apprentices, who serve them until reaching the twenty-first year. The small employers are in about the same situation as those of Birmingham; but the apprentices, as a rule, are much worse off. They get almost exclusively meat from diseased animals or such as have died a natural death, or tainted meat, or fish to eat, with veal from calves killed too young, and pork from swine smothered during transportation, and such food is furnished not by small employers only, but by large manufacturers, who employ from thirty to forty apprentices. The custom seems to be universal in Wolverhampton, and its natural consequence is frequent bowel complaints and other diseases. Moreover, the children usually do not get enough to eat, and have rarely other clothing than their working rags, for which reason, if for no other, they cannot go to Sunday school. The dwellings are bad and filthy, often so much so that they give rise to disease; and in spite of the not materially unhealthy work, the children are puny, weak, and, in many cases, severely crippled. In Willenhall, for instance, there are countless

[1] Grainger Report and Evidence.

persons who have, from perpetually filing at the lathe, crooked backs and one leg crooked, 'hind-leg' as they call it, so that the two legs have the form of a K; while it is said that more than one-third of the working men there are ruptured. Here, as well as in Wolverhampton, numberless cases were found of retarded puberty among girls (for girls, too, work at the forges), as well as among boys, extending even to the nineteenth year. In Sedgeley and its surrounding district, where nails form almost the sole product, the nailers live and work in the most wretched stable-like huts, which for filth can scarcely be equalled. Girls and boys work from the tenth or twelfth year, and are accounted fully skilled only when they make a thousand nails a day. For twelve hundred nails the pay is 5¾d. Every nail receives twelve blows, and since the hammer weighs 1¼ pounds, the nailer must lift 18,000 pounds to earn this miserable pay. With this hard work and insufficient food, the children inevitably develop ill-formed, undersized frames, and the commissioners' depositions confirm this. As to the state of education in this district, data have already been furnished in the foregoing chapters. It is upon an incredibly low plane; half the children do not even go to Sunday school, and the other half go irregularly; very few, in comparison with the other districts, can read, and in the matter of writing the case is much worse. Naturally, for between the seventh and tenth years, just when they are beginning to get some good out of going to school, they are set to work, and the Sunday school teachers, smiths or miners, frequently cannot read, and write their names with difficulty. The prevailing morals correspond with these means of education. In Willenhall, Commissioner Horne asserts, and supplies ample proofs of his assertion, that there exists absolutely no moral sense among the workers. In general, he found that the children neither recognized duties to their parents nor felt any affection for them. They were so little capable of thinking of what they said, so stolid, so hopelessly stupid, that they often asserted that they were well treated, were coming on famously, when they were forced to work twelve to fourteen hours, were clad in rags, did not get enough to eat, and were beaten so that they felt it several days afterwards. They knew nothing of a different kind of life than that in which they toil from morning until they are allowed to stop at night, and did not even understand the question never heard before, whether they were tired.[1]

In Sheffield wages are better, and the external state of the workers also. On the other hand, certain branches of work are to be noticed here, because of their extraordinarily injurious influence upon health. Certain operations require the constant pressure of tools against the chest, and engender consumption in many cases; others, file-cutting among them, retard the general development of the body and produce digestive disorders; bone-cutting for knife handles brings with it headache, biliousness, and among girls, of whom many are employed, anaemia. By far the most unwholesome work is the grinding of knife-blades and forks, which, especially when done with a dry stone, entails certain early death. The unwholesomeness of this work lies in part in the bent posture, in which chest and stomach are cramped; but especially in the quantity of sharp-edged metal dust particles freed in the cutting, which fill the atmosphere, and are necessarily inhaled. The dry grinders' average life is hardly 35 years, the wet grinders' rarely exceeds 45. Dr Knight, in Sheffield, says:

I can convey some idea of the injuriousness of this occupation only by asserting that the hardest drinkers among the grinders are the longest lived among them, because they are longest and oftenest absent from their work. There are, in all, some 2,500 grinders in Sheffield. About 150 (80 men and 70 boys) are fork grinders; these die between the twenty-eighth and thirty-second years of age. The razor grinders, who grind wet as well as dry, die between forty and forty-five years, and the table cutlery grinders, who grind wet, die between the fortieth and fiftieth year.

The same physician gives the following description of the course of the disease called grinders' asthma:

They usually begin their work with the fourteenth year, and, if they have good constitutions, rarely notice any symptoms before the twentieth year. Then the symptoms of their peculiar disease appear. They suffer from shortness of breath at the slightest effort in going up hill or up stairs, they habitually raise the shoulders to relieve the permanent and increasing want of breath; they bend forward, and seem, in general, to feel most comfortable in the crouching position

---

[1] Horne Report and Evidence.

in which they work. Their complexion becomes dirty yellow, their features express anxiety, they complain of pressure upon the chest. Their voices become rough and hoarse, they cough loudly, and the sound is as if air were driven through a wooden tube. From time to time they expectorate considerable quantities of dust, either mixed with phlegm or in balls or cylindrical masses, with a thin coating of mucus. Spitting blood, inability to lie down, night sweat, colliquative diarrhoea, unusual loss of flesh, and all the usual symptoms of consumption of the lungs finally carry them off, after they have lingered months, or even years, unfit to support themselves or those dependent upon them. I must add that all attempts which have hitherto been made to prevent grinders' asthma, or to cure it, have wholly failed.

All this Knight wrote ten years ago; since then the number of grinders and the violence of the disease have increased, though attempts have been made to prevent it by covered grindstones and carrying off the dust by artificial draught. These methods have been at least partially successful, but the grinders do not desire their adoption, and have even destroyed the contrivance here and there, in the belief that more workers may be attracted to the business and wages thus reduced; they are for a short life and a merry one. Dr Knight has often told grinders who came to him with the first symptoms of asthma that a return to grinding means certain death, but with no avail. He who is once a grinder falls into despair, as though he had sold himself to the devil. Education in Sheffield is upon a very low plane. A clergyman, who had occupied himself largely with the statistics of education, was of the opinion that of 16,500 children of the working class who are in a position to attend school, scarcely 6,500 can read. This comes of the fact that the children are taken from school in the seventh, and, at the very latest, in the twelfth year, and that the teachers are good for nothing; one was a convicted thief who found no other way of supporting himself after being released from jail than teaching school! Immorality among young people seems to be more prevalent in Sheffield than anywhere else. It is hard to tell which town ought to have the prize, and in reading the report one believes of each one that this certainly deserves it! The younger generation spend the whole of Sunday lying in the street tossing coins or fighting dogs, go regularly to the gin palace, where they sit with their sweethearts until late at night, when they take walks in solitary couples. In an alehouse which the commissioner visited, there sat forty to fifty young people of both sexes, nearly all under 17 years of age, and each lad beside his lass. Here and there cards were played, at other places dancing was going on, and everywhere drinking. Among the company were openly avowed professional prostitutes. No wonder, then, that, as all the witnesses testify, early, unbridled sexual intercourse, youthful prostitution, beginning with persons of 14 to 15 years, is extraordinarily frequent in Sheffield. Crimes of a savage and desperate sort are of common occurrence; one year before the commissioner's visit, a band, consisting chiefly of young persons, was arrested when about to set fire to the town, being fully equipped with lances and inflammable substances. We shall see later that the labour movement in Sheffield has this same savage character.[1]

Besides these two main centres of the metal industry, there are needle factories in Warrington, Lancashire, where great want, immorality, and ignorance prevail among the workers, and especially among the children; and a number of nail forges in the neighbourhood of Wigan, in Lancashire, and in the east of Scotland. The reports from these latter districts tell almost precisely the same story as those of Staffordshire. There is one more branch of this industry carried on in the factory districts, especially in Lancashire, the essential peculiarity of which is the production of machinery by machinery, whereby the workers crowded out elsewhere, are deprived of their last refuge, the creation of the very enemy which supersedes them. Machinery for planing and boring, cutting screws, wheels, nuts, etc., with power lathes, has thrown out of employment a multitude of men who formerly found regular work at good wages; and whoever wishes to do so may see crowds of them in Manchester.

North of the iron district of Staffordshire lies an industrial region to which we shall now turn our attention, the Potteries, whose headquarters are in the borough of Stoke, embracing Henley, Burslem, Lane End, Lane Delph, Etruria, Coleridge, Langport, Tunstall, and Golden Hill, containing

---

[1] Symons Report and Evidence.

together 60,000 inhabitants. The Children's Employment Commission reports upon this subject that in some branches of this industry, in the production of stoneware, the children have light employment in warm, airy rooms; in others, on the contrary, hard, wearing labour is required, while they receive neither sufficient food nor good clothing. Many children complain: 'Don't get enough to eat, get mostly potatoes with salt, never meat, never bread, don't go to school, haven't got no clothes.' 'Haven't got nothin' to eat today for dinner, don't never have dinner at home, get mostly potatoes and salt, sometimes bread.' 'This is all the clothes I have, no Sunday suit at home.' Among the children whose work is especially injurious are the mould-runners, who have to carry the moulded article with the form to the drying-room, and afterwards bring back the empty form, when the article is properly dried. Thus they must go to and fro the whole day, carrying burdens heavy in proportion to their age, while the high temperature in which they have to do this increases very considerably the exhaustiveness of the work. These children, with scarcely a single exception, are lean, pale, feeble, stunted; nearly all suffer from stomach troubles, nausea, want of appetite, and many of them die of consumption. Almost as delicate are the boys called 'jiggers', from the 'jigger' wheel which they turn. But by far the most injurious is the work of those who dip the finished article into a fluid containing great quantities of lead, and often of arsenic, or have to take the freshly dipped article up with the hand. The hands and clothing of these workers, adults and children, are always wet with this fluid, the skin softens and falls off under the constant contact with rough objects, so that the fingers often bleed, and are constantly in a state most favourable for the absorption of this dangerous substance. The consequence is violent pain, and serious disease of the stomach and intestines, obstinate constipation, colic, sometimes consumption, and, most common of all, epilepsy among children. Among men, partial paralysis of the hand muscles, colica pictonum, and paralysis of whole limbs are ordinary phenomena. One witness relates that two children who worked with him died of convulsions at their work; another who had helped with the dipping two years while a boy, relates that he had violent pains in the bowels at first, then convulsions, in consequence of which he was confined to his bed two months, since when the attacks of convulsions have increased in frequency, are now daily, accompanied often by ten to twenty epileptic fits, his right arm is paralysed, and the physicians tell him that he can never regain the use of his limbs. In one factory were found in the dipping-house four men, all epileptic and afflicted with severe colic, and eleven boys, several of whom were already epileptic. In short, this frightful disease follows this occupation universally: and that, too, to the greater pecuniary profit of the bourgeoisie! In the rooms in which the stoneware is scoured, the atmosphere is filled with pulverized flint, the breathing of which is as injurious as that of the steel dust among the Sheffield grinders. The workers lose breath, cannot lie down, suffer from sore throat and violent coughing, and come to have so feeble a voice that they can scarcely be heard. They, too, all die of consumption. In the Potteries district, the schools are said to be comparatively numerous, and to offer the children opportunities for instruction; but as the latter are so early set to work for twelve hours and often more per day, they are not in a position to avail themselves of the schools, so that three-fourths of the children examined by the commissioner could neither read nor write, while the whole district is plunged in the deepest ignorance. Children who have attended Sunday school for years could not tell one letter from another, and the moral and religious education, as well as the intellectual, is on a very low plane.[1]

In the manufacture of glass, too, work occurs which seems little injurious to men, but cannot be endured by children. The hard labour, the irregularity of the hours, the frequent nightwork, and especially the great heat of the working place (100 to 130 Fahrenheit), engender in children general debility and disease, stunted growth, and especially affections of the eye, bowel complaint, and rheumatic and bronchial affections. Many of the children are pale, have red eyes, often blind for weeks at a time, suffer from violent nausea,

[1] Scriven Report and Evidence.

vomiting, coughs, colds, and rheumatism. When the glass is withdrawn from the fire, the children must often go into such heat that the boards on which they stand catch fire under their feet. The glass-blowers usually die young of debility and chest affections.[1]

As a whole, this report testifies to the gradual but sure introduction of the factory system into all branches of industry, recognizable especially by the employment of women and children. I have not thought it necessary to trace in every case the progress of machinery and the superseding of men as workers. Everyone who is in any degree acquainted with the nature of manufacture can fill this out for himself, while space fails me to describe in detail an aspect of our present system of production, the result of which I have already sketched in dealing with the factory system. In all directions machinery is being introduced, and the last trace of the working man's independence thus destroyed. In all directions the family is being dissolved by the labour of wife and children, or inverted by the husband's being thrown out of employment and made dependent upon them for bread; everywhere the inevitable machinery bestows upon the great capitalist command of trade and of the workers with it. The centralization of capital strides forward without interruption, the division of society into great capitalists and non-possessing workers is sharper every day, the industrial development of the nation advances with giant strides towards the inevitable crisis.

I have already stated that in the handicrafts the power of capital, and in some cases the division of labour too, has produced the same results, crushed the small tradesmen, and put great capitalists and non-possessing workers in their place. As to these handicraftsmen there is little to be said, since all that relates to them has already found its place where the proletariat in general was under discussion. There has been but little change here in the nature of the work and its influence upon health since the beginning of the industrial movement. But the constant contact with the factory oper-

---

[1] Leifchild Report Append., Part II., p. L 2, ss. 11, 12; Franks Report Append., Part II., p. K 7, s. 48; Tancred Evid. Append., Part II., p. I 76, etc.; all Children's Employment Commission's Report.

atives, the pressure of the great capitalists, which is much more felt than that of the small employer to whom the apprentice still stood in a more or less personal relation, the influences of life in towns, and the fall of wages, have made nearly all the handicraftsmen active participators in labour movements. We shall soon have more to say on this point, and turn meanwhile to one section of workers in London who deserve our attention by reason of the extraordinary barbarity with which they are exploited by the money-greed of the bourgeoisie. I mean the dressmakers and sewing-women.

It is a curious fact that the production of precisely those articles which serve the personal adornment of the ladies of the bourgeoisie involves the saddest consequences for the health of the workers. We have already seen this in the case of the lace-makers, and come now to the dress-making establishments of London for further proof. They employ a mass of young girls—there are said to be 15,000 of them in all—who sleep and eat on the premises, come usually from the country, and are therefore absolutely the slaves of their employers. During the fashionable season, which lasts some four months, working hours, even in the best establishments, are fifteen, and, in very pressing cases, eighteen a day; but in most shops work goes on at these times without any set regulation, so that the girls never have more than six, often not more than three or four, sometimes, indeed, not more than two hours in the twenty-four, for rest and sleep, working nineteen to twenty hours, if not the whole night through, as frequently happens! The only limit set to their work is the absolute physical inability to hold the needle another minute. Cases have occurred in which these helpless creatures did not undress during nine consecutive days and nights, and could only rest a moment or two here and there upon a mattress, where food was served them ready cut up in order to require the least possible time for swallowing. In short, these unfortunate girls are kept by means of the moral whip of the modern slave-driver, the threat of discharge, to such long and unbroken toil as no strong man, much less a delicate girl of 14 to 20 years, can endure. In addition to this, the foul air of the workroom and sleeping places, the bent posture, the often bad and indigestible food, all these causes, but above all the long hours of work combined with almost total exclusion from fresh air, entail the saddest consequences for the health of the girls. Enervation, exhaustion, debility, loss of appetite, pains in the shoulders, back, and hips, but especially headache, begin very soon; then follow curvatures of the spine, high, deformed shoulders, leanness, swelled, weeping, and smarting eyes, which soon become short-sighted; coughs, narrow chests, shortness of breath, and all manner of disorders in the development of the female organism.

In many cases the eyes suffer so severely that incurable blindness follows; but if the sight remains strong enough to make continued work possible, consumption usually soon ends the sad life of these milliners and dressmakers. Even those who leave this work at an early age retain permanently injured health, a broken constitution; and, when married, bring feeble and sickly children into the world. All the medical men interrogated by the commissioner agreed that no method of life could be invented better calculated to destroy health and induce early death.

With the same cruelty, though somewhat more indirectly, the rest of the needle-women of London are exploited. The girls employed in stay-making have a hard, wearing occupation, trying to the eyes. And what wages do they get? I do not know; but this I know, that the middleman who has to give security for the material delivered, and who distributes the work among the needle-women, receives 1½d. per piece. From this he deducts his own pay, at least ½d., so that 1d. at most reaches the pocket of the girl. The girls who sew neckties must bind themselves to work sixteen hours a day, and receive 4s. 6d. a week.[1] But the shirtmakers' lot is the worst. They receive for an ordinary shirt 1½d., formerly 2d.–3d.; but since the work-house of St Pancras, which is administered by a Radical board of guardians, began to undertake work at 1⅓d., the poor women outside have been compelled to do the same. For fine, fancy shirts, which can be made in one day of eighteen hours, 6d. is paid. The weekly wage of these sewing-women according to this and according to testimony from many sides, including both

[1] See *Weekly Dispatch*, 17 Mar. 1844.

needle-women and employers, is 2s. 6d. to 3s. for most strained work continued far into the night. And what crowns this shameful barbarism is the fact that the women must give a money deposit for a part of the materials entrusted to them, which they naturally cannot do unless they pawn a part of them (as the employers very well know), redeeming them at a loss; or if they cannot redeem the materials, they must appear before a Justice of the Peace, as happened to a sewing-woman in November 1843. A poor girl who got into this strait and did not know what to do next, drowned herself in a canal in 1844. These women usually live in little garret rooms in the utmost distress, where as many crowd together as the space can possibly admit, and where, in winter, the animal warmth of the workers is the only heat obtainable. Here they sit bent over their work, sewing from four or five in the morning until midnight, destroying their health in a year or two and ending in an early grave, without being able to obtain the poorest necessities of life meanwhile.[1] And below them roll the brilliant equipages of the upper bourgeoisie, and perhaps ten steps away some pitiable dandy loses more money in one evening at faro than they can earn in a year.

Such is the condition of the English manufacturing proletariat. In all directions, whithersoever we may turn, we find want and disease permanent or temporary, and demoralization arising from the condition of the workers; in all directions slow but sure undermining, and final destruction of the human being physically as well as mentally. Is this a state of things which can last? It cannot and will not last. The workers, the great majority of the nation, will not endure it. Let us see what they say of it.

---

[1] Thomas Hood, the most talented of all the English humourists now living, and like all humorists, full of human feeling, but wanting in mental energy, published at the beginning of 1844 a beautiful poem, 'The Song of the Shirt', which drew sympathetic but unavailing tears from the eyes of the daughters of the bourgeoisie. Originally published in *Punch*, it made the round of all the papers. As discussions of the condition of the sewing-women filled all the papers at the time, special extracts are needless.

8

Labour Movements

IT must be admitted, even if I had not proved it so often in detail, that the English workers cannot feel happy in this condition; that theirs is not a state in which a man or a whole class of men can think, feel, and live as human beings. The workers must therefore strive to escape from this brutalising condition, to secure for themselves a better, more human position; and this they cannot do without attacking the interest of the bourgeoisie which consists in exploiting them. But the bourgeoisie defends its interests with all the power placed at its disposal by wealth and the might of the State. In proportion as the working man determines to alter the present state of things, the bourgeois becomes his avowed enemy.

Moreover, the working man is made to feel at every moment that the bourgeoisie treats him as a chattel, as its property, and for this reason, if for no other, he must come forward as its enemy. I have shown in a hundred ways in the foregoing pages, and could have shown in a hundred others, that, in our present society, he can save his manhood only in hatred and rebellion against the bourgeoisie. And he can protest with most violent passion against the tyranny of the propertied class, thanks to his education, or rather want of education, and to the abundance of hot Irish blood that flows in the veins of the English working class. The English working man is no Englishman nowadays; no calculating money-grabber like his wealthy neighbour. He possesses more fully developed feelings, his native northern coldness is overborne by the unrestrained development of his passions and their control over him. The cultivation of the understanding which so greatly strengthens the selfish tendency of the English bourgeois, which has made selfishness his predominant trait and concentrated all his emotional power upon the single point of money-greed, is wanting in the working man, whose passions are therefore strong and mighty as those of the foreigner. English nationality is annihilated in the working man.

Since, as we have seen, no single field for the exercise of his manhood is left him, save his opposition to the whole conditions of his life, it is natural that exactly in this opposition he should be most manly, noblest, most worthy of sympathy. We shall see that all the energy, all the activity of the working men is directed to this point, and that even their attempts to attain general education all stand in direct connection with this. True, we shall have single acts of violence and even of brutality to report, but it must always be kept in mind that the social war is avowedly raging in England; and that, whereas it is in the interest of the bourgeoisie to conduct this war hypocritically, under the disguise of peace and even of philanthropy, the only help for the working men consists in laying bare the true state of things and destroying this hypocrisy; that the most violent attacks of the workers upon the bourgeoisie and its servants are only the open, undisguised expression of that which the bourgeoisie perpetrates secretly, treacherously against the workers.

The revolt of the workers began soon after the first industrial development, and has passed through several phases. The investigation of their importance in the history of the English people I must reserve for separate treatment, limiting myself meanwhile to such bare facts as serve to characterize the condition of the English proletariat.

The earliest, crudest, and least fruitful form of this rebellion was that of crime. The working man lived in poverty and want, and saw that others were better off than he. It was not clear to his mind why he, who did more for society than the rich idler, should be the one to suffer under these conditions. Want conquered his inherited respect for the sacredness of property, and he stole. We have seen how crime increased with the extension of manufacture; how the yearly number of arrests bore a constant relation to the number of bales of cotton annually consumed.

The workers soon realized that crime did not help matters. The criminal could protest against the existing order of society only singly, as one individual; the whole might of society was brought to bear upon each criminal, and crushed him with its immense superiority. Besides, theft was the most primitive form of protest, and for this reason, if for no other, it never became the universal expression of the public opinion of the working man, however much they might approve of it in silence. As a class, they first manifested opposition to the bourgeoisie when they resisted the introduction of machinery at the very beginning of the industrial period. The first inventors, Arkwright and others, were persecuted in this way and their machines destroyed. Later, there took place a number of revolts against machinery, in which the occurrences were almost precisely the same as those of the printers' disturbances in Bohemia in 1844; factories were demolished and machinery destroyed.

This form of opposition also was isolated, restricted to certain localities, and directed against one feature only of our present social arrangements. When the momentary end was attained, the whole weight of social power fell upon the unprotected evil-doers and punished them to its heart's content, while the machinery was introduced none the less. A new form of opposition had to be found.

At this point help came in the shape of a law enacted by the old, unreformed, oligarchic-Tory Parliament, a law which never could have passed the House of Commons later, when the Reform Bill* had legally sanctioned the distinction between bourgeoisie and proletariat, and made the bourgeoisie the ruling class. This was enacted in 1824, and repealed all laws by which coalitions between working men for labour purposes had hitherto been forbidden. The working men obtained a right previously restricted to the aristocracy and bourgeoisie, the right of free association. Secret coalitions had, it is true, previously existed, but could never achieve great results. In Glasgow, as Symons[1] relates, a general strike of weavers had taken place in 1812, which was brought about by a secret association. It was repeated in 1822, and on this occasion vitriol was thrown into the faces of the two working men who would not join the association, and were therefore regarded by the members as traitors to their class. Both the assaulted lost the use of their eyes in consequence of the injury. So, too, in 1818, the association of Scottish miners was powerful enough to carry on a general

[1] *Arts and Artisans*, 137 ff.

strike. These associations required their members to take an oath of fidelity and secrecy, had regular lists, treasurers, bookkeepers, and local branches. But the secrecy with which everything was conducted crippled their growth. When, on the other hand, the working men received in 1824 the right of free association, these combinations were very soon spread over all England and attained great power. In all branches of industry Trade Unions were formed with the outspoken intention of protecting the single working man against the tyranny and neglect of the bourgeoisie. Their objects were: to fix wages and to deal, *en masse*, as a power, with the employers; to regulate the rate of wages according to the profit of the latter, to raise it when opportunity offered, and to keep it uniform in each trade throughout the country. Hence they tried to settle with the capitalists a scale of wages to be universally adhered to, and ordered out on strike the employees of such individuals as refused to accept the scale. They aimed further to keep up the demand for labour by limiting the number of apprentices, and so to keep wages high; to counteract, as far as possible, the indirect wages reductions which the manufacturers brought about by means of new tools and machinery; and finally, to assist unemployed working men financially. This they do either directly or by means of a card to legitimate the bearer as a 'society man', and with which the working man wanders from place to place, supported by his fellow-workers, and instructed as to the best opportunity for finding employment. This is tramping, and the wanderer a tramp. To attain these ends, a President and Secretary are engaged at a salary (since it is to be expected that no manufacturer will employ such persons), and a committee collects the weekly contributions and watches over their expenditure for the purposes of the association. When it proved possible and advantageous, the various trades of single districts united in a federation and held delegate conventions at set times. The attempt has been made in single cases to unite the workers of one branch over all England in one great Union; and several times (in 1830 for the first time) to form one universal trades association for the whole United Kingdom, with a separate organization for each trade. These associations, however, never held together long, and were seldom realized even for the moment, since an exceptionally universal excitement is necessary to make such a federation possible and effective.

The means usually employed by these Unions for attaining their ends are the following: If one or more employers refuse to pay the wage specified by the Union, a deputation is sent or a petition forwarded (the working men, you see, know how to recognize the absolute power of the lord of the factory in his little State); if this proves unavailing, the Union commands the employees to stop work, and all hands go home. This strike is either partial when one or several, or general when all employers in the trade refuse to regulate wages according to the proposals of the Union. So far go the lawful means of the Union, assuming the strike to take effect after the expiration of the legal notice, which is not always the case. But these lawful means are very weak when there are workers outside the Union, or when members separate from it for the sake of the momentary advantage offered by the bourgeoisie. Especially in the case of partial strikes can the manufacturer readily secure recruits from these black sheep (who are known as knobsticks), and render fruitless the efforts of the united workers. Knobsticks are usually threatened, insulted, beaten, or otherwise maltreated by the members of the Union; intimidated, in short, in every way. Prosecution follows, and as the law-abiding bourgeoisie has the power in its own hands, the force of the Union is broken almost every time by the first unlawful act, the first judicial procedure against its members.

The history of these Unions is a long series of defeats of the working men, interrupted by a few isolated victories. All these efforts naturally cannot alter the economic law according to which wages are determined by the relation between supply and demand in the labour market. Hence the Unions remain powerless against all *great* forces which influence this relation. In a commercial crisis the Union itself must reduce wages or dissolve wholly; and in a time of considerable increase in the demand for labour, it cannot fix the rate of wages higher than would be reached spontaneously by the competition of the capitalists among themselves. But in dealing with minor, single influences they are powerful. If the employer had no concentrated, collective opposition to expect, he would in his own interest gradually reduce wages to a lower and lower point; indeed, the battle of competition which he has to wage against his fellow-manufacturers would force him to do so, and wages would soon reach the minimum. But this competition of the manufacturers among themselves is, *under average conditions*, somewhat restricted by the opposition of the working men.

Every manufacturer knows that the consequence of a reduction not justified by conditions to which his competitors also are subjected would be a strike, which would most certainly injure him, because his capital would be idle as long as the strike lasted, and his machinery would be rusting, whereas it is very doubtful whether he could, in such a case, enforce his reduction. Then he has the certainty that if he should succeed, his competitors would follow him, reducing the price of the goods so produced, and thus depriving him of the benefit of his policy. Then, too, the Unions often bring about a more rapid increase of wages after a crisis than would otherwise follow. For the manufacturer's interest is to delay raising wages until forced by competition, but now the working men demand an increased wage as soon as the market improves, and they can carry their point by reason of the smaller supply of workers at his command under such circumstances. But, for resistance to more considerable forces which influence the labour market, the Unions are powerless. In such cases hunger gradually drives the strikers to resume work on any terms, and when once a few have begun, the force of the Union is broken, because these few knobsticks, with the reserve supplies of goods in the market, enable the bourgeoisie to overcome the worst effects of the interruption of business. The funds of the Union are soon exhausted by the great numbers requiring relief, the credit which the shopkeepers give at high interest is withdrawn after a time, and want compels the working man to place himself once more under the yoke of the bourgeoisie. But strikes end disastrously for the workers mostly, because the manufacturers, in their own interest (which has, be it said, become their interest only through the resistance of the workers), are obliged to avoid all useless reductions, while the workers feel in every reduction imposed by the state of trade a deterioration of their condition, against which they must defend themselves as far as in them lies.

It will be asked, 'Why, then, do the workers strike in such cases, when the uselessness of such measures is so evident?' Simply because they *must* protest against every reduction, even if dictated by necessity; because they feel bound to proclaim that they, as human beings, shall not be made to bow to social circumstances, but social conditions ought to yield to them as human beings; because silence on their part would be a recognition of these social conditions, an admission of the right of the bourgeoisie to exploit the workers in good times and let them starve in bad ones. Against this the working men must rebel so long as they have not lost all human feeling, and that they protest in this way and no other, comes of their being practical English people, who express themselves in *action*, and do not, like German theorists, go to sleep as soon as their protest is properly registered and placed *ad acta*,* there to sleep as quietly as the protesters themselves. The active resistance of the English working men has its effect in holding the money-greed of the bourgeoisie within certain limits, and keeping alive the opposition of the workers to the social and political omnipotence of the bourgeoisie, while it compels the admission that something more is needed than Trade Unions and strikes to break the power of the ruling class. But what gives these Unions and the strikes arising from them their real importance is this, that they are the first attempt of the workers to abolish competition. They imply the recognition of the fact that the supremacy of the bourgeoisie is based wholly upon the competition of the workers among themselves; i.e. upon their want of cohesion. And precisely because the Unions direct themselves against the vital nerve of the present social order, however onesidedly, in however narrow a way, are they so dangerous to this social order. The working men cannot attack the bourgeoisie, and with it the whole existing order of society, at any sorer point than this. If the competition of the workers among themselves is destroyed, if all determine not to be further exploited by the bourgeoisie, the rule of property is at an end. Wages depend upon the relation of demand to supply, upon the accidental state of the labour market, simply because the workers have hitherto been content to be treated as chattels, to be bought and sold. The moment the workers resolve to be bought and sold no longer, when, in the determination of the value of labour, they take the part of men possessed of a will as well as of working power, at that moment the whole Political Economy of today is at an end.

The laws determining the rate of wages would, indeed, come into force again in the long run, if the working men did not go beyond this step of abolishing competition among themselves. But they must go beyond that unless they are prepared to recede again and to allow competition among themselves to reappear. Thus once advanced so far, necessity compels them to go further; to abolish not only one kind of competition, but competition itself altogether, and that they will do.

The workers are coming to perceive more clearly with every day how competition affects them; they see far more clearly than the bourgeois that competition of the capitalists among themselves presses upon the workers too, by bringing on commercial crises, and that this kind of competition, too, must be abolished. They will soon learn *how* they have to go about it.

That these Unions contribute greatly to nourish the bitter hatred of the workers against the property-holding class need hardly be said. From them proceed, therefore, with or without the connivance of the leading members, in times of unusual excitement, individual actions which can be explained only by hatred wrought to the pitch of despair, by a wild passion overwhelming all restraints. Of this sort are the attacks with vitriol mentioned in the foregoing pages, and a series of others, of which I shall cite several. In 1831, during a violent labour movement, young Ashton, a manufacturer in Hyde, near Manchester, was shot one evening when crossing a field, and no trace of the assassin discovered. There is no doubt that this was a deed of vengeance of the working men. Incendiarisms and attempted explosions are very common. On Friday, 29 September 1843 an attempt was made to blow up the saw-works of Padgin, in Howard Street, Sheffield. A closed iron tube filled with powder was the means employed, and the damage was considerable. On the following day, a similar attempt was made in Ibbetson's knife and file works at Shales Moor, near Sheffield. Mr Ibbetson had made himself obnoxious by an active participation in bourgeois movements, by low wages, the exclusive employment of knobsticks, and the exploitation of the Poor Law for his own benefit. He had reported, during the crisis of 1842, such operatives as refused to accept reduced wages, as persons who could find work but would not take it, and were, therefore, not deserving of relief, so compelling the acceptance of a reduction. Considerable damage was inflicted by the explosion, and all the working men who came to view it regretted only 'that the whole concern was not blown into the air'. On Friday, 6 October 1843 an attempt to set fire to the factory of Ainsworth and Crompton, at Bolton, did no damage; it was the third or fourth attempt in the same factory within a very short time. In the meeting of the Town Council of Sheffield, on Wednesday, 10 January 1844 the Commissioner of Police exhibited a cast-iron machine, made for the express purpose of producing an explosion, and found filled with four pounds of powder, and a fuse which had been lighted but had not taken effect, in the works of Mr Kitchen, Earl Street, Sheffield. On Sunday, 20 January 1844 an explosion caused by a package of powder took place in the sawmill of Bently & White, at Bury, in Lancashire, and produced considerable damage. On Thursday, 1 February 1944 the Soho Wheel Works, in Sheffield, were set on fire and burnt up.

Here are six such cases in four months, all of which have their sole origin in the embitterment of the working men against the employers. What sort of a social state it must be in which such things are possible I need hardly say. These facts are proof enough that in England, even in good business years, such as 1843, the social war is avowed and openly carried on, and still the English bourgeoisie does not stop to reflect! But the case which speaks most loudly is that of the Glasgow Thugs,[1] which came up before the Assizes from the 3rd to the 11th of January 1838. It appears from the proceedings that the Cotton-Spinners' Union, which

---

[1] So called from the East Indian tribe, whose only trade is the murder of all the strangers who fall into its hands.

existed here from the year 1816, possessed rare organization
and power. The members were bound by an oath to adhere
to the decision of the majority, and had during every turnout
a secret committee which was unknown to the mass of the
members, and controlled the funds of the Union absolutely.
This committee fixed a price upon the heads of knobsticks
and obnoxious manufacturers and upon incendiarisms in
mills. A mill was thus set on fire in which female knobsticks
were employed in spinning in the place of men; a Mrs
McPherson, mother of one of these girls, was murdered,
and both murderers sent to America at the expense of the
association. As early as 1820, a knobstick named McQuarry
was shot at and wounded, for which deed the doer received
£15 from the Union. Later a certain Graham was shot at; the
doer received £20, but was discovered and transported for
life. Finally, in 1837, in May, disturbances occurred in
consequence of a turnout in the Oatbank and Mile End
factories, in which perhaps a dozen knobsticks were maltreated. In July of the same year, the disturbances still
continued, and a certain Smith, a knobstick, was so maltreated that he died. The committee was now arrested, an
investigation begun, and the leading members found guilty of
participation in conspiracies, maltreatment of knobsticks,
and incendiarism in the mill of James and Francis Wood, and
they were transported for seven years. What do our good
Germans say to this story?[1]

The property-holding class, and especially the manufacturing portion of it which comes into direct contact with
the working men, declaims with the greatest violence against
these Unions, and is constantly trying to prove their use-

[1] 'What kind of wild justice must it be in the hearts of these men that
prompts them, with cold deliberation, in conclave assembled, to doom
their brother workman, as the deserter of his order and his order's cause,
to die a traitor's and a deserter's death, have him executed, in default of
any public judge and hangman, then by a secret one; like your old
Chivalry Fehmgericht and Secret Tribunal, suddenly revived in this
strange guise; suddenly rising once more on the astonished eye, dressed
not now in mail shirts, but in fustian jackets meeting not in Westphalian
forests, but in the paved Gallowgate of Glasgow! Such a temper must be
widespread virulent among the many when, even in its worse acme, it
can take such form in the few.' (Carlyle, *Chartism*, 40.)

lessness to the working men upon grounds which are economically perfectly correct, but for that very reason partially mistaken, and for the working-man's understanding totally without effect. The very zeal of the bourgeoisie shows that it is not disinterested in the matter; and apart from the direct loss involved in a turnout, the state of the case is such that whatever goes into the pockets of the manufacturers comes of necessity out of those of the worker. So that even if the working men did not know that the Unions hold the emulation of their masters in the reduction of wages, at least in a measure, in check, they would still stand by the Unions, simply to the injury of their enemies, the manufacturers. In war the injury of one party is the benefit of the other, and since the working men are on a war-footing towards their employers, they do merely what the great potentates do when they get into a quarrel. Beyond all other bourgeois is our friend Dr Ure, the most furious enemy of the Unions. He foams with indignation at the 'secret tribunals' of the cotton-spinners, the most powerful section of the workers, tribunals which boast their ability to paralyse every disobedient manufacturer,[1] 'and so bring ruin on the man who had given them profitable employment for many a year'. He speaks of a time[2] 'when the inventive head and the sustaining heart of trade were held in bondage by the unruly lower members'. A pity that the English working men will not let themselves be pacified so easily with thy fable as the Roman Plebs, thou modern Menenius Agrippa!* Finally, he relates the following: At one time the coarse mule-spinners had misused their power beyond all endurance. High wages, instead of awakening thankfulness towards the manufacturers and leading to intellectual improvement (in harmless study of sciences useful to the bourgeoisie, of course), in many cases produced pride and supplied funds for supporting rebellious spirits in strikes, with which a number of manufacturers were visited one after the other in a purely arbitrary manner. During an unhappy disturbance of this sort in Hyde, Dukinfield, and the surrounding neighbourhood, the manufacturers of the district, anxious lest they should be driven from the market by the French, Belgians, and Americans,

---

[1] Dr Ure, *Philosophy of Manufactures*, 282.
[2] Ibid.

addressed themselves to the machine-works of Sharp, Roberts & Co., and requested Mr Sharp to turn his inventive mind to the construction of an automatic mule in order 'to emancipate the trade from galling slavery and impending ruin'.[1]

He produced in the course of a few months a machine apparently instinct with the thought, feeling, and tact of the experienced workman—which even in its infancy displayed a new principle of regulation, ready in its mature state to fulfil the functions of a finished spinner. Thus the Iron Man, as the operatives fitly call it, sprung out of the hands of our modern Prometheus at the bidding of Minerva—a creation destined to restore order among the industrious classes, and to confirm to Great Britain the empire of art. The news of this Herculean prodigy spread dismay through the Union, and even long before it left its cradle, so to speak, it strangled the Hydra of misrule.[2]

Ure proves further that the invention of the machine, with which four and five colours are printed at once, was a result of the disturbances among the calico printers; that the refractoriness of the yarn-dressers in the power-loom weaving mills gave rise to a new and perfected machine for warp-dressing, and mentions several other such cases. A few pages earlier this same Ure gives himself a great deal of trouble to prove in detail that machinery is beneficial to the workers! But Ure is not the only one; in the Factory Report, Mr Ashworth, the manufacturer, and many another, lose no opportunity to express their wrath against the Unions. These wise bourgeois, like certain governments, trace every movement which they do not understand, to the influence of ill-intentioned agitators, demagogues, traitors, spouting idiots, and ill-balanced youth. They declare that the paid agents of the Unions are interested in the agitation because they live upon it, as though the necessity for this payment were not forced upon them by the bourgeois, who will give such men no employment!

The incredible frequency of these strikes proves best of all to what extent the social war has broken out all over England. No week passes, scarcely a day, indeed, in which

[1] Ibid. 367.

[2] Ibid. 366 ff.

there is not a strike in some direction, now against reduction, then against a refusal to raise the rate of wages, again by reason of the employment of knobsticks or the continuance of abuses, sometimes against new machinery, or for a hundred other reasons. These strikes, at first skirmishes, sometimes result in weighty struggles; they decide nothing, it is true, but they are the strongest proof that the decisive battle between bourgeoisie and proletariat is approaching. They are the military school of the working men in which they prepare themselves for the great struggle which cannot be avoided; they are the pronunciamentos of single branches of industry that these too have joined the labour movement. And when one examines a year's file of the *Northern Star*, the only sheet which reports all the movements of the proletariat, one finds that all the proletarians of the towns and of country manufacture have united in associations, and have protested from time to time, by means of a general strike, against the supremacy of the bourgeoisie. And as schools of war, the Unions are unexcelled. In them is developed the peculiar courage of the English. It is said on the Continent that the English, and especially the working men, are cowardly, that they cannot carry out a revolution because, unlike the French, they do not riot at intervals, because they apparently accept the bourgeois regime so quietly. This is a complete mistake. The English working men are second to none in courage; they are quite as restless as the French, but they fight differently. The French, who are by nature political, struggle against social evils with political weapons; the English, for whom politics exist only as a matter of interest, solely in the interest of bourgeois society, fight, not against the Government, but directly against the bourgeoisie; and for the time, this can be done only in a peaceful manner. Stagnation in business, and the want consequent upon it, engendered the revolt at Lyons, in 1834, in favour of the Republic: in 1842, at Manchester, a similar cause gave rise to a universal turnout for the Charter and higher wages. That courage is required for a turnout, often indeed much loftier courage, much bolder, firmer determination than for an insurrection, is self-evident. It is, in truth, no trifle for a working man who knows want from experience, to face it with wife and children, to endure hunger and wretchedness for months together, and stand firm and unshaken through it all. What is death, what the galleys which await the French revolutionist, in comparison with gradual starvation, with the daily sight of a starving family, with the certainty of future revenge on the part of the bourgeoisie, all of which the English working man chooses in preference to subjection under the yoke of the property-holding class? We shall meet later an example of this obstinate, unconquerable courage of men who surrender to force only when all resistance would be aimless and unmeaning. And precisely in this quiet perseverance, in this lasting determination which undergoes a hundred tests every day, the English working man develops that side of his character which commands most respect. People who endure so much to bend one single bourgeois will be able to break the power of the whole bourgeoisie.

But apart from that, the English working man has proved his courage often enough. That the turnout of 1842 had no further results came from the fact that the men were in part forced into it by the bourgeoisie, in part neither clear nor united as to its object. But aside from this, they have shown their courage often enough when the matter in question was a specific social one. Not to mention the Welsh insurrection of 1839,* a complete battle was waged in Manchester in May 1843, during my residence there. Pauling & Henfrey, a brick firm, had increased the size of the bricks without raising wages, and sold the bricks, of course, at a higher price. The workers, to whom higher wages were refused, struck work, and the Brickmakers' Union declared war upon the firm. The firm, meanwhile, succeeded with great difficulty in securing hands from the neighbourhood, and among the knobsticks, against whom in the beginning intimidation was used, the proprietors set twelve men to guard the yard, all ex-soldiers and policemen, armed with guns. When intimidation proved unavailing, the brick-yard, which lay scarcely a hundred paces from an infantry barracks, was stormed at ten o'clock one night by a crowd of brickmakers, who advanced in military order, the first ranks armed with guns.[1]

[1] At the corner of Cross Lane and Regent Road. See map of Manchester. (*Note in the German edition.*)

They forced their way in, fired upon the watchmen as soon as they saw them, stamped out the wet bricks spread out to dry, tore down the piled-up rows of those already dry, demolished everything which came in their way, pressed into a building, where they destroyed the furniture and maltreated the wife of the overlooker who was living there. The watchmen, meanwhile, had placed themselves behind a hedge, whence they could fire safely and without interruption. The assailants stood before a burning brick-kiln, which threw a bright light upon them, so that every ball of their enemies struck home, while every one of their own shots missed its mark. Nevertheless, the firing lasted half an hour, until the ammunition was exhausted, and the object of the visit—the demolition of all the destructible objects in the yard—was attained. Then the military approached, and the brickmakers withdrew to Eccles, three miles from Manchester. A short time before reaching Eccles they held roll-call, and each man was called according to his number in the section when they separated, only to fall the more certainly into the hands of the police, who were approaching from all sides. The number of the wounded must have been very considerable, but those only could be counted who were arrested. One of these had received three bullets (in the thigh, the calf, and the shoulder), and had travelled in spite of them more than four miles on foot. These people have proved that they, too, possess revolutionary courage, and do not shun a rain of bullets. And when an unarmed multitude, without a precise aim common to them all, are held in check in a shut-off market-place, whose outlets are guarded by a couple of policemen and dragoons, as happened in 1842, this by no means proves a want of courage. On the contrary, the multitude would have stirred quite as little if the servants of public (i.e. of the bourgeois) order had not been present. Where the working people have a specific end in view, they show courage enough; as, for instance, in the attack upon Birley's mill, which had later to be protected by artillery.

In this connection, a word or two as to the respect for the law in England. True, the law is sacred to the bourgeois, for it is his own composition, enacted with his consent, and for his benefit and protection. He knows that, even if an individual law should injure him, the whole fabric protects his interests; and more than all, the sanctity of the law, the sacredness of order as established by the active will of one part of society, and the passive acceptance of the other, is the strongest support of his social position. Because the English bourgeois finds himself reproduced in his law, as he does in his God, the policeman's truncheon which, in a certain measure, is his own club, has for him a wonderfully soothing power. But for the working man quite otherwise! The working man knows too well, has learned from too oft-repeated experience, that the law is a rod which the bourgeois has prepared for him; and when he is not compelled to do so, he never appeals to the law. It is ridiculous to assert that the English working man fears the police, when every week in Manchester policemen are beaten, and last year an attempt was made to storm a station-house secured by iron doors and shutters. The power of the police in the turnout of 1842 lay, as I have already said, in the want of a clearly defined object on the part of the working men themselves.

Since the working men do not respect the law, but simply submit to its power when they cannot change it, it is most natural that they should at least propose alterations in it, that they should wish to put a proletarian law in the place of the legal fabric of the bourgeoisie. This proposed law is the People's Charter, which in form is purely political, and demands a democratic basis for the House of Commons. Chartism is the compact form of their opposition to the bourgeoisie. In the Unions and turnouts opposition always remained isolated: it was single working men or sections who fought a single bourgeois. If the fight became general, this was scarcely by the intention of the working men; or, when it did happen intentionally, Chartism was at the bottom of it. But in Chartism it is the whole working class which arises against the bourgeoisie, and attacks, first of all, the political power, the legislative rampart with which the bourgeoisie has surrounded itself. Chartism has proceeded from the Democratic party which arose between 1780 and 1790 with and in the proletariat, gained strength during the French Revolution, and came forth after the peace as the Radical party. It had its headquarters then in Birmingham and Manchester, and later in London; extorted the Reform Bill from the Oligarchs of the old Parliament by a union with the Liberal bourgeoisie, and has steadily consolidated itself, since then, as a more and more pronounced working-men's party in opposition to the bourgeoisie. In 1835 a committee of the General Working-men's Association of London, with William Lovett at its head, drew up the People's Charter, whose six points are as follows:

(1) Universal suffrage for every man who is of age, sane, and unconvicted of crime;

(2) Annual Parliaments;

(3) Payment of Members of Parliament, to enable poor men to stand for election;

(4) Voting by ballot to prevent bribery and intimidation by the bourgeoisie;

(5) Equal electoral districts to secure equal representation; and

(6) Abolition of the even now merely nominal property qualification of £300 in land* for candidates in order to make every voter eligible.

These six points, which are all limited to the reconstitution of the House of Commons, harmless as they seem, are sufficient to overthrow the whole English Constitution, Queen and Lords included. The so-called monarchical and aristocratic elements of the Constitution can maintain themselves only because the bourgeoisie has an interest in the continuance of their sham existence; and more than a sham existence neither possesses today. But as soon as real public opinion in its totality backs the House of Commons, as soon as the House of Commons incorporates the will, not of the bourgeoisie alone, but of the whole nation, it will absorb the whole power so completely that the last halo must fall from the head of the monarch and the aristocracy. The English working man respects neither Lords nor Queen. The bourgeois, while in reality allowing them but little influence, yet offers to them personally a sham worship. The English Chartist is politically a republican, though he rarely or never mentions the word, while he sympathizes with the republican parties of all countries, and calls himself in preference a democrat. But he is more than a mere republican, his democracy is not simply political.

Chartism was from the beginning in 1835 chiefly a movement among the working men, though not yet sharply separated from the radical petty bourgeoisie. The Radicalism of the workers went hand in hand with the Radicalism of the bourgeoisie; the Charter was the shibboleth of both. They held their National Convention every year in common, seeming to be one party. The lower middle class was just then in a very bellicose and violent state of mind in consequence of the disappointment over the Reform Bill and of the bad business years of 1837–9, and viewed the boisterous Chartist agitation with a very favourable eye. Of the vehemence of this agitation no one in Germany has any idea. The people were called upon to arm themselves, were frequently urged to revolt; pikes were got ready, as in the French Revolution, and in 1838 one Stephens, a Methodist parson, said to the assembled working people of Manchester:

You have no need to fear the power of Government, the soldiers, bayonets, and cannon that are at the disposal of your oppressors; you have a weapon that is far mightier than all these, a weapon against which bayonets and cannon are powerless, and a child of ten years can wield it. You have only to take a couple of matches and a bundle of straw dipped in pitch, and I will see what the Government and its hundreds of thousands of soldiers will do against this one weapon if it is used boldly.[1]

As early as that year the peculiarly social character of the working men's Chartism manifested itself. The same Stephens said, in a meeting of 200,000 men on Kersall Moor, the Mons Sacer of Manchester: 'Chartism, my friends, is no political movement, where the main point is your getting the ballot. Chartism is a knife and fork question: the Charter means a good house, good food and drink, prosperity, and short working-hours.'

The movements against the new Poor Law and for the Ten Hours Bill were already in the closest relation to Chartism. In all the meetings of that time the Tory Oastler was active, and hundreds of petitions for improvements of the social condition of the workers were circulated along with the national petition for the People's Charter adopted in Birmingham. In 1839 the agitation continued as vigorously

[1] We have seen that the workers took this advice seriously. (*Note in the German edition.*)

as ever, and when it began to relax somewhat at the end of the year, Bussey, Taylor, and Frost hastened to call forth uprisings simultaneously in the North of England, in Yorkshire, and Wales. Frost's plan being betrayed, he was obliged to open hostilities prematurely. Those in the North heard of the failure of his attempt in time to withdraw. Two months later, in January 1840, several so-called spy outbreaks* took place in Sheffield and Bradford, in Yorkshire, and the excitement gradually subsided. Meanwhile the bourgeoisie turned its attention to more practical projects, more profitable for itself, namely the Corn Laws. The Anti-Corn Law Association was formed in Manchester, and the consequence was a relaxation of the tie between the Radical bourgeoisie and the proletariat. The working men soon perceived that for them the abolition of the Corn Laws could be of little use, while very advantageous to the bourgeoisie; and they could therefore not be won for the project. The crisis of 1842 came on. Agitation was once more as vigorous as in 1839. But this time the rich manufacturing bourgeoisie, which was suffering severely under this particular crisis, took part in it. The Anti-Corn Law League, as it was now called, assumed a decidedly revolutionary tone. Its journals and agitators used undisguisedly revolutionary language, one very good reason for which was the fact that the Conservative party had been in power since 1841. As the Chartists had previously done, these bourgeois leaders called upon the people to rebel; and the working men who had most to suffer from the crisis were not inactive, as the year's national petition for the charter with its three and a half million signatures proves. In short, if the two Radical parties had been somewhat estranged, they allied themselves once more. At a meeting of Liberals and Chartists held in Manchester on 15 February 1842, a petition urging the repeal of the Corn Laws and the adoption of the Charter was drawn up. The next day it was adopted by both parties. The spring and summer passed amidst violent agitation and increasing distress. The bourgeoisie was determined to carry the repeal of the Corn Laws with the help of the crisis, the want which it entailed, and the general excitement. At this time, the Conservatives being in power, the Liberal bourgeoisie half abandoned their law-abiding habits; they wished to bring about a revolution with the help of the workers. The working men were to take the chestnuts from the fire to save the bourgeoisie from burning their own fingers. The old idea of a 'holy month', a general strike, broached in 1839 by the Chartists, was revived. This time, however, it was not the working men who wished to quit work, but the manufacturers who wished to close their mills and send the operatives into the country parishes upon the property of the aristocracy, thus forcing the Tory Parliament and the Tory Ministry to repeal the Corn Laws. A revolt would naturally have followed, but the bourgeoisie stood safely in the background and could await the result without compromising itself if the worst came to the worst. At the end of July business began to improve; it was high time. In order not to lose the opportunity, three firms in Staleybridge reduced wages in spite of the improvement.[1] Whether they did so of their own motion or in agreement with other manufacturers, especially those of the League, I do not know. Two withdrew after a time, but the third, William Bailey & Brothers, stood firm, and told the objecting operatives that 'if this did not please them, they had better go and play a bit'. This contemptuous answer the hands received with jeers. They left the mill, paraded through the town, and called upon all their fellows to quit work. In a few hours every mill stood idle, and the operatives marched to Mottram Moor to hold a meeting. This was on 5 August. On 8 August they proceeded to Ashton and Hyde five thousand strong, closed all the mills and coal-pits, and held meetings, in which, however, the question discussed was not, as the bourgeoisie had hoped, the repeal of the Corn Laws, but, ' a fair day's wages for a fair day's work'. On 9 August they proceeded to Manchester, unresisted by the authorities (all Liberals), and closed the mills; on the 11th they were in Stockport, where they met with the first resistance as they were storming the workhouse, the favourite child of the bourgeoisie. On the same day there was a general strike and disturbance in Bolton, to which the authorities here, too, made no resistance. Soon the uprising spread throughout the

[1] Compare Report of Chambers of Commerce of Manchester and Leeds at the end of July and beginning of August.

whole manufacturing district, and all employments, except harvesting and the production of food, came to a standstill. But the rebellious operatives were quiet. They were driven into this revolt without wishing it. The manufacturers, with the single exception of the Tory Birley, in Manchester, had, *contrary to their custom*, not opposed it. The thing had begun without the working men's having any distinct end in view, for which reason they were all united in the determination not to be shot at for the benefit of the Corn Law repealing bourgeoisie. For the rest, some wanted to carry the Charter, others who thought this premature wished merely to secure the wages rate of 1840. On this point the whole insurrection was wrecked. If it had been from the beginning an intentional, determined working men's insurrection, it would surely have carried its point; but these crowds who had been driven into the streets by their masters, against their own will, and with no definite purpose, could do nothing. Meanwhile the bourgeoisie, which had not moved a finger to carry the alliance of 15 February into effect, soon perceived that the working men did not propose to become its tools, and that the illogical manner in which it had abandoned its law-abiding standpoint threatened danger. It therefore resumed its law-abiding attitude, and placed itself upon the side of Government as against the working men.

It swore in trusty retainers as special constables (the German merchants in Manchester took part in this ceremony, and marched in an entirely superfluous manner through the city with their cigars in their mouths and thick truncheons in their hands). It gave the command to fire upon the crowd in Preston, so that the unintentional revolt of the people stood all at once face to face, not only with the whole military power of the Government, but with the whole property-holding class as well. The working men, who had no especial aim, separated gradually, and the insurrection came to an end without evil results. Later, the bourgeoisie was guilty of one shameful act after another, tried to white-wash itself by expressing a horror of popular violence by no means consistent with its own revolutionary language of the spring; laid the blame of insurrection upon Chartist instigators, whereas it had itself done more than all of them together to bring about the uprising; and resumed its old attitude of sanctifying the name of the law with a shame-lessness perfectly unequalled. The Chartists, who were all but innocent of bringing about this uprising, who simply did what the bourgeoisie meant to do when they made the most of their opportunity, were prosecuted and convicted, while the bourgeoisie escaped without loss, and had, besides, sold off its old stock of goods with advantage during the pause in work.

The fruit of the uprising was the decisive separation of the proletariat from the bourgeoisie. The Chartists had not hitherto concealed their determination to carry the Charter at all costs, even that of a revolution; the bourgeoisie, which now perceived, all at once, the danger with which any violent change threatened its position, refused to hear anything further of physical force, and proposed to attain its end by moral force, as though this were anything else than the direct or indirect threat of physical force. This was one point of dissension, though even this was removed later by the assertion of the Chartists (who are at least as worthy of being believed as the bourgeoisie) that they, too, refrained from appealing to physical force. The second point of dissension and the main one, which brought Chartism to light in its purity, was the repeal of the Corn Laws. In this the bourgeoisie was directly interested, the proletariat not. The Chartists therefore divided into two parties whose political programmes agreed literally, but which were nevertheless thoroughly different and incapable of union. At the Birmingham National Convention, in January 1843, Sturge, the representative of the Radical bourgeoisie, pro-posed that the name of the Charter be omitted from the rules of the Chartist Association,* nominally because this name had become connected with recollections of violence during the insurrection, a connection, by the way, which had existed for years, and against which Mr Sturge had hitherto advanced no objection. The working men refused to drop the name, and when Mr Sturge was outvoted, that worthy Quaker suddenly became loyal, betook himself out of the hall, and founded a 'Complete Suffrage Association' within the Radical bourgeoisie. So repugnant had these recollections become to the Jacobinical bourgeoisie, that he altered even the name Universal Suffrage into the ridiculous title, Complete Suffrage. The working men laughed at him and quietly went their way.

From this moment Chartism was purely a working-man's cause freed from all bourgeois elements. The 'Complete' journals, the *Weekly Dispatch*, *Weekly Chronicle*, *Examiner*, etc., fell gradually into the sleepy tone of the other Liberal sheets, espoused the cause of Free Trade, attacked the Ten Hours Bill and all exclusively working-men's demands, and let their Radicalism as a whole fall rather into the background. The Radical bourgeoisie joined hands with the Liberals against the working men in every collision, and in general made the Corn Law question, which for the English is the Free Trade question, their main business. They thereby fell under the dominion of the Liberal bourgeoisie, and now play a most pitiful role.

The Chartist working men, on the contrary, espoused with redoubled zeal all the struggles of the proletariat against the bourgeoisie. Free competition has caused the workers suffering enough to be hated by them; its apostles, the bourgeoise, are their declared enemies. The working man has only disadvantages to await from the complete freedom of competition. The demands hitherto made by him, the Ten Hours Bill, protection of the workers against the capitalist, good wages, a guaranteed position, repeal of the new Poor Law, all of the things which belong to Chartism quite as essentially as the 'Six Points', are directly opposed to free competition and Free Trade. No wonder, then, that the working men will not hear of Free Trade and the repeal of the Corn Laws (a fact incomprehensible to the whole English bourgeoisie), and while at least wholly indifferent to the Corn Law question, are most deeply embittered against its advocates. This question is precisely the point at which the proletariat separates from the bourgeoisie, Chartism from Radicalism; and the bourgeois understanding cannot comprehend this, because it cannot comprehend the proletariat.

Therein lies the difference between Chartist democracy and all previous political bourgeois democracy. Chartism is of an essentially social nature, a class movement. The 'Six Points' which for the Radical bourgeois are the beginning and end of the matter, which are meant, at the utmost, to call forth certain further reforms of the Constitution, are for the proletarian a mere means to further ends. 'Political power our means, social happiness our end', is now the clearly formulated war-cry of the Chartists. The 'knife and fork question' of the preacher Stephens was a truth for a part of the Chartists only, in 1838; it is a truth for all of them in 1845. There is no longer a mere politician among the Chartists, and even though their Socialism is very little developed, though their chief remedy for poverty has hitherto consisted in the land-allotment system,* which was superseded by the introduction of manufacture, though their chief practical propositions are apparently of a reactionary nature, yet these very measures involve the alternative that they must either succumb to the power of competition once more and restore the old state of things, or they must themselves entirely overcome competition and abolish it. On the other hand, the present indefinite state of Chartism, the separation from the purely political party, involves that precisely the characteristic feature, its social aspect, will have to be further developed. The approach to Socialism cannot fail, especially when the next crisis directs the working men by force of sheer want to social instead of political remedies. And a crisis must follow the present active state of industry and commerce in 1847 at the latest, and probably in 1846; one, too, which will far exceed in extent and violence all former crises. The working men will carry their Charter, naturally; but meanwhile they will learn to see clearly with regard to many points which they can make by means of it and of which they now know very little.

Meanwhile the socialist agitation also goes forward. English Socialism comes under our consideration so far only as it affects the working class. The English Socialists demand the gradual introduction of possession in common in home colonies* embracing two to three thousand persons who shall carry on both agriculture and manufacture and enjoy equal rights and equal education. They demand greater facility of obtaining divorce, the establishment of a rational government, with complete freedom of conscience and the abolition of punishment, the same to be replaced by a rational treatment of the offender. These are their practical measures, their theoretical principles do not concern us here. English Socialism arose with Owen, a manufacturer, and proceeds therefore with great consideration towards the bourgeoisie and great injustice towards the proletariat in its methods, although it culminates in demanding the abolition of the class antagonism between bourgeoisie and proletariat.

The Socialists are thoroughly tame and peaceable, accept our existing order, bad as it is, so far as to reject all other methods but that of winning public opinion. Yet they are so dogmatic that success by this method is for them, and for their principles as at present formulated, utterly hopeless. While bemoaning the demoralization of the lower classes, they are blind to the element of progress in this dissolution of the old social order, and refuse to acknowledge that the corruption wrought by private interests and hypocrisy in the property-holding class is much greater. They acknowledge no historic development, and wish to place the nation in a state of Communism at once, overnight, not by the unavoidable march of its political development up to the point at which this transition becomes both possible and necessary. They understand, it is true, why the working man is resentful against the bourgeois, but regard as unfruitful this class hatred, which is, after all, the only moral incentive by which the worker can be brought nearer the goal. They preach instead, a philanthropy and universal love far more unfruitful for the present state of England. They acknowledge only a psychological development, a development of man in the abstract, out of all relation to the Past, whereas the whole world rests upon that Past, the individual man included. Hence they are too abstract, too metaphysical, and accomplish little. They are recruited in part from the working class, of which they have enlisted but a very small fraction representing, however, its most educated and solid elements. In its present form, Socialism can never become the common creed of the working class; it must condescend to return for a moment to the Chartist standpoint. But the true proletarian Socialism having passed through Chartism, purified of its bourgeois elements, assuming the form which it has already reached in the minds of many Socialists and Chartist leaders (who are nearly all Socialists[1]), must, within a short time, play a weighty part in the history of the devel-

---

[1] Socialists, naturally, in the general, not the specifically Owenistic sense. (*Note in the German edition.*)

opment of the English people. English Socialism, the basis of which is much more ample than that of the French, is behind it in theoretical development, will have to recede for a moment to the French standpoint in order to proceed beyond it later. Meanwhile the French, too, will develop further. English Socialism affords the most pronounced expression of the prevailing absence of religion among the working men, an expression so pronounced indeed that the mass of the working men, being unconsciously and merely practically irreligious, often draw back before it. But here, too, necessity will force the working men to abandon the remnants of a belief which, as they will more and more clearly perceive, serves only to make them weak and resigned to their fate, obedient and faithful to the vampire property-holding class.

Hence it is evident that the working-men's movement is divided into two sections, the Chartists and the Socialists. The Chartists are theoretically the more backward, the less developed, but they are genuine proletarians all over, the representatives of their class. The Socialists are more far-seeing, propose practical remedies against distress, but, proceeding originally from the bourgeoisie, are for this reason unable to amalgamate completely with the working class. The union of Socialism with Chartism, the reproduction of French Communism in an English manner, will be the next step, and has already begun. Then only, when this has been achieved, will the working class be the true intellectual leader of England. Meanwhile, political and social development will proceed, and will foster this new party, this new departure of Chartism.

These different sections of working men, often united, often separated, Trade Unionists, Chartists, and Socialists, have founded on their own hook numbers of schools and reading-rooms for the advancement of education. Every Socialist, and almost every Chartist institution, has such a place, and so too have many trades. Here the children receive a purely proletarian education, free from all the influences of the bourgeoisie; and, in the reading-rooms, proletarian journals and books alone, or almost alone, are to be found. These arrangements are very dangerous for the bourgeoisie, which has succeeded in withdrawing several such institutes, 'Mechanics' Institutes',* from proletarian influences, and making them organs for the dissemination of the sciences useful to the bourgeoisie. Here the natural sciences are now taught, which may draw the working men away from the opposition to the bourgeoisie, and perhaps place in their hands the means of making inventions which bring in money for the bourgeoisie; while for the working man the acquaintance with the natural sciences is utterly useless *now* when it too often happens that he never gets the slightest glimpse of Nature in his large town with his long working hours. Here Political Economy is preached, whose idol is free competition, and whose sum and substance for the working man is this, that he cannot do anything more rational than resign himself to starvation. Here all education is tame, flabby, subservient to the ruling politics and religion, so that for the working man it is merely a constant sermon upon quiet obedience, passivity, and resignation to his fate.

The mass of working men naturally have nothing to do with these institutes, and betake themselves to the proletarian reading-rooms and to the discussion of matters which directly concern their own interests, whereupon the self-sufficient bourgeoisie says its *Dixi et Salvavi,** and turns with contempt from a class which 'prefers the angry ranting of ill-meaning demagogues to the advantages of solid education'. That, however, the working men appreciate solid education when they can get it unmixed with the interested cant of the bourgeoisie, the frequent lectures upon scientific, aesthetic, and economic subjects prove which are delivered especially in the Socialist institutes, and very well attended. I have often heard working men, whose fustian jackets scarcely held together, speak upon geological, astronomical, and other subjects, with more knowledge than most 'cultivated' bourgeois in Germany possess. And in how great a measure the English proletariat has succeeded in attaining independent education is shown especially by the fact that the epochmaking products of modern philosophical, political, and poetical literature are read by working men almost exclusively. The bourgeois, enslaved by social conditions and the prejudices involved in them, trembles, blesses, and crosses himself before everything which really paves the way for progress; the proletarian has open eyes for it, and studies it with pleasure and success. In this respect the Socialists, especially, have done wonders for the education of the proletariat. They have translated the French materialists, Helvétius, Holbach, Diderot, etc., and disseminated them, with the best English works, in cheap editions. Strauss's *Life of Jesus* and Proudhon's *Property* also circulate among the working men only. Shelley, the genius, the prophet, Shelley, and Byron, with his glowing sensuality and his bitter satire upon our existing society, find most of their readers in the proletariat; the bourgeoisie owns only castrated editions, family editions, cut down in accordance with the hypocritical morality of today. The two great practical philosophers of latest date, Bentham and Godwin, are, especially the latter, almost exclusively the property of the proletariat; for though Bentham has a school within the Radical bourgeoisie, it is only the proletariat and the Socialists who have succeeded in developing his teachings a step forward. The proletariat has formed upon this basis a literature, which consists chiefly of journals and pamphlets, and is far in advance of the whole bourgeois literature in intrinsic worth. On this point more later.

One more point remains to be noticed. The factory operatives, and especially those of the cotton district, form the nucleus of the labour movement. Lancashire, and especially Manchester, is the seat of the most powerful Unions, the central point of Chartism, the place which numbers most Socialists. The more the factory system has taken possession of a branch of industry, the more the working men employed in it participate in the labour movement; the sharper the opposition between working men and capitalists, the clearer the proletarian consciousness in the working men. The small masters of Birmingham, though they suffer from the crises, still stand upon an unhappy middle ground between proletarian Chartism and shopkeepers' Radicalism. But, in general, all the workers employed in manufacture are won for one form or the other of resistance to capital and bourgeoisie; and all are united upon this point, that they, as working men, a title of which they are proud, and which is the usual form of address in Chartist meetings, form a separate class, with separate interests and principles, with a separate way of looking at things in contrast with that of all property-owners; and that in this class reposes the strength and the capacity of development of the nation.

9

The Mining Proletariat

THE production of raw materials and fuel for a manufacture so colossal as that of England requires a considerable number of workers. But of all the materials needed for its industries (except wool, which belongs to the agricultural districts), England produces only the minerals: the metals and the coal. While Cornwall possesses rich copper-, tin-, zinc-, and lead-mines, Staffordshire, Wales, and other districts yield great quantities of iron, and almost the whole North and West of England, central Scotland, and certain districts of Ireland, produce a superabundance of coal.[1]

In the Cornish mines about 19,000 men, and 11,000 women and children are employed, in part above and in part below ground. Within the mines below ground, men and boys above 12 years old are employed almost exclusively.

[1] According to the census of 1841, the number of working men employed in mines in Great Britain, without Ireland, was:

	Men over 20 Years	Men under 20 Years	Women over 20 Years	Women under 20 Years	Together
Coal-mines	83,408	32,475	1,185	1,165	118,233
Copper-mines	9,866	3,428	913	1,200	15,407
Lead	9,427	1,932	40	20	11,419
Iron	7,773	2,679	424	73	10,949
Tin	4,602	1,349	68	82	6,101
Various, the mineral not specified	24,162	6,591	472	491	31,716
Total	139,238	48,454	3,102	3,031	193,825

As the coal and iron-mines are usually worked by the same people, a part of the miners attributed to the coal-mines, and a very considerable part of those mentioned under the last heading, are to be attributed to the iron-mines.

The condition of these workers seems, according to the Children's Employment Commission's Report, to be comparatively endurable, materially, and the English often enough boast of their strong, bold miners, who follow the veins of mineral below the bottom of the very sea. But in the matter of the health of these workers, this same Children's Employment Commission's Report judges differently. It shows in Dr Barham's intelligent report how the inhalation of an atmosphere containing little oxygen, and mixed with dust and the smoke of blasting powder, such as prevails in the mines, seriously affects the lungs, disturbs the action of the heart, and diminishes the activity of the digestive organs; that wearing toil, and especially the climbing up and down of ladders, upon which even vigorous young men have to spend in some mines more than an hour a day, and which precedes and follows daily work, contributes greatly to the development of these evils, so that men who begin this work in early youth are far from reaching the stature of women who work above ground; that many die young of galloping consumption, and most miners at middle age of slow consumption; that they age prematurely and become unfit for work between the thirty-fifth and forty-fifth years; that many are attacked by acute inflammations of the respiratory organs when exposed to the sudden change from the warm air of the shaft (after climbing the ladder in profuse perspiration) to the cold wind above ground; and that these acute inflammations are very frequently fatal. Work above ground, breaking and sorting the ore, is done by girls and children, and is described as very wholesome, being done in the open air.

In the North of England, on the borders of Northumberland and Durham, are the extensive lead-mines of Alston Moor. The reports from this district[1] agree almost wholly with those from Cornwall. Here, too, there are complaints of want of oxygen, excessive dust, powder smoke, carbonic acid gas, and sulphur, in the atmosphere of the workings. In consequence, the miners here, as in Cornwall, are small of stature, and nearly all suffer from the thirtieth year

[1] Also found in the Children's Employment Commission's Report: Commissioner Mitchell's Report.

throughout life from chest affections, which end, especially when this work is persisted in, as is almost always the case, in consumption, so greatly shortening the average of life of these people. If the miners of this district are somewhat longer lived than those of Cornwall, this is the case, because they do not enter the mines before reaching the nineteenth year, while in Cornwall, as we have seen, this work is begun in the twelfth year. Nevertheless, the majority die here, too, between 40 and 50 years of age, according to medical testimony. Of 79 miners, whose death was entered upon the public register of the district, and who attained an average of 45 years, 37 had died of consumption and 6 of asthma. In the surrounding districts, Allendale, Stanhope, and Middleton, the average length of life was 49, 48, and 47 years respectively, and the deaths from chest affections composed 48, 54, and 56 per cent of the whole number. It must be borne in mind that all the data refer only to miners who did not begin to work *until they were 19 years old*. Let us compare these figures with the so-called Swedish tables, detailed tables of mortality embracing all the inhabitants of Sweden, and recognized in England as the most correct standard hitherto attainable for the average length of life of the British working class. According to them, male persons who survive the nineteenth year attain an average of 57½ years; but, according to this, the North of England miners are robbed by their work of an average of ten years of life. Yet the Swedish tables are accepted as the standard of longevity of the *workers*, and present, therefore, the average chances of life as affected by the unfavourable conditions in which the proletariat lives, a standard of longevity less than the normal one. In this district we find again the lodging-houses and sleeping-places with which we have already become acquainted in the towns, and in quite as filthy, disgusting, and overcrowded a state as there. Commissioner Mitchell visited one such sleeping barrack, 18 feet long, 13 feet wide, and arranged for the reception of 42 men and 14 boys, or 56 persons altogether, one-half of whom slept above the other in berths as on shipboard. There was no opening for the escape of the foul air; and, although no one had slept in this pen for three nights preceding the visit, the smell and the atmosphere were such that Commissioner Mitchell could not endure it a moment. What must it be through a hot summer night, with 56 occupants? And this is not the steer-age of an American slave ship, it is the dwelling of free-born Britons!

Let us turn now to the most important branch of British mining, the iron- and coal-mines, which the Children's Employment Commission treats in common, and with all the detail which the importance of the subject demands. Nearly the whole of the first part of this report is devoted to the condition of the workers employed in these mines. After the detailed description which I have furnished of the state of the industrial workers, I shall, however, be able to be as brief in dealing with this subject as the scope of the present work requires.

In the coal- and iron-mines which are worked in pretty much the same way, children of 4, 5, and 7 years are employed. They are set to transporting the ore or coal loosened by the miner from its place to the horse-path or the main shaft, and to opening and shutting the doors (which separate the divisions of the mine and regulate its ventilation) for the passage of workers and material. For watching the doors the smallest children are usually employed, who thus pass twelve hours daily, in the dark, alone, sitting usually in damp passages without even having work enough to save them from the stupefying, brutalizing tedium of doing nothing. The transport of coal and iron-stone, on the other hand, is very hard labour, the stuff being shoved in large tubs, without wheels, over the uneven floor of the mine; often over moist clay, or through water, and frequently up steep inclines and through paths so low-roofed that the workers are forced to creep on hands and knees. For this more wearing labour, therefore, older children and half-grown girls are employed. One man or two boys per tub are employed, according to circumstances; and, if two boys, one pushes and the other pulls. The loosening of the ore or coal, which is done by men or strong youths of 16 years or more, is also very weary work. The usual working day is eleven to twelve hours, often longer; in Scotland it reaches fourteen hours, and double time is frequent, when all the employees are at work below ground twenty-four, and even thirty-six hours at a stretch. Set times for meals are almost unknown, so that these people eat when hunger and time permit.

The standard of living of the miners is in general described as fairly good and their wages high in comparison with those of the agricultural labourers surrounding them (who, however, live at starvation rates), except in certain parts of Scotland and in the Irish mines, where great misery prevails: we shall have occasion to return later to this statement, which, by the way, is merely relative, implying comparison to the poorest class in all England. Meanwhile, we shall consider the evils which arise from the present method of mining, and the reader may judge whether any pay in money can indemnify the miner for such suffering.

The children and young people who are employed in transporting coal and iron-stone all complain of being overtired. Even in the most recklessly conducted industrial establishments there is no such universal and exaggerated overwork. The whole report proves this, with a number of examples on every page. It is constantly happening that children throw themselves down on the stone hearth or the floor as soon as they reach home, fall asleep at once without being able to take a bite of food, and have to be washed and put to bed while asleep; it even happens that they lie down on the way home, and are found by their parents late at night asleep on the road. It seems to be a universal practice among these children to spend Sunday in bed to recover in some degree from the over-exertion of the week. Church and school are visited by but few, and even of these the teachers complain of their great sleepiness and the want of all eagerness to learn. The same thing is true of the elder girls and women. They are overworked in the most brutal manner. This weariness, which is almost always carried to a most painful pitch, cannot fail to affect the constitution. The first result of such over-exertion is the diversion of vitality to the one-sided development of the muscles, so that those especially of the arms, legs, and back, of the shoulders and chest, which are chiefly called into activity in pushing and pulling, attain an uncommonly vigorous development, while all the rest of the body suffers and is atrophied from want of nourishment. More than all else the stature suffers, being stunted and retarded; nearly all miners are short, except those of Leicestershire and Warwickshire, who work under exceptionally favourable conditions. Further, among boys as well as girls, puberty is retarded, among the former often until the eighteenth year; indeed, a 19-year-old boy appeared before Commissioner Symons, showing no evidence beyond that of the teeth, that he was more than 11 or 12 years old. This prolongation of the period of childhood is at bottom nothing more than a sign of checked development, which does not fail to bear fruit in later years. Distortions of the legs, knees bent inwards and feet bent outwards, deformities of the spinal column and other malformations, appear the more readily in constitutions thus weakened, in consequence of the almost universally constrained position during work; and they are so frequent that in Yorkshire and Lancashire, as in Northumberland and Durham, the assertion is made by many witnesses, not only by physicians, that a miner may be recognized by his shape among a hundred other persons. The women seem to suffer especially from this work, and are seldom, if ever, as straight as other women. There is testimony here, too, to the fact that deformities of the pelvis and consequent difficult, even fatal, child-bearing arise from the work of women in the mines. But apart from these local deformities, the coal-miners suffer from a number of special affections easily explained by the nature of the work. Diseases of the digestive organs are first in order; want of appetite, pains in the stomach, nausea, and vomiting, are most frequent, with violent thirst, which can be quenched only with the dirty, lukewarm water of the mine; the digestion is checked and all the other affections are thus invited. Diseases of the heart, especially hypertrophy, inflammation of the heart and pericardium, contraction of the auriculo-ventricular communications and the entrance of the aorta are also mentioned repeatedly as diseases of the miners, and are readily explained by overwork; and the same is true of the almost universal rupture which is a direct consequence of protracted over-exertion. In part from the same cause and in part from the bad, dust-filled atmosphere mixed with carbonic acid and hydrocarbon gas, which might so readily be avoided, there arise numerous painful and dangerous affections of the lungs, especially asthma, which in some districts appears in the fortieth, in others in the thirtieth year in most of the miners, and makes them unfit for work in a short time. Among those employed in wet workings the oppression in the chest naturally appears much earlier; in some districts of Scotland between the twentieth and thirtieth years, during which time the affected lungs are especially susceptible to inflammations and diseases of a feverish nature. The peculiar disease of workers of this sort is 'black spittle', which arises from the saturation of the whole lung with coal particles, and manifests itself in general debility, headache, oppression of the chest, and thick, black mucous expectoration. In some districts this disease appears in a mild form; in others, on the contrary, it is wholly incurable, especially in Scotland. Here, besides the symptoms just mentioned, which appear in an intensified form, short, wheezing breathing, rapid pulse (exceeding 100 per minute), and abrupt coughing, with increasing leanness and debility, speedily make the patient unfit for work. Every case of this disease ends fatally. Dr Makellar, in Pencaitland, East Lothian, testified that in all the coal-mines which are properly ventilated this disease is unknown, while it frequently happens that miners who go from well- to ill-ventilated mines are seized by it. The profit-greed of mine owners which prevents the use of ventilators is therefore responsible for the fact that this working-men's disease exists at all. Rheumatism, too, is, with the exception of the Warwick and Leicestershire workers, a universal disease of the coal-miners, and arises especially from the frequently damp working-places. The consequence of all these diseases is that, in all districts *without exception*, the coal-miners age early and become unfit for work soon after the fortieth year, though this is different in different places. A coal-miner who can follow his calling after the forty-fifth or fiftieth year is a very great rarity indeed. It is universally recognized that such workers enter upon old age at 40. This applies to those who loosen the coal from the bed; the loaders, who have constantly to lift heavy blocks of coal into the tubs, age with the twenty-eighth or thirtieth year, so that it is proverbial in the coal-mining districts that the loaders are old before they are young. That this premature old age is followed by the early death of the colliers is a matter of course, and a man who reaches 60 is a great exception among them. Even in South Staffordshire, where the mines are comparatively wholesome, few men reach their fifty-first year. Along with this early superannuation of the workers we naturally find, just as in the case of the mills, frequent lack of employment of the elder men, who are often supported by very young children. If we sum up briefly the results of the work in coal-mines, we find, as Dr Southwood Smith, one of the commissioners, does, that through prolonged childhood on the one hand and premature age on the other, that period of life in which the human being is in full possession of his powers, the period of manhood, is greatly shortened, while the length of life in general is below the average. This, too, on the debit side of the bourgeoisie's reckoning!

All this deals only with the average of the English coal-mines. But there are many in which the state of things is much worse, those, namely, in which thin seams of coal are worked. The coal would be too expensive if a part of the adjacent sand and clay were removed; so the mine owners permit only the seams to be worked; whereby the passages which elsewhere are 4 or 5 feet high and more are here kept so low that to stand upright in them is not to be thought of. The working man lies on his side and loosens the coal with his pick; resting upon his elbow as a pivot, whence follow inflammations of the joint, and in cases where he is forced to kneel, of the knee also. The women and children who have to transport the coal crawl upon their hands and knees, fastened to the tub by a harness and chain (which frequently passes between the legs), while a man behind pushes with hands and head. The pushing with the head engenders local irritations, painful swellings, and ulcers. In many cases, too, the shafts are wet, so that these workers have to crawl through dirty or salt water several inches deep, being thus exposed to a special irritation of the skin. It can be readily imagined how greatly the diseases already peculiar to the miners are fostered by this especially frightful, slavish toil.

But these are not all the evils which descend upon the head of the coal-miner. In the whole British Empire there is no occupation in which a man may meet his end in so many diverse ways as in this one. The coal-mine is the scene of a multitude of the most terrifying calamities, and these come directly from the selfishness of the bourgeoisie. The hydro-carbon gas, which develops so freely in these mines, forms, when combined with atmospheric air, an explosive which takes fire upon coming into contact with a flame, and kills every one within its reach. Such explosions take place, in one mine or another, nearly every day; on 28 September 1844 one killed 96 men in Haswell Colliery, Durham. The carbonic acid gas, which also develops in great quantities, accumulates in the deeper parts of the mine, frequently reaching the height of a man, and suffocates everyone who gets into it. The doors which separate the sections of the mines are meant to prevent the propagation of explosions and the movement of the gases; but since they are entrusted to small children, who often fall asleep or neglect them, this means of prevention is illusory. A proper ventilation of the mines by means of fresh air-shafts could almost entirely remove the injurious effects of both these gases. But for this purpose the bourgeoisie has no money to spare, preferring to command the working men to use the Davy lamp, which is wholly useless because of its dull light, and is, therefore, usually replaced by a candle. If an explosion occurs, the recklessness of the miner is blamed, though the bourgeois might have made the explosion well-nigh impossible by supplying good ventilation. Further, every few days the roof of a working falls in, and buries or mangles the workers employed in it. It is the interest of the bourgeois to have the seams worked out as completely as possible, and hence the accidents of this sort. Then, too, the ropes by which the men descend into the mines are often rotten, and break, so that the unfortunates fall, and are crushed. All these accidents, and I have no room for special cases, carry off yearly, according to the *Mining Journal*, some 1,400 human beings. The *Manchester Guardian* reports at least two or three accidents every week for Lancashire alone. In nearly all mining districts the people composing the coroner's juries are, in almost all cases, dependent upon the mine owners, and where this is not the case, immemorial custom ensures that the verdict shall be: 'Accidental Death'. Besides, the jury takes very little interest in the state of the mine, because it does not understand anything about the matter. But the Children's Employment Commission does not hesitate to make the mine owners directly responsible for the greater number of these cases.

As to the education and morals of the mining population, they are, according to the Children's Employment Commission, pretty good in Cornwall, and excellent in Alston Moor; in the coal districts, in general, they are, on the contrary, reported as on an excessively low plane. The workers live in the country in neglected regions, and if they do their weary work, no human being outside the police force troubles himself about them. Hence, and from the tender age at which children are put to work, it follows that their mental education is wholly neglected. The day schools are not within their reach, the evening and Sunday schools mere shams, the teachers worthless. Hence, few can read and still fewer write. The only point upon which their eyes are as yet open is the fact that their wages are far too low for their hateful and dangerous work. To church they go seldom or never; all the clergy complain of their irreligion as beyond comparison. As a matter of fact, their ignorance of religious and of secular things, alike, is such that the ignorance of the factory operatives, shown in numerous examples in the foregoing pages, is trifling in comparison with it. The categories of religion are known to them only from the terms of their oaths. Their morality is destroyed by their work itself. That the overwork of all miners must engender drunkenness is self-evident. As to their sexual relations, men, women, and children work in the mines, in many cases, wholly naked, and in most cases, nearly so, by reason of the prevailing heat, and the consequences in the dark, lonely mines may be imagined. The number of illegitimate children is here disproportionately large, and indicates what goes on among the half-savage population below ground; but proves, too, that the illegitimate intercourse of the sexes has not here, as in the great cities, sunk to the level of prostitution. The labour of women entails the same consequences as in the factories, dissolves the family, and makes the mother totally incapable of household work.

When the Children's Employment Commission's Report was laid before Parliament, Lord Ashley hastened to bring in a bill wholly forbidding the work of women in the mines, and greatly limiting that of children. The bill was adopted,* but has remained a dead letter in most districts, because no mine inspectors were appointed to watch over its being carried into effect. The evasion of the law is very easy in the country districts in which the mines are situated; and no one need be surprised that the Miners' Union laid before the Home Secretary an official notice, last year, that in the Duke of Hamilton's coal-mines in Scotland, more than sixty women were at work; or that the *Manchester Guardian* reported that a girl perished in an explosion in a mine near Wigan, and no one troubled himself further about the fact that an infringement of the law was thus revealed. In single cases the employment of women may have been discontinued, but in general the old state of things remains as before.

These are, however, not all the afflictions known to the coal-miners. The bourgeoisie, not content with ruining the health of these people, keeping them in danger of sudden loss of life, robbing them of all opportunity for education, plunders them in other directions in the most shameless manner. The truck system is here the rule, not the exception, and is carried on in the most direct and undisguised manner. The cottage system,* likewise, is universal, and here almost a necessity; but it is used here, too, for the better plundering of the workers. To these means of oppression must be added all sorts of direct cheating. While coal is sold by weight, the worker's wages are reckoned chiefly by measure; and when his tub is not perfectly full he receives no pay whatever, while he gets not a farthing for over-measure. If there is more than a specified quantity of dust in the tub, a matter which depends much less upon the miner than upon the nature of the seam, he not only loses his whole wage but is fined besides. The fine system in general is so highly perfected in the coal-mines that a poor devil who has worked the whole week and comes for his wages, sometimes learns from the overseer, who fines at discretion and without summoning the workers, that he not only has no wages but must pay so and so much in fines extra! The overseer has, in general, absolute power over wages; he notes the work done, and can please himself as to what he pays the worker, who is forced to take his word. In some mines, where the pay is according to weight, false decimal scales are used, whose weights are not subject to the inspection of the authorities; in one coal-mine there was actually a regulation that any workman who intended to complain of the falseness of the scales *must give notice to the overseer three weeks in advance*! In many districts, especially in the North of England, it is customary to engage the workers by the year; they pledge themselves to work for no other employer during that time, but the mine owner by no means pledges himself to give them work, so that they are often without it for months together, and if they seek elsewhere, they are sent to the treadmill for six weeks for breach of contract. In other contracts, work to the amount of 26s. every 14 days, is promised the miners, but not furnished; in others still, the employers advance the miners small sums to be worked out afterwards, thus binding the debtors to themselves. In the North, the custom is general of keeping the payment of wages one week behindhand, chaining the miners in this way to their work. And to complete the slavery of these enthralled workers nearly all the Justices of the Peace in the coal districts are mine owners themselves, or relatives or friends of mine owners, and possess almost unlimited power in these poor, uncivilized regions where there are few newspapers, these few in the service of the ruling class, and but little other agitation. It is almost beyond conception how these poor coal-miners have been plundered and tyrannized over by Justices of the Peace acting as judges in their own cause.

So it went on for a long time. The workers did not know any better than that they were there for the purpose of being swindled out of their very lives. But gradually, even among them, and especially in the factory districts, where contact with the more intelligent operatives could not fail of its effect, there arose a spirit of opposition to the shameless oppression of the 'coal kings'. The men began to form Unions and strike from time to time. In civilized districts they joined the Chartists body and soul. The great coal district of the North of England, shut off from all industrial intercourse, remained backward until, after many efforts, partly of the Chartists and partly of the more intelligent miners themselves, a general spirit of opposition arose in 1843. Such a movement seized the workers of Northumberland and Durham that they placed themselves at the forefront of a general Union of coal-miners throughout the kingdom, and appointed W. P. Roberts, a Chartist solicitor, of Bristol, their 'Attorney-General', he having distinguished himself in earlier Chartist trials. The Union soon spread over a great majority of the districts; agents were appointed in all directions, who held meetings everywhere and secured new members; at the first conference of delegates, in Manchester, in 1844, there were 60,000 members represented, and at Glasgow, six months later, at the second conference, 100,000. Here all the affairs of the coal-miners were discussed and decisions as to the greater strikes arrived at. Several journals were founded, especially the *Miner's Advocate*, at Newcastle upon Tyne, for defending the rights of the miners. On 31 March 1844 the contracts of all the miners of Northumberland and Durham expired. Roberts was empowered to draw up a new agreement, in which the men demanded:

(1) Payment by weight instead of measure;
(2) Determination of weight by means of ordinary scales subject to the public inspectors;
(3) Half-yearly renewal of contracts;
(4) Abolition of the fines system and payment according to work actually done;
(5) The employers to guarantee to miners in their exclusive service at least four days' work per week, or wages for the same.

This agreement was submitted to the 'coal kings', and a deputation appointed to negotiate with them; they answered, however, that for them the Union did not exist, that they had to deal with single workmen only, and should never recognize the Union. They also submitted an agreement of their own which ignored all the foregoing points, and was, naturally, refused by the miners. War was thus declared. On 31 March 1844 40,000 miners laid down their picks, and every mine in the country stood empty. The funds of the Union were so considerable that for several months a weekly contribution of 2s. 6d. could be assured to each family. While the miners were thus putting the patience of their masters to the test, Roberts organized with uncomparable perseverance both strike and agitation, arranged for the holding of meetings, traversed England from one end to the other, preached peaceful and legal agitation, and carried on a crusade against the despotic Justices of the Peace and truck masters, such as had never been known in England. This he had begun at the beginning of the year. Wherever a miner had been condemned by a Justice of the Peace, he obtained a habeas corpus from the Court of Queen's Bench, brought his client to London, and always secured an acquittal. Thus, on 13 January, Judge Williams of Queen's Bench acquitted three miners condemned by the Justices of the Peace of Bilston, South Staffordshire; the offence of these people was that they refused to work in a place which threatened to cave in, and had actually caved in before their return! On an earlier occasion, Judge Patteson had acquitted six working men, so that the name Roberts began to be a terror to the mine owners. In Preston four of his clients were in jail. In the first week of January he proceeded thither to investigate the case on the spot, but found, when he arrived, the condemned all released before the expiration of the sentence. In Manchester there were seven in jail; Roberts obtained a habeas corpus and acquittal for all from Judge Wightman. In Prescott nine coal-miners were in jail, accused of creating a disturbance in St Helens, South Lancashire, and awaiting trial; when Roberts arrived upon the spot, they were released at once. All this took place in the first half of February. In April, Roberts released a miner from jail in Derby, four in Wakefield, and four in Leicester. So it went on for a time until these Dogberries* came to have some respect for the miners. The truck system shared the same fate. One after another Roberts brought the disreputable mine owners before the courts, and compelled the reluctant Justices of the Peace to condemn them; such dread of this 'lightning' 'Attorney-General' who seemed to be everywhere at once spread among them, that at Belper, for instance, upon Roberts' arrival, a truck firm published the following notice:

NOTICE!
Pentrich Coal-Mine.

The Messrs. Haslam think it necessary, in order to prevent all mistakes, to announce that all persons employed in their colliery will receive their wages wholly in cash, and may expend them when and as they choose to do. If they purchase goods in the shops of Messrs. Haslam they will receive them as heretofore at wholesale prices, but they are not expected to make their purchases there, and work and wages will be continued as usual whether purchases are made in these shops or elsewhere.

This triumph aroused the greatest jubilation throughout the English working class, and brought the Union a mass of new members. Meanwhile the strike in the North was proceeding. Not a hand stirred, and Newcastle, the chief coal port, was so stripped of its commodity that coal had to be brought from the Scottish coast, in spite of the proverb. At first, while the Union's funds held out, all went well, but towards summer the struggle became much more painful for the miners. The greatest want prevailed among them; they had no money, for the contributions of the workers of all branches of industry in England availed little among the vast number of strikers, who were forced to borrow from the small shopkeepers at a heavy loss. The whole press, with the single exception of the few proletarian journals, was against them; the bourgeois, even the few among them who might have had enough sense of justice to support the miners, learnt from the corrupt Liberal and Conservative sheets only lies about them. A deputation of twelve miners who went to London received a sum from the proletariat there, but this, too, availed little among the mass who needed support. Yet, in spite of all this, the miners remained steadfast, and what is even more significant, were quiet and peaceable in the face of all the hostilities and provocation of the mine owners and their faithful servants. No act of revenge was carried out, not a renegade was maltreated, not one single theft committed. Thus the strike had continued well on towards four months, and the mine owners still had no prospect of getting the upper hand. One way was, however, still open to them. They remembered the cottage system; it occurred to them that the houses of the rebellious spirits were THEIR property. In July, notice to quit was served the workers, and, in a week, the whole 40,000 were put out of doors. This measure was carried out with revolting cruelty. The sick, the feeble, old men and little children, even women in child-birth, were mercilessly turned from their beds and cast into the roadside ditches. One agent dragged by the hair from her bed, and into the street, a woman in the pangs of child-birth. Soldiers and police in crowds were present, ready to fire at the first symptom of resistance, on the slightest hint of the Justices of the Peace, who had brought about the whole brutal procedure. This, too, the working men endured without resistance. The hope had been that the men would use violence; they were spurred on with all force to infringements of the laws, to furnish an excuse for making an end of the strike by the intervention of the military. The homeless miners, remembering the warnings of their Attorney-General, remained unmoved, set up their household goods upon the moors or the harvested fields, and held out. Some, who had no other place, encamped on the roadsides and in ditches, others upon land belonging to other people, whereupon they were prosecuted, and, having caused 'damage of the value of a half-penny', were fined a pound, and, being unable to pay it, worked it out on the treadmill. Thus they lived eight weeks and more of the wet fag-end of last summer under the open sky with their families, with no further shelter for themselves and their little ones than the calico curtains of their beds; with no other help than the scanty allowances of their Union and the fast shrinking credit with the small dealers. Hereupon Lord Londonderry, who owns considerable mines in Durham, threatened the small tradesmen in 'his' town of Seaham with his most high displeasure if they should continue to give credit to 'his' rebellious workers. This 'noble' lord made himself the first clown of the turnout in consequence of the ridiculous, pompous, ungrammatical ukases* addressed to the workers, which he published from time to time, with no other result than the merriment of the nation. When none of their efforts produced any effect, the mine owners imported, at great expense, hands from Ireland and such remote parts of Wales as have as yet no labour movement. And when the competition of workers against workers was thus restored, the strength of the strikers collapsed. The mine owners obliged them to renounce the Union, abandon Roberts, and accept the conditions laid down by the employers. Thus ended at the close of September the great five months' battle of the coal-miners against the mine owners, a battle fought on the part of the oppressed with an endurance, courage, intelligence, and coolness which demands the highest admiration. What a degree of true human culture, of enthusiasm and strength of character, such a battle implies on the part of men who, as we have seen in the Children's Employment Commission's Report, were described as late as 1840, as being thoroughly brutal and wanting in moral sense! But how hard, too, must have been the pressure which brought these 40,000 colliers to rise as one man and to fight out the battle like an army not only well-disciplined but enthusiastic, an army possessed of one single determination, with the greatest coolness and composure, to a point beyond which further resistance would have been madness. And what a battle! Not against visible, mortal enemies, but against hunger, want, misery, and homelessness, against their own passions provoked to madness by the brutality of wealth. If they had revolted with violence, they, the unarmed and defenceless, would have been shot down, and a day or two would have decided the victory of the owners. This law-abiding reserve was no fear of the constable's staff, it was the result of deliberation, the best proof of the intelligence and self-control of the working men.

Thus were the working men forced once more, in spite of their unexampled endurance, to succumb to the might of capital. But the fight had not been in vain. First of all, this nineteen week's strike had torn the miners of the North of England forever from the intellectual death in which they had hitherto lain; they have left their sleep, are alert to defend their interests, and have entered the movement of civilization, and especially the movement of the workers. The strike, which first brought to light the whole cruelty of the owners, has established the opposition of the workers here, forever, and made at least two-thirds of them Chartists; and the acquisition of 30,000 such determined experienced men is certainly of great value to the Chartists. Then, too, the endurance and law-abiding which characterized the whole strike, coupled with the active agitation which accompanied it, has fixed public attention upon the miners. On the occasion of the debate upon the export duty on coal, Thomas Duncombe, the only decidedly Chartist member of the House of Commons, brought up the condition of the coal-miners, had their petition read, and by his speech forced the bourgeois journals to publish, at least in their reports of Parliamentary proceedings, a correct statement of the case. Immediately after the strike, occurred the explosion at Haswell; Roberts went to London, demanded an audience with Peel, insisted as representative of the miners upon a thorough investigation of the case, and succeeded in having the first geological and chemical notabilities of England, Professors Lyell and Faraday, commissioned to visit the spot. As several other explosions followed in quick succession, and Roberts again laid the details before the Prime Minister, the latter promised to propose the necessary measures for the protection of the workers, if possible, in the next session of Parliament, i.e. the present one of 1845. All this would not have been accomplished if these workers had not, by means of the strike, proved themselves freedom-loving men worthy of all respect, and if they had not engaged Roberts as their counsel.

Scarcely had it become known that the coal-miners of the North had been forced to renounce the Union and discharge Roberts, when the miners of Lancashire formed a Union of some 10,000 men, and guaranteed their Attorney-General a salary of £1,200 a year. In the autumn of last year they collected more than £700, rather more than £200 of which they expended upon salaries and judicial expenses, and the rest chiefly in support of men out of work, either through want of employment or through dissensions with their employers. Thus the working men are constantly coming to see more clearly that, united, they too are a respectable power, and can, in the last extremity, defy even the might of the bourgeoisie. And this insight, the gain of all labour movements, has been won for all the miners of England by the Union and the strike of 1844. In a very short time the difference of intelligence and energy which now exists in favour on the factory operatives will have vanished, and the miners of the kingdom will be able to stand abreast of them in every respect.[1] Thus one piece of standing ground after another is undermined beneath the feet of the bourgeoisie; and how long will it be before their whole social and political edifice collapses with the basis upon which it rests?

But the bourgeoisie will not take warning. The resistance of the miners does but embitter it the more. Instead of appreciating this forward step in the general movement of the workers, the property-holding class saw in it only a

[1] The coal-miners have at this moment, 1886, six of their body sitting in the House of Commons.

source of rage against a class of people who are fools enough to declare themselves no longer submissive to the treatment they had hitherto received. It saw in the just demands of the non-possessing workers only impertinent discontent, mad rebellion against 'Divine and human order'; and, in the best case, a success (to be resisted by the bourgeoisie with all its might) won by 'ill-intentioned demagogues who live by agitation and are too lazy to work'. It sought, of course, without success, to represent to the workers that Roberts and the Union's agents, whom the Union very naturally had to pay, were insolent swindlers, who drew the last farthing from the working men's pockets. When such insanity prevails in the property-holding class, when it is so blinded by its momentary profit that it no longer has eyes for the most conspicuous signs of the times, surely all hope of a peaceful solution of the social question for England must be abandoned. The only possible solution is a violent revolution, which cannot fail to take place.

10

The Agricultural Proletariat

WE have seen in the introduction how, simultaneously with the small bourgeoisie and the modest independence of the former workers, the small peasantry also was ruined when the former Union of industrial and agricultural work was dissolved, the abandoned fields thrown together into large farms, and the small peasants superseded by the overwhelming competition of the large farmers. Instead of being landowners or leaseholders, as they had been hitherto, they were now obliged to hire themselves as labourers to the large farmers or the landlords. For a time this position was endurable, though a deterioration in comparison with their former one. The extension of industry kept pace with the increase of population until the progress of manufacture began to assume a slower pace, and the perpetual improvement of machinery made it impossible for manufacture to absorb the whole surplus of the agricultural population. From this time forward, the distress which had hitherto existed only in the manufacturing districts, and then only at times, appeared in the agricultural districts too. The twenty-five years' struggle with France came to an end at about the same time; the diminished production at the various seats of the wars, the shutting off of imports, and the necessity of providing for the British army in Spain, had given English agriculture an artificial prosperity, and had besides withdrawn to the army vast numbers of workers from their ordinary occupations. This check upon the import trade, the opportunity for exportation, and the military demand for workers, now suddenly came to an end; and the necessary consequence was what the English call agricultural distress. The farmers had to sell their corn at low prices, and could, therefore, pay only low wages. In 1815, in order to keep up prices, the Corn Laws were prohibiting the importation of corn so long as the price of wheat continued less than 80 s. per quarter. These naturally ineffective laws were several times modified, but did not succeed in ameliorating the distress in the agricultural districts. All that they did was to change the disease, which, under free competition from abroad, would have assumed an acute form, culminating in a series of crises, into a chronic one which bore heavily but uniformly upon the farm labourers.

For a time after the rise of the agricultural proletariat, the patriarchal relation between master and man, which was being destroyed for manufacture, developed here the same relation of the farmer to his hands which still exists almost everywhere in Germany. So long as this lasted, the poverty of the farm-hands was less conspicuous; they shared the fate of the farmer, and were discharged only in cases of the direst necessity. But now all this is changed. The farm-hands have become day-labourers almost everywhere, are employed only when needed by the farmers, and, therefore, often have no work for weeks together, especially in winter. In the patriarchal time, the hands and their families lived on the farm, and their children grew up there, the farmer trying to find occupation on the spot for the oncoming generation; day-labourers, then, were the exception, not the rule. Thus there was, on every farm, a larger number of hands than were strictly necessary. It became, therefore, the interest of the farmers to dissolve this relation, drive the farm-hand from the farm, and transform him into a day-labourer. This took place pretty generally towards the year 1830, and the consequence was that the hitherto latent over-population was set free, the rate of wages forced down, and the poor-rate enormously increased. From this time the agricultural districts became the headquarters of permanent, as the manufacturing districts had long been of periodic, pauperism; and the modification of the Poor Law was the first measure which the State was obliged to apply to the daily increasing impoverishment of the country parishes. Moreover, the constant extension of farming on a large scale, the introduction of threshing and other machines, and the employment of women and children (which is now so general that its effects have recently been investigated by a special official commission), threw a large number of men out of employment. It is manifest, therefore, that here, too, the system of industrial production has made its entrance, by means of farming on a large scale, by the abolition of the patriarchal relation, which is of the greatest importance just here, by the introduction of machinery, steam, and the labour of women and children. In so doing, it has swept the last and most stationary portion of working humanity into the revolutionary movement. But the longer agriculture had remained stationary, the heavier now became the burden upon the worker, the more violently broke forth the results of the disorganization of the old social fabric. The 'over-population' came to light all at once, and could not, as in the manufacturing districts, be absorbed by the needs of an increasing production. New factories could always be built, if there were consumers for their products, but new land could not be created. The cultivation of waste common land was too daring a speculation for the bad times following the conclusion of peace. The necessary consequence was that the competition of the workers among each other reached the highest point of intensity, and wages fell to the minimum. So long as the old Poor Law existed,[1] the workers received relief from the rates; wages naturally fell still lower, because the farmers forced the largest possible number of labourers to claim relief. The higher poor-rate, necessitated by the surplus population, was only increased by this measure, and the new Poor Law, of which we shall have more to say later, was now enacted as a remedy. But this did not improve matters. Wages did not rise, the surplus population could not be got rid of, and the cruelty of the new law did but serve to embitter the people to the utmost. Even the poor-rate, which diminished at first after the passage of the new law, attained its old height after a few years. Its only effect was that whereas previously three to four million half paupers had existed, a million of total paupers now appeared, and the rest, still half paupers, merely went without relief. The poverty in the agricultural districts has increased every year. The people live in the greatest want, whole families must struggle along with 6, 7, or 8 s. a week, and at times have nothing. Let us hear a description of this population given by a Liberal Member of Parliament as early as 1830:[2]

[1] Extracts from Information received from the Poor Law Commissioners. Published by authority (London, 1833).

[2] E. G. Wakefield, MP, *Swing Unmasked; or, The Cause of Rural Incendiarism.* (London, 1831). Pamphlet. The foregoing extracts may be found on pp. 9–13, the passage dealing in the original with the then still existing Old Poor Law being here omitted.

An English agricultural labourer and an English pauper, these words are synonymous. His father was a pauper and his mother's milk contained no nourishment. From his earliest childhood he had bad food, and only half enough to still his hunger, and even yet he undergoes the pangs of unsatisfied hunger almost all the time that he is not asleep. He is half clad, and has not more fire than barely suffices to cook his scanty meal. And so cold and damp are always at home with him, and leave him only in fine weather. He is married, but he knows nothing of the joys of the husband and father. His wife and children, hungry, rarely warm, often ill and helpless, always careworn and hopeless like himself, are naturally grasping, selfish, and troublesome, and so, to use his own expression, he hates the sight of them, and enters his cot only because it offers him a trifle more shelter from rain and wind than a hedge. He must support his family, though he cannot do so, whence come beggary, deceit of all sorts, ending in fully developed craftiness. If he were so inclined, he yet has not the courage which makes of the more energetic of his class wholesale poachers and smugglers. But he pilfers when occasion offers, and teaches his children to lie and steal. His abject and submissive demeanour towards his wealthy neighbours shows that they treat him roughly and with suspicion; hence he fears and hates them, but he never will injure them by force. He is depraved through and through, too far gone to possess even the strength of despair. His wretched existence is brief, rheumatism and asthma bring him to the workhouse, where he will draw his last breath without a single pleasant recollection, and will make room for another luckless wretch to live and die as he has done.

Our author adds that besides this class of agricultural labourers, there is still another, somewhat more energetic and better endowed physically, mentally, and morally; those, namely, who live as wretchedly, but were not born to this condition. These he represents as better in their family life, but smugglers and poachers who get into frequent bloody conflicts with the gamekeepers and revenue officers of the coast, become more embittered against society during the prison life which they often undergo, and so stand abreast of the first class in their hatred of the property-holders. 'And', he says, in closing, 'this whole class is called, by courtesy, the bold peasantry of England.'

Down to the present time, this description applies to the greater portion of the agricultural labourers of England. In June 1844 *The Times* sent a correspondent into the agricultural districts to report upon the condition of this class, and the report which he furnished agreed wholly with the foregoing. In certain districts wages were not more than 6s. a week; not more, that is, than in many districts in Germany, while the prices of all the necessaries of life are at least twice as high. What sort of life these people lead may be imagined; their food scanty and bad, their clothing ragged, their dwellings cramped and desolate, small, wretched huts, with no comforts whatsoever; and, for young people, lodging-houses, where men and women are scarcely separated, and illegitimate intercourse thus provoked. One or two days without work in the course of a month must inevitably plunge such people into the direst want. Moreover, they cannot combine to raise wages, because they are scattered, and if one alone refuses to work for low wages, there are dozens out of work, or supported by the rates, who are thankful for the most trifling offer, while to him who declines work, every other form of relief than the hated workhouse is refused by the Poor Law guardians as to a lazy vagabond; for the guardians are the very farmers from whom or from whose neighbours and acquaintances alone he can get work. And not from one or two special districts of England do such reports come. On the contrary, the distress is general, equally great in the North and South, the East and West. The condition of the labourers in Suffolk and Norfolk corresponds with that of Devonshire, Hampshire, and Sussex. Wages are as low in Dorsetshire and Oxfordshire as in Kent and Surrey, Buckinghamshire and Cambridgeshire.

One especially barbaric cruelty against the working class is embodied in the Game Laws, which are more stringent than in any other country, while the game is plentiful beyond all conception. The English peasant who, according to the old English custom and tradition, sees in poaching only a natural and noble expression of courage and daring, is stimulated still further by the contrast between his own poverty and the *car tel est notre plaisir** of the lord, who preserves thousands of hares and game birds for his private enjoyment. The labourer lays snares, or shoots here and there a piece of game. It does not injure the landlord as a matter of fact, for he has a vast superfluity, and it brings the poacher a meal for himself and his starving family. But if he is caught he goes to jail, and for a second offence receives at the least seven years' transportation. From the severity of these laws arise the frequent bloody conflicts with the gamekeepers, which lead to a number of murders every year. Hence the post of game-keeper is not only dangerous, but of ill-repute and despised. Last year, in two cases, gamekeepers shot themselves rather than continue their work. Such is the moderate price at which the landed aristocracy purchases the noble sport of shooting; but what does it matter to the lords of the soil? Whether one or two more or less of the 'surplus' live or die matters nothing, and even if in consequence of the Game Laws half the surplus population could be put out of the way, it would be all the better for the other half—according to the philanthropy of the English landlords.

Although the conditions of life in the country, the isolated dwellings, the stability of the surroundings and occupations, and consequently of the thoughts, are decidedly unfavour-able to all development, yet poverty and want bear their fruits even here. The manufacturing and mining proletariat emerged early from the first stage of resistance to our social order, the direct rebellion of the individual by the perpetra-tion of crime; but the peasants are still in this stage at the present time. Their favourite method of social warfare is incendiarism. In the winter which followed the Revolution of July, in 1830–1, these incendiarisms first became general. Disturbances had taken place, and the whole region of Sussex and the adjacent counties had been brought into a state of excitement in October, in consequence of an increase of the coastguard (which made smuggling much more dif-ficult and 'ruined the coast'—in the words of a farmer), changes in the Poor Law, low wages, and the introduction of machinery. In the winter the farmers' hay and corn-stacks were burnt in the fields, and the very barns and stables under their windows. Nearly every night a couple of such fires blazed up, and spread terror among the farmers and land-lords. The offenders were rarely discovered, and the workers attributed the incendiarism to a mythical person whom they named 'Swing'. Men puzzled their brains to discover who this Swing could be and whence this rage among the poor of the country districts. Of the great motive power, Want, Oppression, only a single person here and there thought, and certainly no one in the agricultural districts. Since that year the incendiarisms have been repeated every winter, with each recurring unemployed season of the agricultural labourers. In the winter of 1843–4, they were once more extraordinarily frequent. There lies before me a series of numbers of the *Northern Star* of that time, each one of which contains a report of several incendiarisms, stating in each case its authority. The numbers wanting in the following list I have not at hand; but they, too, doubtless contain a number of cases. Moreover, such a sheet cannot possibly ascertain all the cases which occur. 25 November 1843, two cases; several earlier ones are discussed. 16 December, in Bedfordshire, general excitement for a fortnight past in consequence of frequent incendiarisms, of which several take place every night. Two great farmhouses burnt down within the last few days; in Cambridgeshire four great farmhouses, Hertfordshire one, and besides these, fifteen other incendiarisms in different districts. 30 December, in Norfolk one, Suffolk two, Essex two, Cheshire one, Lancashire one, Derby, Lincoln, and the South twelve. 6 January 1844, in all ten. 13 January, seven. 20 January, four incendiarisms. From this time forward, three or four incendiarisms per week are reported, and not as formerly until the spring only, but far into July and August. And that crimes of this sort are increasing in the approaching hard season of 1844–5, the English papers already indicate.

What do my readers think of such a state of things in the quiet, idyllic country districts of England? Is this social war, or is it not? Is it a natural state of things which can last? Yet here the landlords and farmers are as dull and stupefied, as blind to everything which does not directly put money into their pockets, as the manufacturers and the bourgeoisie in general in the manufacturing districts. If the latter promise their employees salvation through the repeal of the Corn Laws,* the landlords and a great part of the farmers promise theirs heaven upon earth from the maintenance of the same laws. But in neither case do the property-holders succeed in winning the workers to the support of their pet hobby. Like the operatives, the agricultural labourers are thoroughly indifferent to the repeal or non-repeal of the Corn Laws. Yet the question is an important one for both. That is to say—by the repeal of the Corn Laws, free competition, the present social economy is carried to its extreme point; all further development within the present order comes to an end, and the only possible step further is a radical transformation of the social order.[1] For the agricultural labourers the question has, further, the following important bearing: Free importation of corn involves (how, I cannot explain *here*) the emancipation of the farmers from the landlords, their transformation into Liberals. Towards this consummation the Anti-Corn Law League has already largely contributed, and this is its only real service. When the farmers become Liberals, i.e. conscious bourgeois, the agricultural labourers will inevitably become Chartists and Socialists; the first change involves the second. And that a new movement is already beginning among the agricultural labourers is proved by a meeting which Earl Radnor, a Liberal landlord, caused to be held in October 1844, near Highworth, where his estates lie, to pass resolutions against the Corn Laws. At this meeting, the labourers, perfectly indifferent as to these laws, demanded something wholly different, namely smallholdings, at low rent, for themselves, telling Earl Radnor all sorts of bitter truths to his face. Thus the movement of the working class is finding its way into the remote, stationary, mentally dead agricultural districts; and, thanks to the general distress, will soon be as firmly rooted and energetic as in the manufacturing districts.[2]

As to the religious state of the agricultural labourers, they are, it is true, more pious than the manufacturing operatives; but they, too, are greatly at odds with the Church—for in these districts members of the Established Church almost exclusively are to be found. A correspondent of the *Morning Chronicle*, who, over the signature, 'One who has whistled at the plough', reports his tour through the agricultural districts, relates, among other things, the following conversation with some labourers after service.

---

[1] This has been literally fulfilled. After a period of unexampled extension of trade, Free Trade has landed England in a crisis, which began in 1878, and is still increasing in energy in 1886.

[2] The agricultural labourers have now a Trade Union; their most energetic representative, Joseph Arch, was elected MP in 1885.

I asked one of these people whether the preacher of the day was their own clergyman. 'Yes, blast him! He is our own parson, and begs the whole time. He's been always a-begging as long as I've known him.' (The sermon had been upon a mission to the heathen.) 'And as long as I've known him too,' added another; 'and I never knew a parson but what was begging for this or the other.' 'Yes,' said a woman, who had just come out of the church, 'and look how wages are going down, and see the rich vagabonds with whom the parsons eat and drink and hunt. So help me God, we are more fit to starve in the workhouse than pay the parsons as go among the heathen.' 'And why,' said another, 'don't they send the parsons as drones every day in Salisbury Cathedral, for nobody but the bare stones? Why don't *they* go among the heathen?' 'They don't go,' said the old man whom I had first asked, 'because they are rich, they have all the land they need, they want the money in order to get rid of the poor parsons. I know what they want. I know them too long for that.' 'But, good friends,' I asked, 'you surely do not always come out of the church with such bitter feelings towards the preacher? Why do you go at all?' 'What for do we go?' said the woman. 'We must, if we do not want to lose everything, work and all, we must.' I learned later that they had certain little privileges of fire-wood and potato land (which they paid for!) on condition of going to church.

After describing their poverty and ignorance, the correspondent closes by saying: 'And now I boldly assert that the condition of these people, their poverty, their hatted of the church, their external submission and inward bitterness against the ecclesiastical dignitaries, is the rule among the country parishes of England, and its opposite is the exception.'

If the peasantry of England shows the consequences which a numerous agricultural proletariat in connection with large farming involves for the country districts, Wales illustrates the ruin of the smallholders. If the English country parishes reproduce the antagonism between capitalist and proletarian, the state of the Welsh peasantry corresponds to the progressive ruin of the small bourgeoisie in the towns. In Wales are to be found, almost exclusively, smallholders, who cannot with like profit sell their products as cheaply as the larger, more favourably situated English farmers, with whom, however, they are obliged to compete. Moreover, in some places the quality of the land admits of the raising of livestock only, which is but slightly profitable. Then, too, these Welsh farmers, by reason of their separate nationality, which they retain pertinaciously, are much more stationary than the English farmers. But the competition among themselves and with their English neighbours (and the increased mortgages upon their land consequent upon this) has reduced them to such a state that they can scarcely live at all; and because they have not recognized the true cause of their wretched condition, they attribute it to all sorts of small causes, such as high tolls, etc., which do check the development of agriculture and commerce, but are taken into account as standing charges by everyone who takes a holding, and are therefore really ultimately paid by the landlord. Here, too, the new Poor Law is cordially hated by the tenants, who hover in perpetual danger of coming under its sway. In 1843 the famous 'Rebecca' disturbances broke out among the Welsh peasantry; the men dressed in women's clothing, blackened their faces, and fell in armed crowds upon the toll-gates, destroyed them amidst great rejoicing and firing of guns, demolished the toll-keepers' houses, wrote threatening letters in the name of the imaginary 'Rebecca', and once went so far as to storm the workhouse of Carmarthen. Later, when the militia was called out and the police strengthened, the peasants drew them off with wonderful skill upon false scents; demolished toll-gates at one point while the militia, lured by false signal bugles, was marching in some opposite direction; and betook themselves finally, when the police was too thoroughly reinforced, to single incendiarisms and attempts at murder. As usual, these greater crimes were the end of the movement. Many withdrew from disapproval, others from fear, and peace was restored of itself. The Government appointed a commission to investigate the affair and its causes, and there was an end of the matter. The poverty of the peasantry continues, however, and will one day, since it cannot under existing circumstances grow less, but must go on intensifying, produce more serious manifestations than these humorous Rebecca masquerades.

If England illustrates the results of the system of farming on a large scale and Wales on a small one, Ireland exhibits the consequences of overdividing the soil. The great mass of the population of Ireland consists of small tenants who occupy a sorry hut without partitions, and a potato patch just large enough to supply them most scantily with potatoes through the winter. In consequence of the great competition which prevails among these small tenants, the rent has reached an unheard-of height, double, treble, and quadruple that paid in England. For every agricultural labourer seeks to become a tenant-farmer, and though the division of land has gone so far, there still remain numbers of labourers in competition for plots. Although in Great Britain 32,000,000 acres of land are cultivated, and in Ireland but 14,000,000; although Great Britain produces agricultural products to the value of £150,000,000, and Ireland of but £36,000,000, there are in Ireland 75,000 agricultural proletarians *more* than in the neighbouring island.[1] How great the competition for land in Ireland must be is evident from this extraordinary disproportion, especially when one reflects that the labourers in Great Britain are living in the utmost distress. The consequence of this competition is that it is impossible for the tenants to live much better than the labourers, by reason of the high rents paid. The Irish people is thus held in crushing poverty, from which it cannot free itself under our present social conditions. These people live in the most wretched clay huts, scarcely good enough for cattle-pens, have scant food all winter long, or, as the report above quoted expresses it, they have potatoes half enough thirty weeks in the year, and the rest of the year nothing. When the time comes in the spring at which this provision reaches its end, or can no longer be used because of its sprouting, wife and children go forth to beg and tramp the country with their kettle in their hands. Meanwhile the husband, after planting potatoes for the next year, goes in search of work either in Ireland or England, and returns at the potato harvest to his family. This is the condition in which nine-tenths of the Irish country folks live. They are poor as church mice, wear the most wretched rags, and stand upon the lowest plane of intelligence possible in a half-civilized country. According to the report quoted, there are, in a population of 8½ millions, 585,000

---

[1] Report of the Poor Law Commission on Ireland [Parliamentary Session of 1837. (*Added in the German edition.*)]

heads of families in a state of total destitution; and according to other authorities, cited by Sheriff Alison,[1] there are in Ireland 2,300,000 persons who could not live without public or private assistance—or 27 per cent of the whole population paupers!

The cause of this poverty lies in the existing social conditions, especially in competition here found in the form of the subdivision of the soil. Much effort has been spent in finding other causes. It has been asserted that the relation of the tenant to the landlord who lets his estate in large lots to tenants, who again have their sub-tenants, and sub-sub-tenants, in turn, so that often ten middlemen come between the landlord and the actual cultivator—it has been asserted that the shameful law which gives the landlord the right of expropriating the cultivator who may have paid his rent duly, if the first tenant fails to pay the landlord, that this law is to blame for all this poverty. But all this determines only the form in which the poverty manifests itself. Make the small tenant a landowner himself and what follows? The majority could not live upon their holdings even if they had no rent to pay, and any slight improvement which might take place would be lost again in a few years in consequence of the rapid increase of population. The children would then live to grow up under the improved conditions who now die in consequence of poverty in early childhood. From another side comes the assertion that the shameless oppression inflicted by the English is the cause of the trouble. It is the cause of the somewhat earlier appearance of this poverty, but not of the poverty itself. Or the blame is laid on the Protestant Church forced upon a Catholic nation; but divide among the Irish what the Church takes from them, and it does not reach 6s. a head. Besides, tithes are a tax upon landed property, not upon the tenant, though he may nominally pay them; now, since the Commutation Bill of 1838, the landlord pays the tithes directly and reckons so much higher rent, so that the tenant is none the better off. And in the same way a hundred other causes of this poverty are brought forward, all proving as little as these. This poverty is the result of our social conditions; apart from

---

[1] *Principles of Population*, vol. ii.

these, causes may be found for the manner in which it manifests itself, but not for the fact of its existence. That poverty manifests itself in Ireland thus and not otherwise, is owing to the character of the people, and to their historical development. The Irish are a people related in their whole character to the Latin nations, to the French, and especially to the Italians. The bad features of their character we have already had depicted by Carlyle. Let us now hear an Irishman, who at least comes nearer to the truth than Carlyle, with his prejudice in favour of the Teutonic character:[1] 'They are restless, yet indolent, clever and indiscreet, stormy, impatient, and improvident; brave by instinct, generous without much reflection, quick to revenge and forgive insults, to make and to renounce friendships, gifted with genius prodigally, sparingly with judgement.' With the Irish, feeling and passion predominate; reason must bow before them. Their sensuous, excitable nature prevents reflection and quiet, persevering activity from reaching development—such a nation is utterly unfit for manufacture as now conducted. Hence they held fast to agriculture, and remained upon the lowest plane even of that. With the small subdivisions of land, which were not here artificially created, as in France and on the Rhine, by the division of great estates,[2] but have existed from time immemorial, an improvement of the soil by the investment of capital was not to be thought of; and it would, according to Alison, require £120 million to bring the soil up to the not very high state of fertility already attained in England. The English immigration, which might have raised the standard of Irish civilization, has contented itself with the most brutal plundering of the Irish people; and while the Irish, by their immigration into England, have furnished England a leaven which will produce its own results in the future, they have little for which to be thankful to the English immigration.

---

[1] *The State of Ireland*, (London, 1807; 2nd edn., 1821). Pamphlet.

[2] Mistake. Small-scale agriculture had been the prevailing form of farming ever since the Middle Ages. Thus the small peasant farm existed even before the Revolution. The only thing the latter changed was its ownership; that it took away from the feudal lords and transferred, directly or indirectly, to the peasants. (*Added in the German edition of 1892.*)

The attempts of the Irish to save themselves from their present ruin, on the one hand, take the form of crimes. These are the order of the day in the agricultural districts, and are nearly always directed against the most immediate enemies, the landlords' agents, or their obedient servants, the Protestant intruders, whose large farms are made up of the potato patches of hundreds of ejected families. Such crimes are especially frequent in the South and West. On the other hand, the Irish hope for relief by means of the agitation for the repeal of the Legislative Union with England.* From all the foregoing, it is clear that the uneducated Irish must see in the English their worst enemies; and their first hope of improvement in the conquest of national independence. But quite as clear is it, too, that Irish distress cannot be removed by any Act of Repeal. Such an Act would, however, at once lay bare the fact that the cause of Irish misery, which now seems to come from abroad, is really to be found at home. Meanwhile, it is an open question whether the accomplishment of repeal will be necessary to make this clear to the Irish. Hitherto, neither Chartism nor Socialism has had marked success in Ireland.

I close my observations upon Ireland at this point the more readily, as the Repeal Agitation of 1843 and O'Connell's trial* have been the means of making the Irish distress more and more known in Germany.

We have now followed the proletariat of the British Isles through all branches of its activity, and found it everywhere living in want and misery under totally inhuman conditions. We have seen discontent arise with the rise of the proletariat, grow, develop, and organize; we have seen open bloodless and bloody battles of the proletariat against the bourgeoisie. We have investigated the principles according to which the fate, the hopes, and fears of the proletariat are determined, and we have found that there is no prospect of improvement in their condition.

We have had an opportunity, here and there, of observing the conduct of the bourgeoisie towards the proletariat, and we have found that it considers only itself, has only its own advantage in view. However, in order not to be unjust, let us investigate its mode of action somewhat more exactly.

11

The Attitude of the Bourgeoisie
Towards the Proletariat

IN speaking of the bourgeoisie I include the so-called aristocracy, for this is a privileged class, an aristocracy, only
in contrast with the bourgeoisie, not in contrast with the
proletariat. The proletarian sees in both only the property-
holder—i.e. the bourgeois. Before the privilege of property
all other privileges vanish. The sole difference is this, that the
bourgeois proper stands in active relations with the manufacturing, and, in a measure, with the mining proletarians,
and, as farmer, with the agricultural labourers, whereas
the so-called aristocrat comes into contact with part of the
mining and with the agricultural labourers only.

I have never seen a class so deeply demoralized, so incurably debased by selfishness, so corroded within, so incapable
of progress, as the English bourgeoisie; and I mean by this,
especially the bourgeoisie proper, particularly the Liberal,
Corn Law repealing bourgeoisie. For it, nothing exists in this
world, except for the sake of money, itself not excluded. It
knows no bliss save that of rapid gain, no pain save that of
losing gold.[1] In the presence of this avarice and lust of gain,
it is not possible for a single human sentiment or opinion to
remain untainted. True, these English bourgeois are good
husbands and family men, and have all sorts of other private
virtues, and appear, in ordinary intercourse, as decent and
respectable as all other bourgeois; even in business they are
better to deal with than the Germans; they do not higgle and
haggle so much as our own pettifogging merchants; but how
does this help matters? Ultimately it is self-interest, and
especially money gain, which alone determines them. I once

---

[1] Carlyle gives in his *Past and Present* (London, 1843) a splendid
description of the English bourgeoisie and its disgusting money-greed.
[Part of this description I translated for the *Deutsch-Französische
Jahrbücher*, to which I refer the reader.* (*Added in the German
edition.*)]

went into Manchester with such a bourgeois, and spoke to him of the bad, unwholesome method of building, the frightful condition of the working-people's quarters, and asserted that I had never seen so ill-built a city. The man listened quietly to the end, and said at the corner where we parted: 'And yet there is a great deal of money made here; good morning, sir.' It is utterly indifferent to the English bourgeois whether his working men starve or not, if only he makes money. All the conditions of life are measured by money, and what brings no money is nonsense, unpractical, idealistic bosh. Hence, Political Economy, the Science of Wealth, is the favourite study of these bartering Jews. Every one of them is a Political Economist. The relation of the manufacturer to his operatives has nothing human in it; it is purely economic. The manufacturer is Capital, the operative Labour. And if the operative will not be forced into this abstraction, if he insists that he is not Labour, but a man who possesses, among other things, the attribute of labour-force, if he takes it into his head that he need not allow himself to be sold and bought in the market, as the commodity 'Labour', the bourgeois reason comes to a standstill. He cannot comprehend that he holds any other relation to the operatives than that of purchase and sale; he sees in them not human beings, but hands, as he constantly calls them to their faces; he insists, as Carlyle says, that 'Cash Payment is the only nexus between man and man'. Even the relation between himself and his wife is, in ninety-nine cases out of a hundred, mere 'Cash Payment'. Money determines the worth of the man; he is 'worth ten thousand pounds'. He who has money is of 'the better sort of people', is 'influential', and what *he* does counts for something in his social cricle. The huckstering spirit penetrates the whole language, all relations are expressed in business terms, in economic categories. Supply and demand are the formulas according to which the logic of the English bourgeois judges all human life. Hence free competition in every respect, hence the regime of *laissez-faire*, *laissez-aller** in government, in medicine, in education, and soon to be in religion, too, as the State Church collapses more and more. Free competition will suffer no limitation, no State supervision; the whole State is but a burden to it. It would reach its highest perfection in a wholly ungoverned anarchic society, where each might exploit the other to his heart's content. Since, however, the bourgeoisie cannot dispense with government, but must have it to hold the equally indispensable proletariat in check, it turns the power of government against the proletariat and keeps out of its way as far as possible.

Let no one believe, however, that the 'cultivated' Englishman openly brags with his egotism. On the contrary, he conceals it under the vilest hypocrisy. What? The wealthy English fail to remember the poor? They who have founded philanthropic institutions, such as no other country can boast of! Philanthropic institutions forsooth! As though you rendered the proletarians a service in first sucking out their very life-blood and then practising your self-complacent, Pharisaic philanthropy upon them, placing yourselves before the world as mighty benefactors of humanity when you give back to the plundered victims the hundreth part of what belongs to them! Charity which degrades him who gives more than him who takes; charity which treads the down-trodden still deeper in the dust, which demands that the degraded, the pariah cast out by society, shall first surrender the last that remains to him, his very claim to manhood, shall first beg for mercy before your mercy deigns to press, in the shape of an alms, the brand of degradation upon his brow. But let us hear the English bourgeoisie's own words. It is not yet a year since I read in the *Manchester Guardian* the following letter to the editor, which was published without comment as a perfectly natural, reasonable thing:

MR. EDITOR,—For some time past our main streets are haunted by swarms of beggars, who try to awaken the pity of the passers-by in a most shameless and annoying manner, by exposing their tattered clothing, sickly aspect, and disgusting wounds and de-formities. I should think that when one not only pays the poor-rate, but also contributes largely to the charitable institutions, one had done enough to earn a right to be spared such disagreeable and impertinent molestations. And why else do we pay such high rates for the maintenance of the municipal police, if they do not even protect us so far as to make it possible to go to or out of town in peace? I hope the publication of these lines in your widely-circulated paper may induce the authorities to remove this nuisance; and I remain,—Your obedient servant.

A LADY.

There you have it! The English bourgeoisie is charitable out of self-interest; it gives nothing outright, but regards its gifts as a business matter, makes a bargain with the poor, saying: 'If I spend this much upon benevolent institutions, I thereby purchase the right not to be troubled any further, and you are bound thereby to stay in your dusky holes and not to irritate my tender nerves by exposing your misery. You shall despair as before, but you shall despair unseen, this I require, this I purchase with my subscription of twenty pounds for the infirmary!' It is infamous, this charity of a Christian bourgeois! And so writes 'A Lady'; she does well to sign herself such, well that she has lost the courage to call herself a woman! But if the 'Ladies' are such as this, what must the 'Gentlemen' be? It will be said that this is a single case; but no, the foregoing letter expresses the temper of the great majority of the English bourgeoisie, or the editor would not have accepted it, and some reply would have been made to it, which I watched for in vain in the succeeding numbers. And as to the efficiency of this philanthropy, Canon Parkinson himself says that the poor are relieved much more by the poor than by the bourgeoisie; and such relief given by an honest proletarian who knows himself what it is to be hungry, for whom sharing his scanty meal is really a sacrifice, but a sacrifice borne with pleasure, such help has a wholly different ring to it from the carelessly tossed alms of the luxurious bourgeois.

In other respects, too, the bourgeoisie assumes a hypocritical, boundless philanthropy, but only when its own interests require it; as in its Politics and Political Economy. It has been at work now well on towards five years to prove to the working men that it strives to abolish the Corn Laws solely in their interest. But the long and short of the matter is this: the Corn Laws keep the price of bread higher than in other countries, and thus raise wages; but these high wages render difficult competition of the manufacturers against other nations in which bread, and consequently wages, are cheaper. The Corn Laws being repealed, the price of bread falls, and wages gradually approach those of other European countries, as must be clear to everyone from our previous exposition of the principles according to which wages are determined. The manufacturer can compete more readily, the demand for English goods increases, and, with it, the demand for labour. In consequence of this increased demand wages would actually rise somewhat, and the unemployed workers be re-employed; but for how long? The 'surplus population' of England, and especially of Ireland, is sufficient to supply English manufacture with the necessary operatives, even if it were doubled; and, in a few years, the small advantage of the repeal of the Corn Laws would be balanced, a new crisis would follow, and we should be back at the point from which we started, while the first stimulus to manufacture would have increased population meanwhile. All this the proletarians understand very well, and have told the manufacturers to their faces; but, in spite of that, the manufacturers have in view solely the immediate advantage which the Corn Laws would bring them. They are too narrow-minded to see that, even for themselves, no permanent advantage can arise from this measure, because their competition with each other would soon force the profit of the individual back to its old level; and thus they continue to shriek to the working men that it is purely for the sake of the starving millions that the rich members of the Liberal party pour hundreds and thousands of pounds into the treasury of the Anti-Corn Law League, while everyone knows that they are only sending the butter after the cheese, that they calculate upon earning it all back in the first ten years after the repeal of the Corn Laws. But the workers are no longer to be misled by the bourgeoisie, especially since the insurrection of 1842. They demand of every one who presents himself as interested in their welfare, that he should declare himself in favour of the People's Charter as proof of the sincerity of his professions, and in so doing, they protest against all outside help, for the Charter is a demand for the power to help themselves. Whoever declines so to declare himself they pronounce their enemy, and are perfectly right in so doing, whether he be a declared foe or a false friend. Besides, the Anti-Corn Law League has used the most despicable falsehoods and tricks to win the support of the workers. It has tried to prove to them that the money price of labour is in inverse proportion to the price of corn; that wages are high when grain is cheap, and vice versa, an assertion which it pretends to prove with the most ridiculous arguments, and one which is, in itself, more ridiculous than any other that has proceeded from the mouth of an Economist. When this failed to help matters, the workers were promised bliss supreme in consequence of the increased demand in the labour market; indeed, men went so far as to carry through the streets two models of loaves of bread, on one of which, by far the larger, was written: 'American Eightpenny Loaf, Wages Four Shillings per Day', and upon the much smaller one: 'English Eightpenny Loaf, Wages Two Shillings a Day'. But the workers have not allowed themselves to be misled. They know their lords and masters too well.

But rightly to measure the hypocrisy to these promises, the practice of the bourgeoisie must be taken into account. We have seen in the course of our report how the bourgeoisie exploits the proletariat in every conceivable way for its own benefit! We have, however, hitherto seen only how the single bourgeois maltreats the proletariat upon his own account. Let us turn now to the manner in which the bourgeoisie as a party, as the power of the State, conducts itself towards the proletariat. It is quite obvious that all legislation is calculated to protect those that possess property against those who do not. Laws are necessary only because there are persons in existence who own nothing; and although this is directly expressed in but few laws, as, for instance, those against vagabonds and tramps, in which the proletariat as such is outlawed, yet enmity to the proletariat is so emphatically the basis of the law that the judges, and especially the Justices of the Peace, who are bourgeois themselves, and with whom the proletariat comes most in contact, find this meaning in the laws without further consideration. If a rich man is brought up, or rather summoned, to appear before the court, the judge regrets that he is obliged to impose so much trouble, treats the matter as favourably as possible, and, if he is forced to condemn the accused, does so with extreme regret, etc., etc., and the end of it all is a miserable fine, which the bourgeois throws upon the table with contempt and then departs. But if a poor devil gets into such a position as involves appearing before the Justice of the Peace—he has almost always spent the night in the station-house with a crowd of his peers—he is regarded from the beginning as guilty; his defence is set aside with a contemptuous 'Oh! we know the excuse', and a fine imposed which he cannot pay and must work out with several months on the treadmill. And if nothing can be proved against him, he is sent to the treadmill, none the less, 'as a rogue and a vagabond'. The partisanship of the Justices of the Peace, especially in the country, surpasses all description, and it is so much the order of the day that all cases which are not too utterly flagrant are quietly reported by the newspapers, without comment. Nor is anything else to be expected. For on the one hand, these Dogberries do merely construe the law according to the intent of the farmers, and, on the other, they are themselves bourgeois, who see the foundation of all true order in the interests of their class. And the conduct of the police corresponds to that of the Justices of the Peace. The bourgeois may do what he will and the police remain ever polite, adhering strictly to the law, but the proletarian is roughly, brutally treated; his poverty both casts the suspicion of every sort of crime upon him and cuts him off from legal redress against any caprice of the administrators of the law; for him, therefore, the protecting forms of the law do not exist, the police force their way into his house without further ceremony, arrest and abuse him; and only when a working-men's association, such as the miners, engages a Roberts, does it become evident how little the protective side of the law exists for the working man, how frequently he has to bear all the burdens of the law without enjoying its benefits.

Down to the present hour, the property-holding class in Parliament still struggles against the better feelings of those not yet fallen a prey to egotism, and seeks to subjugate the proletariat still further. One piece of common land after another is appropriated and placed under cultivation, a process by which the general cultivation is furthered, but the proletariat greatly injured. Where there were still commons, the poor could pasture an ass, a pig, or geese, the children and young people had a place where they could play and live out of doors; but this is gradually coming to an end. The earnings of the worker are less, and the young people, deprived of their playground, go to the beer-shops. A mass of Acts for enclosing and cultivating commons is passed at every session of Parliament. When the Government determined during the session of 1844 to force the all-monopolizing railways to make travelling possible for the workers by means of charges proportionate to their means, a penny a mile, and proposed therefore to introduce such a third class train upon every railway daily, the 'Reverend Father in God', the Bishop of London, proposed that Sunday, the only day upon which working men in work *can* travel, be exempted from this rule, and travelling thus be left open to the rich and shut off from the poor. This proposition was, however, too direct, too undisguised to pass through Parliament, and was dropped. I have no room to enumerate the many concealed attacks of even one single session upon the proletariat. One from the session of 1844 must suffice. An obscure member of Parliament, a Mr Miles, proposed a bill regulating the relation of master and servant which seemed comparatively unobjectionable. The Government became interested in the bill, and it was referred to a committee. Meanwhile the strike among the miners in the North broke out, and Roberts made his triumphal passage through England with his acquitted working men. When the bill was reported by the committee, it was discovered that certain most despotic provisions had been interpolated in it, especially one conferring upon the employer the power to bring before any Justice of the Peace every working man who had contracted verbally or in writing to do any work whatsoever, in case of refusal to work or other misbehaviour, and have him condemned to prison with hard labour for two months, upon the oath of the employer or his agent or overlooker, i.e. upon the oath of the accuser. This bill aroused the working men to the utmost fury, the more so as the Ten Hours Bill was before Parliament at the same time, and had called forth a considerable agitation. Hundreds of meetings were held, hundreds of working-men's petitions forwarded to London to Thomas Duncombe, the representative of the interests of the proletariat. This man was, except for Ferrand, the representative of 'Young England',* the only vigorous opponent of the bill; but when the other Radicals saw that the people were declaring against it, one after the other crept forward and took his place by Duncombe's side; and as the Liberal bourgeoisie had not the courage to defend the bill in the face of the excitement among the working men, it was ignominiously lost.

Meanwhile the most open declaration of war of the bourgeoisie upon the proletariat is Malthus's Law of Population and the New Poor Law framed in accordance with it. We have already alluded several times to the theory of Malthus. We may sum up its final result in these few words, that the earth is perennially overpopulated, whence poverty, misery, distress, and immorality must prevail; that it is the lot, the eternal destiny of mankind, to exist in too great numbers, and therefore in diverse classes, of which some are rich, educated, and moral, and others more or less poor, distressed ignorant, and immoral. Hence it follows in practice, and Malthus himself drew this conclusion, that charities and poor-rates are, properly speaking, nonsense, since they serve only to maintain, and stimulate the increase of, the surplus population whose competition crushes down wages for the employed; that the employment of the poor by the Poor Law Guardians is equally unreasonable, since only a fixed quantity of the products of labour can be consumed, and for every unemployed labourer thus furnished employment, another hitherto employed must be driven into enforced idleness, whence private undertakings suffer at cost of Poor Law industry; that, in other words, the whole problem is not how to support the surplus population, but how to restrain it as far as possible. Malthus declares in plain English that the right to live, a right previously asserted in favour of every man in the world, is nonsense. He quotes the words of a poet, that the poor man comes to the feast of Nature and finds no cover laid for him, and adds that 'she bids him begone', for he did not before his birth ask of society whether or not he is welcome. This is now the pet theory of all genuine English bourgeois, and very naturally, since it is the most specious excuse for them, and has, moreover, a good deal of truth in it under existing conditions. If, then, the problem is not to make the 'surplus population' useful, to transform it into available population, but merely to let it starve to death in the least objectionable way and to prevent its having too many children, this, of course, is simple enough, provided the surplus population perceives its own superfluousness and takes kindly to starvation. There is, however, in spite of the violent exertions of the humane bourgeoisie, no immediate prospect of its succeeding in bringing about such a disposition among the workers. The workers have taken it into their heads that they, with their busy hands, are the necessary, and the rich capitalists, who do nothing, the surplus population.

Since, however, the rich hold all the power, the proletarians must submit, if they will not good-temperedly perceive it for themselves, to have the law actually declare them superfluous. This has been done by the New Poor Law. The Old Poor Law which rested upon the Act of 1601 (the 43rd of Elizabeth), naïvely started from the notion that it is the duty of the parish to provide for the maintenance of the poor. Whoever had no work received relief, and the poor man regarded the parish as pledged to protect him from starvation. He demanded his weekly relief as his right, not as a favour, and this became, at last, too much for the bourgeoisie. In 1833, when the bourgeoisie had just come into power through the Reform Bill, and pauperism in the country districts had just reached its full development, the bourgeoisie began the reform of the Poor Law according to its own point of view. A commission was appointed, which investigated the administration of the Poor Laws, and revealed a multitude of abuses. It was discovered that the whole working class in the country was pauperized and more or less dependent upon the rates, from which they received relief when wages were low; it was found that this system by which the unemployed were maintained, the ill-paid and the parents of large families relieved, fathers of illegitimate children required to pay alimony, and poverty, in general, recognized as needing protection, it was found that this system was ruining the nation, was

A check upon industry, a reward for improvident marriage, a stimulus to increased population, and a means of counterbalancing the effect of an increased population upon wages; a national provision for discouraging the honest and industrious, and protecting the lazy, vicious, and improvident; calculated to destroy the bonds of family life, hinder systematically the accumulation of capital, scatter that which is already accumulated, and ruin the taxpayers. Moreover, in the provision of aliment, it sets a premium upon illegitimate children.[1]

[1] Extracts from Information received from the Poor Law Commissioners. Published by authority (London, 1883).

This description of the action of the Old Poor Law is certainly correct; relief fosters laziness and increase of 'surplus population'. Under present social conditions it is perfectly clear that the poor man is compelled to be an egotist, and when he can choose, living equally well in either case, he prefers doing nothing to working. But what follows therefrom? That our present social conditions are good for nothing, and not as the Malthusian Commissioners conclude, that poverty is a crime, and, as such, to be visited with heinous penalties which may serve as a warning to others.

But these wise Malthusians were so thoroughly convinced of the infallibility of their theory that they did not for one moment hesitate to cast the poor into the Procrustean bed of their economic notions and treat them with the most revolting cruelty. Convinced with Malthus and the rest of the adherents of free competition that it is best to let each one take care of himself, they would have preferred to abolish the Poor Laws altogether. Since, however, they had neither the courage nor the authority to do this, they proposed a Poor Law constructed as far as possible in harmony with the doctrine of Malthus, which is yet more barbarous than that of *laissez-faire*, because it interferes actively in cases in which the latter is passive. We have seen how Malthus characterizes poverty, or rather the want of employment, as a crime under the title 'superfluity', and recommends for it punishment by starvation. The commissioners were not quite so barbarous; death outright by starvation was something too terrible even for a Poor Law Commissioner. 'Good,' said they, 'we grant you poor a right to exist, but only to exist; the right to multiply you have not, nor the right to exist as befits human beings. You are a pest, and if we cannot get rid of you as we do of other pests, you shall feel, at least, that you are a pest, and you shall at least be held in check, kept from bringing into the world other "surplus", either directly or through inducing in others laziness and want of employment. Live you shall, but live as an awful warning to all those who might have inducements to become "superfluous".'

They accordingly brought in the New Poor Law, which was passed by Parliament in 1834, and continues in force down to the present day. All relief in money and provisions was abolished; the only relief allowed was admission to the workhouses immediately built. The regulations for these workhouses, or, as the people call them, Poor Law Bastilles, is such as to frighten away every one who has the slightest prospect of life without this form of public charity. To make sure that relief be applied for only in the most extreme cases and after every other effort had failed, the workhouse has been made the most repulsive residence which the refined ingenuity of a Malthusian can invent. The food is worse than that of the most ill-paid working man while employed, and the harder, or they might prefer the workhouse to their wretched existence outside. Meat, especially fresh meat, is rarely furnished, chiefly potatoes, the worst possible bread and oatmeal porridge, little or no beer. The food of criminal prisoners is better, as a rule, so that the paupers frequently commit some offence for the purpose of getting into jail. For the workhouse is a jail too; he who does not finish his task gets nothing to eat; he who wishes to go out must ask permission, which is granted or not, according to his behaviour or the inspector's whim; tobacco is forbidden, also the receipt of gifts from relatives or friends outside the house; the paupers wear a workhouse uniform, and are handed over, helpless and without redress, to the caprice of the inspectors. To prevent their labour from competing with that of outside concerns, they are set to rather useless tasks: the men break stones, 'as much as a strong man can accomplish with effort in a day'; the women, children, and aged men pick oakum, for I know not what insignificant use. To prevent the 'superfluous' from multiplying, and 'demoralized' parents from influencing their children, families are broken up; the husband is placed in one wing, the wife in another, the children in a third, and they are permitted to see one another only at stated times after long intervals, and then only when they have, in the opinion of the officials, behaved well. And in order to shut off the external world from contamination by pauperism within these bastilles, the inmates are permitted to receive visits only with the consent of the officials, and in the reception-rooms; to communicate in general with the world outside only by leave and under supervision.

Yet the food is supposed to be wholesome and the treatment humane with all this. But the intent of the law is too loudly outspoken for this requirement to be in any wise fulfilled. The Poor Law Commissioners and the whole English bourgeoisie deceive themselves if they believe the administration of the law possible without these results. The treatment, which the letter of the law prescribes, is in direct contradiction of its spirit. If the law in its essence proclaims the poor criminals, the workhouses prisons, their inmates beyond the pale of the law, beyond the pale of humanity, objects of disgust and repulsion, then all commands to the contrary are unavailing. In practice, the spirit and not the letter of the law is followed in the treatment of the poor, as in the following few examples:

In the workhouse at Greenwich, in the summer of 1843, a boy five years old was punished by being shut into the deadroom, where he had to sleep upon the lids of the coffins. In the workhouse at Herne, the same punishment was inflicted upon a little girl for wetting the bed at night, and this method of punishment seems to be a favourite one. This workhouse, which stands in one of the most beautiful regions of Kent, is peculiar, in so far as its windows open only upon the court, and but two, newly introduced, afford the inmates a glimpse of the outer world.

The author, who relates this in the *Illuminated Magazine*, closes his description with the words: 'If God punished men for crimes as man punishes man for poverty, then woe to the sons of Adam!'

In November 1843 a man died at Leicester, who had been dismissed two days before from the workhouse at Coventry. The details of the treatment of the poor in this institution were revolting. The man, George Robson, had a wound upon the shoulder, the treatment of which was wholly neglected; he was set to work at the pump, using the sound arm; was given only the usual workhouse fare, which he was utterly unable to digest by reason of the unhealed wound and his general debility; he naturally grew weaker, and the more he complained, the more brutally he was treated. When his wife tried to bring him her drop of beer, she was reprimanded, and forced to drink it herself in the presence of the female warder. He became ill, but received no better treatment. Finally, at his own request, and under the most insulting epithets, he was discharged, accompanied by his wife. Two days later he died at Leicester, in consequence of the neglected wound and of the food given him, which was utterly indigestible for one in his condition, as the surgeon present at the inquest testified. When he was discharged, there were handed to him letters containing money, which had been kept back six weeks, and opened, according to a rule of the establishment, by the inspector! In Birmingham such scandalous occurrences took place, that finally, in 1843, an official was sent to investigate the case. He found that four tramps had been shut up naked under a staircase in a black hole, eight to ten days, often deprived of food until noon, and that at the severest season of the year. A little boy had been passed through all grades of punishment known to the institution; first locked up in a damp, vaulted, narrow lumber-room; then in the dog-hole twice, the second time three days and three nights; then the same length of time in the old dog-hole, which was still worse; then the tramp-room, a stinking, disgustingly filthy hole, with wooden sleeping stalls, where the official, in the course of his inspection, found two other tattered boys, shrivelled with cold, who had been spending three days there. In the dog-hole there were often seven, and in the tramp-room, twenty men huddled together. Women, also, were placed in the dog-hole, because they refused to go to church; and one was shut four days into the tramp-room, with God knows what sort of company, and that while she was ill and receiving medicine! Another woman was placed in the insane department for punishment, though she was perfectly sane. In the work-house at Bacton, in Suffolk, in January 1844, a similar investigation revealed the fact that a feeble-minded woman was employed as nurse, and took care of the patients accordingly; while sufferers, who were often restless at night, or tried to get up, were tied fast with cords passed over the covering and under the bedstead, to save the nurses the trouble of sitting up at night. One patient was found dead, bound in this way. In the St Pancras workhouse in London (where the cheap shirts already mentioned are made), an epileptic died of suffocation during an attack in bed, no one coming to his relief; in the same house, four to six, sometimes eight children, slept in one bed. In Shoreditch workhouse a man was placed, together with a fever patient violently ill, in a bed teeming with vermin. In Bethnal Green workhouse, London, a woman in the sixth month of pregnancy was shut up in the reception-room with her 2-year-old child, from 28 February to 20 March, without being admitted into the workhouse itself, and without a trace of a bed or the means of satisfying the most natural wants. Her husband, who was brought into the workhouse, begged to have his wife released from this imprisonment, whereupon he received twenty-four hours imprisonment, with bread and water, as the penalty of his insolence. In the workhouse at Slough, near Windsor, a man lay dying in September 1844. His wife journeyed to him, arriving at midnight; and hastening to the workhouse, was refused admission. She was not permitted to see her husband until the next morning, and then only in the presence of a female warder, who forced herself upon the wife at every succeeding visit, sending her away at the end of half an hour. In the workhouse at Middleton, in Lancashire, twelve, and at times eighteen paupers, of both sexes, slept in one room. This institution is not embraced by the New Poor Law, but is administered under an old special act (Gilbert's Act).* The inspector had instituted a brewery in the house for his own benefit. In Stockport, on 31 July 1844, a man, 72 years old, was brought before the Justice of the Peace for refusing to break stones, and insisting that, by reason of his age and a stiff knee, he was unfit for this work. In vain did he offer to undertake any work adapted to his physical strength; he was sentenced to two weeks upon the treadmill. In the work-house at Basford, an inspecting official found that the sheets had not been changed in thirteen weeks, shirts in four weeks, stockings in two to ten months, so that of forty-five boys but three had stockings, and all their shirts were in tatters. The beds swarmed vermin, and the tableware was washed in the slop-pails. In the west of London workhouse, a porter who had infected four girls with syphilis was not discharged, and another who had concealed a deaf and dumb girl four days and nights in his bed was also retained.

As in life, so in death. The poor are dumped into the earth like infected cattle. The pauper burial-ground of St Brides, London, is a bare morass, in use as a cemetery since the time of Charles II, and filled with heaps of bones; every Wednesday the paupers are thrown into a ditch 14 feet deep; a curate rattles through the Litany at the top of his speed;

the ditch is loosely covered in, to be reopened the next Wednesday, and filled with corpses as long as one more can be forced in. The putrefaction thus engendered contaminates the whole neighbourhood. In Manchester, the pauper burial-ground lies opposite to the Old Town, along the Irk: this, too, is a rough, desolate place. About two years ago a rail-road was carried through it. If it had been a respectable cemetery, how the bourgeoisie and the clergy would have shrieked over the desecration! But it was a pauper burial-ground, the resting-place of the outcast and superfluous, so no one concerned himself about the matter. It was not even thought worth while to convey the partially decayed bodies to the other side of the cemetery; they were heaped up just as it happened, and piles were driven into newly made graves, so that the water oozed out of the swampy ground, pregnant with putrefying matter, and filled the neighbourhood with the most revolting and injurious gases. The disgusting brutality which accompanied this work I cannot describe in further detail.

Can anyone wonder that the poor decline to accept public relief under these conditions? That they starve rather than enter these bastilles? I have the reports of five cases in which persons actually starving, when the guardians refused them outdoor relief, went back to their miserable homes and died of starvation rather than enter these hells. Thus far have the Poor Law Commissioners attained their object. At the same time, however, the workhouses have intensified, more than any other measure of the party in power, the hatred of the working class against the property-holders, who very generally admire the New Poor Law.

From Newcastle to Dover, there is but one voice among the workers—the voice of hatred against the new law. The bourgeoisie has formulated so clearly in this law its conception of its duties towards the proletariat, that it has been appreciated even by the dullest. So frankly, so boldly had the conception never yet been formulated, that the non-possessing class exists solely for the purpose of being ex-ploited, and of starving when the property-holders can no longer make use of it. Hence it is that this New Poor Law has contributed so greatly to accelerate the labour move-ment, and especially to spread Chartism: and, as it is carried out most extensively in the country, it facilitates the development of the proletarian movement which is arising in the agricultural districts.

Let me add that a similar law in force in Ireland since 1838 affords a similar refuge for 80,000 paupers. Here, too, it has made itself disliked, and would have been intensely hated if it had attained anything like the same importance as in England. But what difference does the ill-treatment of 80,000 proletarians make in a country in which there are two and a half millions of them? In Scotland there are, with local exceptions, no Poor Laws.

I hope that after this picture of the New Poor Law and its results, no word which I have said of the English bourgeoisie will be thought too stern. In this public measure, in which it acts *in corpore*, as the ruling power, it formulates its real intentions, reveals the animus of those smaller transactions with the proletariat, of which the blame apparently attaches to individuals. And that this measure did not originate with any one section of the bourgeoisie, but enjoys the approval of the whole class, is proved by the parliamentary debates of 1844. The Liberal party had enacted the New Poor Law; the Conservative party, with its Prime Minister Peel at the head, defends it, and only alters some pettyfogging trifles in the Poor Law Amendment Bill of 1844. A Liberal majority carried the bill, a Conservative majority approved it, and the 'Noble Lords' gave their consent each time. Thus is the expulsion of the proletariat from State and society outspoken, thus is it publicly proclaimed that proletarians are not human beings, and do not deserve to be treated as such. Let us leave it to the proletarians of the British Empire to reconquer their human rights.[1]

[1] To prevent misconstructions and consequent objections, I would observe that I have spoken of the bourgeoisie as a *class*, and that all such facts as refer to individuals serve merely as evidence of the way of thinking and acting of a *class*. Hence I have not entered upon the distinctions between the diverse sections, subdivisions, and parties of the bourgeoisie, which have a mere historical and theoretical significance. And I can, for the same reason, mention but casually the few members of the bourgeoisie who have shown themselves honourable exceptions. These are, on the one hand, the pronounced Radicals, who are almost Chartists, such as a few members of the House of Commons, the manu-

Such is the state of the British working class as I have come to know it in the course of twenty-one months, through the medium of my own eyes, and through official and other trustworthy reports. And when I call this condition, as I have frequently enough done in the foregoing pages, an utterly unbearable one, I am not alone in so doing. As early as 1833, Gaskell declared that he despaired of a peaceful issue, and that a revolution can hardly fail to follow. In 1838 Carlyle explained Chartism and the revolutionary activity of the working men as arising out of the misery in which they live, and only wondered that they have sat so quietly eight long years at the Barmecide feast,* at which they have been regaled by the Liberal bourgeoisie with empty promises. And in 1844 he declared that the work of organizing labour must be begun at once 'if Europe, or at least England, is long to remain inhabitable'. And *The Times*, the 'first journal of Europe', said in June, 1844: 'War to palaces, peace unto cabins—that is a battle-cry of terror which may come to resound throughout our country. Let the wealthy beware!'

Meanwhile, let us review once more the chances of the English bourgeoisie. In the worst case, foreign manufacture,

facturers Hindley of Ashton, and Fielden of Todmordon (Lancashire), and, on the other hand, the philanthropic Tories, who have recently constituted themselves 'Young England', among whom are the Members of Parliament, Disraeli, Borthwick, Ferrand, Lord John Manners, etc. Lord Ashley, too, is in sympathy with them. The hope of Young England is a restoration of the old 'merry England' with its brilliant features and its romantic feudalism. This object is of course unattainable and ridiculous, a satire upon all historic development; but the good intention, the courage to resist the existing state of things and prevalent prejudices, and to recognize the vileness of our present condition, is worth something anyhow. Wholly isolated is the half-German Englishman, Thomas Carlyle, who, originally a Tory, goes beyond all those hitherto mentioned. He has sounded the social disorder more deeply than any other English bourgeois, and demands the organization of labour. [I hope that Carlyle, who has found the right path, will be capable of following it. He has my best wishes and those of many other Germans. (*Omitted in the authorized English edition.*)] [But the February Revolution made him an out-and-out reactionary. His righteous wrath against the Philistines turned into sullen Philistine grumbling at the tide of history that cast him ashore. (*Added in the German edition of 1892.*)]

especially that of America, may succeed in withstanding English competition, even after the repeal of the Corn Laws, inevitable in the course of a few years. German manufacture is now making great efforts, and that of America has developed with giant strides. America, with its inexhaustible resources, with its unmeasured coal- and iron-fields, with its unexampled wealth of water-power and its navigable rivers, but especially with its energetic, active population, in comparison with which the English are phlegmatic dawdlers—America has in less than ten years created a manufacture which already competes with England in the coarser cotton goods, has excluded the English from the markets of North and South America, and holds its own in China, side by side with England. If any country is adapted to holding a monopoly of manufacture, it is America. Should English manufacture be thus vanquished—and in the course of the next twenty years, if the present conditions remain unchanged, this is inevitable—the majority of the proletariat must become forever superfluous, and has no other choice than to starve or to rebel. Does the English bourgeoisie reflect upon this contingency? On the contrary; its favourite economist, MacCulloch, teaches from his student's desk, that a country so young as America, which is not even properly populated, cannot carry on manufacture successfully or dream of competing with an old manufacturing country like England. It were madness in the Americans to make the attempt, for they could only lose by it; better far for them to stick to their agriculture, and when they have brought their whole territory under the plough, a time may perhaps come for carrying on manufacture with a profit. So says the wise economist, and the whole bourgeoisie worships him, while the Americans take possession of one market after another, while a daring American speculator recently even sent a shipment of American cotton goods to England, where they were sold for re-exportation.

But assuming that England retained the monopoly of manufactures, that its factories perpetually multiply, what must be the result? The commercial crises would continue, and grow more violent, more terrible, with the extension of industry and the multiplication of the proletariat. The proletariat would increase in geometrical proportion, in consequence of the progressive ruin of the lower middle class and the giant strides with which capital is concentrating itself in the hands of the few; and the proletariat would soon embrace the whole nation, with the exception of a few millionaires. But in this development there comes a stage at which the proletariat perceives how easily the existing power may be overthrown, and then follows a revolution.

Neither of these supposed conditions may, however, be expected to arise. The commercial crises, the mightiest levers for all independent development of the proletariat, will probably shorten the process, acting in concert with foreign competition and the deepening ruin of the lower middle class. I think the people will not endure more than one more crisis. The next one, in 1846 or 1847, will probably bring with it the repeal of the Corn Laws[1] and the enactment of the Charter. What revolutionary movements the Charter may give rise to remains to be seen. But, by the time of the next following crisis, which, according to the analogy of its predecessors, must break out in 1852 or 1853, unless delayed perhaps by the repeal of the Corn Laws or hastened by other influences, such as foreign competition—by the time this crisis arrives, the English people will have had enough of being plundered by the capitalists and left to starve when the capitalists no longer require their services. If, up to that time, the English bourgeoisie does not pause to reflect—and to all appearance it certainly will not do so—a revolution will follow with which none hitherto known can be compared. The proletarians, driven to despair, will seize the torch which Stephens has preached to them; the vengeance of the people will come down with a wrath of which the rage of 1793 gives no true idea. The war of the poor against the rich will be the bloodiest ever waged. Even the union of a part of the bourgeoisie with the proletariat, even a general reform of the bourgeoisie, would not help matters. Besides, the change of heart of the bourgeoisie could only go as far as a lukewarm *juste-milieu*;* the more determined, uniting with the workers, would only form a new Gironde,* and succumb in the course of the mighty development. The prejudices of a whole class cannot be laid aside like an old coat: least of all, those of the

[1] And it did.

stable, narrow, selfish English bourgeoisie. These are all inferences which may be drawn with the greatest certainty; conclusions, the premisses for which are undeniable facts, partly of historical development, partly facts inherent in human nature. Prophecy is nowhere so easy as in England, where all the component elements of society are clearly defined and sharply separated. The revolution must come; it is already too late to bring about a peaceful solution; but it can be made more gentle than that prophesied in the foregoing pages. This depends, however, more upon the development of the proletariat than upon that of the bourgeoisie. In proportion, as the proletariat absorbs socialistic and communistic elements, will the revolution diminish in bloodshed, revenge, and savagery. Communism stands, in principle, above the breach between bourgeoisie and proletariat, recognizes only its historic significance for the present, but not its justification for the future: wishes, indeed, to bridge over this chasm, to do away with all class antagonisms. Hence it recognizes as justified, so long as the struggle exists, the exasperation of the proletariat towards its oppressors as a necessity, as the most important lever for a labour movement just beginning; but it goes beyond this exasperation, because Communism is a question of humanity and not of the workers alone. Besides, it does not occur to any Communist to wish to revenge himself upon individuals, or to believe that, in general, the single bourgeois can act otherwise, under existing circumstances, than he does act. English Socialism, i.e. Communism, rests directly upon the irresponsibility of the individual. Thus the more the English workers absorb communistic ideas, the more superfluous becomes their present bitterness, which, should it continue so violent as at present, could accomplish nothing; and the more their action against the bourgeoisie will lose its savage cruelty. If, indeed, it were possible to make the whole proletariat communistic before the war breaks out, the end would be very peaceful; but that is no longer possible, the time has gone by. Meanwhile, I think that before the outbreak of open, declared war of the poor against the rich, there will be enough intelligent comprehension of the social question among the proletariat, to enable the communistic party, with the help of events, to conquer the brutal element of the revolution and prevent a 'Ninth Thermidor'. In any case, the experience of the French will not have been undergone in vain, and most of the Chartist leaders are, moreover, already Communists. And as Communism stands above the strife between bourgeoisie and proletariat, it will be easier for the better elements of the bourgeoisie (which are, however, deplorably few, and can look for recruits only among the rising generation) to unite with it than with purely proletarian Chartism.

If these conclusions have not been sufficiently established in the course of the present work, there may be other opportunities for demonstrating that they are necessary consequences of the historical development of England. But this I maintain, the war of the poor against the rich now carried on in detail and indirectly will become direct and universal. It is too late for a peaceful solution. The classes are divided more and more sharply, the spirit of resistance penetrates the workers, the bitterness intensifies, the guerilla skirmishes become concentrated in more important battles, and soon a slight impulse will suffice to set the avalanche in motion. Then, indeed, will the war-cry resound through the land: 'War to the palaces, peace to the cottages!'—but then it will be too late for the rich to beware.

APPENDIX

The Labour Movement in America.
Preface to the American Edition

TEN months have elapsed since, at the translator's wish, I wrote the Appendix* to this book; and during these ten months, a revolution has been accomplished in American society such as, in any other country, would have taken at least ten years. In February 1885, American public opinion was almost unanimous on this one point; that there was no working class, in the European sense of the word, in America;[1] that consequently no class struggle between workmen and capitalists, such as tore European society to pieces, was possible in the American Republic; and that, therefore, Socialism was a thing of foreign importation which could never take root on American soil. And yet, at that moment, the coming class struggle was casting its gigantic shadow before it in the strikes of the Pennsylvania coal-miners,* and of many other trades, and especially in the preparations, all over the country, for the great Eight Hours movement which was to come off, and did come off, in the May following.* That I then duly appreciated these symptoms, that I anticipated a working-class movement on a national scale, my 'Appendix' shows; but no one could then foresee that in such a short time the movement would burst out with such irresistible force, would spread with the

[1] An English edition of my book, which was written in 1844, was justified precisely because the industrial conditions in present-day America correspond almost exactly to those which obtained in England in the 1840s, i.e. those which I described. How much this is the case is evident from the articles on 'The Labour Movement in America' by Edward and Eleanor Marx-Aveling published in the March, April, May, and June issues of *Time*, the London monthly. I am referring to these excellent articles with all the greater pleasure because it offers me an opportunity at the same time to reject the miserable slanderous accusations against Aveling which the Executive of the American Socialist Labor party was unscrupulous enough to circulate.

rapidity of a prairie-fire, would shake American society to its very foundations.

The fact is there, stubborn and indisputable. To what an extent it had struck with terror the American ruling classes, was revealed to me, in an amusing way, by American journalists who did me the honour of calling on me last summer; the 'new departure' had put them into a state of helpless fright and perplexity. But at that time the movement was only just on the start; there was but a series of confused and apparently disconnected upheavals of that class which, by the suppression of negro slavery and the rapid development of manufactures, had become the lowest stratum of American society. Before the year closed, these bewildering social convulsions began to take a definite direction. The spontaneous, instinctive movements of these vast masses of working people, over a vast extent of country, the simultaneous outburst of their common discontent with a miserable social condition, the same everywhere and due to the same causes, made them conscious of the fact, that they formed a new and distinct class of American society; a class of—practically speaking—more of less hereditary wage-workers, proletarians. And with true American instinct this consciousness led them at once to take the next step towards their deliverance: the formation of a political working men's party, with a platform of its own, and with the conquest of the Capitol and the White House for its goal. In May the struggle for the Eight Hours' working day, the troubles in Chicago, Milwaukee, etc., the attempts of the ruling class to crush the nascent uprising of Labour by brute force and brutal class-justice; in November the new Labor party organized in all great centres, and the New York, Chicago, and Milwaukee elections. May and November have hitherto reminded the American bourgeoisie only of the payment of coupons of US bonds; henceforth May and November will remind them, too, of the dates on which the American working class presented *their* coupons for payment.

In European countries, it took the working class years and years before they fully realized the fact that they formed a distinct and, under the existing social conditions, a permanent class of modern society; and it took years again until this class-consciousness led them to form themselves into a distinct political party, independent of, and opposed to, all the old political parties formed by the various sections of the ruling classes. On the more favoured soil of America, where no medieval ruins bar the way, where history begins with the elements of modern bourgeois society as evolved in the seventeenth century, the working class passed through these two stages of its development within ten months.

Still, all this is but a beginning. That the labouring masses should feel their community of grievances and of interests, their solidarity as a class in opposition to all other classes; that in order to give expression and effect to this feeling, they should set in motion the political machinery provided for that purpose in every free country—that is the first step only. The next step is to find the common remedy for these common grievances, and to embody it in the platform of the new Labor party. And this—the most important and the most difficult step in the movement—has yet to be taken in America.

A new party must have a distinct positive platform; a platform which may vary in details as circumstances vary and as the party itself develops, but still one upon which the party, for the time being, is agreed. So long as such a platform has not been worked out, or exists but in a rudimentary form, so long the new party, too, will have but a rudimentary existence; it may exist locally but not yet nationally; it will be a party potentially but not actually.

That platform, whatever may be its first initial shape, must develop in a direction which may be determined beforehand. The causes that brought into existence the abyss between the working class and the capitalist class are the same in America as in Europe; the means of filling up that abyss are equally the same everywhere. Consequently, the platform of the American proletariat will in the long run coincide, as to the ultimate end to be attained, with the one which, after sixty years of dissensions and discussions, has become the adopted platform of the great mass of the European militant proletariat. It will proclaim, as the ultimate end, the conquest of political supremacy by the working class, in order to effect the direct appropriation of all means of production—land, railways, mines, machinery, etc.—by society at large, to be worked in common by all for the account and benefit of all.

But if the new American party, like all political parties everywhere, by the very fact of its formation aspires to the conquest of political power, it is as yet far from agreed upon what to do with that power when once attained. In New York and the other great cities of the East, the organization of the working class has proceeded upon the lines of Trades' Societies, forming in each city a powerful Central Labor Union. In New York the Central Labor Union, last November, chose for its standard-bearer Henry George, and consequently its temporary electoral platform has been largely imbued with his principles. In the great cities of the North-West the electoral battle was fought upon a rather indefinite labour platform, and the influence of Henry George's theories was scarcely, if at all, visible. And while in these great centres of population and of industry the new class movement came to a political head, we find all over the country two wide-spread labour organizations: the 'Knights of Labor'* and the 'Socialist Labor party', of which only the latter has a platform in harmony with the modern European standpoint as summarized above.

Of the three more or less definite forms under which the American labour movement thus presents itself, the first, the Henry George movement in New York, is for the moment of a chiefly local significance. No doubt New York is by far the most important city of the States; but New York is not Paris and the United States are not France. And it seems to me that the Henry George platform, in its present shape, is too narrow to form the basis for anything but a local movement, or at best for a short-lived phase of the general movement. To Henry George, the expropriation of the mass of the people from the land is the great and universal cause of the splitting up of the people into Rich and Poor. Now this is not quite correct historically. In Asiatic and classical antiquity, the predominant form of class oppression was slavery, that is to say, not so much the expropriation of the masses from the land as the appropriation of their persons. When, in the decline of the Roman Republic, the free Italian peasants were expropriated from their farms, they formed a class of 'poor whites' similar to that of the Southern Slave States before 1861; and between slaves and poor whites, two classes equally unfit for self-emancipation, the old world went to pieces. In the Middle Ages, it was not the expropriation of the people *from*, but on the contrary, their appropriation to the land which became the source of feudal oppression. The peasant retained his land, but was attached to it as a serf or villein, and made liable to tribute to the lord in labour and in produce. It was only at the dawn of modern times, towards the end of the fifteenth century, that the expropriation of the peasantry on a large scale laid the foundation for the modern class of wage-workers who possess nothing but their labour-power and can live only by the selling of that labour-power to others. But if the expropriation from the land brought this class into existence, it was the development of capitalist production, of modern industry and agriculture on a large scale which perpetuated it, increased it, and shaped it into a distinct class with distinct interests and a distinct historical mission. All this has been fully expounded by Marx (*Das Kapital*, Part VIII: 'The So-Called Primitive Accumulation'). According to Marx, the cause of the present antagonism of the classes and of the social degradation of the working class is their expropriation from *all* means of production, in which the land is of course included.

If Henry George declares land-monopolization to be the sole cause of poverty and misery, he naturally finds the remedy in the resumption of the land by society at large. Now, the Socialists of the school of Marx, too, demand the resumption, by society, of the land, and not only of the land but of all other means of production likewise. But even if we leave these out of the question, there is another difference. What is to be done with the land? Modern Socialists, as represented by Marx, demand that it should be held and worked in common and for common account, and the same with all other means of social production, mines, railways, factories, ect.; Henry George would confine himself to letting it out to individuals as at present, merely regulating its distribution and applying the rents for public, instead of, as at present, for private purposes. What the Socialists demand, implies a total revolution of the whole system of social production; what Henry George demands, leaves the present mode of social production untouched, and has, in fact, been anticipated by the extreme section of Ricardian bourgeois economists who, too, demanded the confiscation of the rent of land by the State.

It would of course be unfair to suppose that Henry George has said his last word once for all. But I am bound to take his theory as I find it.

The second great section of the American movement is formed by the Knights of Labor. And that seems to be the section most typical of the present state of the movement, as it is undoubtedly by far the strongest. An immense association spread over an immense extent of country in innumerable 'assemblies', representing all shades of individual and local opinion within the working class; the whole of them sheltered under a platform of corresponding indistinctness and held together much less by their impracticable constitution than by the instinctive feeling that the very fact of their clubbing together for their common aspiration makes them a great power in the country; a truly American paradox clothing the most modern tendencies in the most medieval mummeries, and hiding the most democratic and even rebellious spirit behind an apparent, but really powerless despotism—such is the picture the Knights of Labor offer to a European observer. But if we are not arrested by mere outside whimsicalities, we cannot help seeing in this vast agglomeration an immense amount of potential energy evolving slowly but surely into actual force. The Knights of Labor are the first national organization created by the American working class as a whole; whatever be their origin and history, whatever their shortcomings and little absurdities, whatever their platform and their constitution, here they are, the work of practically the whole class of American wage-workers, the only national bond that holds them together, that makes their strength felt to themselves not less than to their enemies, and that fills them with the proud hope to future victories. For it would not be exact to say that the Knights of Labor are liable to development. They are constantly in full process of development and revolution; a heaving, fermenting mass of plastic material seeking the shape and form appropriate to its inherent nature. That form will be attained as surely as historical evolution has, like natural evolution, its own immanent laws. Whether the

Knights of Labor will then retain their present name or not, makes no difference, but to an outsider it appears evident that here is the raw material out of which the future of the American working-class movement, and along with it, the future of American society at large, has to be shaped.

The third section consists of the Socialist Labor party. This section is a party but in name, for nowhere in America has it, up to now, been able actually to take its stand as a political party. It is, moreover, to a certain extent foreign to America, having until lately been made up almost exclusively by German immigrants, using their own language and for the most part, little conversant with the common language of the country. But if it came from a foreign stock, it came, at the same time, armed with the experience earned during long years of class struggle in Europe, and with an insight into the general conditions of working-class emancipation, far superior to that hitherto gained by American working men. This is a fortunate circumstance for the American proletarians who thus are enabled to appropriate, and to take advantage of, the intellectual and moral fruits of the forty years' struggle of their European class-mates, and thus to hasten on the time of their own victory. For, as I said before, there cannot be any doubt that the ultimate platform of the American working class must and will be essentially the same as that now adopted by the whole militant working class of Europe, the same as that of the German-American Socialist Labor party. So far this party is called upon to play a very important part in the movement. But in order to do so they will have to doff every remnant of their foreign garb. They will have to become out and out American. They cannot expect the Americans to come to them; they, the minority and the immigrants, must go to the Americans, who are the vast majority and the natives. And to do that, they must above all things learn English.

The process of fusing together these various elements of the vast moving mass—elements not really discordant, but indeed mutually isolated by their various starting-points— will take some time and will not come off without a deal of friction, such as is visible at different points even now. The Knights of Labor, for instance, are here and there, in the Eastern cities, locally at war with the organized Trade

Unions. But then this same friction exists within the Knights of Labor themselves, where there is anything but peace and harmony. These are not symptoms of decay, for capitalists to crow over. They are merely signs that the innumerable hosts of workers, for the first time set in motion in a common direction, have as yet found out neither the adequate expression for their common interests, nor the form of organization best adapted to the struggle, nor the discipline required to ensure victory. They are as yet the first levies *en masse* of the great revolutionary war, raised and equipped locally and independently, all converging to form one common army, but as yet without regular organization and common plan of campaign. The converging columns cross each other here and there: confusion, angry disputes, even threats of conflict arise. But the community of ultimate purpose in the end overcomes all minor troubles; ere long the straggling and squabbling battalions will be formed in a long line of battle array, presenting to the enemy a well-ordered front, ominously silent under their glittering arms, supported by bold skirmishers in front and by unshakeable reserves in the rear.

To bring about this result, the unification of the various independent bodies into one national Labour Army, with no matter how inadequate a provisional platform, provided it be a truly working-class platform—that is the next great step to be accomplished in America. To effect this, and to make that platform worthy of the cause, the Socialist Labor party can contribute a great deal, if they will only act in the same way as the European Socialists have acted at the time when they were but a small minority of the working class. That line of action was first laid down in the 'Communist Manifesto' of 1847 in the following words:

'The Communists'—that was the name we took at the time and which even now we are far from repudiating—'the Communists do not form a separate party opposed to other working-class parties.

'They have no interests separate and apart from the interests of the whole working class.

'They do not set up any sectarian principles of their own, by which to shape and model the proletarian movement.

'The Communists are distinguished from the other

working-class parties by this only: (1) In the national struggles of the proletarians of the different countries they point out, and bring to the front, the common interests of the whole proletariat, interests independent of all nationality; (2) In the various stages of development which the struggle of the working class against the capitalist class has to pass through, they always and everywhere represent the interests of the movement as a whole.

'The Communists, therefore, are on the one hand, practically the most advanced and resolute section of the working-class parties of all countries, that section which ever pushes forward all others; on the other hand, theoretically, they have, over the great mass of the proletarians, the advantage of clearly understanding the line of march, the conditions, and the ultimate general results of the proletarian movement.

'Thus they fight for the attainment of the immediate ends, for the enforcement of the momentary interests of the working class; but in the movement of the present, they represent and take care of the future of the movement.'*

That is the line of action which the great founder of Modern Socialism, Karl Marx, and with him, I and the Socialists of all nations who worked along with us, have followed for more than forty years, with the result that it has led to victory everywhere, and that at this moment the mass of European Socialists, in Germany and in France, in Belgium, Holland, and Switzerland, in Denmark and Sweden as well as in Spain and Portugal, are fighting as one common army under one and the same flag.

Frederick Engels

London, 26 January 1887

Preface to the English Edition

THE book, an English translation of which is here re-published, was first issued in Germany in 1845. The author, at that time, was young, 24 years of age, and his production bears the stamp of his youth with its good and its faulty features, of neither of which he feels ashamed. It was translated into English, in 1885, by an American lady, Mrs F. Kelley-Wischnewetzky, and published in the following year in New York. The American edition being as good as exhausted, and having never been extensively circulated on this side of the Atlantic, the present English copyright edition is brought out with the full consent of all parties interested.

For the American edition, a new Preface and an Appendix were written in English by the author. The first had little to do with the book itself; it discussed the American Working-Class Movement of the day, and is, therefore, here omitted as irrelevant; the second—the original preface—is largely made use of in the present introductory remarks.

The state of things described in this book belongs today, in many respects, to the past, as far as England is concerned. Though not expressly stated in our recognized treatises, it is still a law of modern Political Economy that the larger the scale on which capitalistic production is carried on, the less can it support the petty devices of swindling and pilfering which characterize its early stages. The pettifogging business tricks of the Polish Jew, the representative in Europe of commerce in its lowest stage, those tricks that serve him so well in his own country, and are generally practised there, he finds to be out of date and out of place when he comes to Hamburg or Berlin; and, again, the commission agent who hails from Berlin or Hamburg, Jew or Christian, after frequenting the Manchester Exchange for a few months, finds out that in order to buy cotton yarn or cloth cheap, he, too, had better drop those slightly more refined but still miserable wiles and subterfuges which are considered the acme of cleverness in his native country. The fact is, those tricks do not pay any longer in a large market, where time is money, and where a certain standard of commercial morality is unavoidably developed, purely as a means of saving time and trouble. And it is the same with the relation between the manufacturer and his 'hands'.

The revival of trade, after the crisis of 1847, was the dawn of a new industrial epoch. The repeal of the Corn Laws and the financial reforms subsequent thereon gave to English industry and commerce all the elbow-room they had asked for. The discovery of the Californian and Australian goldfields followed in rapid succession. The colonial markets developed at an increasing rate their capacity for absorbing English manufactured goods. In India millions of handweavers were finally crushed out by the Lancashire power-loom. China was more and more being opened up. Above all, the United States—then, commercially speaking, a mere colonial market, but by far the biggest of them all—underwent an economic development astounding even for that rapidly progressive country. And, finally, the new means of communication introduced at the close of the preceding period—railways and ocean steamers—were now worked out on an international scale; they realized actually what had hitherto existed only potentially, a world-market. This world-market, at first, was composed of a number of chiefly or entirely agricultural countries grouped around one manufacturing centre—England—which consumed the greater part of their surplus raw produce, and supplied them in return with the greater part of their requirements in manufactured articles. No wonder England's industrial progress was colossal and unparalleled, and such that the status of 1844 now appears to us as comparatively primitive and insignificant. And in proportion as this increase took place, in the same proportion did manufacturing industry become apparently moralized. The competition of manufacturer against manufacturer by means of petty thefts upon the workpeople did no longer pay. Trade had outgrown such low means of making money; they were not worth while practising for the manufacturing millionaire, and served merely to keep alive the competition of smaller traders, thankful to pick up a penny wherever they could. Thus the truck system* was suppressed, the Ten Hours' Bill* was enacted, and a number of other secondary reforms introduced—much against the spirit of Free Trade and unbridled competition, but quite as much in favour of the giant-capitalist in his competition with his less favoured brother. Moreover, the larger the concern, and with it the number of hands, the greater the loss and inconvenience caused by every conflict between master and men; and thus a new spirit came over the masters, especially the large ones, which taught them to avoid unnecessary squabbles, to acquiesce in the existence and power of Trade Unions, and finally even to discover in strikes—at opportune times—a powerful means to serve their own ends. The largest manufacturers, formerly the leaders of the war against the working class, were now the foremost to preach peace and harmony. And for a very good reason. The fact is that all these concessions to justice and philanthropy were nothing else but means to accelerate the concentration of capital in the hands of the few, for whom the niggardly extra extortions of former years had lost all importance and had become actual nuisances; and to crush all the quicker and all the safer their smaller competitors, who could not make both ends meet without such perquisites. Thus the development of production on the basis of the capitalistic system has of itself sufficed—at least in the leading industries, for in the more unimportant branches this is far from being the case—to do away with all those minor grievances which aggravated the workman's fate during its earlier stages. And thus it renders more and more evident the great central fact that the cause of the miserable condition of the working class is to be sought, not in these minor grievances, but in *the capitalistic system itself*. The wage-worker sells to the capitalist his labour-force for a certain daily sum. After a few hours' work he has reproduced the value of that sum; but the substance of his contract is, that he has to work another series of hours to complete his working day; and the value he produces during these additional hours of surplus labour is surplus value, which costs the capitalist nothing, but yet goes into his pocket. That is the basis of the system which tends more and more to split up civilized society into a few Rothschilds and Vanderbilts, the owners of all the means of production and subsistence, on the one hand, and an immense number of wage-workers, the owners of nothing but their labour-force, on the other. And that this result is caused, not by this or that secondary grievance, but by the system itself—this fact has been brought out in bold relief by the development of Capitalism in England since 1847.

Again, the repeated visitations of cholera, typhus, smallpox, and other epidemics have shown the British bourgeois the urgent necessity of sanitation in his towns and cities, if he wishes to save himself and family from falling victims to such diseases. Accordingly, the most crying abuses described in this book have either disappeared or have been made less conspicuous. Drainage has been introduced or improved, wide avenues have been opened out athwart many of the worst 'slums' I had to describe. 'Little Ireland' had disappeared, and the 'Seven Dials'* are next on the list for sweeping away. But what of that? Whole districts which in 1844 I could describe as almost idyllic have now, with the growth of the towns, fallen into the same state of dilapidation, discomfort, and misery. Only the pigs and the heaps of refuse are no longer tolerated. The bourgeoisie have made further progress in the art of hiding the distress of the working class. But that, in regard to their dwellings, no substantial improvement has taken place is amply proved by the Report of the Royal Commission 'on the Housing of the Poor', 1885. And this is the case, too, in other respects. Police regulations have been plentiful as blackerries; but they can only hedge in the distress of the workers, they cannot remove it.

But while England has thus outgrown the juvenile state of capitalist exploitation described by me, other countries have only just attained it. France, Germany, and especially America are the formidable competitors who, at this moment—as foreseen by me in 1844—are more and more breaking up England's industrial monopoly. Their manufactures are young as compared with those of England, but increasing at a far more rapid rate than the latter; and, curious enough, they have at this moment arrived at about the same phase of development as English manufacture in 1844. With regard to America, the parallel is indeed most striking. True, the external surroundings in which the working class is placed in America are very different, but the same economical laws are at work, and the results, if not identical in every respect, must still be of the same order. Hence we find in America the same struggles for a shorter working day, for a legal limitation of the working time, especially of women and children in factories; we find the truck system in full blossom, and the cottage system,* in rural districts, made use of by the 'bosses' as a means of domination over the workers. When I received, in 1886, the American papers with accounts of the great strike of 12,000 Pennsylvanian coal-miners in the Connellsville district, I seemed but to read my own description of the North of England colliers' strike of 1844. The same cheating of the workpeople by false measure; the same truck system; the same attempt to break the miners' resistance by the capitalists' last, but crushing, resource—the eviction of the men out of their dwellings, the cottages owned by the companies.

I have not attempted, in this translation, to bring the book up to date, or to point out in detail all the changes that have taken place since 1844. And for two reasons: First, to do this properly, the size of the book must be about doubled; and, secondly, the first volume of *Das Kapital*, by Karl Marx, an English translation of which is before the public, contains a very ample description of the state of the British working class, as it was about 1865, that is to say, at the time when British industrial prosperity reached its culminating point. I should, then, have been obliged again to go over the ground already covered by Marx's celebrated work.

It will be hardly necessary to point out that the general theoretical standpoint of this book—philosophical, economical, political—does not exactly coincide with my standpoint of today. Modern international Socialism, since fully developed as a science, chiefly and almost exclusively through the efforts of Marx, did not as yet exist in 1844. My book represents one of the phases of its embryonic development; and as the human embryo, in its early stages, still reproduces the gill-arches of our fish-ancestors, so this book exhibits everywhere the traces of the descent of Modern Socialism from one of its ancestors, German philosophy. Thus great stress is laid on the dictum that Communism is not a mere party doctrine of the working class, but a theory compassing the emancipation of society at large, including the capitalist class, from its present narrow conditions. This is true enough in the abstract, but absolutely useless, and sometimes worse, in practice. So long as the wealthy classes not only do not feel the want of any emancipation, but strenuously oppose the self-emancipation of the working class, so long the social revolution will have to be prepared and fought out by the working class alone. The French bourgeois of 1789, too, declared the emancipation of the bourgeoisie to be the emancipation of the whole human race; but the nobility and clergy would not see it; the proposition—though for the time being, with respect to feudalism, an abstract historical truth—soon became a mere sentimentalism, and disappeared from view altogether in the fire of the revolutionary struggle. And today, the very people who, from the 'impartiality' of their superior standpoint, preach to the workers a Socialism soaring high above their class interests and class struggles, and tending to reconcile in a higher humanity the interests of both the contending classes—these people are either neophytes, who have still to learn a great deal, or they are the worst enemies of the workers—wolves in sheep's clothing.

The recurring period of the great industrial crisis is stated in the text as five years. This was the period apparently indicated by the course of events from 1825 to 1842. But the industrial history from 1842 to 1868 has shown that the real period is one of ten years; that the intermediate revulsions were secondary, and tended more and more to disappear. Since 1868 the state of things has changed again, of which more anon.

I have taken care not to strike out of the text the many prophecies, amongst others that of an imminent social revolution in England, which my youthful ardour induced me to venture upon. The wonder is, not that a good many of them proved wrong, but that so many of them have proved right, and that the critical state of English trade, to be brought on by Continental and especially American competition, which I then foresaw—though in too short a period—has now actually come to pass. In this respect I can, and am bound to, bring the book up to date, by placing here an article which I published in the London *Commonweal* of 1 March 1885, under the heading: 'England in 1845 and in 1885'. It gives at the same time a short outline of the history of the English working class during these forty years, and is as follows:

'Forty years ago England stood face to face with a crisis, solvable to all appearances by force only. The immense and rapid development of manufactures had outstripped the extension of foreign markets and the increase of demand. Every ten years the march of industry was violently interrupted by a general commercial crash, followed, after a long period of chronic depression, by a few short years of prosperity, and always ending in feverish over-production and consequent renewed collapse. The capitalist class clamoured for Free Trade in corn, and threatened to enforce it by sending the starving population of the towns back to the country districts whence they came, to invade them, as John Bright said, not as paupers begging for bread, but as an army quartered upon the enemy. The working masses of the towns demanded their share of political power—the People's Charter; they were supported by the majority of the small trading class, and the only difference between the two was whether the Charter should be carried by physical or by moral force. Then came the commercial crash of 1847 and the Irish famine, and with both the prospect of revolution.

'The French Revolution of 1848 saved the English middle class. The Socialistic pronunciamentos of the victorious French workmen frightened the small middle class of England and disorganized the narrower, but more matter-of-fact movement of the English working class. At the very moment when Chartism was bound to assert itself in its full strength, it collapsed internally before even it collapsed externally, on 10 April 1848.* The action of the working class was thrust into the background. The capitalist class triumphed along the whole line.

'The Reform Bill of 1831* had been the victory of the whole capitalist class over the landed aristocracy. The repeal of the Corn Laws was the victory of the manufacturing capitalist not only over the landed aristocracy, but over those sections of capitalists, too, whose interests were more or less bound up with the landed interest—bankers, stockjobbers, fund-holders, etc. Free Trade meant the readjustment of the whole home and foreign, commercial and financial policy of England in accordance with the interests of the manufacturing capitalists—the class which now represented the nation. And they set about this task with a will. Every obstacle to industrial production was mercilessly removed. The tariff and the whole system of taxation were revolutionized. Everything was made subordinate to one end, but that end of the utmost importance to the manufacturing capitalist: the cheapening of all raw produce, and especially of the means of living of the working class; the reduction of the cost of raw material, and the keeping down—if not as yet the *bringing down*—of wages. England was to become the "workshop of the world"; all other countries were to become for England what Ireland already was—markets for her manufactured goods, supplying her in return with raw materials and food. England, the great manufacturing centre of an agricultural world, with an ever-increasing number of corn- and cotton-growing Irelands revolving around her, the industrial sun. What a glorious prospect!

'The manufacturing capitalists set about the realization of this their great object with that strong common sense and that contempt for traditional principles which has ever distinguished them from their more narrow-minded compeers on the Continent. Chartism was dying out. The revival of commercial prosperity, natural after the revulsion of 1847 had spent itself, was put down altogether to the credit of Free Trade. Both these circumstances had turned the English working class, politically, into the tail of the "great Liberal Party", the party led by the manufacturers. This advantage, once gained, had to be perpetuated. And the manufacturing capitalists, from the Chartist opposition, not to Free Trade, but to the transformation of Free Trade into the one vital national question, had learnt, and were learning more and more, that the middle class can never obtain full social and political power over the nation except by the help of the working class. Thus a gradual change came over the relations between both classes. The Factory Acts, once the bugbear of all manufacturers, were not only willingly submitted to, but their expansion into acts regulating almost all trades was tolerated. Trade Unions, hitherto considered inventions of the devil himself, were now petted and patronized as perfectly legitimate institutions, and as useful means of spreading sound economical doctrines amongst the workers. Even strikes, than which nothing had been more nefarious up to 1848, were now gradually found out to be occasionally very useful, especially when provoked by the masters themselves, at their own time. Of the legal enactments, placing the workman at a lower level or at a disadvantage with regard to the master, at least the most revolting were repealed. And, practically, that horrid "People's Charter" actually became the political programme of the very manufacturers who had opposed it to the last. "The Abolition of the Property Qualification" and "Vote by Ballot" are now the law of the land. The Reform Acts of 1867 and 1884* make a near approach to "universal suffrage", at least such as it now exists in Germany; the Redistribution Bill now before Parliament creates "equal electoral districts"—on the whole not more unequal than those of Germany; "payment of members", and shorter, if not actually "annual Parliaments", are visibly looming in the distance—and yet there are people who say that Chartism is dead.

'The Revolution of 1848, not less than many of its predecessors, has had strange bedfellows and successors. The very people who put it down have become, as Karl Marx used to say, its testamentary executors. Louis Napoleon had to create an independent and united Italy, Bismarck had to revolutionize Germany and to restore Hungarian independence, and the English manufacturers had to enact the People's Charter.

'For England, the effects of this domination of the manufacturing capitalists were at first startling. Trade revived and extended to a degree unheard of even in this cradle of modern industry; the previous astounding creations of steam and machinery dwindled into nothing compared with the immense mass of productions of the twenty years from 1850 to 1870, with the overwhelming figures of exports and imports, of wealth accumulated in the hands of capitalists and of human working power concentrated in the large towns. The progress was indeed interrupted, as before, by a crisis every ten years, in 1857 as well as in 1866; but these revulsions were now considered as natural, inevitable events, which must be fatalistically submitted to, and which always set themselves right in the end.

'And the condition of the working class during this period? There was temporary improvement even for the great mass.

But this improvement always was reduced to the old level by the influx of the great body of the unemployed reserve, by the constant superseding of hands by new machinery, by the immigration of the agricultural population, now, too, more and more superseded by machines.

'A permanent improvement can be recognized for two "protected" sections only of the working class. First, the factory-hands. The fixing by Act of Parliament of their working day within relatively rational limits has restored their physical constitution and endowed them with a moral superiority, enhanced by their local concentration. They are undoubtedly better off than before 1848. The best proof is that, out of ten strikes they make, nine are provoked by the manufacturers in their own interests, as the only means of securing a reduced production. You can never get the masters to agree to work "short time", let manufactured goods be ever so unsaleable; but get the work-people to strike, and the masters shut their factories to a man.

'Secondly, the great Trade Unions. They are the organizations of those trades in which the labour of *grown-up men* predominates, or is alone applicable. Here the competition neither of women and children nor of machinery has so far weakened their organized strength. The engineers, the carpenters and joiners, the bricklayers, are each of them a power, to that extent that, as in the case of the bricklayers and bricklayers' labourers, they can even successfully resist the introduction of machinery. That their condition has remarkably improved since 1848 there can be no doubt, and the best proof of this is in the fact that for more than fifteen years not only have their employers been with them, but they with their employers, upon exceedingly good terms. They form an aristocracy among the working class; they have succeeded in enforcing for themselves a relatively comfortable position, and they accept it as final. They are the model working men of Messrs. Leone Levi & Giffen, and they are very nice people indeed nowadays to deal with, for any sensible capitalist in particular and for the whole capitalist class in general.

'But as to the great mass of working people, the state of misery and insecurity in which they live now is as low as ever, if not lower. The East End of London is an everspreading pool of stagnant misery and desolation, of starvation when out of work, and degradation, physical and moral, when in work. And so in all other large towns—abstraction made of the privileged minority of the workers; and so in the smaller towns and in the agricultural districts. The law which reduces the *value* of labour-power to the value of the necessary means of subsistence, and the other law which reduces its *average price*, as a rule, to the minimum of those means of subsistence, these laws act upon them with the irresistible force of an automatic engine which crushes them between its wheels.

'This, then was the position created by the Free Trade policy of 1847, and by twenty years of the rule of the manufacturing capitalists. But then a change came. The crash of 1866 was, indeed, followed by a slight and short revival about 1873; but that did not last. We did not, indeed, pass through the full crisis at the time it was due, in 1877 or 1878; but we have had, ever since 1876, a chronic state of stagnation in all dominant branches of industry. Neither will the full crash come; nor will the period of longed-for prosperity to which we used to be entitled before and after it. A dull depression, a chronic glut of all markets for all trades, that is what we have been living in for nearly ten years. How is this?

'The Free Trade theory was based upon one assumption: that England was to be the one great manufacturing centre of an agricultural world. And the actual fact is that this assumption has turned out to be a pure delusion. The conditions of modern industry, steam-power and machinery, can be established wherever there is fuel, especially coals. And other countries besides England—France, Belgium, Germany, America, even Russia—have coals. And the people over there did not see the advantage of being turned into Irish pauper farmers merely for the greater wealth and glory of English capitalists. They set resolutely about manufacturing, not only for themselves, but for the rest of the world; and the consequence is that the manufacturing monopoly enjoyed by England for nearly a century is irretrievably broken up.

'But the manufacturing monopoly of England is the pivot

of the present social system of England. Even while that monopoly lasted, the markets could not keep pace with the increasing productivity of English manufacturers; the decennial crises were the consequence. And new markets are getting scarcer every day, so much so that even the Negroes of the Congo are now to be forced into the civilization attendant upon Manchester calicos, Staffordshire pottery, and Birmingham hardware. How will it be when Continental, and especially American, goods flow in in ever-increasing quantities—when the predominating share, still held by British manufacturers, will become reduced from year to year? Answer, Free Trade, thou universal panacea.

'I am not the first to point this out. Already in 1883, at the Southport meeting of the British Association, Mr Inglis Palgrave, the President of the Economic section, stated plainly that "the days of great trade profits in England were over, and there was a pause in the progress of several great branches of industrial labour. *The country might almost be said to be entering the non-progressive state.*" But what is to be the consequence? Capitalist production *cannot* stop. It must go on increasing and expanding, or it must die. Even now the mere reduction of England's lion's share in the supply of the world's markets means stagnation, distress, excess of capital here, excess of unemployed work people there. What will it be when the increase of yearly production is brought to a complete stop?

'Here is the vulnerable place, the heel of Achilles, for capitalistic production. Its very basis is the necessity of constant expansion, and this constant expansion now becomes impossible. It ends in a deadlock. Every year England is brought nearer face to face with the question: either the country must go to pieces, or capitalist production must. Which is it to be?

'And the working class? If even under the unparalleled commercial and industrial expansion, from 1848 to 1868, they have had to undergo such misery; if even then the great bulk of them experienced at best but a temporary improvement of their condition, while only a small, privileged, "protected" minority was permanently benefited, what will it be when this dazzling period is brought finally to a close;

when the present dreary stagnation shall not only become intensified, but this, its intensified condition, shall become the permanent and normal state of English trade?

'The truth is this: during the period of England's industrial monopoly the English working class have, to a certain extent, shared in the benefits of the monopoly. These benefits were very unequally parcelled out amongst them; the privileged minority pocketed most, but even the great mass had, at least, a temporary share now and then. And that is the reason why, since the dying-out of Owenism, there has been no Socialism in England. With the breakdown of that monopoly, the English working class will lose that privileged position; it will find itself generally—the privileged and leading minority not excepted—on a level with its fellow-workers abroad. And that is the reason why there will be Socialism again in England.'

To this statement of the case, as that case appeared to me in 1885, I have but little to add. Needless to say that today there is indeed 'Socialism again in England', and plenty of it—Socialism of all shades: Socialism conscious and unconscious, Socialism prosaic and poetic, Socialism of the working class and of the middle class, for, verily, that abomination of abominations, Socialism, has not only become respectable, but has actually donned evening dress and lounges lazily on drawing-room *causeuses*.* That shows the incurable fickleness of that terrible despot of 'society', middle-class public opinion, and once more justifies the contempt in which we Socialists of a past generation always held that public opinion. At the same time we have no reason to grumble at the symptom itself.

What I consider far more important than this momentary fashion among bourgeois circles of affecting a mild dilution of Socialism, and even more than the actual progress Socialism has made in England generally, that is the revival of the East End of London. That immense haunt of misery is no longer the stagnant pool it was six years ago. It has shaken off its torpid despair, has returned to life, and has become the home of what is called the 'New Unionism', that is to say, of the organization of the great mass of 'unskilled' workers. This organization may to a great extent adopt the form of the old Unions of 'skilled' workers but it is essentially different in character. The old Unions preserve the traditions of the time when they were founded, and look upon the wages system as a once-for-all established, final fact, which they at best can modify in the interest of their members. The new Unions were founded at a time when the faith in the eternity of the wages system was severely shaken; their founders and promoters were Socialists either consciously or by feeling; the masses, whose adhesion gave them strength, were rough, neglected, looked down upon by the working-class aristocracy; but they had this immense advantage, that *their minds were virgin soil*, entirely free from the inherited 'respectable' bourgeois prejudices which hampered the brains of the better situated 'old' Unionists. And thus we see now these new Unions taking the lead of the working-class movement generally, and more and more taking in tow the rich and proud 'old' Unions.

Undoubtedly, the East Enders have committed colossal blunders; so have their predecessors, and so do the doctrinaire Socialists who pooh-pooh them. A large class, like a great nation, never learns better or quicker than by undergoing the consequences of its own mistakes. And for all the faults committed in past, present, and future, the revival of the East End of London remains one of the greatest and most fruitful facts of this *fin de siècle*, and glad and proud I am to have lived to see it.

F. Engels

11 January 1892

EXPLANATORY NOTES

9   *dedication*: Engels wrote this dedication in English and published it in the German editions (though not the American and English editions) of his book. He told Marx, in a letter of 19 November 1844, that he intended to have it printed separately and to send it to 'English party leaders, men of letters, and Members of Parliament'.

13   *the Silesian and Bohemian disturbances*: in June 1844 there were riots by weavers in Silesia and by textile workers in other industrial parts of Bohemia. They involved the destruction of machinery and were put down by government troops.

25   *the first iron bridge*: in fact, the first iron bridge in England was built over the River Severn at Coalbrookdale in 1779. Paine designed parts which were used to build the second great iron bridge erected over the River Wear in 1796.

30   *the Reform Bill*: the Reform Bill, passed in 1832, extended the franchise to the better-off sections of the middle class.

34   *industrial Micawbers*: Micawber is a character in Dickens's *David Copperfield* who, when faced with a financial crisis, was wont to hope that something would 'turn up'.

37   *Stirner's recent book*: Max Stirner's *The Ego and Its Own* (1844) which advocated an extreme anarchist individualism.

57   *Kersallmoor . . . Manchester*: Kersallmoor is a hill near Manchester where workers used to hold meetings. Engels compares it to the 'mons sacer' or 'sacred mountain' outside Rome to which, according to tradition, the plebeians withdrew after their revolt against the patricians in 494 BC.

82   *tout comme chez nous*: just as in our country.

101   *Milesian*: from Milesius, a fabulous Spanish king, whose sons were reputed to have conquered and reorganized the kingdom of Ireland around 1300 BC.

120   *Metropolitan Buildings Act*: this Act, which regulated buildings in London, was passed in 1844.

132   *pur sang*: pure blooded.

152   *Ten Hours Bill*: this bill put a legal limit of ten hours on the working day.

159   *Apprentices' Bill . . . removed*: this law limited to twelve hours the working day of child apprentices not resident with their

parents and also prohibited their employment at night. But it only affected wool- and cotton-mills—and only those who employed at least three apprentices and twenty adults.

176   *à tout prix*: at any price.

178   *the Factory Acts . . . never enforced*: the Factory Act (1819) forbade the employment of children under 9 in cotton-spinning mills and also night work for children under 16 whose working day was limited to twelve hours. In 1825 this working day was shortened by law by half an hour. Neither law was enforced.

183   *Fleet Papers*: weekly pamphlets written as letters by R. Oastler to T. Thornhill. Thornhill kept Oastler in the Fleet debtors prison from 1841 to 1843.

       dissenters: members of Protestant Churches, such as the Methodists or Baptists, who had broken with the Anglican Church.

184   *There remains . . . be adopted*: the Ten Hours Bill was eventually passed in June 1847.

       Sugar Question: this refers to the Cabinet's proposal to lower tariffs on sugar imported from the West Indies in order to encourage sugar imports from India.

194   *The Steam King*: this poem by Edward Mead was printed in the *Northern Star*, February 1843.

222   *the Reform Bill*: see note to p. 30 above.

226   *ad acta*: filed.

230   *Menenius Agrippa*: a Roman patrician, who is said to have persuaded the plebeians who withdrew to the *mons sacer* in 494 BC to return by telling them the story of the other parts of the human body rebelling against the stomach on the grounds that it consumed food without producing it, but then seeing that they could not exist without it.

233   *the Welsh insurrection of 1839*: this refers to the rising, and severe repression, of Welsh miners in Newport in 1839, caused by Parliament's rejection of the Chartist petition and the arrest of the Chartist agitators.

236   *property qualification of £300 in land*: under a law of 1710 parliamentary candidates in borough seats had to have an income from land of at least £300 a year, and £600 a year in country seats.

238   *spy outbreaks*: clashes between Chartists and the police said to be caused by *agents provocateurs*.

241 *Chartist Association*: the *National Charter Association*, founded in July 1840, was the first mass working-class political party.

243 *the land-allotment system*: Feargus O'Connor and other Chartist leaders had proposed a return to the land by industrial workers as a remedy for industrial exploitation.

 home colonies: this was the name given to the communes, such as New Lanark, founded by Robert Owen and his followers.

245 '*Mechanics' Institutes*': these institutes, which first appeared in 1820, provided evening classes for workers in general and technical subjects.

246 *Dixi et Salvavi*: the full quotation is *dixi et salvavi animam meam*: I have spoken out and saved my soul. Considerable effort has failed to reveal the source of the quotation.

257 *a bill...was adopted*: this law forbade the employment underground of women and of children under 10 and was passed in August 1842.

288 *truck system...cottage system*: for a description of these, see above, pp. 190 ff.

261 *Dogberries*: Dogberry is a foolish court officer in Shakespeare's *Much Ado About Nothing*.

263 *ukases*: a Russian word meaning 'arbitrary commands'.

271 *car tel est notre plaisir*: for such is our pleasure.

273 *repeal of the Corn Laws*: the Corn Laws, which imposed high tariffs on grain imports and thus protected the interests of big landlords as opposed to those engaged in industry, were repealed in 1846.

280 *the repeal...with England*: the Union of Ireland with Great Britain was imposed by the British government after the suppression of the Irish rising in 1798. Agitation for the repeal of the Union, led by Daniel O'Connell, had immense popular support in Ireland from the 1820s onwards.

 O'Connell's trial: Daniel O'Connell and twelve of his supporters were sentenced to up to twelve months' imprisonment in February 1844 but the sentence was quashed by the House of Lords.

281 *Part of this description...refer the reader*: Engels refers to his article 'The Condition of England, *Past and Present* by Thomas Carlyle'. See K. Marx, F. Engels, *Collected Works* (New York, 1975), iii. 444 ff.

282 *laissez-faire, laissez-aller*: a slogan advocating non-interference by the State in economic affairs.

288 '*Young England*': the name of a group of Conservative writers and politicians, such as Carlyle and Disraeli, who were concerned to alleviate the social disruption caused by the industrial revolution.

295 *Gilbert's Act*: the Gilbert Act of 1782 authorized the creation of workhouses for the disabled poor and pauper children.

298 *the Barmecide feast*: an expression taken from a tale in the *Arabian Nights* where a beggar is humiliated by being told of an imaginary feast.

300 *juste-milieu*: golden mean.

Gironde: the more moderate party of French revolutionaries, led by Danton, who eventually succumbed to the more extreme faction of Robespierre.

303 *the Appendix*: this Appendix was included by Engels in the Preface to the English edition of 1892. See above, pp. 312 ff.

strikes of the Pennsylvania coal-miners: the five-week strike of the Pennsylvania miners in early 1886.

Eight Hours' movement . . . following: the general strike movement for an eight-hour working day which began on 1 May 1886 and was largely, if temporarily, successful.

306 '*Knights of Labor*': a working-class organization, founded in Philadelphia in 1869, which reached the peak of its influence in the strike movements of the 1880s.

311 '*The Communists . . . future of the movement*': see K. Marx and F. Engels, *Collected Works* (New York, 1975), iii. 418 f.

313 *the truck-system*: for a description of this, see above, pp. 190–1.

the Ten-Hours Bill: see note to p. 152 above.

315 '*Little Ireland*' . . . '*Seven Dials*': Little Ireland was a particularly deprived working-class district in Manchester, as was Seven Dials in central London.

316 *the cottage system*: for a description of this, see above, pp. 191–2.

318 *it collapsed internally . . . 10 April 1848*: on this date a mass meeting and demonstration called by the Chartist Convention ended in failure due to strong paramilitary counter-measures by the government and irresolution on the part of the Chartist leaders.

The Reform Bill of 1831: the Reform Bill modestly extended the franchise by some 200,000 voters and redistributed the parliamentary sects in England and Wales more fairly.

320 *The Reform Acts of 1867 and 1884*: the second Reform Act of 1867 extended the franchise for the first time to sections of the male working class—but not to most male unskilled or rural workers. Most of these were enfranchised in the 1884 Act, but still millions of men and all women had to wait until well into the next century to get the vote.

324 *causeuses*: small sofas or settees (French).

INDEX

The Oxford World's Classics Website

www.worldsclassics.co.uk

- Information about new titles
- Explore the full range of Oxford World's Classics
- Links to other literary sites and the main OUP webpage
- Imaginative competitions, with bookish prizes
- Peruse the Oxford World's Classics Magazine
- Articles by editors
- Extracts from Introductions
- A forum for discussion and feedback on the series
- Special information for teachers and lecturers

www.worldsclassics.co.uk